高校专门用途英语（ESP）系列教材

LEGAL ENGLISH
Comprehensive Course Book
法律英语综合教程

主　编　杨俊峰
副主编　屈文生　李　群
编　者（按姓氏笔画顺序排列）
　　　　冯　婧　邢彩霞
　　　　李　群　杨俊峰
　　　　张　丽　屈文生

第二版
SECOND EDITION

清华大学出版社
北京

内 容 简 介

本书涉及法的概念、法的渊源、司法制度、主要法学流派、美国法学教育、美国宪法、行政法、美国刑法、诉讼法、国际法概述，以及WTO与国际经济法概述等。

本书分上下两篇，共22课。每课包括课文正文、注释、词汇表和课后练习等，除个别情况外，都提供补充阅读材料，另外还在附录中提供常用刑事法律英语术语。本书作为学习法律专业英语的综合教程，在巩固和提高学生语言基本功的同时，还注重培养学生对法律英语的口语、阅读、写作和翻译能力。

本书适用于已具有一定英语水平的英语院校和法学院本科生、研究生、涉外律师、法律翻译工作者以及法律英语爱好者。

图书在版编目（CIP）数据

法律英语综合教程 / 杨俊峰主编. —2版. --北京：清华大学出版社，2015（2023.7重印）
高校专门用途英语（ESP）系列教材
ISBN 978-7-302-41511-4

Ⅰ.①法… Ⅱ.①杨… Ⅲ.①法律–英语–高等学校–教材 Ⅳ.①H31

中国版本图书馆CIP数据核字（2015）第209701号

责任编辑：刘细珍
封面设计：覃一彪
责任校对：王凤芝
责任印制：朱雨萌

出版发行：清华大学出版社
网　　址：http://www.tup.com.cn，http://www.wqbook.com
地　　址：北京清华大学学研大厦A座　　邮　　编：100084
社 总 机：010-83470000　　邮　　购：010-62786544
投稿与读者服务：010-62776969，c-service@tup.tsinghua.edu.cn
质量反馈：010-62772015，zhiliang@tup.tsinghua.edu.cn

印 装 者：天津鑫丰华印务有限公司
经　　销：全国新华书店
开　　本：170mm×230mm　　印　张：23.75　　字　数：560千字
版　　次：2005年9月第1版　2015年8月第2版　印　次：2023年7月第5次印刷
印　　数：4201-4800
定　　价：69.00元

产品编号：064980-02

第二版前言
Foreword (2nd Edition)

　　随着我国法制改革的不断深入和加入WTO后中国社会和经济的不断发展，中国已正式进入了法律服务的全球化时代。人才市场对人才的定义及需求不断地细化。在涉外法律服务领域，对既精通法律又能运用英语处理对外法律实务的人才的需求与日俱增，但真正满足这一需求的人才却是凤毛麟角。谁能攻克法律英语，谁就能赢得先机，在国际人才的竞争中脱颖而出。在这一时代背景下，作为全国外语院校的佼佼者——大连外国语大学，一直在探索适应这种市场需求的人才培养模式。通过近十年的探索和实践，大连外国语大学的专门用途英语（ESP）教学已经日臻成熟，拥有一批既懂理论又有实践经验的优秀教师队伍，并不断地为社会输送"复合型"的精英法律英语人才。本书的编者即来自这批优秀教师团队。《法律英语综合教程》第一版出版距今已接近十年，用"十年磨一剑"来形容编者们这些年来对该书的精雕细琢并不为过。相信本次的再版会更好地满足广大法律英语爱好者的需求。

　　作为ESP的分支学科之一，法律英语（Legal English）是应用型、功能型英语。为了使读者更准确和有效地学习法律语言，本书选择英美法系著名法律学者的论著及教程作为学习资料，详细介绍了普通法系的概念、法律流派、法学教育、法律职业、法院体系、宪法、行政法、合同法、侵权法、家庭法、WTO与国际经济法概况等。读者在学习法律英语的同时，还能够了解普通法系的重要法律制度、原则和规范，可谓一石多鸟。

　　《法律英语综合教程》一书出版以来，一直受到法律英语爱好者的厚爱，同时也收到了广大读者的建议和指正，在此，感谢读者的鼓励与鞭策。此次新版的《法律英语综合教程》保留了原书的基本风貌，全书分为上下两篇，共22课。每课包括课文正文、注释、词汇表、课后练习等，除个别情况外，都提供补充阅读材料。同时为了更好地顺应时代的需求，本书在再版时对部分过时的内容进行了更新，对不准确的知识点进行了修订，对版式进行了优化，对个别印刷瑕疵进行了订正，希望它能更好地服务广大读者。

  本书在再版修订过程中收到了来自大连外国语大学、华东政法大学等全国多所使用过该教材的教师和学生们的诸多宝贵建议，得到了清华大学出版社刘细珍编辑的协助，在此表示深深的谢意。

  由于编者的水平有限，再次恳请读者们对于本书的错误和不当之处予以指正，以便再版时更正。

主编：杨俊峰

2015年6月于大连

第一版前言
Foreword (1st Edition)

  随着我国对外开放力度的不断加大，信息化社会、知识与经济全方位的迅猛发展，尤其是我国加入WTO之后，人才市场对英语专业人才的需求也从单纯的语言技能走向多元化，社会诸多领域都在渴望得到既精通英语又掌握某种专业的复合型人才。因此，全国诸多专门的外语类院校近些年加大了这方面人才的培养力度。有人可能会有这样的疑问：外语类院校能培养出外语以外的专业人才吗？其实，这个问题早在十多年前就已经随着多学科的发展迎刃而解了。不少人已经看到，近年来外语类院校不仅培养出了高水平的外语人才，还培养出了深受用人单位钟情的经贸、法律、新闻等专门人才。目前工作在涉外经贸、涉外法律和国际新闻战线上的优秀人才又有哪一个不是英语顶呱呱。

  大连外国语学院作为外语类院校的佼佼者，近些年来同全国其他各大院校一样，也在加快人才培养模式调整的步伐，在深入探讨和实践双语、三语人才培养模式的基础上，又开设了法律、经贸、新闻等。而这些专业的最大特点是用英语学习专门知识，也许他们的法律（新闻、经贸）专业知识不及法律（新闻、经贸）专业的学生，但他们的外语水平，尤其是口语和笔头水平普遍受到用人单位的一致好评。对人才市场的调查也给了我们同样的启示，复合型外语人才不仅比单一的语言人才受欢迎，甚至比单一的专业人才更受欢迎（例如，同样是经贸专业，外语类院校的毕业生就比财经类院校的毕业生更具竞争力），这已是不争的事实。利用英语来教授和学习法律知识的模式势必会提高学生将来从事涉外法律事务相关工作的能力。也正是因为这个缘由，我们精心组织了一批"复合型老师"编写了这本《法律英语综合教程》，以满足广大法律英语爱好者的需求。

  《法律英语综合教程》涉及法的概念、法的渊源、司法制度、主要法学流派、美国法学教育、美国宪法、行政法、美国刑法、诉讼法、国际法概述、WTO与国际经济法概述等。

  本书的内容广泛、选材新颖、语言地道，是获得法律知识和提高对法律英语学习兴趣的首推教材。其中被告人权利、沉默权制度等课文都具有浓厚的趣味性和广泛的知识性。

本书分上下两篇，共22课。每课均包括课文正文、注释、词汇表、课后练习等，除个别情况外，都提供补充阅读材料。本书作为学习法律和英语的综合教程，在巩固和提高学生语言基本功的同时，还注重培养学生对法律英语的口语、阅读、写作以及翻译能力。

鉴于各学校的学期长短不一，周课时和学生的英语水平不一，在使用本教材时可根据本校的情况自行确定进度。一般情况下，如果只注重知识的获得，在提前预习较充分的情况下（包括课后练习都应在课前完成），每课可用2学时完成；如果知识和语言并重，建议每课4学时。两者相比，我们更主张后者，这样，教师既可以将知识的获得交给学生完成，又可以腾出时间讲解语言难点和用法。

通过本书的学习，学习者可以在法律术语以及英语语言运用方面打下一个坚实的基础，为下一步较高阶段的学习做好精神和物质准备，进而增强实际运用法律英语的能力，如用英语进行谈判、起草法律文书、开展辩论等。

参加本书编写的有屈文生（上篇第1、2、5、6、9课；下篇第1、2课）、冯婧（上篇第4课；下篇第6、7、8课）、邢彩霞（下篇第3、4课）、张丽（上篇第3、9课；下篇第5、9、12课）、李群（上篇第7、10课；下篇第10、11课）、黄涛（上篇第8课）。

清华大学出版社刘细珍编辑为本书的出版付出了辛勤的劳动，在此表示衷心的感谢。

由于编者水平有限，加之时间仓促，错误和不当之处在所难免，恳请使用者指正，以便再版时更正。

主编：杨俊峰
2005年6月于大连

目录
Contents

上篇 Part One

Lesson 1	Law and Its Classifications	2
Lesson 2	Sources of Law	15
Lesson 3	The American Court System	26
Lesson 4	The Jury System	37
Lesson 5	A Survey on Schools of Jurisprudence	49
Lesson 6	The Doctrine of Stare Decisis	60
Lesson 7	Two Major Legal Systems in the World	69
Lesson 8	Legal Education in America	80
Lesson 9	The American Constitution	90
Lesson 10	Administrative Law	102

下篇 Part Two

Lesson 1	Criminal Law: An Overview	116
Lesson 2	Criminal Law: Types of Defenses to a Criminal Charge	126
Lesson 3	Defendant's Rights: Key Aspects of Modern Criminal Procedure	140
Lesson 4	The Right to Remain Silent	150
Lesson 5	Property Law	159
Lesson 6	Contract Law	171
Lesson 7	Tort Law	180
Lesson 8	Company Law	195
Lesson 9	Intellectual Property Law	210
Lesson 10	Civil Procedure Law	221
Lesson 11	International Law	233
Lesson 12	WTO and International Economic Law	245
Appendix I	Text Translation & Key to Exercises (Part One)	257
Appendix II	Text Translation & Key to Exercises (Part Two)	289
Appendix III	Common Terms Used in Criminal Law	333
Appendix IV	Glossary	359
Appendix V	References	370

上 篇
Part One

Lesson 1
Law and Its Classifications

Law is a rule of conduct, a contract, an ideal of reason.
—*Aristotle*
法是行为的准则，是契约，是理性的典范。
——亚里士多德（古希腊，公元前384—332）

I. What Is Law

There have been and will continue to be different definitions of law. Aristotle saw law as a rule of conduct. Plato believed that law was a form of social control. Cicero contended that law was the agreement of reason and nature, the distinction between the just and the unjust. The British jurist Sir William Blackstone described law as "a rule of civil conduct prescribed by the supreme power in a state, commanding what is right, and prohibiting what is wrong". In America, the eminent jurist Oliver Wendell Holmes[1], Jr., contended that law was a set of rules that allowed one to predict how a court would resolve a particular dispute: "the prophecies of what the courts will do in fact, and nothing more pretentious, are what I mean by law."

Although these definitions vary in their particulars, all are based on the following general observation: *law consists of enforceable rules governing relationships among individuals and between individuals and their society*. This very broad definition of law implies the following:

- To have law, there must be established rules[2], such as constitutions, statutes,

---

1 Oliver Wendell Holmes（1841—1935）：奥利弗·温德尔·霍姆斯，1902年西奥多·罗斯福总统任命他为联邦最高法院法官，任期直到1932年。其传世之作首推1881年《普通法》（*The Common Law*, 1881）。
2 established rules：固定下来的规则，成文规则。

Lesson 1
Law and Its Classifications

administrative agency[1] regulations, and judicial decisions[2].

• These rules must be capable of enforcement; that is, law and order must prevail with resolution in a judicial system.

• The rules must establish approved conduct by which individuals deal with each other and participate in society.

National laws are made in Congress[3], which is part of the legislative[4] branch and is made up of the House of Representatives[5] and the Senate[6]. Congress can make laws on all kinds of matters, such as setting speed limits on highways or regulating how much radon may be found in drinking water. During each Congress, senators and representatives introduce[7] numerous bills. Bills are passed by Congress and then signed into law[8] by the president.

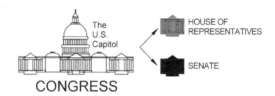

Figure 1-1

---

1. administrative agency：行政机关。A governmental body with the authority to implement and administer particular legislation. 在英国，该词更多用于指19世纪末兴起的行政裁判机构。
2. judicial decisions：司法判决。decision：裁定，判决。A judicial determination after consideration of facts and the law; esp., a ruling, order, or judgment pronounced by a court when considering or disposing of a case.
3. Congress：国会。The legislative body of the federal government, created under U.S. Constitution Article I, and consisting of the Senate and the House of Representatives.
4. legislative：关于立法的，有立法权的，立法的。Of or relating to lawmaking or to the power to enact laws. legislative department：立法部门。legislative power：立法权。legislature：立法机关。The branch of government responsible for making statutory laws. The U.S. federal government and most states have bicameral legislatures（两院制立法机关）, usu. consisting of a house of representatives and a senate.
5. House of Representatives：众议院。众议院的席位按照各州人口分配，每州至少要有一名议员。House of Representatives: the lower chamber of the U.S. Congress, composed of 435 members—apportioned among the states on the basis of population—who are elected to two-year term. 此外，House of Representatives也可以指美国各州的下院。House of Representatives可以缩写为H.R.。
6. Senate：参议院。Senate为美国国会的上院，参议院议员共有100名，每州2名，任期为6年，每两年更换全部议席的1/3。Senator：参议员。The upper chamber of a bicameral legislature. In U.S.A., it is the upper house of the U.S. Congress, composed of 100 members—two from each state—who are elected to six-year term.
7. introduce：提出议案等。To bring forward (a plan, a bill for example) for consideration.
8. sign into law：签署成为法律。

II. Classifications of Law

There are several different ways in which laws can be classified, depending on the criteria or characteristics which are applied for setting up the categories. One is to distinguish between public law and private law. Another important distinction is between criminal and civil law. Other classifications include civil law versus common law and substantive law versus procedural law. This section examines these legal classifications.

a. Public Law v. Private Law

Law can be divided into two main branches: public law and private law[1]. Public law is the body of law dealing with the relations between private individuals and the government, and with the structure and operation of the government itself; it includes constitutional law, criminal law, and administrative law. Private law is the body of law dealing with private persons and their property and relationships. Private law can be divided into six major branches according to the kinds of legal rights and obligations involved. These branches are contract and commercial law, tort law, property law, inheritance law, family law, and corporation law[2].

b. Criminal Law v. Civil Law

Criminal law defines breaches of duty to society at large. It is society, through government employees called prosecutors[3] (such as district attorneys), that brings court action against violators. If you are found guilty of a crime such as theft, you will be punished by imprisonment or a fine[4]. When a fine is paid, the money generally goes to the state, not the victim of the crime.

Private duties owed by one person (including corporations) to another are established by civil law. For example, we have a duty to carry out our contractual promises. Tort law defines a host of duties people owe to each other. One of the most common duties is a duty to exercise reasonable care[5] with regard to others. Failure to

---

1 private law: 私法。public law: 公法。罗马法学家乌尔比安（Ulpianus）将法律划分为公法与私法。
2 私法所包括的这六个部门依次是合同与商法、侵权行为法、财产法、继承法、家庭法以及公司法。
3 prosecutor: 检察官。A legal officer who represents the government in criminal proceedings.
4 fine: 罚金。A sum of money required to be paid as a criminal penalty.
5 a duty to exercise reasonable care: 尽合理注意义务。reasonable care也可以称作是 "due care" 或 "ordinary care"。"Reasonable care" is the degree of care that a person of ordinary intelligence and prudence would exercise under the given circumstances. This is the standard of care expected of virtually everyone at all times; a failure to exercise reasonable care is negligence.

Lesson 1
Law and Its Classifications

do so is the tort of negligence.

Suit for the breach of a civil duty must be brought by the person wronged[1]. Generally, the court does not seek to punish the wrongdoer but rather to make the wronged party whole through a money award called damages[2]. For example, if someone carelessly runs a car into yours, that person has committed the civil wrong (tort) of negligence. If you have suffered a broken leg, you will be able to recover damages from the driver (or his or her insurance company). The damages will be amount of money sufficient to repair your auto, to pay your medical bills, to pay for wages you have lost, and to give you something for any permanent disability such as a limp. Damages for "pain and suffering"[3] also may be awarded.

Although the civil law generally does not aim to punish, there is an exception. If the behavior of someone who commits a tort is outrageous, that person can be made to pay punitive damages[4] (also called "exemplary damages"). Unlike a fine paid in a criminal case, punitive damages go to the injured party.

Sometimes, the same behavior can violate both the civil law and the criminal law. For instance, a person whose drunken driving causes the death of another may face both a criminal prosecution by the state and a civil suit for damages by the survivors of the victim. If both suits are successful, the driver would pay back society for the harm done with a criminal fine and/or prison sentence, and compensate the survivors with the payment of money damages.

See Table 1-1 criminal law versus civil law, for a general comparison of criminal and civil cases.

---

1 wrong：不法行为。The violation of or failure to perform a legal duty, or the infringement of another's legal rights. wrongdoer：不法行为人。One who violates the law.
2 damages：损害赔偿金。Money claimed or allowed as compensation for injury or loss. 例如，① nominal damages 象征性损害赔偿金；②liquidated damages 预定损害赔偿金。
3 pain and suffering："痛苦与创伤"（精神损害赔偿金）。在美国《侵权行为法》中，损害赔偿金通常指经济损失，例如医疗开支、康复开支，以及财产损失。但损害赔偿金有时还包括非经济损害，基本上指被告的过失给身体受到伤害的原告所带来的"痛苦与创伤"（pain and suffering）。痛苦与创伤补偿通常会大大超过经济损失补偿。"拇指原则"（rule of thumb）就是指，假定原告完全康复，痛苦与创伤补偿至少应该是经济损失的四倍。
4 punitive damages：惩罚性损害赔偿金；exemplary damages：惩戒性损害赔偿金。"Punitive damages or exemplary damages" refers to money damages awarded to punish the other's conduct, as well as to deter others from such conduct in the future.

Table 1-1

	Criminal Cases	**Civil Cases**
Elements	Intentional or negligent violation of a statute	Harm to another person or property (tort) or breach of a contract
Actors	Prosecutor v. Defendant (government) (accused)	Plaintiff v. Defendant (wronged party) (wrong party)
Punishment	Fines, imprisonment, execution etc.	Defendant may have to pay the plaintiff compensatory and punitive damages

c. Civil Law v. Common Law

We have already seen that our system of law can be divided into two branches: Criminal law and non-criminal, or civil law. However, although "non-criminal" is indeed one meaning of the term "civil law", it is not the one with which we are concerned here. Civil law is the name of a particular system of jurisprudence[1] that is followed in a great many countries of the world. Put in its simplest form, we can say that civil-law systems are those based on legal codes (or statutes) that spell out a society's basic laws on a variety of subjects, such as acts that constitute crimes, tax obligations, and rules about owning and transferring property.

The term "civil law" and the basis of the law itself are derived originally from the law of ancient Rome, the jus civile[2]. As time passed, ancient Roman law was reworked into comprehensive legal codes. The code of the emperor Justinian (483—565 A.D.)[3] was revived after the Dark Ages[4], and it became the basis of modern law in Italy, the German Empire, the Netherlands, France, and Spain, as well as in their colonial offshoots. State of Louisiana historically also shares the civil-law tradition. Today, most Western European countries have civil-law systems, as do the countries of Latin America, most African countries, Japan, Thailand, and Turkey.

---

1 jurisprudence（法律体系）: a system, body, or division of law. jurisprudence, 这是个意义多变的词，除"法律体系"这个意思之外，jurisprudence还有"法理学""法哲学"之意，在德国法中，它指the whole of legal knowledge；在英美法中，它还有"判例法"（case law）之意。
2 jus civile：市民法。与之相对应的是"万民法"（jus gentium）。
3 罗马皇帝查士丁尼一世（Justinian I，公元483—565年）。
4 Dark Ages：黑暗世纪。指黑暗的中世纪年代，大约从西罗马帝国灭亡（A.D. 476）到中世纪文明的复兴（A.D. 1000）这一段时间。宽泛的讲，它等同于Middle Ages，即大约从公元476年到1450年。

Lesson 1
Law and Its Classifications

Besides the United States and England, a system known as common law prevails in Australia, Burma, Canada, India, Iraq, Liberia, Malaya, New Zealand, Singapore, and in Britain's former colonies in Africa, such as Ghana and Nigeria. The basis of common law is not a comprehensive code: Rather, the basic building block[1] of common-law system is case law, which is composed of decisions handed down by judges who rule on individual cases. Because each judicial opinion serves as a precedent[2] for later decisions, as a result, common law is sometimes called judge-made law. Common-law judges have very wide powers of interpretation to apply previous judicial rulings and to interpret statutes.

The most obvious distinction between civil law and common law systems is that civil law system is a codified system, whereas the common law is not created by means of legislation but is based mainly on case law. The principle is that earlier judicial decisions, usually of the higher courts, made in a similar case, should be followed in the subsequent cases, i.e. that precedents should be respected. This principle is known as stare decisis. The claim that common law is created by the case law is only partly true, as the common law is based in large part on statutes, which the judges are supposed to apply and interpret in much the same way as the judges in civil law (eg the Sale of Goods Act 1979, the Uniform Commercial Code).

d. Substantive Law v. Procedural Law

The branches of our legal system can be divided into substantive law and procedural law.

Procedural law establishes the rules or the guidelines—that is, the procedures—under which our legal system operates. In our legal system, for example, procedural law specifies the length of a statute of limitations[3] for instituting a lawsuit[4]. Procedural law can be divided into criminal procedures, such as the list of rights that

---

1 building block:（本义）积木；这里指组成部分。
2 precedent: 先例。A decided case that furnishes a basis for determining later cases involving similar facts or issues.
3 statute of limitations: 时效；诉讼时效。A statute establishing a time for suing in a civil case, based on the date when the claim accrued (as when the injury occurred or was discovered); a statue establishing a time limit for prosecuting a crime, based on the date when the offense occurred. 与"诉讼时效"相混淆的另一个概念"除斥期间"可以表述为"statue of repose"。
4 a lawsuit: 提起法律诉讼。

must be read to a suspect before being questioned by the police[1], and civil procedures such as pleadings[2], the written statements of the positions to be advanced at trial by the parties in lawsuit. Some procedures are common to both civil and criminal law.

Substantive law embraces rights, obligations, or limitations applicable to people and businesses in a variety of situations. Substantive law may be based in the Constitution of the United States, in legislative enactments such as statutes, or in case law developed by judges. In criminal law, for example, the actual definitions of the acts that constitute crimes are substantive law. In the law of contracts, substantive law includes the rights and remedies[3] that are available when one party to a contract violates the terms of the agreement.

III. Goddess of Law

A common representation of Justice is a blind-folded woman holding a set of scales[4]. The origin of the Goddess of Justice goes back to antiquity. She was referred to as Maat by the ancient Egyptians and was often depicted carrying a sword with an ostrich feather in her hair (but no scales) to symbolize truth and justice. The term magistrate is derived from Maat because she assisted Osiris[5] in the judgment of the dead by weighing their hearts.

To the ancient Greeks she was known as Themis, originally the organizer of the "communal affairs of humans, particularly assemblies." Her ability to foresee the future enabled her to become one of the oracles at Delphi (Temple of Apollo),

---

1 事实上,这里所讲的主要是"米兰达警示原则"。Miranda Warnings: "1. You have the right to remain silent. 2. Anything you say can and will be used against you in a court of law. 3. You have the right to have an attorney present before any questioning. 4. If you cannot afford an attorney, one will be appointed to represent you before any questioning." ("你有权保持沉默,否则你所说的一切,都可能作为指控你的不利证据。你有权请律师在你受审时到场。如果你请不起律师,法庭将为你指派一位。")本书在"沉默权制度"一文中对此有专门论述。
2 pleadings: 诉讼文件,民事诉状;答辩状。A formal document in which a party to a legal proceeding (esp. a civil lawsuit) sets forth or responds to allegations, claims, denials, or defenses.
3 remedy: 救济。Redress sought from or awarded by a court.
4 a set of scales: 天平。法律女神,又称作正义女神。正义女神的样子一般被描述为:"眼睛上蒙着布,一手执衡器(以权正义),一手执宝剑(以实现正义——法律)"。宝剑而无衡器,不过是暴力;衡器而无宝剑,只是有名无实的正义,二者相依相辅,运用宝剑的威力与运用衡器的技巧协调,而后法律才能见诸实行。
5 奥西里斯神,尼罗河之神,也是幽冥界之王。在古希腊神话中,心脏被认为是人的意识栖身之所,于是将死者的心放到天平的一边,在天平的另一边放上象征正义的羽毛,如果心脏重于羽毛,则通不过审判,被交给长着鳄鱼头的魔鬼;如果羽毛重于心脏,则通过审判,获得永生。

Lesson 1
Law and Its Classifications

which in turn led to her establishment as "the goddess of divine justice." Classical representations of Themis did not show her blindfolded (because of her talent for prophecy, she had no need to be blinded) nor was she holding a sword (because she represents common consent, not coercion).

The Roman goddess of justice was called Justitia and was often portrayed as evenly balancing both scales and a sword and wearing a blindfold. She was sometimes portrayed holding the fasces (a bundle of rods around an ax symbolizing judicial authority) in one hand and a flame in the other (symbolizing truth).

Glossary

administrative agency 行政机关
administrative law 行政法
antiquity 古代
assembly 大会；公民大会
building block （本义）积木；这里指组成部分
Congress 国会
constitutional law 宪法
criminal law 刑法
damages 损害赔偿金
Dark Ages 黑暗世纪
exemplary damages 惩戒性损害赔偿金
fine 罚金
House of Representatives 众议院
introduce 提出议案等
judicial decisions 司法判决
Jurisprudence 法律体系；法理学；法哲学
jus civile 市民法

legislative 关于立法的；有立法权的；立法的
pain and suffering 痛苦与创伤
pleadings 诉讼文件；民事诉状；答辩状
precedent 先例
private law 私法
prosecutor 检察官
public law 公法
punitive damages 惩罚性损害赔偿金
radon ［化］氡
remedy 救济
scales 天平
Senate 参议院
spell out 详细规定；详细说明
statute of limitations 时效；诉讼时效
survivor 尚存者
violator 违法者；违反者

EXERCISES

I. Answer the following questions.

1. Name the appropriate category of law to fit each of the following descriptions:
   a) law that regulates relationships between two or more different countries.
   b) law that operates within a single country.
   c) a codified legal system deriving largely from Napoleon's law code, and mostly operating within a European country.
   d) law deriving from the English legal system and operating in a Commonwealth country and the U.S.

2. Under which category (or categories) of law would each of the following be dealt with?
   a) Who will care for the young children when a man and woman divorce?
   b) Can I sue the builder who undertook to build my house but did not finish the job?
   c) Can I seek any compensation if my neighbor's fierce dog attacked and savagely bit me as I was walking along the footpath?
   d) How does the country get a new Prime Minister?

3. Explain briefly what matters are dealt with by each of the following categories of law:
   a) Administrative law
   b) Constitutional law
   c) Property law
   d) Tort law
   e) Criminal law

4. What is "common law"? Why is the United States a "common law country"?

5. What is the primary distinction between common law and civil law legal systems?

6. What is public law? Give three examples of public law.

7. Explain private law. Give three examples.

8. What is the difference between civil law and criminal law?

9. Explain the two ways that the words civil law are used in this chapter.

10. Define substantive law and procedural law.

11. Is contract law substantive law or procedural law? What about a rule specifying that a defendant has 30 days to respond to a complaint?

Lesson 1
Law and Its Classifications

II. Translate the following terms into English.

1. 国会
2. 参议院
3. 众议院
4. 检察官
5. 先例
6. 答辩状
7. 正义女神
8. 程序法
9. 实体法
10. 继承法

III. Translate the following sentences into Chinese.

1. The term "common law" is also used to distinguish one segment of Anglo-American law from another part called "equity". Today the terms refer to different sets of legal doctrines.
2. When one person, organization, corporation, or branch of government sues another to obtain a remedy for a supposed injury, the case is a civil case, leading to a possible remedy in money damages or an order to do or not to do a certain act.
3. Public law defines a person's rights and obligations in relation to government. Public law also describes the various divisions of government and their powers.
4. Most nations have a written constitution. A major exception is Great Britain. The British constitution is unwritten.
5. The most obvious distinction between civil law and common law systems is that civil law system is a codified system, whereas the common law is not created by means of legislation but is based mainly on case law.

IV. Dictation.

Law can also be broken down into public and private law. Public law addresses issues and incidents that are of interest to society as a whole. One important branch of public law is administrative law, which defines the structure and functioning of government agencies such as the National Labor Relations Board. Private law is concerned only with disputes that arise between private parties.

Supplementary Reading

Contract and commercial law deals with the rights and obligations of people who make contracts. A contract is an agreement between two or more persons that can be enforced by law. A wide variety of business activities depend on the use of contracts. A business firm makes contracts both with other firms, such as suppliers and transporters[1], and with private persons, such as customers and employees.

Tort law. A tort is a wrong or injury that a person suffers because of someone else's action. The action may cause bodily harm; damage a person's property, business, or reputation; or make unauthorized use of a person's property. The victim may sue the person or persons responsible. Tort law deals with the rights and obligations of the persons involved in such cases. Many torts are unintentional, such as damages in traffic accidents. But if a tort is deliberate and involves serious harm, it may be treated as a crime.

Property law governs the ownership and use of property. Property may be real, such as land and buildings, or personal, such as an automobile and clothing. The law ensures a person's right to own property. However, the owner must use the property lawfully. People also have the right to sell or lease their property and to buy or rent the property of others. Property law determines a person's rights and obligations involved in such dealings.

Inheritance law, or succession law[2], concerns the transfer of property upon the death of the owner. Nearly every country has basic inheritance laws, which list the relatives or other persons who have first rights of inheritance. But in most Western nations, people may will their property to persons other than those specified by law. In such cases, inheritance law also sets the rules for the making of wills.

Family law determines the legal rights and obligations of husbands and wives and of parents and children. It covers such matters as marriage, divorce, adoption, and child support.

Corporation law governs the formation and operation of business corporations.

1　suppliers and transporters：供货商和运输商。
2　inheritance law：也叫succession law 继承法。testate succession：遗嘱继承；hereditary succession：法定继承。

Lesson 1
Law and Its Classifications

It deals mainly with the powers and obligations of management and the rights of stockholders[1]. Corporation law is often classed together with contract and commercial law as business law.

Public law involves government directly. It defines a person's rights and obligations in relation to government. Public law also describes the various divisions of government and their powers.

Public law can be divided into four branches[2]: (1) criminal law, (2) constitutional law, (3) administrative law, and (4) international law. In many cases, the branches of public law, like those of private law, overlap. For example, a violation of administrative law may also be a violation of criminal law.

Criminal law deals with crimes—that is, actions considered harmful to society. Crimes range in seriousness from disorderly conduct to murder. Criminal law defines these offenses and sets the rules for the arrest, the possible trial, and the punishment of offenders. Some crimes are also classed as torts because the victim may sue for damages under private law.

In the majority of countries, the central government makes most of the criminal laws. In the United States, each state, as well as the federal government, has its own set of criminal laws. However, the criminal laws of each state must protect the rights and freedoms guaranteed by the federal constitutional law.

Constitutional law. A constitution is a set of rules and principles that define the powers of a government and the rights of the people. The principles outlined in a constitution form the basis of constitutional law. The law also includes official rulings on how the principles of a nation's constitution are to be interpreted and carried out.

Most nations have a written constitution[3]. A major exception is Great Britain. The British constitution is unwritten. It consists of all the documents and traditions that have contributed to Britain's form of government. In most democracies, the national constitution takes first place over all other laws. In the United States, the federal Constitution has force over all state constitutions as well as over all other national and state laws.

---

1 stockholder：股东。
2 公法包括的四个部门法依次是：刑法、宪法、行政法以及国际法。
3 written constitution：成文宪法；unwritten constitution：不成文宪法；rigid constitution：刚性宪法；flexible constitution：柔性宪法；英国宪法（British Constitution）是柔性宪法、不成文宪法。

Conflicts between a constitution and other laws are settled by constitutional law. In the United States, the courts have the power of judicial review[1], under which they may overturn any laws that are judged to be unconstitutional. A law is declared unconstitutional if the court determines that it violates the United States Constitution or a state constitution. The United States Supreme Court is the nation's highest court of judicial review.

Administrative law centers on the operations of government agencies. Administrative law ranks as one of the fastest-growing and most complicated branches of the law.

National, state or provincial, and local governments set up many administrative agencies to do the work of government. Some of these agencies regulate such activities as banking, communications, trade, and transportation. Others deal with such matters as education, public health, and taxation. Still other agencies administer social welfare programs, such as old-age and unemployment insurance. In most cases, the agencies are established in the executive branch of government under powers granted by the legislature.

Administrative law consists chiefly of (1) the legal powers that are granted to administrative agencies by the legislature and (2) the rules that the agencies make to carry out their powers. Administrative law also includes court rulings in cases between the agencies and private citizens.

International law deals with the relationships among nations both in war and in peace. It concerns trade, communications, boundary disputes, methods of warfare, the uses of the ocean, and many other matters. Laws to regulate international relations have been developed over the centuries by customs and treaties. But international law, unlike other branches of law, is difficult to enforce.

---

1 power of judicial review：司法审查权；违宪审查权。

Lesson 2
Sources of Law

The origin of a thing ought to be regarded.
事物的本源应该得到尊重。

Although the Constitution of the United States is the supreme law of the land, it is only one of the many sources of American law. In addition to the Constitution, American law comprises common law, statutes, and administrative rules and regulations[1].

I. Constitutions (Constitutional Law)

The constitutions of the states and federal government are the highest laws of the nation and override[2] all other sources. The U.S. Constitution establishes the federal government, and its amendments[3] guarantee basic rights and liberties to the people of the nation.

State constitutions also provide a general structure for state government, dividing it into legislative, executive, and judicial branches, giving each branch checks

---

1 administrative rules and regulations：行政规则与规章。rule 应该译为"规则"，例如，美国刑法中精神病（insanity）抗辩事由中的"The M'Naghten Rule"（麦那顿规则）、"The Durham Rule"（德赫姆规则），都可以译为"规则"。再如，Federal Rules of Civil Procedure, 译作《联邦民事诉讼规则》，Rules of Evidence译作"证据规则"等。regulation则应译为"条例、规章"。依据*Black's Law Dictionary*，Regulation一词在美国指"A rule or order, having legal force, issued by an administrative agency or a local government"。所以，它是指行政机构颁发的法规，在我国行政机关颁布的法规一般称为"条例"或"规章"。
2 override：优先于，不顾，使无效。To prevail over; to nullify or set aside.
3 amendment：修正案；补充条款。A formal revision or addition proposed or made to a statute, constitution, or other instrument.

and balances[1] on the others, and defining the powers and functions of the various branches. Like the U.S. Constitution, the state constitutions guarantee various rights and liberties.

If your constitutional rights[2] are violated, the laws violating them are void, (i.e., these laws have no legal effect on you).

The law that interprets the Constitution of the United States and enforces rights under the Constitution is classified as Constitutional law[3]. The judicial branch of the government has the power to review the Constitution or other laws of the federal and state governments. This is known as the doctrine of judicial review. The power of judicial review was established in the landmark case of *Marbury v. Madison*, 5U.S.(1 Cranch) 137(1803)[4], wherein the Supreme Court established the power of the judicial branch of the government to review actions and decisions made by the executive and legislative branches and to determine the constitutionality[5] of those actions. The

---

1. check：制约；牵制。举例：Thus, under this scheme of government, the legislative and executive branches are independent from and exercise a mutual check upon each other. （于是，在这种政府体系中，立法和行政部门彼此独立而又互相制约。）
2. constitutional right：宪法性权利。A right guaranteed by a constitution; esp., one guaranteed by the Constitution.
3. constitutional law：宪法性法律。此外，constitutional law还有宪法学的意思，指以宪法的内容、制定、解释、结构以及宪法作为根本法的法律效力等为研究对象的法律学。
4. Official court reporting began in 1790 with the inception of the United States Reports, cited U.S., which remains the official edition of U.S. Supreme Court decisions. Citations to volumes of the U.S. Reports before volume 91 (1875) must include a reference to the particular official reporter of the Court. There were seven such reporters, as follows:

Reporter	Volumes	Years	U.S. Reports
Dallas	1—4	1790—1800	1—4
Cranch	1—9	1801—1815	5—13
Wheaton	1—12	1816—1827	14—25
Peters	1—16	1828—1842	26—41
Howard	1—24	1843—1860	42—65
Black	1—2	1861—1862	66—67
Wallace	I—23	1863—1874	68—90

Hence, for example, *Marbury v. Madison*, 5 U.S. (1 Cranch) 137 (1803). 这表示该案收集在美国案例汇编第5卷（克兰奇汇编1卷），第137页，1803年形成审判意见。"马伯里诉麦迪逊"一案的背景是当时美国第二任总统约翰·亚当斯（John Adams）竞选败给了托马斯·杰弗逊（Thomas Jefferson）。亚当斯代表的是联邦党。亚当斯在卸任之前，行使了自己的司法提名权，将尽可能多的联邦党人坐上法官的位子。就在新总统上任的三星期前，联邦党控制的参议院通过法案，新增42个法官职位。威廉·马伯里是其中之一。亚当斯命令约翰·马歇尔（John Marshall），时任国务卿来完成这些任命，但是马歇尔尚未完成任命，托马斯·杰弗逊（Thomas Jefferson）就入主了白宫（White House）。杰弗逊对这些尚未发出去的任命状毫不理会，并命令新上任的国务卿詹姆斯·麦迪逊（James Madison）不要发那些没有发出去的任命状。于是就有了"马伯里诉麦迪逊"这一著名案例。

5. constitutionality：合宪性。The quality or state of being constitutional.

ability of a court to review the actions of the other branches of the government is the heart of the American legal system and is instrumental to the development of its laws.

II. Common Law (Case Law)

Judges make the common law. In general, the court begins with rules that have been established in earlier cases precedents, then applies those rules to the case before it, and announces the rule of that case as shaped by those particular facts. In reaching this new rule, the court compares the facts of the case before it with facts of other cases to find similarities and distinctions. Following the principle of *stare decisis*[1], the court attempts in this way to decide similar cases similarly.

According to the doctrine of stare decisis ("let the decision stand"), once a court has set down a legal principle applicable to a certain set of facts, judges will follow that principle in future cases, when the facts are the same or substantially similar. The doctrine establishes stability and consistency in our legal system, for without the doctrine of stare decisis, the system would be chaotic and arbitrary. It is important to note that the doctrine of stare decisis is not carved in stone. As case law develops and changes, some decisions lose their controlling effect because of changing social values or amendments to statues and constitutions.

III. Statutory Law (Legislation)

Statutory law[2] (formal written laws) is one of the most significant sources of law. Laws passed by a legislature to regulate the conduct of citizens are called statues. Under the American legal system at the federal level, Congress passes statutes that are signed by the President of the United States of America. States can pass laws through their state legislatures to be signed by their respective governors[3]. The laws passed

---

1 *stare decisis*: 〈拉丁语〉遵循先例原则；判例拘束原则。The doctrine of precedent, under which it is necessary for a court to follow earlier judicial decisions when the same points arise again in litigation.
2 statutory law: 制定法。The body of law derived from statutes rather than from constitutions or judicial decisions.指非宪法或法院判决的法律总称。也可以写作"statute law""legislative law""ordinary law"。
3 governor: 州长。The chief executive official of a U.S. State. Governors are elected and usually serve a two-or- four-year term.

must conform to the U.S. Constitution and that state's constitution, otherwise they risk being declared void[1] by the judicial branch.

Legislative bodies exist at all levels of government, including not only the federal Congress but also state general assemblies[2], city councils[3], and many other local government bodies that adopt or enact[4] laws. Laws passed by cities and towns are often called ordinances[5] and are considered a form of statute. Legislation in its broad sense also includes treaties[6] entered into by the executive branch of government and ratified[7] by the Senate. Compilations of legislation at all levels of government are called codes[8]. For example, we have local traffic codes covering such matters as speed limits, and state laws, such as the Uniform Commercial Code[9], which covers all aspects of commercial transactions. The statutes of our federal government are compiled in the United States Code[10].

---

1 void：无效。Of no legal effect; null. 例如：void contract：无效合同；void legacy：无效遗赠；void transaction：无效交易。
2 general assembly：州议会。The name of the legislative body in many states. 注意该词大写时，General Assembly表示"联合国大会"（The deliberative body of United Nations）。
3 city council：市政会；市议会。A city's legislative body, usu. responsible for passing ordinances, levying taxes, appropriating funds, and generally administering city government.
4 adopt or enact：通过或颁布。"Adopt" here means to vote to accept; "enact" means to pass into law or to make into a statute.
5 ordinance：条例。ordinance有时也写为bylaw或municipal ordinance。
6 treaty：条约。A formally signed and ratified agreement between two nations or sovereigns; an international agreement concluded between two or more states in written form and governed by international law.
7 ratify：批准。To manifest approval of a previous action by oneself or another so as to make it legally binding. For example, treaties negotiated by the President must be ratified by the Senate; constitutional amendments adopted by Congress must be ratified by three-quarters of the states; a contract entered into by a party under a legal age may be ratified by that party after reaching legal age; a contract entered into on behalf a principal（本人，被代理人）by an agent（代理人）who lacked authority to do so may be ratified by the principal. In the contract situations, ratification may be either expressed (by announcing one's intent to adhere to the contract) or implied (by continuing to perform under the contract or by accepting benefits under it).
8 code：制定法的汇编，法典。An organized compilation of statutes or rules.
9 Uniform Commercial Code：《统一商法典》，简称U.C.C.。它是1952年在统一州法全国委员会(National Conference of Commissioners on Uniform State Laws)和美国法学会（American Law Society）的共同努力下所取得的最成功和最重要的成果。《统一商法典》共十一编，其内容主要包括（1）总则；（2）买卖；（3）商业票据；（4）银行存款和收款；（5）信用证；（6）大宗转让；（7）仓单、提单和其他所有权凭证；（8）投资证券；（9）担保交易，账债和动产契据的买卖；（10）生效日期及废除效力；（11）生效日及过渡规定。美国50个州（包括哥伦比亚特区和维尔京岛）都采纳了这部法典，不过路易斯安那州只采用了法典中第一、三、四、五、七、八编。
10 United States Code：《美国法典》。United States Code: A multivolume published codification of federal statutory law. 在卷宗号（citation）中，United States Code常常缩写为"USC"。

Lesson 2
Sources of Law

a. Uniformity of Legislation

Because Congress, 50 state legislatures, and countless local governments enact statutes and ordinances, there is concern about lack of uniformity in the law. If the law lacks uniformity, it decreases the certainty necessary for the conduct of business and the general ordering of society[1].

Legislators[2] can achieve uniformity in the law through two methods:

- Congress can enact a single law that preempts (overrides) varying state laws.
- The state legislatures can all adopt a single uniform law in a particular area.

The latter method has been attempted by a legislative drafting group known as the National Conference of Commissioners on Uniform State Laws. These commissioners endeavor to promote uniformity by drafting model acts[3]. When approved by the National Conference, proposed uniform acts are recommended to the state legislatures for adoption.

More than 100 uniform laws, mostly related to business activities, have been drafted and presented to the various state legislatures. The response of the states in adopting these proposed laws has varied. A few of the uniform laws have been adopted by all the states. Sometimes a state adopts the uniform law in principle but changes some of the provisions to meet local needs. The most significant uniform law for business is the Uniform Commercial Code (UCC).

b. Interpretation of Legislation

Legislation often is written in general terms. The precise meaning of the law often is unclear. In our legal system, it is up to the judiciary[4] to determine the

---

1 商事行为以及社会整体秩序所必需的确定性。
2 legislator：立法者；立法机关的成员。One who makes laws within a given jurisdiction; a member of a legislative body. 例如，我国的全国人大常委会委员长可译为 "the top-legislator of the National People's Congress(NPC)"，因为NPC and its Standing Committee 是China's top legislature。
3 model act：模范法。A statute drafted by the National Conference of Commissioners on Uniform State Laws and proposed as guideline legislation for the states to borrow from or adapt to suit their individual needs. Examples of model acts include the Model Employment Termination Act (《模范就业中止法》), the Model Punitive Damages Act (《模范惩罚性赔偿法》) and Model Penal Code (《模范刑法典》).
4 judiciary：司法机构，司法机关。The branch of government responsible for interpreting the laws and administering justice. "立法机构" 用一个词表示为 "legislature"；"行政机构" 用一个词来表示是 "executive" (the branch of government responsible for effecting and enforcing laws; the person or persons who constitute this branch.), 等同于executive branch。

meaning of general language in a legislative enactment and apply it to the limited facts of a case. The court's purpose in interpreting a statute or an ordinance is to determine the intent of the legislature when the statute was enacted. Such a process is called statutory construction[1].

IV. Administrative Regulation (Administrative Law)

An agency is a governmental entity that has the power to make rules, regulate conduct, and adjudicate[2] violations of agency rules and regulations. Administrative regulation is unique in that, as a result of the delegation of powers[3] from the federal and state governments, agencies perform many functions of the three branches of government: Agencies may legislate by making rules and regulations, agencies may supervise compliance with regulations by acting as an executive power, and agencies may render decisions the way a court does—through adjudication.

Since, in the early stages of development the agencies' power went virtually unchecked, Congress passed a statute in 1946 which set standards according to which agencies must act. The statute is called the Administrative Procedure Act[4], which is divided into four areas known as the Freedom of Information Act[5], the Privacy Act[6], the Government in the Sunshine Act[7], and the Regulatory Flexibility Act[8]. Under the Administrative Procedure Act, agencies regulate and supervise the activities of

---

1 statutory construction：制定法的解释；法定解释。The act or process of interpreting a statute；也可称为"statutory interpretation"。Construction在法律英语中常作"解释"讲，即the act or process of interpreting or explaining the sense or the intention of a writing (usu. a statute, opinion, or instrument)。
2 adjudicate：判决，裁判。To rule upon... judicially.
3 delegation of powers：权力的委托，授权。A transfer of authority by one branch of government to another branch or to an administrative agency.
4 为了确保行政权力不至于滥用，美国于1946年制定了一部重要的《联邦行政程序法》（APA），该法从重视行政程序上对行政行为予以规范，并且guarantees the right of judicial review（保证司法审查权）。
5 Freedom of Information Act：《情报自由法》。The federal statute that establishes guidelines for public disclosure of documents and materials created and held by federal agencies.
6 Privacy Act：《隐私权法》，该法保护个人私生活权利（protect a person's right to be left alone），限制公众获悉个人纳税申报表、医疗档案等信息（restrict public access to personal information such as tax return and medical records）。有时称为Privacy Law。
7 Government in the Sunshine Act：《阳光下的政府法》。The Government in the Sunshine Act is a U.S. law passed in 1976. It is one of a number of so-called sunshine laws, intended to create greater openness in government.
8 Regulatory Flexibility Act：《管理弹性法案》，主要是立法对中小企业实施调整。

Lesson 2
Sources of Law

federal agencies such as Environmental Protection Agency[1] and the Federal Aviation Administration[2], subject to compliance with the U.S. Constitution.

Glossary

adjudicate 判决；裁判
administration 行政机关；局（署）
adopt 通过
amendment 修正案；补充条款
check 制约；牵制
city council 市政会；市议会
code 制定法的汇编；法典
constitutional right 宪法性权利
constitutionality 合宪性
delegation of powers 权力的委托；授权
enact 颁布
enter into 订立
Freedom of Information Act 《情报自由法》
general assembly 州议会
governor 州长
judiciary 司法机构；司法机关

legislator 立法者；立法机关的成员
model act 模范法
ordinance 条例
override 优先于；不顾；使无效
Privacy Act 《隐私权法》
ratify 批准
regulation 条例、规章
rule 规则
stare decisis 〈拉丁语〉遵循先例原则；判例拘束原则
statutory construction 制定法的解释；法定解释
statutory law 制定法
treaty 条约
Uniform Commercial Code 《统一商法典》
United States Code 《美国法典》
void 无效

EXERCISES

I. Answer the following questions.

1. What are the main sources of American law according to this text?
2. Which law provides the structure of government and basic rights of a citizen in U.S.?
3. What is a precedent?
4. Define the following terms: statute, ordinance, and code. Are there any differences among these words?

---

[1] Environmental Protection Agency：联邦环境保护局，成立于1970年。
[2] Federal Aviation Administration：联邦航空管理局。Administration一词本身有"executive branch of a government"的意思，即"行政机关、局（署）等"。

5. What is an agency? What is the basic function of the Administrative Procedure Act (APA)?
6. Who makes law in America?
7. Through which two ways can legislators achieve the uniformity in law according to this text?

II. Translate the following sentences into Chinese.

1. The courts have the power to assess not only the actions of individuals and agencies but laws enacted by Congress, states, and localities in order to determine whether they are in accord with the Constitution, this power of judicial review is now widely considered an essential check on both Congress and the president.
2. Congress and the state legislature can delegate some of their lawmaking power to a government agency.
3. The term "common law" comes from English origins. The Normans conquered England in 1066, and one of the principal devices William the Conqueror and his successors used to unite the country was to send royal judges around to hold court in the various cities.
4. If your constitutional rights are violated, the laws violating them are void.
5. Many prohibitions against government regulation are contained in the Bill of Rights (the first ten amendments to the Constitution). These amendments guarantee certain rights to the people, including the familiar rights of speech, freedom of religion, and the privilege against unreasonable search and seizure.

III. Cloze.

The 1_____, which developed in Great Britain after the Norman Conquest, was based on the decisions of judges in the royal courts. It is called 2_____ law because it is a system of rules based on "precedent". Whenever a judge makes a decision that is to be legally enforced, this decision becomes a 3_____: a rule that will guide judges in making subsequent decisions in similar cases. The common law is unique in the world because it cannot be found in any "code" or "legislation"; it exists only in past 4_____.

However, this also makes it flexible and adaptable to changing circumstances. The tradition of 5_____ is quite different. It is based on 6_____, which was consolidated by the Roman Emperor Justinian（查士丁尼皇帝）. The law in ancient Rome was scattered about in many places: in books, in statutes, in proclamations. Justinian ordered his legal experts to put all the law into a single book to avoid confusion. Ever since, the civil law has been associated with a "7_____", containing almost all private law. Quebec's Civil Code was first enacted in 1866, just before Confederation (as the Civil Code of Lower Canada), and periodically amended over the years. The reformed Civil Code of Quebec came into 8_____ in 1994. Like all civil codes, such as the Code Napoléon in France, it contains a comprehensive statement of rules, many of which are framed as broad, general principles so as to deal with any 9_____ that may arise. Unlike common-law courts, courts in a civil-law system first look to the 10_____, and then refer to previous decisions for consistency.

IV. Dictation.

Making laws through legislation can be a complicated process. Suppose, for example, the federal government wanted to create a law that would help control pollution. First, government ministers or senior public servants would be asked to examine the problem carefully and suggest ways in which, under federal jurisdiction, a law could deal with pollution. Next, a draft of the proposed law would be made. This text would then have to be approved by the Cabinet, which is composed of members of Parliament chosen by the Prime Minister. This version would then be presented to Parliament as a "bill", and would be studied and debated by members. Bills only become laws if they are approved by a majority in both the House of Commons and the Senate, and assented to by the Governor General in the name of the Queen. (139 words)

Supplementary Reading

Although never so important as in the civil law, doctrinal writings hold an important place as a secondary source[1] of law in the Anglo-American legal system. For the very earliest periods, indeed, they are equivalent to true law, for there are no other sources.

Overt legal writing began in England in the reign of Henry I (1100—1135), when several attempts were made to restate the Anglo-Saxon laws[2] in the light of Norman changes.

Glanvill and Bracton In or about 1187 a treatise[3] appeared which has been attributed to Ranulph de Glanvill, one of Henry's favorites, soon to become his Chief Justiciar[4]. The next great book on the common law was the unfinished treatise of 1256 attributed to Bracton[5]. It, too, was a commentary on the writs, which by that time numbered about two hundred and fifty. Bracton's work was much more inclusive than the earlier one, and in some places he appeared to have inserted civil-law concepts in order to fill the gaps in the still incomplete English law.

Lord Coke drew upon Bracton's influence and antiquity in his famous conflicts with the Crown, particularly in invoking his famous statement, "The King is King under God and the law."[6] In the time of Bracton, of course, concepts of divine right in the king were still unknown, and the reaffirmation of Bracton's statement at a time when such claims were being made had a salutary effect.

Littleton, Coke and Blackstone Perhaps in 1481, or only a half-dozen years after the introduction of printing in England, appeared the first edition of Thomas de Littleton's Tenures[7]. Its subject, land law, was one with which the author, as a Common Pleas judge, was closely familiar. The book initiated a new trend in legal writing: organizing a text on a particular object, not in the form of a commentary on writs but by subject, divided into

---

1 secondary source：次要渊源。
2 Anglo-Saxon laws：盎格鲁—撒克逊法。
3 指Treatise on the Laws and Customs of the Realm of England《论英格兰王国的法律和习惯》。
4 Chief Justiciar：司法长官；首席摄政官。地位仅次于国王，国王离国不在时，摄政国事。
5 指On the Laws and Customs of England《论英格兰的法律和习惯》。
6 国王是上帝与法律之下的国王。
7 利特尔顿的《土地法》（Tenures）。Tenures也有人译为《土地保有法》。

Lesson 2
Sources of Law

chapters. After almost a century and a half of use, it was brought up to date and translated from its original law French by Lord Coke in 1628. English legal language is a composite of Latin, French, and English. Latin was the formal language of court documents until 1731; French was the language spoken in the courts until 1362 and did not disappear as the language of legal literature until the sixteenth century[1]. Various editions of *Coke on Littleton* were produced by later editors, adding modern annotations to the prior writings. The work was actively used in the United States until the beginning of the nineteenth century.

The seventeenth century saw various minor but important legal treatises, some of a practical nature and others concerned with general matter particularly legal history.

In 1765 appeared the book that was to constitute a major text for American lawyers until the twentieth century—Blackstone's *Commentaries on the laws of England*[2].

Kent and Story The 1820s saw the publication of two important works in the United States. James Kent published his *Commentaries on American Law* in four volumes between 1826 and 1830. He had been a Justice of the New York Supreme Court and Chancellor of the Court of Equity. Although he followed the four volume format of Blackstone's *Commentaries*, his work differed. He traced the development of American law from English law and, unlike Blackstone, appreciated continental civil law.

Although Joseph Story also called his work commentaries, they were the first legal textbooks. The influence of these men is often so great that they have cast the line of development of the law in many areas. The law schools of this country produce considerable legal writings in their law reviews. Virtually all law schools publish journals, usually staffed by senior students. Eminent lawyers, judges, and law professors[3] write the lead articles, and students comment on topics and cases of interest. For close analysis, the law reviews are probably more valuable than any other secondary legal source.

---

1 英语法律语言是拉丁语、法语和英语的综合体。拉丁语到1731年一直是法庭文件的正式语言，法语到1362年一直是法庭上使用的语言，法语直到16世纪才在法律文学语言中消失。
2 布莱克斯通的《英国法释义》。
3 eminent lawyers, judges, and law professors：杰出的律师、法官、法学教授。

Lesson 3
The American Court System

The perfect judge fears nothing—he could go front to front before God.
—Walt Whitman(1818-1892)

完美的法官无所畏惧,他可以直面上帝。
——华尔特·惠特曼(1819—1892)

Unlike most countries in the world, actually, there are fifty-two court systems in America—one for each of the fifty states, one for the District of Columbia, plus a federal system—similarities abound. The state court systems are established according to the constitution of each state. The federal courts are not superior to the state courts; they are simply independent systems of courts, which derives its authority from Article III, Section 2, of the U.S. Constitution. Although state court systems differ, Figure 3-1 illustrates the basic organizational structure characteristic of the court system in many states. The figure also shows how federal court system is structured.

I. State Court System

Typically, a state court system will include several levels, or tiers, of courts. State courts may include (1) trial courts of limited jurisdiction[1], (2) trial courts of general jurisdiction, (3) appellate courts, and (4) the state's highest court (often

---

1 jurisdiction:司法管辖权。A court's power to decide a case or issue a decree. 包括有限管辖权 limited jurisdiction: jurisdiction that is confined to a particular type of case or that may be exercised only under statutory limits and prescription; 普遍管辖权 general jurisdiction: a court's authority to hear a wide range of cases, civil or criminal, that arise within its geographic area.

Lesson 3
The American Court System

called the state supreme court). Generally, any person who is a party[1] to a lawsuit[2] has the opportunities to plead[3] the case before a trial court and then, if he or she loses, before at least one level of appellate court. Finally, if a federal statute or federal constitutional issue is involved in the decision of the state supreme court, that decision can be further pleaded before the Federal Supreme Court.

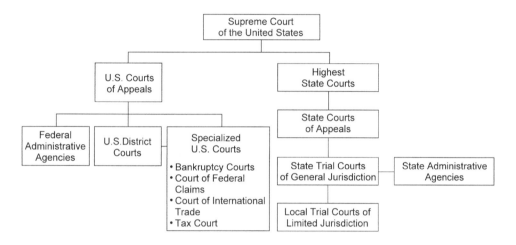

Figure 3-1

a. Trial Courts[4]

Trial courts are exactly what their name implies, courts in which trials are held and testimony[5] taken. State trial courts have either general or limited jurisdiction.

---

1 party: 当事人, 指进行一定事务或诉讼的人。One by or against whom a lawsuit is brought or one who takes part in a transaction. 本文指诉讼当事人, 即原告和被告。
2 lawsuit (or suit, suit at law): 诉讼; Any proceeding by a party or parties against another in a court of law, e.g., enter/bring in a lawsuit against sb. (对某人起诉); v. to proceed against (an adversary) in a lawsuit; to sue.
3 plead: 辩护、抗辩。Address a court of law as an advocate on behalf of either the plaintiff or the defendant; e.g., plead for/against sb.
4 trial court: 初审法院。A court of original jurisdiction where the evidence is first received and considered.
5 testimony: 证据 (指证人以誓言口头提供证明) ; 口供; 证言。Evidence that a complete witness under oath or affirmation gives at trial or in an affidavit or deposition e.g., testimony of a witness(证人证言), testimony of the accused(被告人供述).

Trial courts that have general jurisdiction as to subject matter[1] may be called county, district, superior, or circuit courts[2]. The jurisdiction of these courts is often determined by the size of the county in which the courts sit. State trial courts of general jurisdiction have jurisdiction over a wide variety of subjects, including both civil disputes and criminal prosecutions[3]. In some cases, trial courts of general jurisdiction may hear appeals from courts of limited jurisdiction.

Some courts of limited jurisdiction are called special inferior trial courts or minor judiciary courts. Small claims courts[4] are inferior trial courts that hear only civil cases involving claims of less than a certain amount, such as $5,000(the amount varies from state to state). Suits brought in small claims courts are generally conducted informally, and lawyers are not even allowed to represent people in small claims courts for most purposes. Another example of an inferior trial court is a local municipal court[5] that hears mainly traffic cases. Decisions of small claims courts and municipal courts may be appealed to a state trial court of general jurisdiction.

Other courts of limited jurisdiction as to subject matter include domestic relations courts[6], which handle only divorce actions and child-custody cases, and probate courts[7].

b. Courts of Appeals

Every state has at least one court of appeals (appellate court, or reviewing court), which may be an intermediate appellate court or the state's highest court. About three-fourths of the states have intermediate appellate courts. Generally, courts of appeals do not conduct new trials, in which evidence is submitted to the court and witnesses are examined. Rather, an appellate court panel of three or more judges

---

1 subject matter：争议事项；标的；诉讼标的。The issue presented for consideration; the thing in which a right or duty has been asserted.
2 circuit courts：巡回法院；巡回法庭。在美国，指管辖权涉及几个县或地区，实行巡回审理的法院。
3 criminal prosecution：刑事诉讼。A criminal proceeding in which an accused person is tried.
4 small claims courts：小额索赔法院，旨在便捷的解决小额索赔而设立的法院。
5 municipal court：市镇法院（庭），在美国只有某些州有这类法院，是一种管辖权很小的低级法院，通常拥有刑事管辖权，有时还对小额民事案件拥有管辖权。
6 domestic relations courts：家庭关系法院，为涉及婚姻状况、扶养费（alimony）、离婚（divorce）、子女监护（child-custody）等家事问题拥有管辖权的州法院。
7 probate court：遗嘱检验法庭（有权认证遗嘱与管理死者遗产的特种法庭）。A court with a power to declare wills valid or invalid, to oversee the administration of estates, and in some states to appoint guardians and approve the adoption of minors.

Lesson 3
The American Court System

reviews the record of the case on appeal, which includes a transcript of the trial proceedings, and determines whether the trial court committed an error.

Usually, appellate courts do not look at the questions of fact (such as whether a party did, in fact, commit a certain action, such as burning a flag) but at questions of law[1] (such as whether the act of flag-burning is a form of speech protected by the First Amendment to the Constitution). Only a judge, not a jury, can rule on questions of law. Appellate courts normally defer to a trial court's findings on questions of fact because the trial court judge and jury were in a better position to evaluate testimony—by directly observing witnesses' gestures, demeanor, and nonverbal behavior during the trial. At the appellate level, the judges review the written transcription of the trial, which does not include these nonverbal elements.

An appellate court will challenge a trial court's finding of fact only when the finding is clearly erroneous (that is, when it is contrary to the evidence presented at trial) or when there is no evidence to support the finding. If a jury concluded that a manufacturer's product harmed the plaintiff but no evidence was submitted to the court to support that conclusion, the appellate court would hold[2] that the trial court's decision was erroneous.

c. State Supreme (Highest) Courts

The highest appellate court in a state is usually called the supreme court but may be called by some other names. For example, in both New York and Maryland, the highest state court is called the court of appeals. The decisions of each state's highest court on all questions of state law are final. Only when issues of federal law are involved can a decision made by a state's highest court be overruled[3] by the United Stated Supreme Court.

---

[1] question of fact: 事实问题。An issue that has not been predetermined and authoritatively answered by the law. 与此相对的概念是question of law（法律问题）: an issue to be decided by the judge, concerning the application or interpretation.
[2] hold: 认定、认为。To adjudge or decide.
[3] overrule: （上级法院）否决或推翻（下级法院的判决）。To overturn or set aside (a precedent) by expressly deciding that it should no longer be controlling.

II. The Federal Court System

The federal court system is basically a three-tiered model consisting of (1) U.S. district courts (trial courts of general jurisdiction) and various courts of limited jurisdiction, (2) U.S. courts of appeals (intermediate courts of appeals), and (3 the United States Supreme Court.

Unlike state court judges, who are usually elected, federal court judges—including the justices of the Supreme Court—are appointed by the president of the U.S. and must be confirmed by the U.S. Senate. All federal judges receive lifetime appointments (because under Article III they "hold their offices during Good Behavior[1]").

a. U.S. District Courts

At federal level, the equivalent of a state trial court of general jurisdiction is the district court. There is at least one federal district court in every state. The number of judicial districts can vary over time, primarily owing to population changes and corresponding caseloads[2]. Currently, there are ninety-four federal judicial districts.

U.S. District Courts conduct trials concerning federal matters, such as federal crimes and enforcement of federal statutes. Most federal crimes involve crimes against the government or crimes occurring on federal property. For example, one crime, kidnapping, is a federal crime even though it does not occur on federal land. Federal jurisdiction for the crime of kidnapping is based on taking of the victim across state or country lines and the statute provides that the failure to release the victim within twenty-four hours after seizure creates "a rebuttable presumption that such person has been transported to interstate or foreign commerce".

Moreover, it is possible to sue a federal court even though the claim is based on state law when the plaintiff and defendant are from different states or countries.

---

1 Good Behavior：廉洁行为；品行良好；（正在服刑的罪犯）遵守监规。Dictionary Of The Law (p.203)对该词的定义为：1）(of federal judges)absence of corrupt or criminal conduct, 指（联邦法官）没有渎职或刑事犯罪行为。在美国，联邦最高法院、上诉法院和地区法院的联邦法官都是终身制，只有专门法院的联邦法官才是任期制。终身制法官又被称为"第三条款法官"（Article III Judges）；任期制法官被称为"第一条法官"（Article I Judges）。2）(of a prisoner serving a sentence) compliance with prison rules，指（正在服刑的罪犯）遵守监规。

2 caseload：待处理案件的数量。Volume of cases assigned to a given court, judge, ect.

Lesson 3
The American Court System

Diversity of citizenship jurisdiction[1] exists when a plaintiff is a citizen of one state and the defendant is a citizen of another state, or when one party is a foreign country or a citizen of a foreign country and the other is a citizen of the United States. The amount of claimed damages in a diversity of citizenship case must be at least $75,000.

Also, there are other courts with original, but special (or limited) jurisdiction, such as the federal bankruptcy courts and others shown in Figure 3-1.

b. U.S. Courts of Appeals

In federal court system, there are thirteen U.S. courts of appeals—also referred to as U.S. circuit courts of appeals. The federal courts of appeals for twelve of the circuits, including the U.S. Court of Appeals for the District of Columbia Circuit, hear appeals from the federal district courts located within their respective judicial circuits[2]. The Court of Appeal for the Thirteen Circuit, called the Federal Circuit, has national appellate jurisdiction over certain types of cases, such as cases involving patent law and cases in which the U.S. government is a defendant. Also heard before this court are appeals from specialized courts (e.g., the U.S. Claims Court and the U.S. Court of International Trade) and claims arising from decisions of federal administrative agencies.

c. The United States Supreme Court

The highest level of the three-tiered model of the federal court system is the United States Supreme Court. According to the language of the Article III of the U.S. Constitution, there is only one national Supreme Court. All other courts in federal system are considered "inferior". Congress is empowered to create other inferior courts as it deems necessary. The inferior courts that Congress has created include the second tier in our model—the U.S. court of appeals—as well as the district courts and any other courts of limited, or specialized jurisdiction.

The United States Supreme Court consists of nine justices. Although the Supreme

---

1　diversity (of citizenship) jurisdiction：多元管辖。A federal court's exercise of authority over a case involving parties from different states and amount in controversy greater than a statuary minimum.指联邦法院对事管辖权的一种，指联邦法院对双方当事人乃美国不同州常住居民案件以及争议金额大于法定最低数额案件的管辖权。

2　circuit：巡回审判区。A judicial division of the United States—that is, the 13 circuits where the U.S. courts of appeals sit.美国全国共有11个司法巡回区，哥伦比亚特区作为单独的一个巡回区（District of Columbia），此外还有一个联邦巡回区（Federal Circuit）。

Court has original, or trial, jurisdiction in rare instances (e.g., in legal disputes in which a state is a party, cases between two states, and cases involving ambassadors), most of its work is as an appeals court. The Supreme Court can review any case decided by any of the federal courts of appeals, and it also has appellate authority over some cases decided in the state courts.

Appeals to the Supreme Court To bring a case before the Supreme Court, a party requests the Court to issue a writ of certiorari. *A writ of certiorari* is an order issued by the Supreme Court to a lower court requiring the latter to send it the record of the case for review. The Court will not issue a writ of certiorari unless at least four of the nine justices approve of it. This is called the rule of four. Whether the Court will issue a writ of certiorari is entirely within its discretion. The Court is not required to issue one, and most petitions[1] for writs are denied. (Thousands of cases are filled with the Supreme Court each year, yet it hears, on average, fewer than one hundred of these cases.) A denial is not a decision on the merit of a case, nor does it indicate an agreement with the lower court's opinion. When the Supreme Court declines review of a case, the practical effect is an agreement with the lower court decision, which continues binding the parties.

Glossary

appellate 上诉的
caseload 待处理案件的数量
child-custody 子女监护
circuit court 巡回法院
criminal prosecution 刑事诉讼
defer to 服从，遵从
demeanor 行为；举止；风度
domestic relations court 家庭关系法院
good behavior 廉洁行为；品行良好；（正在服刑的罪犯）遵守监规
hold 认定；认为

jurisdiction 司法管辖权；管辖区域
lawsuit 诉讼
lifetime appointments 终身制任命
municipal court 市镇法院（庭）
nonverbal behavior 非语言的行为或举止
overrule （上级法院）否决或推翻（下级法院的判决）
party （诉讼）当事人
petition 诉状；诉请
plead 辩护；抗辩
probate court 遗嘱检验法庭

---

[1] petition：诉状、诉请。Formal application made to a court of law.

Lesson 3
The American Court System

provide 规定
question of fact 事实问题
rebuttable 可以反驳的；可以反证的
small claims court 小额索赔法院
subject matter 争议事项；标的

testimony 证据（指证人以誓言口头提供证明）；证言
trial court 初审法院
writ of certiorari 调案复审令状

EXERCISES

I. Answer the following questions.

1. Describe briefly the state court system.
2. Describe briefly the federal court system.
3. What are small claims courts? How do they hear cases?
4. How does an appellate court hear cases? Does it listen to witness, accept new evidence or utilize a jury?
5. How many U.S. Courts of Appeals are there now in the U.S.? What are they?
6. Could the Supreme Court of the United States review any cases, if it chooses to do so?

II. Translate the following terms into English.

1. 初审法院
2. 有限管辖权
3. 普遍管辖权
4. 诉讼标的
5. 民事纠纷
6. 刑事诉讼
7. 小额索赔法院
8. 市镇法院
9. 子女监护
10. 上诉法院
11. 地方法院
12. 多元管辖权
13. 巡回法院
14. 调案复审令
15. 四人规则

III. Translate the following sentences into Chinese.

1. In ancient times, people used temples, like the Oracle of Delphi, to assist them in making just decisions.

2. The judicial system of the U.S. is a dual court structure consisting of federal and state courts. Coexistence of dual governments (state and federal) gives rise to separate court systems.
3. Jurisdiction is the authorized power of a court to hear a particular case and render a binding decision.
4. A decision by a lower federal court on a federal question is not binding on a state court.
5. Whenever the U.S. government is a party, a lawsuit will be tried in the federal system. The U.S. is a party when it brings suit or is named as a defendant.

IV. Cloze.

While on the state level some justices are popularly 1_____, no federal judge is elected by any constituency. They also do not serve a 2_____ term, but rather hold office for 3_____ "during Good Behavior". These two provisions result from constitutional attempts to isolate judicial 4_____ from political pressures, and contribute to the 5_____ of the judiciary. Originally (in 1789), there were 13 U.S. district courts, but today, there are 95 of them, distributed throughout all 50 states and U.S. territories. District courts are the most common 6_____ courts of the federal system. They have general 7_____ over all federal crimes, bankruptcies, and when somebody 8_____ the constitutionality of a state or federal law. No district court crosses state lines. Large states like California, New York, and Texas each have four U.S. district courts. The number of 9_____ depends on the size and population and workload. Although each district has numerous judges, a single judge 10_____ over each case.

Supplementary Reading

Court procedures are devised to handle a great variety of legal problems ranging from the most complex to the simplest. Not surprisingly, the usual manner[1] of handling legal

---

1 manner: 方式、方法。

Lesson 3
The American Court System

matters is inefficient for small or simple cases. If you have a legal claim for $1,500 worth of minor damage to your automobile in an accident, the cost of hiring an attorney to help you recover that amount through court action would no doubt exceed your hoped-for recovery.

To promote peaceful resolution of disputes where a conventional lawsuit is prohibitively expensive, states have created a special trial court, called the small claims court[1]. Jurisdiction of this court is usually limited to disputes involving small sums of money damages. They are often referred to as the people's court, because an average adult with limited formal education may obtain resolution of minor civil legal disputes in a speedy, informal, and user-friendly forum.[2]

The small claims court may be a separate court, or a designated subdivision of another court. Because it is the creation of each state, particulars vary widely. The maximum amount of recoverable damages ranges from $1,000 to 25,000, depending on the state, the most common maximum being $5,000. State legislatures frequently change the dollar limits of these courts in inflationary times[3] to continue to provide inexpensive access to the courts for civil matters involving modest amounts of money. The purpose of the small claims court is the same as any other trial court: to determine facts and apply the law. However, the dynamics of the small claims court are more relaxed, proceedings are usually faster, and procedures to use the court are less complicated than those found in other courts. This is not to say it is uncomplicated or that the small claims court is a social gathering—only that is less intimidating[4] to the average litigant.

Most small claims cases involve disputes over money, although some are concerned with matters such as eviction from residential rentals. Divorce actions, criminal matters and civil cases involving in rem[5] jurisdiction are examples of cases not accepted in small claims court. The procedural rules differ from those of traditional trial courts. Legal documents are kept to a minimum; often the only formal document required of the plaintiff is a simple pre-printed form with boxes for checking. There are no formal rules of evidence and no

---

1 传统的诉讼方式非常昂贵，使当事人很难负担，为了促使争议和平解决，各州创设了一种特殊的初审法院，叫作小额索赔法院。
2 它们通常被称作"人们的法院"，因为法庭快捷、不拘礼节、对当事人友好，即使受过很少正规教育的普通人也能够在这里解决小额民事法律纠纷。
3 通货膨胀时期。
4 intimidating: 令人感到受胁迫的。
5 in rem: from Latin, against a thing, 对物; in rem jurisdiction: 对物管辖权。

juries. In the interest of economy and simplicity, most states do not permit attorneys at the Bar to represent litigants in small claims courts. Corporations are artificial, legal persons, and so when they use small claims courts to collect debts they must be represented by employees.[1] Most states will not allow attorney to appear for litigants even in such corporate situations unless the attorney at law[2] is the sole shareholder or an officeholder of the corporation.

Each party explains the dispute, calling on witness of corroboration or for additional facts. Each party also presents any supporting documents or other physical evidence. The judge may ask questions and then, without any elaborate commentary or research, decide the case. Sometimes the judge will rule at the conclusion of the trial[3], but often the judge will inform the parties of his or her decision later by mail. In some states parties can appeal the case, but in many situations the small claims court plaintiff does not have that right—use of a small claims court is deemed a waiver of the right to a jury and to appeal. The defendant, however, generally retains a right to a trail *de novo*[4] (*de novo* means "new" and the term means a right to a completely new trial hearing).

Small claims courts help "the little person" get his or her "day in court" without the delays and costs that accompany use of traditional courts. However, because business firms often have a substantial number of small claims, they appear most frequently as plaintiffs in small claims court actions.

Various television programs such as Judge Judy popularize small claims court. Technically these proceedings are arbitrations (a private third party is selected by the parties to hear and resolve in small claims courts). What they do can not illustrate usual judicial behavior. The cases heard are chosen for entertainment value and the television judge's questions and decisions are often rendered in a sarcastic and condescending fashion.

---

1 公司是虚拟的、法律上的人，因此，当它们利用小额索赔法院来追债时必须以员工作为代表。
2 attorney at law: 律师。
3 有时法官在庭审结束时判决。
4 trial *de novo*: a new trial on the entire case—that is, on both questions of fact and issue of law—conducted as if there had been no trial in the first instance. 对整个案件的重新审判。

Lesson 4
The Jury System

Law is a rule of civil conduct prescribed by the supreme power in a state, commanding what is right, and prohibiting what is wrong.
—*William Blackstone*

法是国家最高权力规定的市民的行动准则，它规定正确的事，禁止做违法的事。

——莱克斯通（英国，1723—1780）

The Anglo-American jury is a remarkable political institution. It recruits a group of no more than 12 laypersons[1], chosen at random from the widest population; it convenes them for the purpose of the particular trial; it entrusts them with great official powers of decision; it permits them to carry on deliberations[2] in secret and to report out their final judgment without giving reasons for it; and, after their momentary service to the state has been completed, it orders them to disband[3] and return to private life.

The jury system is traceable to ninth-century France and was imported to England by William the Conqueror. In its earliest form, a jury was a group of the defendant's neighbors, who were expected to answer questions based on their own knowledge. Such jurors functioned as both witnesses and triers of fact. Later, the right to a jury trial was guaranteed by Bill of Rights and U.S. Constitution and by the separate state constitutions.

Nowadays, in any trial at Crown Court[4] where the defendant has pleaded "not guilty" to a charge in the indictment and where the plea has not been accepted by

---

1 layperson: 外行，未受过专业训练的人。A nonprofessional 这里指非法律专业人士。
2 deliberation: 陪审团作出决定前秘密进行的审议。The discussion by the jury members as to whether or not to return an indictment on a given charge against an accused. During deliberations no one except the jury members may be present.
3 disband: 解散。To cease to function as an organization.
4 Crown Court: 英国王室法院，负责审理重罪一审案件。

the prosecution, he or she will be tried in front of a jury. By contrast, an accused in the United States is entitled to a trial by jury whenever the case is originally brought into federal court and involves an offense for which the punishment may exceed six months' imprisonment and in which the defendant is prosecuted as an adult. The jury system for civil cases has been abolished in Great Britain, and there are pressures to abolish it in the United States.

I. The Role of the Jury

The jury's function during a trial is to decide the facts of the case. They are laypersons and have no knowledge of law and are competent to put forward any opinion on law. They have to rely upon their common sense to assess the accused[1] and the evidence against him in order to reach a verdict. It is the judge's function, *inter alia*[2], to explain the law to the jury and they reach a verdict through their understanding of the law explained by him. The relationship between a judge and a jury is very influential. The judge conducts the trial, decides any legal issues that arise during the trial and controls the evidence the jury is allowed to hear. If the evidence is weak the judge can instruct the jury to acquit the accused. At the conclusion of the evidence the judge will sum up the case to the jury before they retire to reach a verdict. The judge at this point can do no more. The judge can use his summing up to indicate to the jury that the only reasonable decision to reach would be a guilty verdict, however, there is no actual judicial power to instruct juries to convict an accused. If the jury's verdict is a perverse one there is nothing more the judge can do; it must be accepted. If the verdict is acquittal, it is unchallengeable. There is no appeal against an acquittal in Crown Court and further, once the accused is acquittal, he can be not be charged with the same offence again.

1　the accused: 被告。The accused is the person accused of the commission of a federal crime. Use of this term does not imply the person under investigation is guilty of any crime. After a person is indicted by the grand jury, that person is referred to as the "defendant".
2　*inter alia*: 〈拉丁语〉除了别的东西；其中。英文为among other things。这里指法官除了其他平常职责之外，在这种情境中还有解释法律的职责。

Lesson 4
The Jury System

II. Selection of the Jury

Anyone who is listed on the electoral register between the ages of 18 and 70 is eligible for jury service. Ineligible persons are members of the judiciary and others involved in the justice system, e.g. barristers and solicitors, the clergy, the mentally ill.

a. Jury Vetting[1]

The panel[2] is selected at random and any party to the proceedings can inspect the panel from which the jurors will be chosen. Jury vetting, as a means to reduce the randomness, is the investigation of jurors' backgrounds to determine whether they are suitable for jury service.

b. Challenging[3] Jury Membership

Either party has the right to challenge the presence of a juror on three grounds:

a. the juror is in fact not qualified; or

b. the juror is biased; or

c. the juror may be reasonably suspected of bias against the defendant.

When people respond to a jury summons[4], they gather at the court house to form a pool of potential jurors from which they are called in groups for specific criminal or civil trials. There they are questioned by attorneys for each side and/or the trial judge about their background, life experiences, and opinions to determine whether they can weigh the evidence fairly and objectively. This process is called "voir dire"[5], an Anglo-French term meaning "to speak the truth".

In the United States, there is no limit to the number that can be rejected. While in UK, only the defense has the opportunity to make a peremptory challenge[6] to the

---

1 vetting: 审查。Thorough examination or evaluation. "jury vetting" 是在确定全体陪审团成员组成的阶段进行的对陪审员背景的全面详细审查。
2 panel: 指法院陪审员名单上列出的全体陪审员，并非某个陪审团全体团员。
3 challenge: 申请（法官或陪审员）回避；对……表示异议。
4 jury summon: 陪审召集令。A jury summon is a notice requesting a person to report to court as a juror.
5 voir dire: 见证人或陪审员在接受审核时的誓语，即"一切照实陈述"。
6 peremptory challenge: 无因回避请求。即可以不说明理由便排除某个陪审员在该案中的陪审资格。在英国，只有辩方才享有这个权利，但申请的回避人数有限制。与之相对的是有因回避请求"challenge for causes"。

potential juror and arbitrarily reject a number. The prosecution has the right to ask a juror to "stand by for the Crown". The "stood by" juror only got on the jury if the entire panel have been used up.

III. Trial by Jury

A jury trial is a trial of a lawsuit or criminal prosecution in which the case is presented to a jury and the factual questions and the final judgment are determined by a jury. This is distinguished from a "court trial" in which the judge decides factual as well as legal questions, and makes the final judgment.

The questions put to those early juries were usually questions of fact or mixed questions of fact and law. Modern juries may deal with questions of law in addition to questions of fact when rendering general verdicts, and Federal juries are usually limited to dealing with questions of fact.

The jury trial finds expression in the American legal system in three places: the grand jury, the criminal petit jury[1], and civil petit jury. Each is guaranteed in the federal courts by the U.S. Constitution, and every state uses them.

IV. Grand Jury

The grand jury as an institution was so firmly established in the traditions of American forebears that they included it in the Bill of Rights. The Fifth Amendment to the Constitution of the United States provides in part that "no person shall be held to answer for a capital, or otherwise infamous crime, unless on a presentment or indictment of a Grand Jury..."

The powers and functions of the federal grand jury differ from those of the federal trial jury, which is called the petit jury. The petit jury listens to the evidence offered by the prosecution and the defense (if it chooses to offer any) during a criminal trial and returns a verdict of guilty or not guilty. The grand jury, on the other hand, does not determine guilt or innocence, but only whether there is probable

---

1 petit jury：普通陪审团，又称小陪审团。The petit jury is a trial jury, composed of 12 members, which hears a case after indictment and renders a verdict or decision after hearing the prosecution's entire case and whatever evidence the defendant chooses to offer. 与大陪审团（grant jury）相对应。

Lesson 4
The Jury System

cause[1] to believe that a crime was committed and that a specific person or persons committed it. If the grand jury finds probable cause to exist, then it will return a written statement of the charges called an "indictment"[2]. After that, the accused will go to trial.

The grand jury normally hears only that evidence presented by an attorney for the government which tends to show the commission of a crime. The grand jury must determine from this evidence, and usually without hearing evidence for the defense, whether a person should be tried for a serious federal crime, referred to in the Bill of Rights as an "infamous crime." An infamous crime is one which may be punished by imprisonment for more than one year. As a general rule, no one can be prosecuted for a serious crime unless the grand jury decides that the evidence it has heard so requires. In this way, the grand jury operates both as a "sword", authorizing the government's prosecution of suspected criminals, and also as a "shield", protecting citizens from unwarranted or inappropriate prosecutions. A person may, however, waive grand jury proceedings and agree to be prosecuted by a written charge of crime called an information[3].

After the grand jurors have been sworn, the presiding judge advises the grand jury of its obligations and how best to perform its duties. This is called the charge to the grand jury[4]. Careful attention must be paid to the charge, for it and any additional instructions that may be given by the court contain the rules and directions the grand jury must follow during its term of service.

Sixteen of the 23 members of the grand jury constitute a quorum for the

---

1　probable cause: 合理依据。The finding necessary in order to return an indictment against a person accused of a federal crime. A finding of probable cause is proper only when the evidence presented to the grand jury, without any explanation being offered by the accused, persuades 12 or more grand jurors that a federal crime has probably been committed by the person accused. 是大陪审团签署起诉书所需要的条件。就是在听取了各种证据（被告提供的除外）之后，大陪审团中12个以上的陪审员认为该犯罪行为有可能是此被告实施的，则认定有"合理依据"。
2　indictment: 大陪审团起诉书。A written formal charge of a crime by the grand jury, returned when 12 or more grand jurors vote in favor of it. 大陪审团签署的支持公诉的起诉书。
3　information: 检察官刑事起诉书。A written formal charge of crime by the United States Attorney, filed against an accused who, if charged with a serious crime, must have knowingly waived the requirement that the evidence first be presented to a grand jury.（由检察官签署的）刑事起诉书。
4　Charge to the Grand Jury: 法官对大陪审团的指示。The Charge to the Grand Jury is given by the judge presiding over the selection and organization of the grand jury, the charge is the court's instructions to the grand jury as to its duties, functions, and obligations, and how to best perform them.

transaction of business. If fewer than this number are present, even for a moment, the proceedings of the grand jury must stop. Much of the grand jury's time is spent hearing testimony by witnesses and examining documentary or other evidence in order to determine whether such evidence justifies an indictment.

Witnesses will be called to testify one after another. The witness will then be questioned after he is sworn by the grand jury. Ordinarily, the attorney for the government questions the witness first, followed next by the foreperson[1] of the grand jury. Then, the other members of the grand jury may question the witness. Prior to answering a question, a witness may ask to leave the grand jury room to consult with his or her attorney. A witness who is appearing before the grand jury may invoke the Fifth Amendment privilege against self-incrimination[2] and refuse to answer a question. In such a situation, the grand jurors may bring the matter before the court in order to obtain a ruling as to whether or not the answer may be compelled. One manner in which an answer may be compelled is by granting the witness immunity from prosecution in exchange for the witness' testimony.

After it has received evidence against a person, the grand jury must decide whether the evidence presented justifies an indictment, or "true bill"[3], which is the formal criminal charge returned by the grand jury. Upon the indictment's being filed in court, the person accused must either plead guilty or *nolo contendere*[4] or stand trial.

If the evidence does not persuade the grand jury that there is probable cause to believe the person committed a crime, the grand jury will vote a "no bill", or "not a true bill." When this occurs, the person is not required to plead to a criminal charge, and no trial is required.

When the grand jury has received all the evidence on a given charge, all persons other than the members of the grand jury must leave the room so that the grand jury may begin its deliberations. The presence of any other person in the grand jury room

---

1 foreperson: 陪审团主席。A member of a jury who acts as the leader and speaks for the jury.
2 self-incrimination: 自证其罪。Making statements or producing evidence which tends to prove that one is guilty of a crime. 做出可能证明自己有罪的陈述或提供这样的证据。美国宪法第五修正案规定，无论任何人都不得在任何刑事案件中被迫自证其罪。
3 true bill: 大陪审团认可的起诉书；准予起诉。
4 *nolo contendere*: 〈拉丁语〉不辩护的无罪申诉（刑事诉讼中，被告不认罪但又放弃申辩）。

Lesson 4
The Jury System

while the grand jury deliberates or votes may nullify[1] an indictment returned on the accusation.

Every grand juror has the right to express his or her view of the matter under consideration, and grand jurors should listen to the comments of all their fellow grand jurors before making up their mind. Only after each grand juror has been given the opportunity to be heard will the vote be taken. At least 16 jurors must be present and 12 members must vote in favor of the indictment before it may be returned.

If an indictment is found, the grand jury will report it to the judge or a magistrate in open court. It will likewise report any "not true bills", or decisions not to indict. A decision not to indict should immediately be reported to the court in writing by the foreperson so that the accused may promptly be released from jail or freed on bail.

The law imposes upon each grand juror a strict obligation of secrecy. This obligation is emphasized in the oath each grand juror takes and in the charge given to the grand jury by the judge. The tradition of secrecy continues as a vital part of the grand jury system for many reasons. It protects the grand jurors from being subjected to pressure by persons who may be subjects of investigations by the grand jury or associates of such persons. It prevents the escape of those against whom an indictment is being considered. It encourages witnesses before the grand jury to give full and truthful information as to the commission of a crime. It also prevents tampering with or intimidation of such witnesses before they testify at trial. Finally, it prevents the disclosure of investigations that result in no action by the grand jury and avoids any stigma the public might attach to one who is the subject of a mere investigation by the grand jury.

The secrecy imposed upon grand jurors is a major source of protection for them. In addition, no inquiry may be made to learn what grand jurors said or how they voted, except upon order of the court. The law gives the members of a grand jury broad immunity for actions taken by them within the scope of their authority as grand jurors. Because of this immunity, all grand jurors must perform their duties with the highest sense of responsibility.

---

1 nullify: 使无效。To invalidate, make null. e.g., nullify a contract, nullify a verdict.

Glossary

challenge 申请（法官或陪审员）回避
Crown Court 英国王室法院；刑事法院
deliberation（陪审团）审议，评议；（刑事案件中）预谋，蓄谋
disband 解散
foreperson 陪审团主席
indictment 大陪审团起诉书；公诉书
information（由检察官签署的）刑事起诉书
inter alia〈拉丁语〉除了别的东西；其中

jury summon 陪审召集令
layperson 外行；非法律专业人士
nullify 使无效
peremptory challenge 无因回避请求
petit jury 小陪审团
probable cause 合理依据
the accused 被告人
true bill 大陪审团认可的起诉书；准予起诉
vetting 彻底审查

EXERCISES

I. Answer the following questions.

1. What is the "probable cause"?
2. What's the function of the Grand Jury?
3. Who can be a juror? Who is excluded?
4. What is the "charge to the Grand Jury"?
5. How will the witnesses be examined before the Grand Jury, and what rights are they entitled to?
6. If the Grand Jury votes a true bill, what can the accused person do?

II. Translate the following terms into English.

1.（陪审团签发的）起诉书
2.（检察官签发的）起诉书
3.（法官发出的）对大陪审团的指示
4. 自证其罪
5. 证人证言
6.（陪审团）评议
7. 裁决
8. 无罪（裁决）
9. 陪审团主席
10. 大陪审团
11. 小陪审团
12. "一切照实陈述"（拉丁法谚）

Lesson 4
The Jury System

13. 合理依据   14. 绝对回避

15. （美国）权利法案

III. Translate the following sentences into Chinese.

1. After the grand jury has been charged, it is taken to the grand jury room, where it will hear testimony and consider documentary evidence in the cases brought to its attention by the government attorney.
2. Because the appearance of an accused before the grand jury may raise complicated legal problems, a grand jury that desires to request or to permit an accused to appear before it should consult with the government attorney.
3. The foreperson of the grand jury must keep a record of the number of jurors concurring in the finding of every indictment and file the record with the Clerk of the Court.
4. The jury is neither required nor allowed to offer their reasoning in court. They are asked only for their verdict.

IV. Discussion.

The jury system has long been a controversy. Judges, as a result of training, discipline, recurrent experience, and superior intelligence, will be better able to understand the law and analyze the facts than laypersons, selected from a wide range of intelligent levels, without experience with matters of this sort nor durable official responsibility. The critics complain that the jury will not follow the law, either because it does not understand it or because it does not like it, and only a very uneven and unequal administration of justice can result form reliance on the jury.

In your point of view, why should the jury system be (actually is) kept, and what is the value or essence of the jury system?

Supplementary Reading

A fundamental requirement of a fair jury system is that no person or class of persons may be excluded from jury service on account of race, color, religion, sex, national origin or economic status. This principle is clearly stated in the federal Jury Selection and Service Act of 1968[1] and has been specifically endorsed by the American Bar Association's[2] Project on Minimum Standards for Criminal Justice.

A specific jury panel need not represent the entire community exactly. Jurors must then be selected strictly at random from the representative list. And how is such a representative list to be secured? The ABA committee concluded that "there is reason to believe that voter registration lists will usually be the most representative comprehensive lists of names available."

Recent data gathered in the state and federal courts of the state of Rhode Island[3] cast significant doubt on the easy assumption of the ABA and others that voter registration lists do in fact accurately represent the total population. This article will endeavor to document some of the areas in which voter registration lists differ from the population as a whole.

The United States District Court[4] for the District of Rhode Island, which includes the entire state within its jurisdiction, selects its jurors at random from the voter registration lists. The Superior Court of Rhode Island, the basic trial court of the state and the only state court which uses juries, also draws its jurors from the voter registration lists. The two selection processes are completely independent.

The Federal District Court maintains a Qualified Jury Wheel[5] from which the names of jurors are selected as they are needed. The state's system differs significantly from the

---

1 Jury Selection and Service Act of 1968，是指1968年根据美国宪法第六次修正案关于"公正陪审团"审判的权利制定的陪审团组成运作规则的联邦法律。
2 American Bar Association: 美国律师协会（缩写为ABA）。除ABA之外，各州以及各县都有律师协会，之间没有隶属关系。美国律师协会是自愿加入的组织，而各州律师协会是必须加入的组织，因为成为某一州律师协会的会员是在该州执业的前提条件。
3 美国罗得岛州。该文中的结论都是以该州联邦法院以及州法院的统计数据为依据。
4 District Court: 美国的联邦地方法院。管辖的案件主要为：涉及联邦宪法、法律或国际条约的案件，一方当事人为联邦政府的案件，涉及外国政府代理人的案件，公海上或国境内供对外贸易和州际贸易之用的通航水域案件，不同州之间、不同州的公民之间的争议以及州政府向他州公民提起的诉讼。一般为独任审理，重大案件由3名法官组成合议庭并召集陪审团进行审理。
5 jury wheel: 预备陪审员名单或确认其人数的清单或电子系统。

Lesson 4
The Jury System

one employed in federal court in that, once names are drawn at random, the office of the jury commissioner sends out a mail-back questionnaire. A number of potential jurors are disqualified at this point. The jury commissioner maintains a staff of investigators who then visit each potential juror at his home or place of business to administer the same questionnaire a second time. This element of individual investigation naturally raises questions as to the impact of the investigator's discretionary evaluation.

Random Selection Both the state and federal procedures claim to rest on the same base—random selection from the list of registered voters. Interestingly, jury venires were found to be disproportionately male and there is virtually no difference between the state and federal venires in this respect. Indeed, survey research has demonstrated that men are more likely to register to vote than women. And the major factor contributing to the result is that both the state statute and the rules of the Federal District Court grant an automatic exemption to any woman who claims it.

Young persons are clearly under-represented[1] in both state and federal venires and middle-aged persons are grossly over-represented on both state and federal venires. This phenomenon is not surprising in view of the known characteristics of registered voters.

Education In general, members of both state and federal venires are better educated than they would be were they strictly representative of the total population. Interestingly, persons who have graduated from college are represented on federal and state venires in their exact proportion to the adult population. Superficially this is surprising, since the college-educated are more likely to register to vote than those with less formal education. The countervailing factor which should be noted, however, is the automatic exclusion of many professionals from jury service. Lawyers, doctors, dentists and clergymen are routinely exempted, (as are university teachers from state juries), thus significantly decreasing the pool of college graduates who are eligible to serve.

Occupation The data gathered demonstrate that state and federal venires are virtually identical in terms of occupations. Upper status positions—professional, technical, and managerial—are more common among the veniremen than among the total population. As to race, blacks clearly appear in venires in representative numbers.

---

1 under-represented: 未得到充分代表的。是指这部分人担当陪审员的比例低于其在总人口中所占的比例。

Other Variables: There is evidence that venires are disproportionately composed of long-term residents, an overwhelming percentage of male veniremen reported having served in the armed forces, and a greater percentage of the veniremen than that of the total population aged 20 and above is married.

These three variables should be handled with great caution. Nevertheless, if one is prepared to regard length of tenure in residence, military service and marriage, as some evidence of a "stable" and/or "conventional" citizen, then the data are consistent with the hypothesis that the veniremen are overly "stable" and "conventional". Again, all three factors may well be another way of saying that a venireman is significantly more likely to be middle-aged than is the average citizen.

Lesson 5
A Survey on Schools of Jurisprudence

 Jurisprudence is the knowledge of things divine and human, the science of what is right and wrong.

法理乃天上人间诸事之知识，亦公正与否之科学。

The word "jurisprudence" derives from the Latin term *juris prudentia*[1], which means "the study, knowledge, or science of law." In the United States jurisprudence commonly means the philosophy of law[2]. Legal philosophy has many aspects, but four of them are the most common. The first and the most prevalent form of jurisprudence seeks to analyze, explain, classify, and criticize entire bodies of law. Law school textbooks and legal encyclopedias[3] represent this type of scholarship. The second type of jurisprudence compares and contrasts law with other fields of knowledge such as literature, economics, religion, and the social sciences. The third type of jurisprudence seeks to reveal the historical, moral, and cultural basis of a particular legal concept. The fourth body of jurisprudence focuses on finding the answers to such abstract questions as What is law? How do judges (properly) decide cases?

Apart from different types of jurisprudence, different schools of jurisprudence

---

1 拉丁语*juris prudentia*在公元2世纪时已被广泛使用。古罗马五大法学家之一乌尔比安（Ulpianus，约160—228）曾对*juris prudentia*下过著名的定义："法学是神事和人事的知识，正与不正的学问。"
2 philosophy of law：法哲学。法哲学是指研究法律的基本原则（general principles）和基本法学理论问题（scholarly study of fundamental legal theories）的学科，有时也称为"法律哲学"（legal philosophy）。
3 legal encyclopedia：法律大百科全书。现代的法律大百科全书有英格兰1897年首版的《英格兰法律大百科全书》（*Encyclopaedia of the Laws of England*）和1907年首版的《霍尔斯伯里英格兰法律全集》（*Halsbury's Laws of England*）。美国的第一部法律百科全书是1883年桑顿（Thorton）的《世界法律百科全书》（*Universal Cyclopedia of Law*）。

exist. There is a classic debate over the appropriate sources of law between positivist and natural law schools of thought[1]. Positivists argue that there is no connection between law and morality and the only sources of law are rules that have been expressly enacted by a governmental entity or court of law. Naturalists, or proponents of natural law, insist that the rules enacted by government are not the only sources of law. They argue that moral philosophy, religion, human reason and individual conscience are also integrating parts of the law.

There are no bright lines between different schools of jurisprudence. The legal philosophy of a particular legal scholar may consist of a combination of strains from many schools of legal thoughts. Some scholars think that it is more appropriate to think about jurisprudence as a continuum.

The above mentioned schools of legal thoughts are only part of a diverse jurisprudential picture of the United States. Other prominent schools of legal thoughts exist.

I. The Natural Law School

The oldest and one of the most significant schools of jurisprudence is the natural law school[2]. Those who adhere to the natural law school of thought believe that government and the legal system should reflect universal moral and ethical principles that are inherent in human nature.

The concept of natural law traces its origins to ancient Greece. The Greek philosopher Aristotle (384—322 B.C.) made the distinction between natural law and conventional law, (also called positive law, or written law). According to Aristotle, natural law "everywhere has the same force…" Thus, natural laws are moral principles that are universal in human societies. Conventional laws, on the other hand, reflect the values and morals that are accepted by a particular society at a particular time. In our own time, for example, laws establishing minimum-age requirements for voting or drinking are not products of some divine scheme, but

---

1 positivist and natural law schools of thought: 实证与自然法学流派思想。
2 natural law school: 自然法学派。Natural law (自然法): a philosophical system of legal and moral principles purportedly deriving from a universalized conception of human nature or divine justice rather than from legislative or judicial action.

Lesson 5

A Survey on Schools of Jurisprudence

rather reflect the prevailing views of a particular society and a particular time. A law prohibiting murder, for example, does not reflect the values accepted by a particular society at a particular time but is based on a universally accepted precept that murder is wrong. To murder someone is thus a violation of natural law.

Because natural law is universal, it takes on a higher order than positive, or conventional law. The ideology of natural law encourages individuals to disobey conventional or written laws if those individuals believe that the laws are in conflict with natural law. Those who protested America's involvement in Vietnam War (1964—1973), for example, used natural law as their reason to violate written laws.

St. Thomas Aquinas (A.D.1225—1274), a medieval theologian[1], tried to reconcile Aristotle's philosophy of natural law with Christianity. According to Aquinas, there are four types of law. Eternal law is God's plan for the universe. Natural law is made up of those aspects of eternal law that are accessible to humans through reason. Divine law is God's direct revelation to humankind through the Scriptures. Finally, human laws are specific rules created by men and women to address particular problems or circumstances.

Aquinas believed that particular laws created by humans were often influenced by such human vices as selfishness and ignorance. Human laws, therefore, must never conflict with natural laws. In fact, Aquinas believed that human laws that conflict with natural laws ought to be disobeyed. Such acts of disobedience vindicated the superiority of natural law[2].

At the basis of natural law is the concept that all persons have natural rights[3]. John Locke[4], an important English political philosopher, argued in 1689 that no one was born with an obligation to obey rulers. He claimed that all individuals were born free, equal, and independent, and that they had a natural right to life, liberty, and property. The purpose of government was to secure those rights.

---

1 theologian：神学家（One who is learned in theology）。
2 superiority of natural law：自然法至上。
3 natural rights：天赋权利，自然权利。由人的本性和自然法则产生的权利，主要包括生命、自由、私有财产、追求幸福等，它与国家实在法产生的权利不同。
4 John Locke：约翰·洛克（1632—1704），英国著名哲学家，著有《政府论》（*Two Treatises of Civil Government*，因为政府论分上下两篇，因而有时也译为《政府二论》）和《人类理智论》（*An Essay Concerning Human Understanding*）。洛克的主要思想是人的自然权利神圣不可侵犯。

In our own time Lon Fuller has attempted to apply natural-law principles to an analysis of the legal system. In *The Morality of Law* (1964), Fuller examined our legal system to understand its "internal morality."[1] In so doing, he laid out certain requirements for an internally moral legal system:

- The legal system should comprise reasonably clear general rules that are known to all citizens in advance.
- These rules should not be retroactive—that is, they should not be applied to situations that occurred before those rules were established.
- Laws should not be contradictory or require the impossible.
- Laws should remain constant over time and should be administered in a consistent manner.

Although Fuller's formulation of natural law certainly differs from that of Aristotle, it shares with it an attempt to identify certain unchangeable moral principles that should form the foundation of every legal system.

II. The Positivist School

At the other end of the spectrum is the positivist school[2] or positivism (or analytical jurisprudence[3]). Those who adhere to this school believe that there can be no higher law than a nation's positive law—law created by a particular society at a particular point in time.

The English philosopher Thomas Hobbes (1588—1679) is viewed by many as the founder of the positivist approach to law. Hobbes believed that in the original state of nature, humans were no better than monkeys killing each other to get at the few bananas on the banana tree, and he concluded that sovereign power[4] was necessary for stability and peace—in fact, for survival. Individuals do not have

---

1. internal morality：内在道德性。Lon Fuller（1902—1978），新自法学派代表人物之一。
2. the positivist school：实证主义法学派。A school of legal thought that holds that there can be no higher law than a nation's positive law—law created by a particular society at a particular point in time. In contrast to the natural law school, the positivist school maintains that there are no "natural" rights; rights come into existence only when there is a sovereign power (government) to confer and enforce those rights.
3. analytical jurisprudence：分析法学，近代法理学的一个流派。
4. sovereign power：主权权力。根据《布莱克法律字典》，Sovereign power is the power to make and enforce laws，因而这一抽象的"主权权力"就是指制定法律、执行法律的权力。

Lesson 5

A Survey on Schools of Jurisprudence

any "natural" rights; rather, they possess only those rights acquired as a result of enforceable law. Whether a particular law is bad or good is irrelevant. The merits or demerits of a given law can be discussed, and laws can be changed in an orderly manner through legitimate lawmaking process. But as long as a law exists, it must be obeyed.

John Austin (1790—1859), one of the most important thinkers in the tradition of legal positivism, did agree that morality should play some role in shaping the law. But Austin, like other positivists, believed that moral theory has no role in defining what law actually is. A bad law is as much a law as a good one: "The existence of law is one thing," he wrote, "its merit or demerit is another."

To Austin, the difference between a law and an opinion lies in the fact that a law must be obeyed on pain of punishment: A law is thus a "command" issued by a "sovereign". A command, according to Austin, has two components. The first is the expression of a desire that someone do or not do something; the other is a threat or implied threat against anyone who does not comply with that desire.

The sovereign, meanwhile, must be an uncommanded commander—that is, a person or institution "not in the habit of rendering habitual obedience" to anyone else and "habitually obeyed by the bulk of the people in that society." In addition, the sovereign must always be "determinate": that is, it must consist of specific individuals or institutions.

Another legal positivist, the Englishman H.L.A. Hart (b. 1907), emphasized the difference between being obligated[1] to do something and being obliged[2] to do it.

According to Hart, a mature legal system also comprises two kinds of rules, primary rules and secondary rules.

Hart suggests in addition that there are three kinds of secondary rules. Rules of adjudication[3] tell us how to settle disputes. Rules of change explain how the system

---

1 obligate：使受（道德或法律）责任约束（to bind by legal or moral duty）。该词的名词形式是 obligation，一般指"债、债权债务关系""义务、责任""债务文书、盖印合同"之意。它来自于拉丁语"obligatio"，罗马法中"债"的意思，与"契约"（contract）意义相近；在罗马法中，债是"法锁"（legal bond），所以债务人（debtor）须要履行特定行为，即履行义务。
2 oblige：（以道德或法律）强使、迫使（to bind by doing a favor or service）。
3 adjudication：审判。The process of judicially deciding a case.

can be modified. Rules of recognition[1] are standards that tell us whether or not a particular law is valid. By "valid", however, Hart does not mean morally valid. Like Austin, Hart was a positivist: He held that although morality can and should influence law, it does not help us decide what is a valid law.

III. Sociological Jurisprudence

Sociological jurisprudence[2] suggests that both the law and judicial interpretations of it should take into account the findings of sociology. Consider, for example, the case of *Brown v. Board of Education* (1954)[3]—the famous case in which the Supreme Court declared racial segregation of the public schools to be illegal. In explaining its decision, the Court introduced information, stemming from the work of sociologists, which suggested that black children learn more readily in integrated than in segregated schools. When the Court put these findings forward as a reason for banning segregation in public schools, its reasoning was an example of sociological jurisprudence.

Perhaps the leading exponent of sociological jurisprudence was Roscoe Pound (1870—1964). Pound argued that legal systems in civilized countries are based upon certain shared assumptions or expectations. In such countries, he believed, we must be able to assume that:

- no one will deliberately harm anyone else;
- property rights, not only in fixed and movable property but also in such intellectual property as patents and copyrights, will be respected;
- anyone who enters into a contract will observe it;
- people will try to prevent needless injury to others;
- people who use dangerous materials and processes will do so only in ways

---

1. recognition: 确认，认可，承认。Confirmation that an act done by another person was authorized.
2. sociological jurisprudence: 社会法学。Legal theory suggesting that the law and its judicial interpretations should consider the findings of sociology.
3. 1954年5月17日，美国最高法院全体一致作出裁决：公立学校的种族隔离（racial segregation）违反宪法。最高法院以前已宣布高等院校中的种族隔离违法。位于美国南北交界地带的几个地区立即采取行动终止种族隔离。但是南方的大部分地区拒不执行裁决。布朗一案裁决的影响远远超出了公立学校的范围。它为法院对美国生活各方面的种族隔离提出挑战提供了法律基础。该裁决废止了各州实行种族隔离的权力，把美国黑人引入政治进程，从而比以往任何一项最高法院裁决更多地改变了美国人民的日常生活。

that do not threaten the public.

IV. Legal Realism

Legal realism[1] was a school of legal thought popular in the 1920s and 1930s, one that left a strong imprint on American jurisprudence. The legal realists questioned the assumption that judges apply the law impartially, logically, and uniformly. If this were true, they argued, then all cases involving similar circumstances and issues should have similar outcomes. But issues involving identical facts are often decided differently by different courts, even when the same legal principles are applied. Why is this? According to the legal realists, different outcomes result because judges are human beings with unique personalities, value systems, and intellects. It would be impossible, therefore, for any two judges to engage in an identical reasoning process when evaluating the same case. In other words, it would be impossible for the law to be applied in a completely impartial, logical, and uniform manner. The task of jurists, from the legal realist's point of view, is to acknowledge this fact and become as objective as possible by becoming aware of, and clarifying, the ways in which their reasoning in particular cases is affected by their personal biases and values.

United States Supreme Court Justice Oliver Wendell Holmes, Jr. (1841—1935), was an influential proponent of legal realism. In one of his best-known works, *The Common Law*, Holmes emphasized the practical nature of the law: "The life of law has not been logic; it has been experience."[2] Another proponent of this legal school of thought was Karl Llewellyn (1893—1962), best known for his work in drafting the Uniform Commercial Code. Llewellyn viewed judges' decisions as being necessarily shaped by the judges' value judgments and their interpretations of the outcomes of previous cases.

---

1 legal realism：法现实主义。A school of legal thought of the 1920s and 1930s that challenged many existing jurisprudential assumptions, particularly the assumption that subjective elements played no part in judicial reasoning. The legal realists, as the term implies, generally advocated a less abstract and more realistic approach to the law, an approach that would take into account customary practices and the circumstances in which transactions take place. This school left a lasting imprint on American jurisprudence.
2 法的生命不在逻辑，而在经验。

Glossary

adjudication 审判；裁判
articulate 清楚明白地说出
conventional law 惯例法
determinate 决定性的；限定性的
divine 神的；敬神的
empirical 完全根据经验的；经验主义的
exponent 倡导者；拥护者
ideology 思维方式；意识形态
legal encyclopedia 法律大百科全书
legitimacy 合法性
medieval 中世纪的
natural law school 自然法学派
natural rights 天赋权利；自然权利

normality 常态；正常
philosophy of law 法哲学
positivist school 实证主义法学派
possess 占有；支配
proponent 提议者；支持者
retroactive 有溯及既往力的
scholarship 学问；学识
sovereign power 主权
strain 种类
theologian 神学家
vehemence 激烈；猛烈
vindicate 辩护；证明有理
violation 违犯；违反

EXERCISES

I. Answer the following questions.

1. Define *jurisprudence*.
2. Describe the natural law perspectives on jurisprudence.
3. Who was St. Thomas Aquinas? What are the four types of law according to him?
4. Who was Lon Fuller? What thoughts did he contribute to the natural law school?
5. Define the *Positivist School*.
6. List some important thinkers in the tradition of legal positivism.
7. Define *sociological jurisprudence*.
8. Define *legal realism*.

II. Translate the following terms into English.

1. 法学流派
2. 自然法
3. 社会法学
4. 自然权利

Lesson 5
A Survey on Schools of Jurisprudence

5. 法哲学   6. 实证法

7. 种族隔离   8. 神法

9. 人法   10. 永恒法

III. Translate the following sentences into Chinese.

1. The natural-law school, which originated in ancient Greece, stresses the moral and absolute basis of law: Only those laws that conform to natural law—that is, absolute moral values—are viewed as valid.

2. Laws that conflict with higher ethics are not laws at all. As opposed to natural laws, conventional laws reflect the values a particular society has accepted at a particular time.

3. Those who adhere to the natural law school of thought believe that government and the legal system should reflect universal moral and ethical principles that are inherent in human nature.

4. The concept of natural law originated with the Greeks and received its most important formulation in Stoicism.

5. The modern idea of natural rights grew out of the ancient and medieval doctrines of natural law, i.e., the belief that people, as creatures of nature and God, should live their lives and organize their society on the basis of rules and precepts laid down by nature or God.

IV. Cloze.

Sociological jurisprudence, dissatisfied with the 1_____ and positivist schools' lack of attention to social circumstances that help create and affect laws, argues that the law and its interpretations must take into account the findings of 2_____. The school of legal realism, much like sociological 3_____, asks that law recognize the impact of social realities on the formation of laws. Legal realism looks to the participants in the legal system—4 _____, lawyers, and juries—as determinants of the law. Its 5_____ believe that law is the product of human beings who are themselves the products of and influenced by social and economic circumstances. Law, this school argues, is separate from absolute 6_____ principles. Although 7_____ and judges apply the same universally accepted values to cases, the conclusions of judges and 8_____ vary. They are influenced by their own values and beliefs.

Supplementary Reading

Economic analysis of law[1] applies the tools of microeconomic theory to the analysis of legal rules and institutions[2]. Ronald Coase and Guido Calabresi are generally identified as the seminal articles but Commons and Hale among others had brought economic thinking to the study of law in the 1910s and 1920s[3]. Moreover, economic analysis of law derives from several different intellectual traditions in economics.

Richard Posner[4] brought economic analysis of law to the attention of the general legal academy; by the late 1970s, his work had provoked a vigorous controversy within the legal academy. That controversy has usually defined the debate around the philosophical foundations of economic analysis of law. Posner made two claims: (I) Common law legal rules are, in fact, efficient; and (II) Legal rules ought to be efficient. In both claims, "efficient" means maximization of the social willingness-to-pay. In the course of the controversy, two other claims were articulated in Kornhauser: (III) Legal processes select for efficient rules; and (IV) individuals respond to legal rules economically. (In this third claim, "efficient" means "Pareto efficient[5]".) Kornhauser identified this last, behavioral claim as central to the enterprise. A fifth claim is also implicit in the literature: (V) on the best interpretation of law, common law doctrines promote efficiency. Notice that (V) differs from (I) in important respects. According to (V), an economic interpretation fits a doctrine not because, as

---

1 economic analysis of law: 经济分析法学。
2 经济分析法学运用微观经济学原理来分析法律规则与法律制度。
3 一般认为罗那德·科斯（Ronald Coase）与盖多·卡拉布来西（Guido Calabresi）是经济分析法学的创始人，但康孟斯（Commons）与海尔（Hale）等是于二十世纪一十年代与二十年代将经济引入法律研究之中的。seminal：精液的、胚胎的、原创的。article 有"人"的意思。
4 理查德·波斯纳（Richard Posner），经济分析法学派代表人物。
5 Pareto efficient：帕莱托效率。An allocation is Pareto efficient if there is no other allocation in which some other individual is better off and no individual is worse off. Pareto efficient是指"既能使某些人境况更好，而又不使任何人处境更坏"的分配；"帕莱托效率"又称为"分配效率"（allocative efficiency）。

Lesson 5
A Survey on Schools of Jurisprudence

asserted in (I), the legal rules in fact induce efficient behavior but because the rule would induce efficient behavior within the view of the world that seems to underlie the judicial decisions. (I) is an empirical claim that requires the analyst to determine whether the actual behavior induced by legal rules is efficient; it requires knowledge of how individuals do, in fact, behave and of which behavior in the real world would, in fact, be efficient. (V) requires only knowledge of the content of judicial opinions; the analyst interprets these opinions to extract an economic model that underlies the decision. (V) might be true even though legal rules induced inefficient behavior in the real world because the announced legal rule might be efficient within the implicit model used by judges.

These five claims do not correspond directly to traditional questions in the philosophy of law[1]. The evaluative claim (II) that legal rules ought to be efficient would, if directed to judges, qualify as a theory of adjudication, one of the central concerns of Anglo-American philosophy of law. Central philosophic questions concerning the concept of law, of its normativity[2], and the obligation to obey the law, however, are not directly addressed. The behavioral claim as well as the evolutionary claim (III) and the positive claim (II), by contrast, concern empirical issues that philosophers of law generally neglect. Nevertheless, the controversy within the legal academy has generally regarded economic analysis of law as providing a comprehensive theory of law that challenges traditional approaches to law[3]. Indeed, an explanation of the vehemence[4] of the controversy should identify differences in fundamental views concerning law.

---

1 philosophy of law: 法哲学。
2 normativity: 规范性；标准性。
3 challenges traditional approaches to law: 对传统的法律研究方法的挑战。
4 vehemence: 激烈、猛烈。

Lesson 6
The Doctrine of Stare Decisis

Like reason makes like law.

相似的理由产生相似的规则。

I. What Is *Stare Decisis*

The most obvious distinction between civil law and common law systems is that civil law system is a codified system, whereas the common law is not created by means of legislation but is based mainly on case law. The principle is that earlier judicial decisions, usually of the higher courts[1], made in a similar case, should be followed in the subsequent cases, i.e. that precedents should be respected. This principle is known as *stare decisis*[2] and has never been legislated but is regarded as binding by the court. Under the doctrine of *stare decisis* (which is Latin for "to abide by[3] decided cases" or let the decision stand), a rule of law framed in one case under common law will serve as binding authority[4] to resolve future cases that are the same or analogous.

Developed in England in the thirteenth century, *stare decisis* is at the heart of

---

1 higher court: 上级法院（a court to which a case is appealed）。也可称为"court above""upper court"。
2 *stare decisis*:〈拉丁语〉遵循先例原则；判例拘束原则。在英美法中判决（判例）的效力在程度上有两种：一种是有说服力的（persuasive）效力，只具有参考价值；另一种是有约束性的（binding）效力，法院应当遵循，后者又有相对效力和绝对效力两种学说。在英美法实践中，the doctrine of precedent和the doctrine of *stare decisis*常常是通用的，美国习惯用后者。
3 abide by: 遵守、依照。To act in accordance with or in conformity to.
4 binding authority: 有约束力的法律依据。authority在法律英语中常有"法院或行政机构之裁定、判例"（a judicial or administrative decision cited as a precedent）之意。与binding authority相对应的是persuasive authority，即有说服力的法律依据（authority that carries some weight but is not binding on a court）。

Lesson 6
The Doctrine of Stare Decisis

the common law system. Under King Edward I, common-law courts began keeping records of previous cases to guide judges in deciding current ones. This practice helped make the common law more objective and predictable. Like statutes, previous cases became forms of notice of illegal or tortious behavior. If you want to bring a lawsuit against someone[1], you can assess your chances for success by reviewing previous, similar lawsuits. In the same way, you can determine which defense[2] will serve you best if you have a suit brought against you.

In contrast to common law, the case law in civil law systems does not have binding force. The doctrine of *stare decisis* does not apply to civil law courts, so that court decisions are not binding on lower courts in subsequent cases, nor are they binding on the same courts, and it is not uncommon for courts to reach opposite conclusions in similar cases. Under civil law, the courts do not create the law, but only apply and interpret it. In practice, however, the higher court decisions certainly have a certain influence on lower courts, since judges of lower courts will usually take into account the risk that their decisions would probably be reversed[3] by the higher court if they contradict the higher court decisions. Judges normally try to avoid the reversal of their decisions by higher courts as if too many of their decisions are reversed their promotion may be adversely affected. Hence, even though in civil law system the case law formally has no binding force, it is generally recognized that courts should take into account prior decisions.

Included under the principle of *stare decisis* is the concept of precedent. A precedent is a decided case that furnishes a basis for determining later cases involving similar facts or issues. Case opinions are collected and published in book volumes known as "reporters[4]", and these opinions now become precedents for future cases involving similar facts and legal issues.

---

1. bring a lawsuit against sb.: 对某人提起诉讼。
2. defense: 抗辩事由。A defendant's stated reason why the plaintiff or prosecutor has no valid case.
3. reverse：撤销，推翻。该词的名词形式是reversal，通常指an appellate court's overturning of a lower court's decision。
4. reporter: 案例汇编。reporter 也可称为report，通常表示a published volume of judicial decisions by a particular court of group of courts. Generally, these decisions are fist printed in temporary paperback volumes, and then printed in hardbound reporter volumes. Law reports may be either official and unofficial(published by a private publisher). Court citations（卷宗号）usually include the names of both the official and unofficial reports.

Stare decisis operates in the context of a hierarchy of courts in a jurisdiction. Rules of law framed by high courts are binding on the lower courts of the jurisdiction. Rulings by divisional courts[1] that have co-equal status are mutually regarded as persuasive authority. Whether the decision is a binding or a persuasive precedent will depend upon the origin of a court decision. Binding precedent must be followed by a court, whereas persuasive precedent need not be followed by a court. Decisions from the highest court in Massachusetts on a certain legal issue would be binding on all lower courts of the state. However, a decision in Maine or any other state on an undecided legal issue would only be persuasive in a Massachusetts court. The exception is that decisions from the U.S. Supreme Court are binding for all state and federal courts. A precedent acts as a legal guide in determining which law to apply to a client's problem. It sets the standards in our society, and it ensures a degree of fairness of judgment by our courts.

II. Advantages and Disadvantages of *Stare Decisis*

To locate prior precedents, it is helpful to know the citation[2] for the case where a

---

1. divisional courts: 高等法院各分庭。在英国，高等法院各分庭大概包括如王座法院（King's Bench Division/Queen's Bench Division）、衡平法庭（Chancery Division）、家庭分庭（Family Division）等。
2. citation: 卷宗号。我们首先来看一下《布莱克法律字典》中citation的定义：A reference to a legal precedent or authority, such as a case, statute, or treatise, that either substantiates or contradicts a given position. (p. 237) 7th edition. 由于a citation is a reference to a legal authority，因此，citation必须要有一个标准，这样以后的参考者才容易检索得到。正如《布莱克法律字典》所指出的一样，Citation formats exist for many different types of legal sources including cases, statutes and secondary legal materials. Understanding the basic format for each of these different types of sources will enable the researcher to more independently locate materials in the law library.
案例之中的卷宗号通常包括下列几个部分：
a. 案件双方当事人姓名（the names of the parties involved in the lawsuit）；
b. 包含案件全文的汇编卷号（the volume number of the reporter containing the full text of the case）；
c. 该案例汇编的缩写名称（the abbreviated name of that case reporter）；
d. 案例开始的页码数（the page number on which the case begins）；
e. 案件判决年份（the year the case was decided）；有时还包括：
f. 案件判决法院（the name of the court deciding the case）。
举例说明：Hebb v. Severson, 201 P.2d 156 (Wash. 1948). 在这个例子当中，Hebb是原告（plaintiff），Severson 是被告（defendant）。我们可以在《太平洋汇编》第二辑201卷第156页（volume 201 of the Pacific Reporter Second Series beginning on page 156）找到这一案例。该案是由华盛顿州最高法院（Washington State Supreme Court）于1948年判决的。
再如：93 N.J324, 461 A. 2d 138 (1983), 这说明该案出自《新西汇编》第93卷，第324页，以及《大西洋汇编》第二辑第138页，该案判决于1983年。此处，A 是Atlantic Reporter的缩写。像这种指明两个或两个以上出处的卷宗号叫作："平行卷宗号"，其英语表达为 "parallel citation"，意思是 "An additional reference to a case that has been reported in more than reporters." 广义上卷宗号包括上述一、案例名称；二、判决法院。

Lesson 6
The Doctrine of Stare Decisis

precedent is found. For example, a case opinion cited as 313 N.W.2d 601 (1982) can be located in volume 313 of the Northwestern Reporter, second edition, page 601. The extensive reliance of our legal system on judicial decisions has both advantages and disadvantages.

a. Advantages

Stare decisis arose from the desire of courts as well as society for certainty and predictability in the law. In addition, following precedent was expedient. The common law, through precedent, settled many legal issues and brought stability into many areas of the law, such as contracts.

b. Disadvantages

First, notwithstanding the fact that common law arose out of a desire for certainty and is designed to create it, common law creates a great deal of uncertainty in the law. The precedent may require hundreds of hours of research time. Furthermore, conflicting precedents frequently are discovered.

Second, in many cases the law cannot be found by searching cases.

Third, there is an important distinction between precedent and unnecessary opinions of judges. Frequently courts make comments on matters not necessary to the decision reached. Such expressions, called dicta[1], lack the force of a judicial settlement. Strictly speaking, they are not precedent that courts will be required to follow within the rule of *stare decisis*. However, dicta may be followed if they are sound and just, and dicta that have been repeated frequently are often given the force of precedent.

Fourth, one of the major reasons that the case law system leads to uncertainty is that a precedent may be changed or reversed. Since case law is susceptible to change, absolute reliance on it is not possible.

III. Qualifications of *Stare Decisis*

The doctrine of *stare decisis* has four important qualifications:

First, the doctrine does not apply if the facts of the later case are materially

---

1 dicta是dictum的复数形式,指法官个人意见,附带意见。这种意见在论证时有说服论述的价值,但不能作为判例约束以后的案件,也称为obiter dictum。

different from the earlier case that created the rule of law. Consequently, if a judge can "distinguish"[1] the facts of the earlier case, it is not used as precedent.

Second, the doctrine does not apply if the state of the law changes. So subsequent legislation can render a common-law decision invalid, after which it has no precedential effect.

Third, only the central aspect of the court decision (called the *ratio decidendi*) is given precedential effect. Extraneous statements of fact or law that appear within a case (called *obiter dicta*) are not binding on later courts.

Finally, the modern view of *stare decisis* allows courts to depart from prior decisions when rigid adherence to precedent would lead to injustice in a particular case and unduly restrict the proper development of the law. This, however, is done in only the most unusual circumstances, since the very reason for relying on judicial precedent is to lend certainty to the law.

The doctrine of *stare decisis* is most limited in constitutional cases. The Constitution reigns supremely over case law as well as statutes. Sometimes, a constitutional amendment changes the precepts on which prior cases were based. (The Civil War Amendments, for example, effectively overruled the Dred Scott[2] decision denying black slaves the rights of citizenship). Sometimes different judges interpret the Constitution differently and write dissents[3]. In any event, judges are bound by the Constitution, not by previous cases construing it.

1　distinguish：识别，通常指先例的识别。
2　南北战争（1861—1865）之前，美国历史上最著名的人身保护令诉讼是"斯科特单方诉讼案"（Ex Parte Dred Scott）。斯科特是一名内科医生的奴隶，他的主人在去世时曾答应释放斯科特。但是，主人死后，斯科特仍被作为奴隶而限制人身自由。斯科特于是向联邦法院发出请求，申请人身保护令状。后来联邦地区法院签发了令状并得到联邦上诉法院的支持。但是，联邦最高法院罗杰·B. 唐尼（Roger Tanney）认为斯科特作为奴隶并不是联邦宪法中的"人"，他认为像斯科特这样的黑人奴隶仅仅是"财产"，因此无权向联邦法院申请人身保护令状。最高法院因而推翻了联邦地区法院所签发的令状。唐尼的判决后来由于美国宪法的第13条修正案的通过被推翻。1868年通过的宪法第十四条修正案赋予黑人奴隶以公民身份。
附美国宪法第13条修正案：Amendment XIII (1865)
Section 1. Neither slavery nor involuntary servitude, except as a punishment for crime whereof the party shall have been duly convicted, shall exist within the United States, or any place subject to their jurisdiction.
Section 2. Congress shall have power to enforce this article by appropriate legislation.
第一款　在合众国境内受合众国管辖的任何地方，奴隶制和强制劳役都不得存在，但作为对于依法判罪的人的犯罪的惩罚除外。
第二款　国会有权以适当立法实施本条。
3　dissent：分歧，异议。常用来指在法官评议案件中，少数法官不同意多数法官的意见，也称为"dissenting opinion"。

Lesson 6
The Doctrine of Stare Decisis

Glossary

abide by 遵守；依照
analogous 类似的；可比拟的
binding authority 有约束力的法律依据
bring a lawsuit against sb. 对某人提起诉讼
decidendi 判决理由
defense 抗辩事由
dicta（dictum的复数形式）法官个人意见；附带意见
dissent 分歧；异议
divisional courts 高等法院各分庭
expedient 有用的；有利的

higher court 上级法院
notwithstanding 尽管；即使
obiter dicta 附带意见
persuasive authority 有说服力的法律依据
persuasive precedent 有说服力的先例
predictability 可预见性
render 正式宣布
reporter 案例汇编
reverse 撤销；推翻
take into account 考虑；重视

EXERCISES

I. Answer the following questions.

1. Can you give the definition of *stare decisis* according to the text?
2. When and where did the *stare decisis* originate?
3. Does *stare decisis* apply to the civil law courts? Why or why not?
4. List the disadvantages of *stare decisis*.
5. What is the persuasive authority? What is the binding authority? Do they have significant differences?
6. What are the qualifications of *stare decisis* according to the text?

II. Translate the following terms into English.

1. 先例
2. 遵循先例原则
3. 遵守已决案例
4. 有约束力的判决
5. 有说服力的判决
6. 案例汇编
7. 卷宗号
8. 法官附带意见
9. 可预见性
10. 异议

III. Translate the following sentences into Chinese.

1. The principle of using precedents to guide future decisions in court cases is called *stare decisis* (Latin for "to stand by decided cases").

2. Much of the time spent by criminal lawyers in preparing for a case is devoted to finding legal precedents that support their arguments. The successful outcome of a case, in turn, depends largely upon the success of lawyers in that endeavor.

3. *Stare decisis* makes for predictability in the law. Defendants walking into a modern courtroom will have the opportunity to be represented by lawyers who are trained in legal precedents as well as procedure.

4. The doctrine of *stare decisis* does not apply to civil law courts, so that court decisions are not binding on lower courts in subsequent cases, nor are they binding on the same courts, and it is not uncommon for courts to reach opposite conclusions in similar cases.

5. Besides the system of judicial precedents, other characteristics of common law are trial by jury and the doctrine of the supremacy of the law.

IV. Cloze.

Our legal system, which is based on common law and employs an adversary system of dispute resolution, can be divided into two branches: 1_____ and substantive law. Procedural law creates the 2_____ by which our legal system operates and spells out the mechanisms for resolving disputes, as well as the 3_____ that must be followed to enforce a certain law or bring a 4_____. Procedural law can be divided into 5_____ procedures and civil procedures. Substantive law embodies the actual rights, 6_____, and limitations upon human action that a society has embraced. 7_____ law is found in Constitution, statutes, and cases; procedural law is generally found in statutes, regulations, and 8_____ rules.

Lesson 6

The Doctrine of Stare Decisis

Supplementary Reading

Common law, system of law that prevails in England and in countries colonized by England. The name is derived from the medieval[1] theory that the law administered by the king's courts represented the common custom of the realm[2], as opposed to the custom of local jurisdiction that was applied in local or manorial courts[3]. In its early development common law was largely a product of three English courts—King's Bench, Exchequer, and the Court of Common Pleas[4]—which competed successfully against other courts for jurisdiction and developed a distinctive body of doctrine. The term "common law" is also used to mean the traditional, precedent-based element in the law of any common-law jurisdiction, as opposed to its statutory law or legislation, and also to signify that part of the legal system that did not develop out of equity, maritime law, or other special branches of practice.

All Canada except Quebec and all of the United States except Louisiana follow common law. U.S. state statutes usually provide that the common law, equity, and statutes in effect in England in 1603, the first year of the reign of James I, shall be deemed part of the law of the jurisdiction. Later decisions of English courts have only persuasive authority.

Characteristic Features of Common Law

The distinctive feature of common law is that it represents the law of the courts as expressed in judicial decisions. The grounds for deciding cases are found in precedents provided by past decisions, as contrasted to the civil law system, which is based on statutes and prescribed texts. Besides the system of judicial precedents, other characteristics of common law are trial by jury and the doctrine of the supremacy of the law. Originally,

---

1 medieval：中世纪的。
2 realm：王国，领域。
3 manorial courts：采邑法院。
4 King's Bench：王座法院；王座法院最初形成时，它是一个刑事法院又是对普通诉讼法院民事案件作出复审的法院。1873—1875年司法改革前，英国的初审法院（trial court）包括三个法院（财政法院、普通诉讼法院、王座法院）。Court of Exchequer 财政法院；亨利一世时著名的宰相罗杰尔组建了财政署（Exchequer），其名称得之于财政署的格子桌布（checkered cloth, resembling a chessboard），财政法院的管辖权最初只限于税收案件，后来通过"拟制"（fiction）获得了对普通臣民之间民事诉讼的管辖权。Court of Common Pleas 普通诉讼法院（亦译普通民事诉讼法院）；普通诉讼法院管辖土地案件以及民事纠纷。

supremacy of the law meant that not even the king was above the law; today it means that acts of governmental agencies are subject to scrutiny in ordinary legal proceedings.

Judicial precedents derive their force from the doctrine of stare decisis (Lat., stand by the decided matter), i.e., that the previous decisions of the highest court in the jurisdiction are binding on all other courts in the jurisdiction. Changing conditions, however, soon make most decisions inapplicable except as a basis for analogy, and a court must therefore often look to the judicial experience of the rest of the English-speaking world. This gives the system flexibility, while general acceptance of certain authoritative materials provides a degree of stability. Nevertheless, in many instances, the courts have failed to keep pace with social developments and it has become necessary to enact statutes to bring about needed changes; indeed, in recent years statutes have superseded much of common law, notably in the fields of commercial, administrative, and criminal law. Typically, however, in statutory interpretation the courts have recourse to the doctrines of common law. Thus increased legislation has limited but has not ended judicial supremacy.

Development of Common Law

Early common law was somewhat inflexible; it would not adjudicate a case that did not fall precisely under the purview[1] of a particular writ and had an unwieldy set of procedural rules. Except for a few types of lawsuits in which the object was to recover real or personal property, the only remedy provided was money damages; the body of legal principles known as equity evolved partly to overcome these deficiencies. Until comparatively recent times there was a sharp division between common law (or legal jurisprudence) and equity (or equitable jurisprudence). In 1848 the state of New York enacted a code of civil procedure (drafted by David Dudley Field) that merged law and equity into one jurisdiction. Thenceforth, actions at law and suits in equity were to be administered in the same courts and under the same procedure. The Field code reforms were adopted by most states of the United States, by the federal government, and by the United Kingdom (in the Judicature Act of 1873[2]).

1　purview：范围。
2　Judicature Act：《司法法》，英国于1873—1875年间对高等法院的组织和审判程序进行改革的法律。1981年的《最高法院法》（Supreme Court Act）取代了《司法法》。

Lesson 7
Two Major Legal Systems in the World

 All law is created for the benefit of human beings.

法之立也，为民造福耳。

I. What Is the Civil Law[1] Tradition?

When we refer to some of the world's legal systems with a common name, such as "Romanist"[2], "Roman-Germanic"[3], or "civil law" systems, we are calling attention to the fact that, despite their similarities to other legal systems and despite national differences among themselves, these systems share a distinctive heritage. The tradition of the civil law is characterized by a particular interaction in its early formative period among Roman law, Germanic and local customs, canon law, and, later, by a distinctive response to the break with feudalism and the rise of nation states, as well as by the specially important role it has accorded to legal science.

II. Roman Law

To use the term Roman law to describe the entire Roman legal output of nearly a millennium stretching from the Twelve Tables[4] (c.450 B.C.) to the Justinian

---

1　civil law: 民法法系。又称大陆法系，与continental law 同义，与common law 对称。Civil law 的另一个含义是民法，与"criminal law, administrative law, commercial law"对称。
2　Romanist: one who is versed in or practices Roman law; a Roman-law specialist.
3　Roman-Germanic: 该术语所指的法系，亦称民法法系，包括以日耳曼部落习惯为基础的法律制度和在西欧发展的罗马法，现在所包括的国家有法国、比利时、荷兰、德国、奥地利、西班牙、葡萄牙等。
4　Twelve Table: 十二铜表法。罗马历史上最早的法典，也是罗马法制的开端。根据传统，《十二铜表法》由10位专员起草，时间在公元前451—450年间。原来只有十表，第二批专员增加了两表补充性法律。传统认为，这批专员访问过希腊，这可能是真实的；因为这被该法典文本中的希腊法规则的风味所佐证。法案由人民大会制定并在广场上的木表或铜表上公布；其目的在于将那些最重要的习惯法规定成文化——因为在此之前，只有牧师才知道这些习惯法，此外还在于减少贵族特权，因此，这既是一项立法改革措施又是对习惯的革新。

compilations[1](c.534 A.D.) is about as helpful as describing the product of English legal minds from 1066 A.D. to the present as "common law". Thus, specialists in ancient Roman law subdivide their subject into various periods. It was as early as the third century B.C., during the Republic, that there appeared a class of men known as Jurisconsults, who made law their specialty. By the end of the Late Republic in the first century B.C., the Jurisconsults had acquired a monopoly of technical information and legal experience. In difficult cases, the lay judges[2] began to turn to these legal specialists for advice. Through this advisory role, the Jurisconsults stayed close to the practice of law and remained in constant contact with actual disputes. They were the world's first professional lawyers (as distinct from orators like Cicero[3] whose main skills were in rhetoric and statesmanship). What we know as Roman law evolved through the accretion of the opinions they rendered case by case. Eventually the principles thus developed by the Jurisconsults were taught and expounded in treatises, all in a distinctive vocabulary and style.

At first rather formal and rigid, Roman law eventually supplemented fixed rules with flexible standards and moved from concrete to more abstract modes of thought. It become characterized by attention to practical details, and by terms of art[4] which caught on and endured. The law of the Classical period (which began around 117 A.D. and came to an end with the period of anarchy, invasions, plague and civil war that commenced around 235 A.D.), represents the fullest development of ancient Roman

---

1　Justinian compilations: 查士丁尼法典。主要是在查士丁尼皇帝时仍有效的历代皇帝赦令的汇集，并充分利用了以前一些法典所提供的资料。
2　lay judges: 非专业法官。履行司法职责，或与受过专门培训的法官共同履行司法职责的、无法律资格或未受过专门法律培训的人。
3　Cicero：西塞罗。罗马政治家、演说家、律师和作家，在雅典从事哲学研究并投身于政治和辩论活动。公元前63年任执政官，并于公元前52年被派往西里西亚任地方总督。公元前43年被视为奥克塔维安的政敌而遭谋杀。西塞罗是当时最博学者之一，留下了大量政治、论辩及修辞学方面的著作、演说稿，其中著名的有《演说术》和《演说家》，其中有各种系列的书信集和政治、哲学论文集。
4　terms of art: 专门术语。

Lesson 7
Two Major Legal Systems in the World

law. Of the Jurisconsults of this period, Ulpian[1], Panpinian[2] and Gaius[3] are chiefly remembered. At its height, classical Roman law constituted a body of practical wisdom of a kind the world had not seen before. It was therefore of the highest interest to Byzantine jurists after the fall of the Western empire, and through them, had great influence on the development of the civil law systems.

Centuries later, Roman law would be called "written reason" by the medieval scholars who "rediscovered" it as Europe began to emerge from the Middle Ages[4]. The Roman law that they "found" when Western society began to be ready for law to play a prominent role once again among the norms that govern human activity, was not the law of the Classical period in its original form. Most of the ancient sources had been lost. What survived was the monumental compilation of Roman law that was made at the direction of the Byzantine Emperor Justinian in the sixth century A.D. By that time, the Roman Empire in the West had been breaking up for more than a century, its fall symbolized by the sack of Roman in 410 A.D. The significance of the work of the Byzantine jurists in preserving the Roman legal heritage would be hard to exaggerate. From Justinian's times to the present, the term Roman law, except to specialists, generally has meant Roman law as it appears in the sixth century Corpus Juris Civilis of Justinian.

The Corpus Juris Civilis included four parts: the Institutes, the Digest, the Code

---

1 Ulpian：乌尔比安，古罗马后期伟大的法学家之一，担任过各种不同的职务。曾任亚历山大·塞维鲁时期的档案官，从222年开始任军政长官直到去世。乌尔比安一生著述颇多，其中知名的有83卷本的《执政官告示评注》，51卷本的《论萨宾民法》，其中包括简明教科书《规范法学阶梯》，《第一规则论》以及各种为法律从业者撰写的入门手册，如《解答篇》《论辩篇》《意见篇》。如果说乌尔比安是位富有独创性的思想家，倒不如说他是编撰者。乌尔比安的著作是查士丁尼《学说汇纂》的主要资料来源，该书中几乎有1/3、共计2462段摘自他的著作。

2 Papinian：帕皮尼安，古罗马最杰出的法学家之一。其出生地址不详，有可能在叙利亚或非洲。他曾有一段辉煌的从政生涯并于公元203年成为地方执政官，但在212年被卡拉卡拉处死。他并未撰写综合性的或系统性的专题研究，而是著有各种各样的集子，其中包括《问题集》和《解答集》。这两部著作完成于公元190—210年，内容涉及从早期法学家和学说讨论中得到的引证。在查士丁尼的学说汇撰中有601篇引证他的著作。他们在著作中表明了帕皮尼安清晰而富有逻辑性的思维，独立的见解和重新考虑他的观点的意愿。

3 Gaius：盖尤斯，著名罗马法学家。对于他本人的了解很少。公元533年由官方颁布的查士丁尼《法学阶梯》的编撰者，其顺序和内容上都主要以盖尤斯的著作为基础。

4 The Middle Ages：中世纪。西方法律的中世纪是指自公元4世纪东罗马帝国兴起，公元476年西罗马帝国衰弱和最终灭亡时起，直至公元15世纪后期这段时期。公元15世纪，发生了君士坦丁堡陷落，1453年拜占庭帝国或东罗马帝国灭亡，被称为文艺复兴的启蒙运动，宗教改革的开始，罗马法的继受，民族国家的兴起，新的地理大发现及标志近代历史开始的一系列变化。在中世纪，西方各国的发展变化具有某种统一性和一致性，并且在这段时期里发生了深刻地影响了近代法律的法律制度和法律思想的发展。

and the Novels. The Digest was by far the most important in terms of its influence on the civil law tradition, particularly in the areas of personal status, torts, unjust enrichment, contracts and remedies. The Digest was a treatise representing the distillation of what, in the judgment of Justinian's jurists, was most valuable from the best Roman legal writings from all previous periods. Since virtually all of the books they used in composing the Digest have been lost, the Digest itself became the principal source of knowledge about what the Roman law of earlier periods had been like. The Institutes were simply a short introductory text for students, the Code was a systematic collection of Roman legislation, and the Novels were the imperial legislation enacted after the Code and the Digest were completed. Together, the Digest and the Code were meant to be a complete and authoritative restatement of Roman law.

Byzantine Roman lawyers did not merely copy the law of earlier periods. The Corpus Juris was the product of a careful process of selection and rejection. In general outlook, as well as in matter of details, it differed from the law of the Classical period. It continued the movement away from formalism, but this move was accompanied by a decline in technique. Equity, which in the Classical period was regarded as a principle of justice animating the whole of the law, degenerated into mere impatience with legal subtleties. After the Lombard and Arab invasions that followed the reign of Justinian, the Corpus Juris Civilis fell into disuse for centuries.

III. Roman Law Survival Amidst Medieval Customs

The fact that Roman law and legal science were left stranded by the collapse of the way of life that had produced them did not mean that Romanist legal influences disappeared altogether during the Middle ages. Certainly the sophistication and technical perfection to which ancient Roman law had been brought over the centuries was not maintained during the legal and political disorder that followed the disintegration of the Roman Empire. For five centuries after the fall of Roman a series of raiders and settlers overran the areas that had once been Roman. There were no strong, centralized states. Kingdoms rose and fell. The condition of the people was one of local self-sufficiency, and local customs displaced formal law. It would be centuries before scholars again would be capable of putting to use the

Lesson 7
Two Major Legal Systems in the World

technical instruments left behind by the Classical Roman and Byzantine jurists. When a reawakening of interest in Roman law did occur and when attention turned to the Corpus Jurist in the eleventh century, the process became known as the "revival" of Roman law.

There was, nevertheless, a considerable "survival" of Roman law within the diverse customary systems that prevailed from the fifth to the tenth centuries. Roman conquerors once had been all over Europe, and many of the Germanic settlers, legionaries[1] and migrating peoples who eventually overran the former Empire had been, to a certain extent, "Romanized". As conquerors and at conquered changed places, Germanic rulers used Roman law to govern their Roman subjects, while applying their own law to their own peoples. Over time, however, the distinctions between these groups disappeared. By the end of the tenth century, the rules were the same for all persons within a given territory. Crude versions of Roman legal rules had intermingled to varying degrees with the customary rules of the Germanic invaders to the point where historians sometimes speak of the laws during this period as "Romanized customary laws" and sometimes as "barbarized Roman laws". Thus, though Roman legal science and Classical Roman law disappeared in the welter, diversity and localism of the Middle Ages, Romanist element survived and served both as a strand of continuity and a latent, potentially universalizing factor in what we now think of as the civil law tradition.

The widely disseminated Germanic customary laws that began to be written down as early as the fifth century A.D., (as well as particular local customs), formed part of this tradition too, particularly influencing aspects of marital property and inheritance law. Many of the most ingenious and useful legal devices of the modern civil law of property and commercial law derive not from Roman, but from customary medieval origins, and thus remind us that the legal confusion of the Middle Ages had its fruitful and creative, as well as its fragmented and disorganized side. The Germanic element evolved through the Middle Ages, as tribal laws became territorial laws, to the point where it produced the beginnings of a legal literature and a new legal culture that was quite different from the Roman. But its further

---

1　legionary: 古罗马军团中的士兵。

development was arrested, partly because of the crudeness of its procedures (e.g., trial by ordeal[1]), and partly because of its limited potential for adaptation to the social and economic changes that were beginning to transform feudal society.

IV. Canon Law

With the break-up of the far-flung system of Roman administration, the Church took over some of the functions of government. Indeed, after the fall of the Roman Empire, and until the revival of Roman law in the eleventh century, the single most important universalizing factor in the diverse and localized legal systems of the civil law tradition was canon law. But canon law itself was a hybrid of sorts. It had been produced by Christian notions interaction reciprocally with Roman law after the Christianization of the Empire, a process during which the reign of Constantine[2] (d.337A.D.) was an important maker. The sixth century Justinian corpus, in particular, was affected by Christian ideas, but the church, for its part, had borrowed freely from the structure, principles and detailed rules of ancient Roman law. Furthermore, just as there was some degree of amalgamation everywhere of Germanic customs, indigenous customs and debased Roman law, there was a certain penetration by canon law into the codes promulgated by German rulers, and later into the legislation of Holy Roman Empires[3] (c.962 A.D.). During the Middle Ages, the church sought and acquired jurisdiction for its own tribunals over matrimonial causes, and over certain aspects of criminal law and succession to personal property. Many of the rules and procedures it developed in these matters were accepted in secular tribunals long after the Church had lost its civil jurisdiction.

---

1 trial by ordeal: 神明裁判，中世纪审判某人有罪的方式，据说它是通过获得上帝的裁决来确定的。神明裁判在世界各地发现存在着多种不同的形式。如果一个人在犯罪现场被捉获不能提供足够的证明他无罪的保证人或曾犯有伪证罪或者不是自由民，则他必须接受神明裁判。神明裁判包含下列几种形式：抓烧红的铁块，假如没有罪，伤口三天之内痊愈；将头或胳膊伸入开水中，烫伤痊愈则无罪；将人投入水池，有罪则浮上来（水拒绝他）；令其吞噬一口祭奉的面包，噎住则有罪。由于神明裁判很可能被滥用并且似乎难以使人信服，因而很早就开始衰落了。
2 康斯坦丁大帝，罗马皇帝，公元306—337年在位，于312年皈依基督教，从而成为第一个基督教皇帝，此后扶持基督教。他颁布了许多与基督教习俗有关的法律，废除了十字架死刑和在某些刑事犯脸上烙印的做法，扩大了僧侣的特权。他主要的贡献是建立了信奉基督教的帝国统治阶级。
3 Holy Roman Empires: 神圣罗马帝国，罗马帝国的称号，5世纪时已在西欧停止使用，但在800年又被恢复，并以教皇利奥三世封授的法兰克国王查理曼为罗马帝国皇帝。这个名称暗示了对从前由奥古斯都建立的罗马帝国的承袭。

Lesson 7
Two Major Legal Systems in the World

Glossary

accretion 增加物；生长部分
advisory 供咨询的；顾问的
amalgamation （指阶级，社会，民族，公司）混合
anarchy 无政府状态；无秩序；混乱
animate 赋予生命；鼓舞；使活泼
barbarize 使变粗野；使语言杂芜
commence 开始
compilation 编辑；编撰；编制；编撰物
debased 贬低（价值，品质，品格等）
degenerate （由于失去被认为是正常和优良的特质而）退步，堕落
disintegration 分裂成小碎片
disseminate 传播；散布（思想，教义等）
distillation 用蒸馏法净化或制造
distinctive 区别的
exaggerate 夸大；夸张
expound 详加解释；详细说明
far-flung 蔓延的；辽阔的
feudalism 封建制度
formalism 形式主义
formative 使成形的；形成的
heritage 遗产；继承物
hybrid 杂种；混合之物
indigenous 土生的；天生的
ingenious 制作精巧的

interaction 相互作用；相互影响
invasion 侵略；侵犯
matrimonial 婚姻的
migrate 迁移；迁居；移居
millennium 一千年
monopoly 垄断；独占
monumental （指著作，研究等）不朽的
orator 演说者；（尤指出色的）演说家
output 生产量
plague 麻烦、困扰或灾祸的原因；祸患
reciprocally 互惠的；交互的；相互的
rejection 被抛弃或被拒绝之物
rhetoric 修辞；修辞学
rigid 僵硬的；坚挺的
secular 尘世的；非宗教的；非精神的
sophistication 精细；复杂；高深；奥妙
statesmanship 政治家的才能，智慧，技巧等
strand （指船）搁浅
be (left) stranded （指人）陷入无交通工具的情况；束手无策
subtlety 微妙；灵巧；细微的差别
supplement 增补；补充
systematic 有系统；有体系的
treatise 论文；论说
virtually 事实上；实际上
welter 混乱；混杂；纷争

EXERCISES

I. Answer the following questions.

1. What are the features of the tradition of the civil law?
2. Which period can represent the fullest development of ancient Roman law?

3. How many parts do the Corpus Juris Civilis of Justinian include? What are they?
4. What does the "revival of Roman law" mean?
5. Why did some historians sometimes speak of the laws during the end of the tenth century as "Romanized customary laws" and sometimes as "barbarized Roman Laws"?

II. Translate the following terms into English.

1. 民法法系
2. 神明裁判
3. 教会法
4. 罗马法学家
5. 十二铜表法
6. 继承法
7. 非专业法官
8. 神圣罗马帝国
9. 普通法
10. 商法
11. 古典时期
12. 主体资格
13. 侵权
14. 不当得利
15. 财产法

III. Translate the following paragraph into Chinese.

Roman law is not only the best-known, the most highly developed, and the most influential of all legal systems of the past; apart from English law, it is also the only one whose entire and unbroken history can be traced from early and primitive beginnings to a stage of elaborate perfection in the hands of skilled specialists.

IV. Choose the suitable words from the box and fill in the blanks.

| expectation   advance   comparative   claim   comparison |

When the first learned societies dealing with cross-national legal _____ were established in France, Germany, and England in the late nineteenth century, their founders took for granted that _____ methods would _____ the understanding of a broad range of legal issues. In that _____, legal scholars were in accord with the best of their counterparts in other disciplines. Emile Durkheim had gone so far as to _____

Lesson 7
Two Major Legal Systems in the World

that, "Comparative sociology is not a particular branch of sociology; it is sociology itself." The great legal historian F.W. Maitland had insisted that, "The English lawyer who knew nothing and cared nothing for any system but his own, hardly came in sight of the idea of legal history."

Supplementary Reading

English common law[1] evolved from necessity, rooting in the centralized administration of William, conqueror at Hastings. A single event, the 1066 Norman Conquest[2], was the progenitor of t his tradition. Its foundation was a unique, "unwritten" constitution and orally rendered, and ultimately recorded, decisions of an extraordinarily gifted and respected judiciary[3]. The harmony of a homogeneous society, tested by internal stresses but free of foreign invasion for nearly a millennium, aided an orderly development of legal institutions. Focusing on the resolution of specific, current issues, English law developed insulated from the continental reception of Roman law, and the later emphasis on codification[4]. As Pollock said, English laws "grew in rugged exclusiveness, disdaining fellowship with the more polished learning of the civilians."

Comprehension of the rule of law in England today, and its litmus role in other common law systems, calls for an understanding of the cardinal incidents in English history which were generative of the slow but persistent development of institutions and concepts which comprise the common law tradition. The contemporary face of English law has numerous lines which compose a road map of the legal system reaching back nearly a millennium.

Roman Occupation

Legal institutions before the Norman Conquest made few lasting contributions to the

---

1　English common law: 普通法系，是指以英国普通法为主要基础的一类国家及地区的法律制度的总称，其中以英国和美国的法律制度最具有代表性。普通法系又称英美法系、判例法系等。
2　Norman Conquest: 1066年，英王爱德华逝世，诺曼底公爵威廉率军进攻英国，英军战败，威廉进入伦敦，加冕称王，史称诺曼征服。
3　judiciary: 审判人员，所有法律系统中职业法官的总称。
4　这句中的English law 是指普通法，它是法官通过判决所宣布的，存在于判决中，其表现形式是判例。而欧洲大陆接受的罗马法的表现形式是法典编撰。

common law. Pre-Conquest law was mostly unwritten, passing through generations by oral tradition. Over centuries the trial laws changed to accord with the times, although little is known with exactitude of when the changes occurred or the precise forces impelling those changes.

Julius Caesar led exploratory expeditions to the Southeast of the island in 55 and 54 B.C. Disparate Celtic tribes[1], about whose legal structures Maine has commented, "One rude folk are much like another," supported periodic revolts in Britain against the Roman dominion. A century later Claudius, timidly seeking status as a conquering Caesar, chose weak Britain to subdue. Romans ruled much of the island for nearly four centuries. Britain was marked indelibly with Roman culture—the rose, road system, Latin language and central heating—but the Romans did not bestow upon the inhabitants the Roman legal system. Britain had not been developed, it had been occupied. Roman law was an incident of occupation. It governed relations between Romans, but it began a decline in 410 A.D. when the legions departed to protect Rome. What Rome contributed to the English legal system was indirect, occurring through the survival of remnants of institutional structures of a civilized society.

Roman-Norman Hiatus: The Anglo-Saxon Period

The Romans departure left the Britons with little more than a few Christian missionaries to face Angles, Jutes and Saxons[2]—again society became dominated by diverse tribal communities, with law predominantly and unwritten local customs. There was sufficient cohesion for Pope Gregory's missionary, St. Augustine, to establish Christianity in the late sixth century, giving English kings, the latter an important reservation in later centuries.

Anglo-Saxon law possessed elements of Teutonic tribal traditions and customs, but personal wealth began to replace "blood and kin" as the measure of political power. England developed feudal attitudes, but not in the continental sense. Landowners rather than the community or state provided protection to and drew loyalty from the dependent

---

1 Celtic tribes：凯尔特部落，公元前5世纪，凯尔特人移居不列颠岛，过着氏族制度生活。正当凯尔特人向阶级社会和国家迈进的时候，罗马人将它的扩张推进到了不列颠。但罗马人的统治主要在东南部平原区，西北部山区为原始的凯尔特人控制。
2 入侵英国的盎格鲁-撒克逊人由盎格鲁人（Angles）、撒克逊人（Saxons）和朱特人（Jutes）组成。居住在日德兰半岛南部的盎格鲁人和居住在易北河下游的撒克逊人，由于两者语言风格很难区分，因此被称为盎格鲁-撒克逊人。

classes. Lords administered justice for their tenants and villain, and their lands provided the source of taxes to defend the nation.

The Norman Conquest

The victory near Hastings by William was more a succession than a conquest. William's claim to the English throne was no less tenuous than Harold's. The law of England, an aggregate of disparate local customs, was left largely intact by the conqueror. But he confiscated all of the land and apportioned possession among his most trustworthy followers, extracting pledges of loyalty and service. William allocated the land in a manner to prevent his barons from concentrating their power and challenging his central authority. This limited holding of the land, with ownership remaining in the sovereign, is today largely theoretical.

William achieved his goal of kingly investiture at Westminster, but duties in Normandy demanded his attention. Establishing centralized rule at Westminster permitted the governance of a large number of Saxons by comparatively few Normans. William's administrative efficiency produced the Domesday survey in 1086, an inventory of all property throughout England, which facilitated a much larger revenue collection.

William resolved conflicts of royal concern at Westminster; local issues remained in the courts of the shires and hundreds. Only judicial disputes of an extraordinary nature were brought before the king as chief justiciar. Administrative necessity rather than legislative design played the central role in fashioning the early structures of the common law. William's legacy was the creation of a highly centralized legal system.

Lesson 8
Legal Education in America

Law is the crystallization of the habit and thought of society.
法律是社会习俗和思想的结晶。

I. A Brief History

Prior to 1865 the intellectual origins of American legal training were predominantly English. Most American attorneys[1] in the 19th century learned law through the English apprenticeship approach. William Blackstone[2] (1723—1780) had established a place for student and practitioner use of legal treatises with his four-volume *Commentaries on the Laws of England,* which was widely used in American editions and emulated in *Commentaries on American Law.*

The first law schools evolved out of law offices that took in apprentice clerks for a fee. A few attorneys preferred instructing clerks rather than practicing law and gained a reputation for teaching. The Litchfield Law School[3], which operated from 1784 to 1833 and attracted students from several states, or the 20 other law office-type schools patterned on it, clearly showed their English parentage.

---

1 attorney: 在本课中的意思是辩护律师，另外，attorney 还有代理人的意思（A person legally appointed by another to act as his or her agent in the transaction of business, specifically one qualified and licensed to act for plaintiffs and defendants in legal proceedings）。
2 William Blackstone: 威廉·布莱克斯通，生于伦敦的一个经商之家，是18世纪英国最伟大的法学家之一。他的著作《英国法释义》从法学史的角度来说，有两大重要意义：第一，将法学从与其他科学分离的状态下解放出来，将其与其他社会科学一起考虑。第二，在他的时代，将普通法予以体系化、定型化。这部作品的影响在18世纪就已超出英国国界，波及了美国。所以西方学者将其誉为"英国法学史上的金字塔"。
3 The Litchfield Law School: 里奇菲尔德法学院是美国历史上第一个正规的法学院。The Litchfield Law School launched the careers of many well-known Americans including two vice-presidents, 101 United States congressmen, twenty-eight United States senators, six cabinet members, three justices of the United States supreme court, fourteen governors and thirteen chief justices of state supreme courts.

Lesson 8
Legal Education in America

Harvard Law School, which opened in 1817, was an ordinary Litchfield-type law school at first. But at last it rose to prominence, which was attributable primarily to the appointment of Charles Eliot (1834—1906) as university president in 1869 and Christopher Columbus Landell[1] (1826—1906) to the newly created post of law school dean in 1870. Of the two men, Eliot was the more important, initiating and supporting reform throughout the university actively. Landell's most significant innovation was the introduction of an instructional method utilizing Socratic dialogue[2] to discuss appellate court cases.

The American law school student population from 1870 to 1900 grew from 1,650 to 12,500 while the number of law schools increased from 31 to 102. At the turn of 20th century three quarters of the schools were affiliated with a college or a university. But there were also 20 night law schools catering to the urban masses and emphasizing local law and practice much more than university law schools. Elite lawyers began to worry about standards and the influx of immigrant attorneys trained at the night schools. State bar associations began to tighten up qualifying examinations. The schools themselves in 1900 created the Association of American Law Schools[3] (AALS), which together with the American Bar Association[4] (ABA) went into the standards and accreditation business. The AALS initially accepted 32 schools as charter members. A school that failed to qualify for either list was at a competitive disadvantage in attracting students.

---

1 Christopher Columbus Landell：克里斯朵夫·哥伦布·兰德尔教授。1870年，美国哈佛大学（Harvard University）校长查尔斯·W.艾略特任命兰德尔教授为法学院院长，1871年兰德尔出版了他的有关契约法的案例教科书，并在哈佛大学首次使用案例教学法，他直接以判例汇编（casebook）作为课程教材，以问答式（the question-and-answer technique）或对话式方法进行教学，由教师与学生就具体案例进行双向讨论和分析。

2 Socratic dialogue：苏格拉底式教学法又称为"案例教学法（case method）"（the Socratic method），它不同于传统的以教师为核心的讲授式（lecture method）教学法。苏格拉底（Socrates）是古希腊的哲学大师，他使用"问答式"（a catechetical system）或对话式方法进行教学，通过问答方式启发受教者发展自己的思维（to develop their own ideas）。

3 the Association of American Law Schools：美国法学院协会，简称AALS。美国法学院协会成立于1900年，1971年被确认为两个全国立案的法律机关（另一个是ABA法律教育和律师资格部）之一，该协会出版的《法律教育季刊》（*Journal of Legal Education*），长期享有声望。

4 the American Bar Association：美国律师协会，简称ABA。美国律师协会成立于1878年，协会下设有法律教育常务委员会（Standing Committee on Legal Education），它负责发"牌照"给要开办法学院的大学，规定对法学院的各种硬件要求。

II. Characteristics of American Legal Education

a. The basis of legal education in America is the common law[1].

The principal distinction between common law and civil law is that the former relies on the English principle of the binding force of precedent[2]. Thus, a case decided by a court today must be consistent with similar cases previously decided, even if the case is very old. The key concept is that the reasoning by the judges in prior cases must be applied to today's cases so that the law is predictable. Yet the common law is flexible since judges can use prior legal reasoning to reach different but equitable outcomes in similar cases.

b. American legal education is general rather than specialized.

Every law school uses nearly the same courses during first year: torts, contracts, property, criminal law, civil procedure, constitutional law, and legal research and writing. In the second and third year, elective courses are chosen by the students but most take other common courses in administrative law, business and commercial law, litigation, family law, intellectual property and technology law, and international and comparative law. Upon graduation, every student has been exposed to a broad spectrum of the law even though he or she may later specialize in some area.

c. The development of the American legal system has been influenced by the kind of education that lawyers have received, and legal education in turn reflects the diversity of that legal system.

The evidence of this diversity flows from several sources: first, America has

---

1　the common law：普通法（the common law）作为一种法律渊源，又称为习惯法、判例法，由习惯和判例组成，最早是指英国12世纪前后开始形成的、一种以判例形式出现的、普遍适用于全英国的法律，是根据以往法院和法庭对具体案件的判决所作的理论概括。所谓"普通"就是通行于全国的普通习惯，它不同于以往的地方习惯法，它是国家确认的、通行于全国的法律。

2　the binding force of precedent："遵循先例"原则。所谓先例（precedent）即是在今后类似案件中可作为标准的司法决定的判例（A judicial decision that may be used as a standard in subsequent similar cases）。所以"遵循先例"原则是普通法系的根本要旨，就是把先前的判例看作一种规范，并且希望从中得到根据惯例应该、并在某种情况下必须遵循和适用的原则或规则。而且大法官所确定规则的判例将会为普通法院所遵循。（The doctrine of precedent is the essence and foundation of the Anglo-American legal system. Where a judge decides that a particular previous decision which compiled and published in law reports, is binding on the case before the court, then that particular previous decision is termed a precedent for the instant case.）

Lesson 8
Legal Education in America

a large number of private university law schools. Virtually all states have a public university, and some large states have several. But there is no federal ministry of education that sets out the law curriculum, faculty salaries, or research project. But the greatest diversity stems from the existence and competition of private law schools. Second, the historic pattern of law school development established a hierarchy of prestige among law schools that further stimulates competition. Third, the composition of the typical student body and faculty changed from essentially a group of white males to more closely represent the diversity of American population.

III. Methods of Instruction

a. Case Method

The case method in legal education began with the publication of Dean Langdell's casebook on contracts and its use at Harvard in 1871. Casebooks used actual appellate cases and arranged them to show scientific principles of law. Langdell argued that these principles transcended local law and could reveal faulty judicial reasoning in a specific instance. The teacher using a casebook became a Socratic guide, who posed questions to students that revealed concepts as essences hidden in appellate opinions. Professors replacing the traditional lecture method with the case or Socratic method required students to truly prepare for class by studying the cases in depth before meeting. By moving from the particular to the general and then the abstract to the concrete, this technique replicates the dialectical common law method itself.

Today the remnants of Langdell's innovation can probably better be described as the discussion method. Casebooks include statutes, court rules, regulations, excerpts from journals and books—even from disciplines outside the law—and other legal materials such as contracts[1] or pleadings[2]. The discussion method in its purest question-and-answer form works best for first year students in the mandatory curriculum. As novices in the analytic reasoning of lawyers, they are more willing to prepare for class.

b. Lecture

The traditional lecture method has found new popularity—especially in the upper division curriculum—as professors strive to explain the complexity of contemporary American legal materials or how these materials might best be utilized in a diverse social matrix. New electronic classrooms, wired to the Internet and with computer generated displays, facilitate the visual side of lecturing. Another motivation is to undercut the moral relativism that adheres to the contemporary case or discussion method, by which students learn to find good legal arguments for either side of any case. Students come to believe, as the pragmatism[3] in American law would suggest, that what wins lawsuits is the most sophisticated or instrumental argument, not necessarily what is just. And lecturing provides the avenue to try to develop a coherent view among their students regarding American law.

c. Problem Method

Some advanced courses and seminars with small enrollment emphasize the solution of current problems. Students study a complex situation—for instance,

---

1 contract：该词的意思是合同，契约，即两个或两个以上当事人之间达成的一种协议，尤指具有法律效力的书面协议（An agreement between two or more parties, especially one that is written and enforceable by law.）此外还有合同法的意思。（The branch of law dealing with formal agreements between parties. 规范当事人各方之间正式协议法律的一个分支）最后也可作婚约作为正式协定的婚姻；订婚的意思（Marriage as a formal agreement; betrothal）。
2 pleadings：该词的意思是诉状，答辩状（A formal statement, generally written, propounding the cause of action or the defense in a case. Or the consecutive statements, allegations, and counterallegations made in turn by plaintiff and defendant, or prosecutor and accused, in a legal proceeding.）提起诉讼或对案件辩护的正式的一般为书面的声明书，即是在法律程序中，分别由原告、被告或检举人和被检举人所作的连续的供述、辩解和反辩解。另外，该词也有辩护法庭中对案件辩护的意思（Advocacy of causes in court）。
3 pragmatism：该词的意思为实用主义。实用主义是由查尔斯·S.皮尔斯及威廉·姆斯所创立的一种由各种不同的但又相互联系的理论组成的哲学运动，其特点是提出了概念或建议的意义存在于其可观察到的实际结果中的学说。（A movement consisting of varying but associated theories, originally developed by Charles S. Peirce and William James and distinguished by the doctrine that the meaning of an idea or a proposition lies in its observable practical consequences.）该词也有实用性的意思，即使用实用观点来分析、估计形势或解决问题的实际的、可行的方法（A practical, matter-of-fact way of approaching or assessing situations or of solving problems.）

Lesson 8
Legal Education in America

related to the environment, business organizations, or human rights violations—and propose solutions using legal rules and institutions. These courses provide a convenient opportunity to combine nonlegal with legal materials. For example, a seminar at Michigan, Globalization and Labor Rights, looks at freedom of association ,collective bargaining ,employment discrimination, and child labor issues. It also questions the use of economic sanctions by the United States against countries that violate labor rights, and the effectiveness of corporate codes of human rights practice.

d. Professional Skills Training Simulation and Clinical Methods

Students complained in the 1960s that legal education was too theoretical and did not offer enough practical experience in the law. The issue had been raised since the days when legal apprenticeship first fell into disfavor, but more professors listened this time to the calls for relevance. The Ford Foundation[1] set aside funds to encourage law schools to experiment with clinical studies. Certain bar committees discussed requiring particular practice courses, such as trial advocacy.

Practical education today takes many forms, but can be divided between simulated exercises in the classroom and live experience with real clients in administrative and judicial proceedings. Students' performances are sometimes video-taped for subsequent discussion and evaluation. The idea is to replicate the roles and responsibilities of practicing attorneys. Students prepare pleadings, beliefs and motions. They present oral argument. They learn to interview and counsel a client, examine a witness, and negotiate with another lawyer. They draft documents. These exercises may occur in specific simulation or clinical courses or in courses as divergent as real estate transactions or welfare law.

e. Externship

Some law schools permit upper-class students to spend a semester serving as a law clerk for a state or federal judge or working in a governmental agency, public

---

1 The Ford Foundation：福特基金会，该基金会最初由亨利和爱德瑟尔·福特的捐赠设立，后来与福特家族有福特公司脱钩。福特基金会是一个致力于国际和平和改善人类福利的慈善机构。基金会以寻求推进民主，减少贫困和不公，促进社会所有成员平等的实现，关注弱势人群的需要和权利为宗旨。生殖健康和性别问题是福特基金会在全世界的关注焦点之一。

interest law firm, or non-profit organization. Judges or attorneys supervise the students' activities.

IV. The Bar Examination

Under the American federal system, admission to and regulation of the legal profession falls to the states. All states except eight require an applicant to graduate from an ABA approved law school (California is the main exception), to satisfy the criteria of an ethics committee, and to pass a written examination of two to three days duration. All but three states use the standardized Multistate Bar Examination as part of this process. Since the remainder of each state's examination process tests for local law, candidates normally pay for a private four to six week cram course on bar subjects. About 75 percent of first-time test takers pass bar examinations nationwide.

To practice in another state a lawyer normally must either take its bar examination or, if he or she has practiced for five years, apply for admission on motion. About 30 states permit this later option. Bar admission includes the right to litigate in federal courts. In response to the globalization of legal services 23 states permit foreign lawyers to take their bar examinations (sometimes also requiring an American LL.M.[1] degree) and thus to become an attorney in that state. New York dominates this trend, passing 977 foreign lawyers (43 percent of their total).

---

[1] LL.M.: "Mater of Laws" 的简写，意思是法学硕士。现简要介绍一下美国法律教育学位授予的情况：Juris Doctor (J.D.)是美国法学院学习法律所取得的第一个学位，20世纪60年代以前，该学位称为 "Bachelor of Laws" (LL.B.)，即法学学士；法学学士之上是法学硕士 "Master of Laws" (LL.M.)；法学硕士之上是法律科学博士 "Doctor of the Science of Law(J.S.D or S.J.D.)，这是真正意义上的法学博士，读法律科学博士的学生通常旨在成为法学教师；要注意它与 Doctor of Laws(L.L.D)的区别，L.L.D只是一个名誉学位。国内的法律硕士（J.M.）全称是Juris Master。

Lesson 8
Legal Education in America

Glossary

apprenticeship 学徒制
practitioner 法律执业者
emulate 仿效
attributable 可归于……的
dean（大学）系主任
appellate 上诉的
affiliated 附属的
hierarchy 层次
litigation 诉讼

remnant 遗留下来的痕迹
matrix 发源地
undercut 削弱
pragmatism 实用主义
conceptualist 概念论者
seminar 研讨会
theoretical 理论的
divergent 分歧的
criteria 标准

EXERCISES

I. Answer the following questions.

1. What does "diversity" mean in the context of "American Legal Education"?
2. Why are American law students usually interested in some form of law practice? And what kind of technical subjects does he study in the law school?
3. What kind of teaching method do you prefer, lecture method or case method? Why?
4. When did the present-day American law school begin to take shape?
5. Could all the law be learned from cases according to the text? Why or why not?
6. Tell the differences of these degrees in America: J.D., L.L.B., L.L.M. and S.J.D.

II. Translate the following paragraph into Chinese.

Each state administers its own written examination to application to applicants for its bar. Almost all states, however, make use of the Multistate Bar Exam. Those who succeed in passing these examinations are admitted to the bar in their respective states. No apprenticeship is required. The rules for admission to practice before the federal courts vary with the court, but generally those entitled to practice before the highest court of a state may be admitted before the federal courts.

III. Choose the suitable words from the box and fill in the blanks.

| advisory | occurred | associated | distinction | abolished |
| solicitors | despite | dominant | assisted | gained |

The separation of 1_____ and barristers evolved during the first two centuries after the Conquest. Persons appearing before the new common law courts were often 2_____ by one of a number of attorneys or advocates who spent their days milling about the courts. The persons initially were 3_____ with the church, which held a 4_____ role in many areas of law. But as church power waned, laymen assumed the 5_____ roles. Sergeants and barristers carved out their niche as courtroom advocates, and were assisted in preparing litigation by persons called attorneys or, in the Court of Chancery, solicitors. The 6_____ between attorneys and solicitors, and the position of sergeant, were later 7_____, leaving only barristers and solicitors. The separate roles for barristers and solicitors have been for the most part preserved but in the last decade, 8_____ the opposition of the Bar, solicitors have 9_____ some rights of audience to appear before the higher courts. Proponents of a full fusion of the two professions have been rebuffed, even though a kind of "creeping" fusion has 10_____ as the prerogatives of advocacy and adjudication have been increasingly shared by solicitors.

IV. Match the definitions from column B with the words in column A.

A   B

1. attorney   a. person who practices a skill or an art
2. bar   b. one employing the services of a lawyer
3. client   c. to engage in legal proceedings
4. litigate   d. a small group of advanced students in a college or graduate school engaged in original research or intensive study under the guidance of a professor who meets regularly with them to discuss their reports and findings
5. apprentice   e. having the power to hear appeals and to review court decisions
6. practitioner   f. different from another

Lesson 8
Legal Education in America

7. seminar   g. collectively all attorneys
8. appellate   h. indicating opposition
9. divergent   i. person who has agreed to work for a skilled employer for a fixed period in return for being taught his trade or craft
10. against   j. lawyer; legal officer with authority to act in all cases in which the State is a party

Lesson 9
The American Constitution

Later laws prevail over those that preceded them.

后法优于先法。

The Constitution in America is a voluntary agreement among citizens that specifies national rules of governance and expresses the fundamental principles of justice. It also lists the inalienable rights of the people that bind them to cooperate for their general welfare. Drafted in 1787, the Constitution contains fewer than 4,400 words, divided into seven short parts, called articles. The Bill of Rights (the first ten amendments to the Constitution) was added in 1791, and only seventeen more amendments have been added in the more than two centuries since. It is the world's oldest effectively functioning written constitution.

When we speak of constitution today, we mean the fundamental law[1] or the supreme law of the country. Constitutional principles accorded special designation as constitutional laws[2] are (1) federalism, (2) separation of powers, (3) judicial review, (4) civil rights and liberties[3]. These four special categories contain the most publicized

---

1 fundamental law: 基本法；根本法。Refers to the organic law（组织法）that establishes the governing principles of a nation or state; esp., constitutional law. 基本法表明一个法律体系中的某些规定，这些规定已牢固树立，不能用普通的立法程序加以废除或修改。
2 constitutional law: 宪法，指作为一个部门法的宪法；而constitution指特定的成文法形式的宪法。
3 civil rights and liberties: 民权与公民自由。civil rights，民权（the individual rights of personal liberty guaranteed by the Bill of Rights and by the 13th, 14th, 15th, and 19th Amendments, as well as by legislation such as the Voting Rights Act（《选举权法》））。典型的民权包括选举权（the right to vote）、正当程序权（the right of due process）以及享受法律平等保护权（the right of equal protection under the law）等。civil liberties公民自由，通常包括言论与出版自由（freedom of speech and press）、宗教自由（freedom of religion），不受政府不当干涉或任意逮捕的权利（freedom from undue interference or restraint）等。

Lesson 9
The American Constitution

and exciting principles of constitutional law.

I. Federalism[1]

There was virtually no central government in 1787. The states each claimed to be sovereign; Massachusetts and Vermont even fought a war. Under the Articles of Confederation[2] drawn up in 1781 to create a loose affiliation of sovereign states governed by a weak unicameral[3] legislature, the central government could not compel the states or their citizens to act according to legislative or regulatory statutes. Although it could make treaties[4], it was powerless to enforce them and could not resolve conflicts between the states. For instance, when New York restricted use of New York harbor, the Confederation could not interfere in the interests of neighboring states and the national economy. By contrast, the federalism regulated by the Constitution ensured that the new government had the power to enforce such actions.

Federalism may be defined as a political arrangement in which two or more levels of government provide a variety of services to a given group of citizens in a special geographic area. For example, Iowans are served by the national government and by their state government as well as by a variety of local governance structures.

Scholars estimate that more than 80,000 state and local governments exist in the United States, each striving to meet the needs and wants of the complex, technologically driven society. Federalism accords to the states' control over purely local issues and the general, inherent power to protect the public health, safety, and welfare. The Constitution delegates to the states authority to establish local governments, conduct elections, and regulate intrastate commerce and further reserves

---

1 federalism：联邦制。A principle of government in which several states or countries are united as a single political entity with a common government while retaining a considerable degree of autonomy with respect to their internal affairs. 与此相对的是centralization, 中央集权的体制。
2 Articles of Confederation：《邦联条例》，美国的第一部宪法性文件，全称《邦联和永久联合条例》(Articles of Confederation and Perpetual Union)。1787年制宪会议（Constitutional Convention）召开，1788年美国新宪法取代了《邦联条例》。
3 unicameral：一院制的；单院的，与之对应的是bicameral两院制的。
4 treaty：条约，指两国政府正式签署（signed）和批准的（ratified）协议，以及两个以上国家达成的（concluded）受国际法约束的国际性协议。也可称为"accord""convention""covenant""declaration""pact"。

to the states all those powers not expressly delegated to the national government. In return, the Constitution specifically delegated enumerated (or express) powers to the national government, granting it authority over national economic development and stability, national security, and foreign policy: The national government is constitutionally authorized to make treaties and declare war, regulate interstate and foreign commerce, coin money, and maintain an army and navy. In addition, the national government has certain inherent or implied powers—powers not mentioned in the Constitution but necessary to its functioning (for example, the authority to regulate arms sales).

In addition, state and federal governments share certain concurrent powers—powers that are exercised at both levels as long as they do not conflict. Both levels of government, for example, have authority to levy taxes, regulate business, and prohibit housing or employment discrimination. The jurisdiction of state and national governments further overlap because the power of the national government has been broadly interpreted to include the power to regulate local activities that affect national interests. Congress cannot, however, regulate domestic affairs simply in the name of the public interest, as the states may. Its domestic acts must be authorized by the Constitution. Despite inevitable confusion and conflict over jurisdiction, the federal form of government has the advantage of keeping substantial political power close to its citizens, allowing regional differences to flourish while enabling a strong central government to provide both national defense and regulation in areas of common concern.

II. Separation of Powers[1]

Separation of powers is an indispensable element of our chapter of Constitution. The constitution allocates powers of government according to function. The functional branches are legislative (law making), executive (law enforcing), and judicial (adjudicating). The Legislative, composed of the House of Representatives and Senate, is set up in Article 1. The Executive, composed of the President, Vice-

---

1 Separation of Powers：三权分立；权利分立。与制衡原则（Checks and Balances）一起构成现代政治制度的基本体制。

Lesson 9
The American Constitution

President, and the Departments, is set up in Article 2. The Judicial, composed of the federal courts and the Supreme Court, is set up in Article 3.

Separation of powers provides an effective balance of power among the three branches of government. Different officials have unique and specific powers, and each branch operates under the direction of different persons. Each branch checks the other two to prevent them from garnering or exercising power illegally. This institutional structure restrains a natural human tendency toward expansion of personal power. While preventing possible tyranny (i.e., despotic abuse of authority), the separation of powers permits officials to execute faithfully their constitutionally delegated powers.

The constitutional doctrine of separation of powers speaks of the relationships among the divisions of government. While there are indeed exclusive functions assigned to each (e.g., tax bills must begin in the House of Representatives), much of the work engaged in by the three branches of government is shared.

Congress may pass a bill; the president may sign or veto[1] it. Congress may override the veto and enact the bill as law. The Supreme Court may strike down the statute as unconstitutional. If necessary, Congress may initiate a campaign to have the Constitution amended to accomplish the purpose of the statute, or more likely it may attempt to pass a new statute that is in conformity with the Constitution. Note too that the president may be able to appoint new members to the Supreme Court (with the advice and consent of the Senate) who are sympathetic to his or her views.

All of these checks and balances, however, are inefficient. But that's by design rather than by accident. By forcing the various branches to be accountable to the others, no one branch can usurp enough power to become dominant.

III. Judicial Review

Judicial review is the power and duty vested in the U.S. Supreme Court to

---

[1] veto: 否决, 否决权。The power or right vested in one branch of a government to cancel or postpone the decisions, enactments, etc. of another branch; especially, the right of a president, governor, or other chief executive to reject bills passed by the legislature, subject to the right of the legislature to override the veto; The Constitution specifically gives the President the power to veto any bill of Congress within ten days of its enactment and return it to Congress for reconsideration.

declare null and void (i.e., of no validity or effect) any statute or act of the federal government or of any state government that violates the U.S. Constitution. American people have become so used to judicial review that it seems a natural, inevitable, and even necessary part of the government structure. The president, Congress, state legislatures, governors, state courts, state and federal administrative agencies, public officials, and all ordinary citizens are subject to the commands of the nine justices on questions of constitutional law.

Remarkably, the power of judicial review is not given to the Supreme Court in the Constitution itself. Article III states that "The judicial power of the United States, shall be vested in one Supreme Court, and in such inferior courts as the Congress may from time to time ordain and establish," and it extends that power to "all cases, in Law and Equity, arising under this Constitution" and to other categories. These provisions are organizational and jurisdictional. They create the Supreme Court, but "supreme" means only "highest", designating a place in the hierarchy but not a grant of authority to exercise constitutional review in hearing them.

Although not specifically authorized in Article III, some form of judicial review was presumably envisioned by framer of the Constitution. According to Alexander Hamilton, the Supreme Court is the "least dangerous branch", because it controls neither sword nor purse. He said the Supreme Court and not the Congress or the president should be custodian of the Constitution. Further, he referred to "the medium of the courts of justice, whose duty it must be to declare all acts contrary to the manifest tenor of the constitution void. Without this, all the reservations of particular rights or privileges would amount to nothing."

What judicial review meant, however, was not articulated until 1803, in case of *Marbury* v. *Madison*[1]. This case did more than validate (i.e., give legal force to) the judicial review of legislative and executive enactments and orders. Chief Justice

---

1 *Marbury* v. *Madison*：马伯里诉麦迪逊，美国著名司法判例，此案确立了美国的司法审查原则。1801年，美国总统亚当斯在其任期的最后一天午夜，突击任命了42位治安法官，但其中16人的任命状未能及时送达；继任总统杰弗逊让国务卿麦迪逊将这16份委任状统统扔掉。其中一名因此未能当上法官的人叫作马伯里，由此提起了对麦迪逊的诉讼。审理该案的法官马歇尔，运用高超的法律技巧和智慧，判决该案原告所援引的《1789年司法条例》第13款因违宪而无效，从而解决了此案，并从此确立了美国最高法院有权解释宪法、裁定政府行为和国会方法行为是否违宪的制度，对美国政治法律制度产生了深远的影响。

Lesson 9
The American Constitution

Marshall enunciated a major power for the Supreme Court, recognizing it as the sole interpreter and custodian of the Constitution, to the exclusion of the president and Congress. With this declaration came the awesome duty of defining what the Constitution means and what it does not mean.

Although the exclusive judicial power of review has engendered heated controversy over the years, it also has been a stabilizing force for a growing and changing society. As national economic, social, and political conditions have changed, so too have attitudes and opinions of the people. This evolution is reflected in the leaders the people elect to office and in the Supreme Court Justices who are appointed. As a result, some long-standing Supreme Court decisions have been changed. What once was ruled constitutional thereafter is declared unconstitutional. For example, as the twentieth century began, racial segregation in schools was accepted and even endorsed by the "separate but equal" rule of *Plessy* v. *Ferguson*. In 1954, however, the "separate but equal" rule was rejected by *Brown* v. *The Board of Education of Topeka*.

IV. The Bill of Rights

During the debates on the adoption of the Constitution, its opponents repeatedly charged that the Constitution as drafted would open the way to tyranny by the central government. Fresh in their minds was the memory of the British violation of civil rights before and during the Revolution. They demanded a "bill of rights" that would spell out the immunities of individual citizens. Several state conventions in their formal ratification of the Constitution asked for such amendments; others ratified the Constitution with the understanding that the amendments would be offered.

On September 25, 1789, the First Congress of the United States therefore proposed to the state legislatures 12 amendments to the Constitution that met arguments most frequently advanced against it. The first two proposed amendments, which concerned the number of constituents for each Representative[1] and the

---

1 Representative: 众议院议员。A member of the U.S. House of Representatives or of the lower house of a state legislature; 与此相对应, Senator, a member of a senate 参议员。

compensation of Congressmen, were not ratified. Articles 3 to 12, however, ratified by three-fourths of the state legislatures, constitute the first 10 amendments of the Constitution, known as the Bill of Rights[1] (see Supplementary Reading). The Bill of Rights mandates specific and general restraints on the government to protect all persons from arbitrary and capricious acts by federal officials. Thus, the Bill of Rights originally applied only as a restraint on the national government. States were bound only by provisions on civil rights if and as specified in their own state constitutions.

Following the Civil War, several amendments were added to the U.S. Constitution to protect and assist the newly freed slaves. In 1865 the thirteenth Amendment formally outlawed slavery. Previously, most African-Americans had been denied liberty despite the contrary words of the Declaration of Independence and despite the mandate of the Fifth Amendment that "No person shall be deprived of life, liberty, or property without due process of law." Three years later, in 1868, the Fourteenth Amendment reiterated the right of all persons to liberty and extended the scope of its protection by binding all state and local governments with these words:

"No state shall make or enforce any law which shall abridge the privileges or immunities of citizens of the United States; nor shall any state deprive any person of life, liberty, or property, without due process of law, nor deny to any person within its jurisdiction the equal protection of the laws."

The clauses guaranteeing due process of law and equal protection of the laws were not defined at the time of the Fourteenth Amendment, leaving the work of definition and specific application to the judicial branch. Ultimately, it is the United States Supreme Court, as the interpreter of the Constitution, that gives meaning to, and determines the boundaries of, the rights guaranteed by the Constitution.

---

1 the Bill of Rights：《权利法案》，美国宪法前十条修正案，于1789年9月25日提出，1791年12月15日批准，也称为"民权法案"。其内容包括保护言论自由、出版自由等公民最基本的权利。美国各州宪法均含有权利法案，大部分内容都与宪法中内容相似。

Lesson 9
The American Constitution

Glossary

abridge 剥夺
accord to 使调和
affiliation 联系；加入
amendment 修正案
civil liberties 公民自由
civil rights 民权
constituent 选民；有权制宪或修宪的
custodian 管理人
declare war 宣战
despotic 专制的；暴虐的
employment discrimination 就业歧视
enactment 法令；条例
endorse（签注）认可；赞成
engender 造成
enunciate 阐明
federalism 联邦制
fundamental law 基本法；根本法
governance 统治；管理
immunity 免除；豁免
inalienable（权利等）不能让与的；不可剥夺的

judicial review 司法审查
jurisdictional 司法权的；管辖权的
maintain 供养；维持
null and void 无效的；无法律约束力的；可撤销的
ordain（法律）规定
outlaw 宣布……为非法
overlap（与……）交叠；重合
racial segregation 种族隔离
regulatory（行政）规章的；制定规章的
reiterate 重申
Representative 众议院议员
tenor 要旨；大意
tyranny 暴政
unicameral 一院制的；单院的
usurp 非法地占有或拥有；篡夺
validate 使生效；使有法律效力
Vermont 佛蒙特州（美国州名）
vest (in)（权力等）属于；归属
veto 否决

EXERCISES

I. Answer the following questions.

1. How does the Constitution fix the boundaries between federal and state law?
2. What is the social background for the drafting of the U.S. Constitution?
3. Describe how power is separated and shared among the three different branches of government.
4. What's the effect of Separation of Powers? And is there any inefficiency in it? If so, what is it?

5. What's judicial review? How did Chief Justice Marshall argue in favor of judicial review?

6. What was the intent of those who called for the top 10 amendments of the U.S Constitution?

7. Did the Fourteenth Amendment give the black people equal protection at first? When was it used to combat racial discrimination?

II. Translate the following terms into English.

1. 基本法
2. 联邦制
3. 邦联条例
4. 权利分立
5. 参议院
6. 否决权
7. 司法审查
8. 人权法案
9. 法律的正当程序
10. 法律的平等保护

III. Translate the following sentences into Chinese.

1. The Separation of Powers devised by the framers of the Constitution was designed to do one primary thing: to prevent the majority from ruling with an iron fist. Based on their experience, the framers shied away from giving any branch of the new government too much power.

2. The president may be impeached by Congress for treason, bribery, or other high crimes and misdemeanors, but not for political acts.

3. The drafting and ratification of the Constitution reflected a growing consensus that the federal government needed to be strengthened.

4. Today the individual rights guaranteed by the Bill of Rights serve as restrictions on state and federal governments alike.

5. The Constitution has continued to develop in response to the demands of an ever-growing society through all these methods. Yet the spirit and wording of the Constitution have remained constant.

Lesson 9
The American Constitution

IV. Cloze.

The courts have the 1_____ to assess not only the actions of individuals and agencies but 2_____ enacted by Congress, states, and localities in order to determine whether they are in accord with the 3_____, this power of judicial review is now widely considered an essential 4_____ on both Congress and the president. The Constitution itself, however, gives only the slightest hint of that power, in Article III:"The judicial power of the United States, shall be vested in one 5_____ Court, and in such inferior Courts as the Congress may...ordain and establish ...The judicial power shall 6_____ to all cases, in law and Equity, arising under this Constitution."

It is clear that many 7_____ to the Constitutional Convention wanted the Supreme Court to 8_____ the constitutionality of state legislation. It is much less clear, however, whether they wanted the Court, not the president or even congress itself, to have the power to review 9_____ of Congress. The problem arises because the Supremacy Clause defines the relationship of federal and state law, not the relationship between the three coequal 10_____ of the federal government.

Supplementary Reading

The Bill of Rights

Amendment 1

Congress shall make no law respecting an establishment of religion, or prohibiting the free exercise thereof; or abridging the freedom of speech, or of the press; or the right of the people peaceably to assemble, and to petition the Government for a redress of grievances.[1]

Amendment 2

A well regulated Militia, being necessary to the security of a free State, the right of

---

1 国会不得制定关于下列事项的法律：确立国教或禁止信教自由；剥夺言论自由或出版自由；或剥夺人民和平集会和向政府请愿申冤的权利。

the people to keep and bear Arms, shall not be infringed.[1]

Amendment 3

No Soldier shall, in time of peace be quartered in any house, without the consent of the Owner; nor in time of war, but in a manner to be prescribed by law.[2]

Amendment 4

The right of the people to be secure in their persons, houses, papers, and effects, against unreasonable searches and seizures, shall not be violated, and no Warrants shall issue, but upon probable cause, supported by Oath or affirmation, and particularly describing the place to be searched, and the persons or things to be seized.[3]

Amendment 5

No person shall be held to answer for a capital, or otherwise infamous crime, unless on a presentment or indictment of a Grand Jury, except in cases arising in the land or naval forces, or in the Militia, when in actual service in time of War or public danger; nor shall any person be subject for the same offence to be twice put in jeopardy of life or limb; nor shall be compelled in any criminal case to be a witness against himself, nor be deprived of life, liberty, or property, without due process of law; nor shall private property be taken for public use without just compensation.[4]

Amendment 6

In all criminal prosecutions, the accused shall enjoy the right to a speedy and public trial, by an impartial jury of the State and district wherein the crime shall have been committed, which district shall have been previously ascertained by law, and to be informed of the nature and cause of the accusation; to be confronted with the witnesses against him; to have compulsory process for obtaining witnesses in his favor, and to have the Assistance of Counsel for his defense.[5]

---

1 管理良好的民兵是保障自由州的安全所必需的，因此人民持有和携带武器的权利不得侵犯。
2 未经房主同意，士兵平时不得驻扎在任何住宅；除依法律规定的方式，战时也不得驻扎。
3 人民的人身、住宅、文件和财产不受无理搜查和扣押的权利，不得侵犯。除依据合理根据，以宣誓或代誓宣言保证，并详细说明搜查地点和扣押的人或物，不得发出搜查和扣押状。
4 无论何人，除非根据大陪审团起诉报告或公诉书，不受死罪或其他重罪的审判，但发生在陆、海军中或发生在战时或出现公共危险时服役的民兵中的案件除外。任何人不得因同一犯罪行为而两次遭受生命或身体的危害；不得在任何刑事案件中被迫自证其罪；不经正当法律程序，不得被剥夺生命、自由或财产。不给予公平赔偿，私有财产不得充作公用。
5 在一切刑事诉讼中，被告有权由犯罪行为发生地的州和地区的公正陪审团予以迅速和公开的审判，该地区应事先由法律确定；得知控告的性质和理由；同原告证人对质；以强制程序取得对其有利的证人；并取得律师帮助为其辩护。

Lesson 9
The American Constitution

Amendment 7

In Suits at common law, where the value in controversy shall exceed twenty dollars, the right of trial by jury shall be preserved, and no fact tried by a jury, shall be otherwise re-examined in any Court of the United States, than according to the rules of the common law.[1]

Amendment 8

Excessive bail shall not be required, nor excessive fines imposed, nor cruel and unusual punishments inflicted.[2]

Amendment 9

The enumeration in the Constitution, of certain rights, shall not be construed to deny or disparage others retained by the people.[3]

Amendment 10

The powers not delegated to the United States by the Constitution, nor prohibited by it to the States, are reserved to the States respectively, or to the people.[4]

---

1 在普通法的诉讼中,争执价额超过20美元的,由陪审团审判的权利应受到保护。由陪审团裁决的事实,合众国的任何法院除非按照普通法规则,不得重新审查。
2 不得要求过多的保释金,不得处以过重的罚金,不得施加残酷和非常的惩罚。
3 本宪法对某些权利的列举,不得被解释为否定或轻视由人民保留的其他权利。
4 宪法未授予合众国、也未禁止各州行使的权力,由各州各自保留,或由人民保留。

Lesson 10
Administrative Law

Upon the plaintiff lies the burden of proof.

举证责任在于原告。

I. The Definition of Administrative Law

The study of administrative law can be viewed as an analysis of the limits placed on the powers and actions of administrative agencies. These limits are imposed in many ways, and it is important to remember that legal controls may be supplemented or replaced by political checks on agency decisions. One set of legal controls that we will examine at length is the procedures that reviewing courts[1] have required the agencies to use. Another is the rules specified by Congress in the Administrative Procedure Act (APA)[2]. Conceptually, however, the first question that should be examined is the amount of legislative or judicial power that can be delegated initially to the agency by the legislature[3].

II. Delegation of Authority

Throughout the modern era of administrative regulation, agencies have been

---

1 reviewing court: 复审法院。The court that gives the judicial review of an administrative proceeding.行使对行政行为的司法审查要点是，被委以权力的人或机构越权或滥用权力，这种行为就可能被法院宣告无效。
2 Administrative Procedure Act:《行政程序法》。A federal statute establishing practices and procedures to be followed in rulemaking and adjudication.
3 legislature: 立法机关。The branch of government responsible for making statutory laws.国家最高统治机构的组成部分，拥有通过立法制定和修改法律的职能，与拥有执行、适用法律职能的行政机关及拥有解释法律并依据法律对特定案件作出裁决的司法机关不同。规定立法机关的组成人员是每一个国家宪法的一部分。

Lesson 10
Administrative Law

delegated sweeping powers. Some of these powers are assigned on an industry-wide basis, as with the Federal Communications Commission[1], the Nuclear Regulatory Commission[2], and the Maritime Administration[3]. Other agencies are charged with enforcing certain norms of conduct throughout the economy. These range from the Federal Trade Commission[4], which since 1914 has enforced a ban on "unfair methods of competition", to newer health and safety regulators, such as the Environmental Protection Agency and the Occupational Safety and Health Administration.

What makes the delegations more dramatic is that these agencies typically wield powers that are characteristic of each of the three principal branches of government. Many agencies operate under statutes that give them legislative power to issue rules which control private behavior, and which carry heavy civil or criminal penalties for violations; executive power to investigate potential violations of rules or statutes and to prosecute[5] offenders; and judicial power to adjudicate particular disputes over whether an individual or a company has failed to comply with the governing standards.

For example, the Securities Exchange Commission[6] (SEC) formulates law by writing rules which spell out what disclosures[7] must be made in a stock prospectus; these rules may have the same effect as a law passed by the legislature. Finally, the SEC also acts as judge and jury in deciding whether its rules have been violated; it

---

1. Federal Communication Commission: 联邦通讯委员会。1934年成立的美国联邦机构，管理州际和海外的海底电缆、电报、电话、广播和电视通讯。委员会成员由总统任命，经参议院批准。
2. Nuclear Regulatory Commission: 核能管理委员会。An independent federal agency that licenses and regulates civilian use of nuclear energy.
3. Maritime Administration: 海事委员会。A unit in the U.S. Department of Transportation responsible for subsidizing certain costs of operating ships under the U.S. flag; constructing or supervising the construction of merchant-type ships for the U.S. government; administering the War Risk Insurance Program; and operating the Merchant Marine Academy, which trains merchant-marine officers.
4. Federal Trade Commission: 联邦贸易委员会。1914年美国国会成立的防范州际商务中不公平贸易的机构；它是非政治团体，五位成员由总统任命、任期7年，有权调查和控制垄断行为、维持转售价格、处理假冒专利；有权要求公司提供报告以调查商业活动；被授权对违章的公司签发停业令。该委员会的工作"对商业管理的收效甚大"。
5. prosecute: 提起公诉。To institute and pursue a criminal action against (a person). 一种法律程序，即准备并提起诉讼指控某人已犯罪的程序。
6. Security Exchange Commission：证券交易委员会。由美国国会设立的执行《1993年联邦证券法》和《1934年证券交易法》的独立机构。证券交易委员会有经任命的5位委员组成，任期5年。委员会的工作主要有：颁发股票交易许可证，搜集证券交易机构和关于交易实践的信息，委员会还拥有相当大部分的准司法权。它因保护投资者的利益而声誉卓著。
7. disclosure: 披露。The act or process of making known something that was previously unknown.

conducts adjudicatory hearings[1] to determine guilt and mete out punishment. In addition, administrative agencies are often unattached to any of the three branches of government (executive, legislative, or judicial). Although the commissioners—agency members—of the SEC are presidential appointees (subject to Senate approval), the SEC is an independent agency; it is not attached to the Congress nor is it a part of any executive department.

Such delegations raise fundamental questions concerning the constitutional distribution of authority in our system of government. The federal Constitution and most state constitutions as well, are based on the principle of separation of powers. Generally, law-making power is assigned to the legislature, law-enforcing power to the executive and law-deciding power to the judiciary. With responsibility divided in this fashion, each branch theoretically provides checks and balances[2] on the exercise of power by the other two branches. The image of administrative agencies as a "fourth branch" seems, at least formally, at odds with this three-part paradigm of government.

III. Justification for Broad Delegations

Justifications for these broad delegations of combined powers can be found in the institutional advantages of the administrative agency. Particularly in novel or rapidly changing fields of activity, the legislature may be unable to specify detailed rules of conduct. An agency, armed with flexible decision-making procedures and charged with continuing responsibility for a limited subject matter, may be better equipped to develop sound and coherent policies. Moreover, effective development and implementation]of regulatory policy may require the exercise of all three kinds of power. A rule or a policy decision can be quickly nullified in practice if investigations and prosecutions are not vigorously pursued, or if adjudications are decided by tribunals which do not understand or support the regulatory goals. When the subject matter of a regulatory program is technical or complex, or when detailed

---

1 hearing：听审。即某人就件正在被进行法律调查的事项，向一位法官或法庭陈述其意见或援引相关的证据。
2 checks and balance: 制约与平衡。将立法权、行政权、司法权加以区分，并试图确保在任何一方滥用或误用其权利时，都能而且会受到来自另外一方或两方的制约和平衡的政体原则。

Lesson 10
Administrative Law

knowledge of the regulated industry is essential to the formulation of sound policy, administrative agencies can bring to bear their superior experience and expertise. Uniformity and predictability are also important in many areas of economic regulation. Businesses need to plan their operations and make their investment decisions with some assurance that the ground rules will not be changed abruptly or applied inconsistently—problems which might well arise if decision-making power were dispersed among the three branches of government.

It should also be noted, however, that a substantial number of legislators, judges, and commentators are unpersuaded by these arguments. They argue that little real justification exists for continued sweeping delegations or for the combination of prosecutorial, rulemaking and adjudicative powers within one agency. Thus there is pressure to separate such functions, to establish an administrative court, or otherwise to limit the delegation of broad authority to the agencies.

IV. The Origins of American Administrative Law

The origins of American administrative law lie in the common law courts of England. In short, administrative law grew out of common law, and the common law has a large and continuing influence on American administrative law.

Officers of the Crown[1], such as bailiffs and sheriffs, were subject to damage liability if (1) an aggrieved citizen could establish[2] that the officer had committed what was prima facie[3] a common law wrong (such as trespass[4] or battery[5]) that (2) the officer was unable to justify by reference to statute or higher authority. This principle—of accountability of government officials to damage suits in the regular courts of law—was a fundamental element of the English lawyer's conception of the "rule of law". But the common law damage remedy was often inadequate. The

---

1 the Crown: 刑事法院。An English court having jurisdiction over major criminal cases.
2 establish: 证明。To prove; to convince.
3 prima facie: 逐步的,表面的。At first sight; on first appearance but subject to further evidence or information. 一般而言,当事人在诉讼中须提出有初步证据的案件,也就是足以要求答辩的案件。表面证据是在不存在任何相反证据的时候,足以确认一项事实的证据,并非确证。
4 trespass: 侵害行为。在现代法律中是一种故意违法行为,即侵犯他人人身,或妨碍他人根据其意愿占有财产。
5 battery: 殴打。The use of force against another, resulting in harmful or offensive contact.

actions of government officials could not always be pigeonholed into the common law forms of action. In addition, courts sensitive to the need for some administrative flexibility built up doctrines of official privilege based on the exercise of discretionary authority. Even if a plaintiff prevailed[1], the defendant official might be unable to satisfy the judgment out of his own pocket, or damages might afford fully adequate relief.

In response to these and other limitations, the common law courts began in the seventeenth century to refashion old writs[2] and develop new ones for the specific purpose of controlling official action. For example, the writ of mandamus was developed to require officials to grant or restore to citizens entitlements. The writ of prohibition was used to preclude administrative authorities from exercising powers not within their jurisdiction. Courts refashioned the writ of certiorari[3] to review particular decisions of administrative bodies and invalidate those decisions found to be without statutory warrant or otherwise in excess of the administrators' "jurisdiction".

These writs were used by the common lawyers to control a growing variety of administrative functions, including the responsibility of local authorities for relief of the poor, the efforts of commissions to drain fens and other wetlands for agriculture, and the governance of the colleges of Oxford and Cambridge. Judicial review of administrative action was also available in cases where administrative officials resorted to courts to enforce their orders. And the Chancellor's court of Equity began to develop the injunctive remedy as a means of controlling unlawful official action when an irreparable injury could be shown. The common law courts, however, continued to play the leading role in checking official power.

---

1 prevail: 胜诉。To obtain the relief sought in an action.
2 writ: 令状。系指书面形式的命令或批准令，13世纪时，主要有3种为法律所认可的令状；特许状，通常用于授予永久性土地或自由权；开封许可状，用于王室官吏的委任和授予特定期限的批准；密封令状，密封并加盖印章，用于传达命令或情报。
3 the writ of certiorari: 调卷令状。以前指一种特权令，现在一般指由英国高等法院签发下级法院的一种命令，要求将某个案件中的诉讼记录移送高等法院审理以便申诉得到迅速处理。

Lesson 10
Administrative Law

V. Solutions to Control Administrative Action

This reliance on the independent judiciary was not an inevitable solution to the need in modern government for an institution—in addition to the overworked legislature and chief executive—for controlling administrative action. Some nations, such as Italy and France, have relied on well-staffed and specialized tribunals, comprised of high-ranking civil servants and located within the administrative bureaucracy itself, to control the actions of administrators. Indeed, in England during the sixteenth and seventeenth centuries the Tudor and Stuart monarchs had developed powerful administrative tribunals, founded on the asserted prerogative powers of the Crown, that were employed to control subordinate officials in their relation to the citizenry. These bodies—like the Court of Star Chamber[1] and the Court of High Commission[2]—might well have evolved into a bureaucratic version of administrative justice analogous to the present French Conseil d'Etat[3]. But this line of development was cut short in Britain by the Glorious Revolution of 1688, the political triumph of parliamentary government, and the related celebration of the independent judiciary as an important check on executive power.

---

1 Court of Star Chamber: 星室法庭。An English court having broad civil and criminal jurisdiction at the king's discretion and noted for its secretive, arbitrary, and oppressive procedures, including compulsory self-incrimination (自证其罪,指刑事案件中的作不利于自己或有可能使自己受到刑事起诉的证言,美国宪法认定此种证言不能作为合法证据), inquisitorial investigation, and the absence of juries.
2 Court of High Commission: 宗教事务高等法院。于1559年经法律授权而设立的机构,行使国王担任英国教会最高首领时所拥有的某些权利。其与教会的关系与星座法庭同政府及一般法院的关系非常相似,而且其与议会和星座法庭的关系亦非常密切。其不仅监督一般宗教法院的活动,而且几乎拥有与一般宗教法院的管辖权一样广泛的初审权。17世纪其招致了普通法专家的憎恶,于1964年被撤销。
3 Conseil d'Etat: 法国最高行政机构,对行政部门起一定的咨询作用,也起一定的司法作用。它由法国文职人员的精华组成,属于政府的行政部门。1799年由拿破仑按照旧的枢密院模式创建,但一直有别于内阁。在行政诉讼提议问题上,它在对政府提供计划和建议方面发挥着重要的作用,同样在检查和控制行政官员以"形式上不合法、没有管辖权、滥用权力或违反行为"为由而滥用权力上也发挥着重要的司法作用。

Glossary

accountability（对……）负有责任（负有义务）
adjudicatory 裁判的
citizenry 公民或市民（集合称）
commentator 评论员；讲解员
commissioners 委员；专员
conceptual 概念的；观念的；构思的
corporate 社团的；法人的；共同的；全体的
disciplinary 惩罚性的；执行纪律的；纪律上的
disclosure 透露；公开
disperse 散布
drain 排出沟外
fen 沼泽；沼池
formulate 确切的阐述（表达、说明）
implementation 执行
injunctive 命令的；指令的
investigate 调查；侦查；审查
investigation 研究；调查
irreparable 不能挽回的

justification 认为有理；认为正当；理由
legislature 立法机关
mandamus 训令令状
mete 给予
norm 标准；规范；准则
novel 新奇的；新颖的
nullified 无效的
paradigm 范例
pigeonhole 把……分类（归档）；分类记存
predictability 可预言性
prerogative 特权
prosecute 对……起诉；检控
prospectus （介绍学校，企业等优点的）说明书，简章，简介资料
specify 指定；详细说明
statute 制定法；成文法
uniformity 一致；均匀
vigorously 精神旺盛地
wield 具有；运用（权利）

EXERCISES

I. Answer the following questions.

1. What does "the study of administrative law" mean according to the author?
2. What are the three principal functions of government?
3. What are the institutional advantages of the administrative agencies?
4. Explain the relationship between the common law and American administrative law.
5. What is the need in modern government to control the administrative action except reliance on the independent judiciary?

Lesson 10
Administrative Law

II. Translate the following terms into English.

1. 复审法院
2. 立法权
3. 司法权
4. 行政权
5. 制约与平衡
6. 自证其罪
7. 令状
8. 听审
9. 侵犯
10. 殴打

III. Translate the following paragraph into Chinese.

The administrative law system does not rely solely on procedural controls to ensure that officials will perform their functions satisfactorily. It also expects the legislative, executive, and judicial branches to supervise the substance of what agencies do. For example, the President appoints officeholders and chooses the overall goals of his administration; Congress conducts oversight hearings and, when necessary, rewrites enabling statutes; courts enforce legal requirements and place outer limits on agencies' use of discretion.

IV. Choose the suitable words from the box and fill in the blanks.

| challenge | review | agency | mission | discharge |
| congress | practice | acquaintance | diagnose | apply |

We have approached the question of choice by asking ourselves what we think students who might _____ administrative law ought to know as an introduction to the field. We concluded the following:

First, they should understand the basic principles _____ by the courts in _____ agency decisions. Students should also know how to get into court to _____ agency decisions. They should understand such traditional principles as "reviewability", standing, ripeness, and exhaustion of remedies, which determine when or whether they can ask a court to review agency action.

Second, students should have some _____ with the agency viewed as governmental bureaucracy. How does the _____ work as an institution? Who are its personnel?

How are they organized? How do they work? Moreover, any agency operates in a political environment. How are its actions affected by political influences? We try to give the student some feeling for the way bureaucratic and political factors affect an agency's ability to carry out its statutory _____.

Third, students should consider the efforts of _____, the president, and the courts to alter traditional administrative law principles to impose new, different, fewer, or greater controls on agency policymaking. Since the early 1970s, there has been a growing sense that agencies have failed to _____ their missions. In this book, we examine various _____ of agency "failure" and the efforts of various institutions, including but emphatically not only the courts, to remedy "failure".

Supplementary Reading

Modern government is administrative government. Much of modern life is a product, in large part, of the activities of administrative agencies. The range of administrative government is remarkably wide, including—for starters[1] and for illustration—energy, air and water quality, prices of consumer goods, conditions in the workplace, airline safety, taxation, and civil rights.

More than 15 million local, state, and federal government employees, organized in a variety of bureaucratic structures, carry out a vast array of functions using many different tools and procedures. The enormous variety and complexity that characterize "government administration" pose hard questions of choice and organization for those providing an introduction to the administrative state as a whole.

Most broadly, administrative law might be defined as legal control of government. More narrowly, we might say that administrative law consist of those legal principles that define the authority and structure of administrative agencies, specify the procedural formalities that agencies use, determine the validity of administrative decisions, and

---

1 for starters: to begin with; initially 首先；起初。

Lesson 10
Administrative Law

outline the role of reviewing courts[1] and other organs of government in their relation to administrative agencies.

Each particular field of administration has its corresponding substantive and procedural law. Labor law[2], for example, deals with the substantive principles and procedures used by the National Labor Relations Board (NLRB)[3] and other administrative agencies having responsibility over labor relations. Environmental law[4] deals similarly with the actions and procedures of the Environmental Protection Agency (EPA)[5], the Nuclear Regulatory Commission (NRC)[6], the Department of Health and Human Services (HHS)[7], the Food and Drug Administration (FDA)[8], and other federal and state regulatory agencies with environmental responsibilities. The growth of the welfare state and the development of "public interest" advocacy has created such fields as welfare law, consumer protection law, and prison law.

Administrative law deals with the more general principles and rules that cut across the particular substantive fields to embrace all forms of administrative activities. These principles and rules include three basic bodies of law: (1) constitutional law; (2) statutory

---

1 reviewing courts: 复审法院。高等法院审查行政权力行使者或行使机构的行政行为，决定其合法性和有效性的权力。行使对行政行为的司法审查的要点是，被委以权力的人或机构越权或滥用权力，这种行为就可能被法院宣告无效。
2 labor law: 劳动法。专指有关劳动雇佣的全部法律原则和法规的体系，大致与工业法同义。其相应调整雇佣合同，包括工资、假日、工作条件，对雇员健康和安全的注意义务，雇主协会和工会、集体谈判、罢工和劳资纠纷，以及其他劳动和工业关系的法律方面的问题。
3 National Labor Relations Board: 国家劳工关系局。美国为实施《国家劳工关系法》而于1935年设立的一个独立的联邦机构。国家劳工关系局的职能是防止或纠正不公平的劳动惯例。通过调查和非正式和解，或采用准司法程序解决劳资争议。
4 Environmental Law: 环境法。The field of law dealing with the maintenance and protection of the environment, including preventive measures such as the requirements of environmental-impact statements, as well as measures to assign liability and provide cleanup for incidents that harm the environment. Because most environmental litigation involves disputes with governmental agencies, environmental law is heavily intertwined with administrative law.
5 Environmental Protection Agency: 环境保护局。An independent federal agency in the executive branch responsible for setting pollution-control standards in the areas of air, water, solid waste, pesticides, radiation, and toxic materials; enforcing laws enacted to protect the environment; and coordinating the antipollution efforts of state and local governments.
6 Nuclear Regulatory Commission: 核能管理委员会。An independent federal agency that licenses and regulates civilian use of nuclear energy.
7 Department of Health and Human Services: 健康及公共事业部。The cabinet-level department of the federal government responsible for matters of health, welfare, and income security.
8 Food and Drug Administration: 食品与药品管理局。A division of the U.S. Public Health Service in the Department of Health and Human Service responsible for ensuring that animal drugs, biological products, and medical devices are safe and effective; and that certain other products, such as electronic products that emit radiation, are safe.

law[1], including above all the Administrative Procedure Act (APA)[2]; and (3) a form of federal common law, embodied in judicial decisions that do not have a clear constitutional or statutory source.

Administrative law can be a difficult and elusive subject, precisely because of its generality and abstraction from the substantive and procedural law governing specific areas of administration. It is hard to deal with administrative law without knowing a fair bit about the underlying issues of substantive law.

An important theme of this book is that we cannot understand the significance of procedural requirements or principles of judicial review apart from the substantive responsibilities of particular agencies and the means available to those agencies for accomplishing their goals. And in applying general principles, courts are sensitive to the identity of the agency whose action is challenged, the reputation and quality of its personnel, its overall mission, the practical difficulties it faces in discharging that mission, the content of the particular action under challenge, and the respective equities of the agency and the affected private parties. Some courts trust some agencies; some courts distrust some agencies. The absence or lack of trust can matter a great deal to the ultimate outcome.

Administrative agencies usually are created to deal with current crises or to redress serious social problems. Throughout the modern era of administrative regulation, which began approximately a century ago, the government's response to a public demand for action has often been to establish a new agency, or to grant new powers to an existing bureaucracy. Near the turn of the century, agencies like the Interstate Commerce Commission[3] and the Federal Trade Commission were created in an attempt to control the anticompetitive conduct of monopolies and powerful corporations. The economic depression of the 1930s was followed by a proliferation of agencies during the New Deal[4] which were designed to stabilize the economy, temper the excesses of

---

1 statutory law: 成文法。The body of law derived from statutes rather than from constitutions or judicial decisions.
2 The Administrative Procedure Law: 行政程序法。行政部门和当局在行使准司法职能，对向他们提起的申诉或者纠纷作出裁决，或者适当的法庭或者个人作出裁决时所遵守的程序。
3 Interstate Commerce Commission: 州际商业委员会。根据1887年宪法创立的一个联邦管理委员会，用来管理各州间的商业，特别是涉及州际或外国商业的铁路运输。这种创立的实践结果起初非常小，因为它的命令对法院没有强制力，但是自20世纪开始，其权威大大增强。1948年以来，它享有规制所有垄断商业活动以及所有州际商业运输的权利。
4 The New Deal: 新政。

Lesson 10
Administrative Law

unregulated markets, and provide some financial security for individuals. Agencies were also established or enlarged in wartime to mobilize manpower and production, and to administer price controls and rationing. The development of new technologies, ranging from radio broadcasting to air transportation to nuclear energy, often led to creation of new government bureaus to promote and supervise these emerging industries. In the 1960s when the injustices of poverty and racial discrimination became an urgent national concern, the development of programs designed to redress these grievances expanded the scope of government administration. More recently, increased public concern about risks to human health and safety and treats to the natural environment have resulted in new agencies and new regulatory programs.

The primary reason why administrative agencies have so frequently been called upon to deal with such diverse social problems is the great flexibility of the regulatory process. In comparison to courts or legislatures or elected executive officials, administrative agencies have several institutional strengths that equip them to deal with complex problems. Perhaps the most important of these strengths is specialized staffing: an agency is authorized to hire people with whatever mix of talents, skills and experience it needs to get the job done. Moreover, because the agency has responsibility for a limited area of public policy, it can develop the expertise that comes from continued exposure to a problem area. An agency's regulatory techniques and decisionmaking procedures can also be tailored to meet the problem at hand. Agencies can control entry into a field by requiring a license to undertake specified activities; they can set standards, adjudicate violations, and impose penalties; they can dispense grants, subsidies or other incentives; they can set maximum or minimum rates; and they can influence conduct through a wide variety of informal methods.

However, these potential strengths of the administrative process can also be viewed as a threat to other important values. Administrative "flexibility" may simply be a mask for unchecked power, and in our society unrestrained government power has traditionally been viewed with great and justifiable suspicion. Thus, the fundamental policy problem of the administrative process is how to design a system of checks which will minimize the risks of bureaucratic arbitrariness and overreaching, while preserving for the agencies the flexibility they need to act effectively. Administrative law concerns the legal checks that are used to control and limit the powers of government agencies.

下 篇
Part Two

Lesson 1
Criminal Law: An Overview

An act is not a crime unless the law says it is one.
法无明文规定者不为罪。

I. Crimes[1]

Fundamental to the concept of criminal law is the assumption that criminal acts injure not just individuals, but society as a whole. Hence, we can define criminal law as a branch of modern law which concerns itself with offenses committed against society, members thereof, their property, and the social order. Criminal law is also called penal law. How then does a crime differ from a civil wrong[2], such as a tort or a breach of contract[3]?

First, unlike torts and contracts, the criminal law involves public law. That is, although the direct and immediate victim of a crime typically is a private party (e.g., a person who is robbed, assaulted, or kidnapped), and other individuals may indirectly be injured (e.g., a spouse of the direct victim), a crime involves more than a private injury: a crime causes "social harm". For this reason, crimes are prosecuted by public attorneys[4] representing the community at large, and not by privately

---

1 crime: 犯罪，罪。A social harm that the law makes punishable; the breach of a legal duty treated as the subject-matter of a criminal proceeding.
2 civil wrong: 民事过错行为。A violation of non-criminal law, such as a tort(侵权行为), a breach of contract or trust（违反合同或信托）, a breach of statutory duty(违反法定义务), or a defect in performing a public duty; the breach of a legal duty treated as the subject matter of a civil proceeding.
3 breach of contract: 违反合同；违约。Violation of a contractual obligation, either by failing to perform one's own promise or by interfering with another party's performance.
4 public attorney还称为attorney at law，为a person who practices law, "律师"之意。此处，public attorney representing the community at large主要想表达的意思是"public prosecutor"（公诉人）或 "prosecuting attorney"（公诉律师），即"a public official appointed or elected to represent the state in criminal cases in a particular district"，因此，public prosecutor在美国还称为"district attorney"。

Lesson 1
Criminal Law: An Overview

retained counsel[1].

In old England, offenders were said to violate the "King's Peace"[2] when they committed a crime. They offended not just their victims, but contravened the peaceful order established under the rule of the monarch. For this reason, in criminal cases the state, as the injured party, begins the official process of bringing the offender to justice. Even if the victim is dead and has no one to speak on his or her behalf, the agencies of justice will investigate the crime and file charges against the offender. Because crimes injure the fabric of society, the state, not the individual victim, becomes the plaintiff in criminal proceedings.

When the fact finder[3] (ordinarily, a jury) determines that a person is guilty of an offense, the resulting conviction[4] is an expression of the community's moral outrage. But do not assume that all morally wrongful conduct is criminal. In a society that values individual liberty, the criminal law serves a minimalist role: it only seeks to identify and regulate wrongful conduct that results in significant social harm; the criminal law does not seek "to purify thoughts and perfect character". The latter is the responsibility of religion, family, and other private institutions. For example, telling a lie may be a character flaw, but the criminal law punishes only the most harmful lies, e.g., material misstatements made under oath[5] in judicial proceedings (perjury[6]).

The English common law divided crimes into two general categories: felonies and misdemeanors[7]. A felony "comprise[d] every species of crime which occasioned

---

1 privately retained counsel: 私人雇用的律师。Counsel means one or more lawyers who represent a client. retain为"雇用、聘请（律师、顾问）"之意。
2 King's Peace: 国王的安宁。由于国王代表国家，所以这里指"国家的安定"。
3 fact finder: 事实调查人。One or more persons such as jurors（陪审员）in a trial or administrative-law judges（听证行政法官）in a hearing—who hear testimony and review evidence to rule on a factual issue.
4 conviction: 有罪判决、定罪。The act or process of judicially finding someone guilty of a crime; the state of having been proved guilty; The judgment (as by a jury verdict) that a person is guilty of a crime.
5 material misstatements made under oath: 在（作出）宣誓后作出的重大虚假陈述。
6 perjury: 作伪证，伪证罪。The act or an instance of a person's deliberately making material false or misleading statements while under oath.
7 felony and misdemeanor: 重罪和轻罪。Because of its special heinousness, treason（叛国罪）was categorized separately, but strictly speaking it was a felony. Felony, a serious crime, usually punishable by imprisonment for more than one year or by death, examples include murder, rape, arson, and burglary. Misdemeanor, a crime that is less serious than a felony and is usually punishable by fine, penalty, forfeiture, or confinement (usually for a brief term) in a place other than prison (such as a county jail). misdemeanor还称为"minor crime"或"summary offense"。

at common law the forfeiture of lands and goods[1]". All common law felonies were punishable by death. The list of felonies was short: felonious homicide[2] (later divided by statute into murder[3] and manslaughter[4]), arson[5], mayhem[6], rape[7], robbery[8], larceny[9], burglary[10], prison escape, and (perhaps) sodomy[11]. All other criminal offenses were misdemeanors.

In modern penal codes, the line distinguishing felonies from misdemeanors is

---

1 forfeiture of lands and goods：没收土地及货物。
2 felonious homicide：重罪杀人，恶意杀人。Homicide committed unlawfully, without legal justification or excuse. This is the category into which murder and manslaughter fall.
3 murder：谋杀。The killing of a human being with malice aforethought（预谋恶意）. Malice（恶意）是指杀人意图；aforethought（预谋）指杀人意图在杀人行为之前产生。美国有些州将murder划分了等级，例如有first—degree murder（一级谋杀）；second-degree murder（二级谋杀）；third-degree murder（三级谋杀）等。其中，first-degree murder是指murder that is willful, deliberate, or premeditated, or that is committed during the course of another serious felony (often limited to rape, kidnapping, robbery, burglary, or arson)；first-degree murder还称为murder one或murder of the first degree。
4 manslaughter：非预谋杀人罪。The unlawful killing of a human being without malice aforethought. 非预谋杀人罪可分为"过失非预谋杀人罪"（involuntary manslaughter）和"故意非预谋杀人罪"（voluntary manslaughter）；involuntary manslaughter是指homicide in which there is no intention to kill or do grievous bodily harm, but that is committed with criminal negligence or during the commission of a crime not included within the felony-murder rule；与之相对应，voluntary manslaughter指an act of murder reduced to manslaughter because of extenuating circumstances such as adequate provocation arousing the "heat of passion"（激情杀人）or diminished capacity。
5 arson：纵火罪，防火罪。The crime of intentionally causing a dangerous fire or explosion, especially for the purpose of a destroying a building of another or of damaging property in order to collect insurance（领取保险）.
6 mayhem：重伤罪。The crime of maiming—that is disabling, dismembering, or disfiguring—a person, either intentionally or in some states, by any conduct intended to cause serious injury.
7 rape：强奸罪。At common law, unlawful carnal knowledge（性交）of a woman by force and without her consent; in modern usage generally, the crime of forcing or causing a person to submit to sexual intercourse (whether vaginal, oral, or anal) against his or her will, or when consent is obtained by unfair and unlawful means (as by putting a drug in a drink), or under circumstances in which the person is incapable of giving legally valid consent (as with a person who is unconscious or underage).
8 robbery：抢劫罪。The crime of taking someone's money or other personal property from the victim's person or in the victim's presence by force or threat of imminent harm.
9 larceny：偷盗罪。The unlawful taking and carrying away of someone else's personal property with the intent to deprive the possessor of it permanently.
10 burglary：夜盗罪；也有学者主张译为"恶意侵入他人住宅罪"。最初，burglary指the common law offense of breaking and entering another's dwelling at night with the intent to commit a felony；现在，已经不再局限于"夜晚"，"住宅"包括了其他一些建筑；按照《布莱克法律字典》，"the modern statutory offense of breaking and entering any building—not just a dwelling, and not only at night—with the intent to commit a felony"。
11 sodomy：反自然性行为。A term varying in meaning from state to state, but generally referring to any type of sex act regarded by legislature as "unnatural" or "perverted". In the narrowest and most traditional sense, the term refers to anal sexual intercourse between men. In most legal contexts today the term includes, at a minimum, oral and anal intercourse between men, but it may extend to those or other acts between men and women (sometimes exempting married couples, sometimes not), or women and women, or people and animals. sodomy originally was punished as an ecclesiastical offense.

Lesson 1
Criminal Law: An Overview

drawn differently than it was in the past. Generally speaking, an offense punishable by death or imprisonment[1] in a state prison is a felony; an offense for which the maximum punishment is a monetary fine, incarceration[2] in a local jail, or both, is a misdemeanor. For sentencing purposes, the Model Penal Code[3], and the statutory schemes of various jurisdictions, divide felonies into degrees.

Violations of the criminal law result in the imposition of punishment. When punishment is imposed in a criminal case, it is for one basic reason: to express society's fundamental displeasure with the offensive behavior and to hold the offender accountable for it.

II. Principles of Criminal Responsibility

As we noted previously, the objective of criminal law is to deter and punish the commission of acts that threaten society's safety and order. The critical concept is that a crime is committed when a person engages in forbidden conduct—neither bad thoughts alone nor mere action, or inaction where there is a duty to act, are criminal. Instead, the law requires the existence of both a bad act (*actus reus*[4]) and a bad state of mind (*mens rea*[5]) as a basis for the imposition of criminal responsibility.

Note that two other conditions must also exist for a crime to have been committed. First, the person's act must have caused a harmful result. Second, state or federal law must define the conduct as criminal.

a. The Criminal Act

The Model Penal Code states that "a person is not guilty of an offense unless his liability is based on conduct that includes (1) a voluntary act or (2) the omission to perform an act of which he is physically capable." In other words, a defendant must

---

1 imprisonment：监禁。The act of confining a person, especially in a prison.
2 incarceration：关押。The act of confining someone.
3 Model Penal Code：《模范刑法典》。A proposed code drafted by the American Law Institute and used as the basis for criminal—law revision by many states.
4 *actus reus*：〈拉丁语〉犯罪行为。Guilty act; the wrongful deed that comprises the physical components of a crime and that generally must be coupled with *mens rea* to establish criminal liability. 也可称为 "deed of crime" 或 "overt act"。
5 *mens rea*：〈拉丁语〉犯罪意图。Guilty mind; the state of mind that the prosecution, to secure a conviction, must prove that a defendant had when committing a crime. 也可称为 "mental element" 或 "criminal intent" 或 "guilty mind"。

have done something illegal or failed to do something legally required. We require a wrongful act, or *actus reus*, because we would otherwise have a system of criminal justice that punishes on the basis of intent. Thus, the mere thought of shooting a professor for assigning a poor grade is not held to be criminal.

Failure to Act. In some circumstances, the failure to act may fulfill the *actus reus* element. The determining factor is whether there is a legal duty to act, not just a moral one. In most circumstances, people are not under a legal duty to warn others that harm may befall them. For example, someone who overhears a murder threat is not legally required to warn the intended victim. However, individuals have legal duty to file an annual income-tax return. Thus, individuals are legally responsible for completing the task even if they are unable to file the return themselves.

Vicarious Liability. Vicarious liability is a no-fault liability that omits the personal *actus reus* requirement: In vicarious liability, the defendant is held liable for the wrongdoing of another person. As in civil law, a principal may be held responsible for the wrongful act of an agent when the agent acts within the scope of the agency. This question often arises in an employer-employee context.

b. The Mental Element

Criminal intent, or *mens rea*, refers to the actor's state of mind. It is different from the perpetrator's motive for the action. The Model Penal Code defines four mental states that apply to the commission of crimes: (1) intent (or purpose) to perform the act or cause the result, (2) knowledge of the act's nature or outcome, (3) recklessness, and (4) negligence.

Strict liability. The *mens rea* requirement is omitted in some circumstances. Thus, criminal liability can be imposed if a legislature has defined a certain behavior as criminal even if fault cannot be proven—that is, strict liability. Penalties for these offenses, however, are usually less severe than for offenses in which *mens rea* is present. Note that strict liability is not the same as vicarious liability.

III. Proof Beyond a Reasonable Doubt

In view of the fact that in criminal cases we are dealing with the life and liberty of the accused person, as well as the stigma accompanying conviction, the

Lesson 1
Criminal Law: An Overview

legal system places strong limits on the power of the state to convict a person of a crime. Criminal defendants are presumed innocent. The state must overcome this presumption of innocence by proving every element of the offense charged against the defendant beyond a reasonable doubt to the satisfaction of all the jurors. This requirement is the primary way our system minimizes the risk of convicting an innocent person.

The state must prove its case within a framework of procedural safeguards that are designed to protect the accused. The state's failure to prove any material element of its case results in the accused being acquitted or found not guilty, even though he or she may actually have committed the crime charged.

Glossary

actus reus 〈拉丁语〉犯罪行为
arson 纵火罪；放火罪
attorney at law 律师
breach of contract 违反合同；违约
burglary 夜盗罪；恶意侵入他人住宅罪
civil wrong 民事过错行为
contravene 违反
conviction 有罪判决；定罪
direct victim 直接受害者
fact finder 事实调查人
felonious homicide 重罪杀人；恶意杀人
felony 重罪
first-degree murder 一级谋杀
forfeiture of lands and goods 没收土地及货物
imprisonment 监禁
incarceration 关押
King's Peace 国王的安宁
larceny 偷盗罪
malice 恶意

manslaughter 非预谋杀人罪
mayhem 重伤罪
mens rea 〈拉丁语〉犯罪意图
misdemeanor 轻罪
Model Penal Code《模范刑法典》
murder 谋杀
perjury 作伪证；伪证罪
prison escape 逃狱；脱狱
privately retained counsel 私人雇用的律师
prosecuting attorney 公诉律师
public prosecutor 公诉人
rape 强奸罪
retain 雇用；聘请（律师，顾问）
robbery 抢劫罪
second-degree murder 二级谋杀
sodomy 反自然性行为
third-degree murder 三级谋杀
vicarious liability 替代责任

EXERCISES

Answer the following questions.

1. How a crime differs from a civil wrong, such as a tort or a breach of contract?
2. What is the line which distinguishes a felony from a misdemeanor according to the Model Penal Code?
3. What is the objective of criminal law according to this text?
4. What is *mens rea*? How many kinds of mental states are there according to the Model Penal Code?
5. What are the two fundamental conditions for a crime committed?
6. Who must prove the defendant guilty in a criminal action in U.S.A., the victim or the prosecutor? Why?

II. Translate the following terms into English.

1. 伪证罪
2. 重罪杀人
3. 二级谋杀
4. 《模范刑法典》
5. 犯罪行为
6. 犯罪意图
7. 纵火罪
8. 非预谋杀人罪
9. 监禁
10. 轻罪

III. Translate the following sentences into Chinese.

1. In the U.S., there are three basic forms of law: constitutional, statutory, and judicial. Moreover, there are three levels of government with three branches each, and all the levels promulgate laws.
2. Thus, our society has many sources of laws: the federal and the state constitutions, legislative enactments, judicial decisions, and executive orders. Statues are laws promulgated by Congress or state legislatures. Ordinances are laws promulgated at the local level.
3. Case law, unlike statues, is comprised of court decisions, both at the federal and state levels. A less common form of law is the executive order, an order pursuant to

Lesson 1
Criminal Law: An Overview

a president's constitutional powers or to a particular statute.

4. In modern penal codes, the line distinguishing felonies from misdemeanors is drawn differently than it was in the past. Generally speaking, an offense punishable by death or imprisonment in a state prison is a felony.
5. A person is not guilty of an offense unless his liability is based on conduct that includes (1) a voluntary act or (2) the omission to perform an act of which he is physically capable.

IV. Fill in the blanks with proper word(s).

1. The Latin term mens rea refers to _____ or a guilty state of mind. It is the mental aspect of a crime.
2. In some cases, offenders lack the capacity or competence to form mens rea. If they do not have that _____ or competence, they are not to held _____ for their criminal conduct.
3. If an individual did not intend to _____ a crime but was forced or coerced to do so against his or her will, he or she committed the crime under duress and is generally _____ from criminal liability.
4. _____ is the unlawful killing of one human being by another. Few murders are committed by strangers.
5. Violent crimes include murder, forcible rape, robbery, and aggravated _____. _____ crimes are burglary, larceny, and motor vehicle theft.
6. _____, sometimes confused with burglary, is a personal crime and involves face-to-face confrontation between victim and _____. Weapons may be used, or strong-armed robbery may occur through intimidation.
7. Violations of the _____ can be more or less serious. Felonies are serious crimes. The _____ category includes crimes such as murder, rape, aggravated assault, robbery, burglary, arson, and so on.
8. _____ are relatively minor crimes, consisting of offenses such as petty theft (the theft of items of little worth), simple assault (in which the victim suffers no serious _____, and in which none was intended), breaking and entering, the possessions of burglary tools, disorderly conduct, disturbing the peace, filing a _____ crime

report, and writing bad checks.
9. _____ is also a crime under the laws of most states. Hence, treason can be more generally defined as the attempt to overthrow the government of the society of which one is a member.
10. A necessary first feature of any crime is some act in violation of the law. Such an act is termed the _____ of a crime. The term means a "guilty act".

Supplementary Reading

The Corpus Delicti of a Crime The term *corpus delicti*[1] literally means "body of crime" The term is often confused with the statutory elements of a crime. Sometimes the concept is mistakenly thought to mean the body of a murder victim or some other physical result of criminal activity. It actually means something quite different.

One way to understand the concept of *corpus delicti* is to realize that a person cannot be tried for a crime unless it can first be shown that the offense has, in fact, occurred. In other words, to establish the *corpus delicti* of a crime, the state has to demonstrate that a criminal law has been violated and that someone violated it. Hence, there are only two aspects to the *corpus delicti* of an offense: (1) that a certain result has been produced and (2) that a person is criminally responsible for its production. As one court said, *corpus delicti* consists of a showing of (1) the occurrence of the specific kind of injury and (2) someone's criminal as the cause of the injury. So, for example, the crime of larceny requires proof that the property of another has been stolen—that is, unlawfully taken by someone whose intent it was to permanently[2] deprive the owner of its possession. Hence, evidence offered to prove the *corpus delicti* in a trial for larceny is insufficient where the evidence fails to prove that any property has been stolen or where property found in a defendant's possession cannot be identified as having been stolen. Similarly, "in an arson case, the *corpus delicti* consists of (1) a burned building or other property, and (2) some

---

1 *corpus delicti*：〈拉丁语〉犯罪事实；犯罪构成。通常，如果检察机关只有被告人的口供，而不能提供犯罪的事实证据，则指控不能成立。
2 permanently：永久性的。

Lesson 1
Criminal Law: An Overview

criminal agency[1] which caused the burning... In other words, the *corpus delicti* includes not only the fact of burning, but it must also appear that the burning was by the willful act of some person, and not as a result of a natural or accidental cause..."

We might add to the requirement to establish the *corpus delicti* of a crime before a successful prosecution can occur, the observation that the identity of the perpetrator[2] is not an element of the *corpus delicti* of an offense. Hence, the fact that a crime has occurred can be established without having any idea who committed it or even why it was committed. *Black's Law Dictionary* puts it another way: "the *corpus delicti* of a crime is the fact of its having been actually committed."

---

1 criminal agency: 应受刑法追究的力量,指并非意外事件。
2 perpetrator: 侵害者。

Lesson 2
Criminal Law: Types of Defenses to a Criminal Charge

Law should be like death, which spares no one.
　　　　　　　　　　　　　　　　—Montesquieu (1689—1755)

法律应如同死神一般，它不宽恕任何人。
——孟德斯鸠（Charles, 1689—1755，法国政治哲学家、法学家、启蒙思想家）

When a person is charged[1] with a crime, he or she typically offers[2] some defense[3]. A defense consists of evidence and arguments offered by a defendant and his or her attorneys[4] to show why that person should not be held liable for a criminal charge. American legal system generally recognizes four broad categories of defenses: (1) alibi; (2) justifications; (3) excuses; and (4) procedural defenses.

1　法律英语中charge这个词可用作名词，也可用作动词。我们在此简述一下该词的用法。I. *n.* 1）指控。A formal accusation of a crime as a preliminary step to prosecution.例如"故意杀人指控"（a murder charge），在这个意义上，charge 也用作criminal charge；2）陪审团指示。jury charge；3）担保。an encumbrance, lien, or claim；II. *v.* 1）提起指控。To accuse (a person) of criminal conduct, 例如，the police charged him with murder. 2）（向陪审团）作出指示。To instruct a jury on matters of law, 例如: the judge charged the jury on self-defense. 3）设定留置权或权利请求。To impose a lien or claim.

2　offer: 提出，提供。To present for acceptance. 此外，在法律英语中，offer通常有"（发出）要约、发盘、报价"等意思，既可以作名词，也可以作动词。如果合同一方当事人发出offer，另一方当事人作出acceptance（承诺），通常可以产生一个有约束力的合同（a binding contract）。

3　defense: 答辩，抗辩。A defendant's（被告人）stated reason why the plaintiff（原告）or prosecutor（公诉人、检察官）has no valid case; esp., a defendant's answer, denial, or plea. 此外，defense还有"被告方"、（商法）"票据抗辩权"（Commercial law, a basis for avoiding liability on a negotiable instrument（可流通票据））等意思。再如：defense attorney: 辩护律师。defense of insanity: 精神病辩护。self-defense: 自我防卫。

4　attorney: 律师。在美国，律师通常称为"attorney"，在英国，律师则常称为"barrister"或"solicitor"。美国人常用"attorney"来指律师，而"attorney"不仅指律师，还可以指检察官（prosecutor），因为从某种意义上讲，检察官被视为是政府工作的律师，因而"Attorney General"指美国检察总长。而按照英国传统的律师划分法，律师有barrister与solicitor之分。barrister传统译为"巴律师"，在香港为"大律师"或"出庭律师"；solicitor传统译为"沙律师"，在香港为"律师"或"事务律师"。

Lesson 2
Criminal Law: Types of Defenses to a Criminal Charge

I. Alibi

A current reference book for criminal trial[1] lawyers says, "Alibi is different from all of the other defenses...because...it is based upon the premise that the defendant is truly innocent..." The defense of alibi denies that the defendant committed the act in question. All of the other defenses we are about to discuss grant that the defendant committed the act, but they deny that he or she should be held criminally responsible.

Alibi is best supported by witnesses and documentation[2]. A person charged with a crime can use the defense of alibi to show that they were not present at the scene when the crime was alleged[3] to have occurred. Hotel receipts, eyewitness[4] identification, and participation in social events have all been used to prove alibis.

II. Justifications

Justifications may be offered by people who find themselves facing a choice between a "lesser of two evils"[5]. Included under the broad category of "justifications" are (1) self-defense, (2) the defense of others, (3) defense of home and property, (4) necessity, (5) consent, and (6) resisting unlawful arrest.

a. Self-defense

Self-defense is probably the best known of the justifications. This defense strategy makes the claim that it was necessary to inflict[6] some harm on another in order to ensure one's own safety in the face of near-certain injury or death. A person who harms an attacker can generally use this defense. However, the courts have held that where a "path of retreat" exists for a person being attacked, it should be taken. In other words, the safest use of self-defense is only when "cornered", with no path

---

1 criminal trial：刑事审判。Trial有审判、庭审、初审之意，例如trial court（初审法院）；trail by battle（决斗断讼）；trial by jury（陪审团审判）；trial by wager of law（宣誓断讼）。
2 witnesses and documentation：证人和证据资料。
3 allege一词在法律英语中使用频繁。alleged是指"指控的、宣称的、陈述的"等意。根据《布莱克法律字典》（74），alleged, *adj.*, 1）asserted to be true as described <alleged offenses>. 2）Accused but not yet tried<alleged murder>.
4 eyewitness：目击证人。One who personally observes an event. "目击证人"有别于"耳闻证人"。earwitness: A witness who testifies about something that he or she heard but not see.
5 a choice between a "lesser of two evils"：英语中的成语，两害相权取其轻。
6 inflict：强加于。To mete out (something punishing or burdensome).

of escape.

The amount of defensive force used must be proportionate to the amount of force[1] or perceived degree of threat that one is seeking to defend against. Hence, reasonable force is that degree of force that is appropriate in a given situation and is not excessive. Reasonable force can also be thought of as the minimum degree of force necessary to protect oneself, one's property, a third party, or the property of another in the face of a substantial threat. Deadly force[2], the highest degree of force, is considered reasonable only when used to counter an immediate[3] threat of death or great bodily harm. Deadly force cannot be used against non-deadly force.

Force, as the term is used within the context of self-defense, means physical force and does not extend to emotional, psychological, economic, psychic, or other forms of coercion. A person who turns the tables on a robber and assaults[4] him during a robbery attempt[5], for example, may be able to claim self-defense, while the business person who physically assaults a financial rival to prevent a hostile takeover of her company will have no such recourse[6].

---

1 the amount of force：武力程度。perceived degree of threat：所觉察到的威胁程度。

2 deadly force：致命武力。Force likely to cause death or great bodily harm.

3 immediate：及时的，立即的。1）Occurring without delay; instant <an immediate acceptance>. 2）紧接的。Not separated by other persons or things, <her immediate neighbor>. 3）直接的 Having a direct impact; without an intervening agency <the immediate cause of the accident>. 例如，"immediate cause of injury"（损害的直接原因）；"immediate family"（近亲属）；"immediate payment"（即期付款）等。

4 assault：常译为"恐吓；侵犯；殴击"。《布莱克法律字典》（P. 109）的四个释义项，assault: 1) Criminal & tort law. The threat or use of force on another that causes that person to have a reasonable apprehension of imminent harmful or offensive contact; the act of putting another person in reasonable fear or apprehension of imminent harmful or offensive contact; the act of putting another person in reasonable fear or apprehension of an immediate battery by means of an act amounting to an attempt or threat to commit a battery. 2) Criminal law. An attempt to commit battery, requiring the specific intent to cause physical injury.—Also termed (in senses 1 and 2) simple assault. 3) Loosely, a battery. 4) Popularly, any attack.

5 attempt：企图；犯罪未遂。注意：attempt与attempted相去甚远。Attempted crime 通常是指与attempt（未遂）相对立的"既遂犯罪"。请参考《布莱克法律字典》（123）对该词的解释。attempt, n. 1）The act or an instance of making an effort to accomplish something, esp. without success. 2）Criminal Law. An overt act that is done with the intent to commit a crime but that falls short of completing the crime. Attempt is an inchoate offense（不完整罪）distinct from the attempted crime.

6 recourse：权力的行使。Enforcement of, or a method for enforcing, a right 但recourse一词在法律英语中更为常见的意思是"（票据）追索权"，即"The right of a holder of a negotiable instrument to demand payment from the drawer（出票人）or indorser（背书人）if the instrument is dishonored（拒付）"。

Lesson 2
Criminal Law: Types of Defenses to a Criminal Charge

b. Defense of Others

The defense of others, however, sometimes called "defense of a third person", is circumscribed in some jurisdictions by the alter ego rule[1]. Defense of others cannot be claimed by an individual who joins an illegal fight merely in order to assist a friend or family member. Under the law, defense of third persons always requires that the defender be free from fault[2] and that he or she act to aid an innocent person who is in the process of being victimized. Also, the same restrictions that apply to self-defense also apply to the defense of a third party. Hence, a defender must only act in the face of an immediate threat to another person, cannot use deadly force against non-deadly force, and must only act to the extent and use only the degree of force needed to repel the attack.

c. Defense of Home and Property

In most jurisdictions[3] the owner of property can justifiably use reasonable, non-deadly force to prevent others from unlawfully taking or damaging it. As a general rule, however, the preservation of human life outweighs protection of property and the use of deadly force to protect property is not justified unless the perpetrator of the illegal act may intend to commit, or is in the act of committing, a violent act against another human being. A person who shoots an unarmed trespasser[4], for example, could not claim "defense of property" in order to avoid criminal liability. However, one who shoots and kills an armed robber while being robbed can.

The use of mechanical devices to protect property is a special area of law. Since,

---

1. the alter ego rule：他我规则。A rule of law that, in some jurisdictions, holds that a person can only defend a third party under circumstances and only to the degree that the third party could act on their own behalf.
2. fault：过错。Any deviation from prudence or duty resulting from inattention, incapacity, perversity, bad faith, or mismanagement.
3. jurisdiction：司法管辖区域。A geographic area within which political or judicial authority maybe exercised. 例如，the accused fled to another jurisdiction; other jurisdictions have decided the issue differently. 通常，jurisdiction还有"司法管辖权"之意。
4. trespasser：侵害人。trespass是侵权行为法上一个十分重要的概念。In English common law the action of trespass first developed (13th century) to afford a remedy for injuries to property. The two early forms were trespass *quare clausum fregit*, used in instances of breaking into real property(不动产), and trespass *de bonis asportatis*, used when personal property（动产） was removed without consent（同意）. 根据台湾学者潘维大、刘文琦著《英美法导读》，trespass译为"直接侵权行为"，这个词由拉丁文"transgression"演变而来，其原意是"破坏社会秩序的行为"。与之相对应的是"间接侵权行为"（trespass on the case）。

generally speaking, deadly force is not permitted in defense of property, the setting of booby traps such as spring-loaded shotguns, electrified grates, explosive devices, and the like, is generally not permitted to protect property which is unattended and unoccupied.

On the other hand, acts which would otherwise be criminal may carry no criminal liability if undertaken to protect one's home. For purposes of the law, one's "home" is one's dwelling, whether owned, rented, or merely "borrowed". Hotel rooms, rooms on board vessels, and rented rooms in houses belonging to others are all considered, for purposes of the law, one's "dwelling". The retreat rule, referred to earlier, which requires a person under attack to retreat when possible before resorting to deadly force, is subject to what some call the castle exception[1]. The castle exception can be traced to the writings of the sixteenth-century English jurist Sir Edward Coke[2], who said, "A man's house is his castle—for where shall a man be safe if it be not in his house?" The castle exception generally recognizes that a person has a fundamental right to be in his or her home and also recognizes the home as a final and inviolable place of retreat (that is, the home offers a place of retreat from which a person can be expected to retreat no further). Hence, it is not necessary for one to retreat from one's home in the face of an immediate threat, even where such retreat is possible, before resorting to deadly force in protection of the home. A number of court decisions have extended the castle exception to include one's place of business,

---

1 the castle exception：城堡例外规则。Castle doctrine is also termed dwelling defense, defense of habitation.

2 Coke, Sir Edward：爱德华·科克爵士, (1552—1634), English jurist, one of the most eminent（杰出的）in the history of English law. He entered Parliament（议会）in 1589 and rose rapidly, becoming solicitor general and speaker of the House of Commons（下议院）. In 1593 he was made attorney general（司法部长，律政司司长）. His rival for that office was Sir Francis Bacon（培根）, thereafter one of Coke's bitterest enemies. He earned a reputation as a severe prosecutor（检察官）, notably at the trial of Sir Walter Raleigh（沃尔特·拉雷格爵士）, and held a favorable position at the court of King James I（詹姆斯一世国王）. In 1606 he became chief justice of the common pleas. In this position, and (after 1613) as chief justice（大法官）of the king's bench, Coke became the champion of common law against the encroachments of the royal prerogative（皇室特权的侵害）and declared null and void（宣布无效）royal proclamations that were contrary to law. Although his historical arguments were frequently based on false interpretations of early documents, as in the case of the Magna Carta（大宪章）, his reasoning was brilliant and his conclusions impressive. By personal and political influence, Coke got himself back on the privy council（枢密院）and was elected (1620) to Parliament, where he became a leader of the popular faction in opposition to James I and Charles I. He was prominent in the drafting of the Petition of Right (1628)（《权利请愿书》）. His most important writings are the Reports（《汇编》）, a series of detailed commentaries on cases in common law, and the Institutes（《法学阶梯》）, which includes his commentary on Littleton's Tenures.

Lesson 2
Criminal Law: Types of Defenses to a Criminal Charge

such as a store or office.

d. Necessity

Necessity, or the claim that some illegal action was needed to prevent an even greater harm, is a useful defense in cases which do not involve serious bodily harm. One of the most famous uses of this defense occurred in *Crown* v. *Dudly & Stephens* in the late 1800s[1]. The case involved a shipwreck in which three sailors and a cabin boy were set adrift in a lifeboat. After a number of days at sea without rations, two of the sailors decided to kill and eat the cabin boy. At their trial, they argued that it was necessary to do so, or none of them would have survived. The court, however, reasoned that the cabin boy was not a direct threat to the survival of the men and rejected the defense. Convicted of murder, they were sentenced to death, although they were spared the gallows by royal intervention[2].

Although cannibalism is usually against the law, courts have sometimes recognized the necessity of consuming human flesh where survival was at issue. Those cases, however, involved only "victims" who had already died of natural causes[3].

e. Consent

The defense of consent claims that whatever harm was done occurred only after the injured person gave their permission for the behavior in question.

f. Resisting Unlawful Arrest

All jurisdictions consider resistance in the face of an unlawful arrest justifiable. Some have statutory provisions detailing the limits imposed on such resistance and the conditions under which it can be used. Such laws generally state that a person may use a reasonable amount of force, other than deadly force, to resist an unlawful arrest or an unlawful search by a law enforcement officer[4] if the officer uses or attempts to use greater force than necessary to make the arrest or search. Deadly force to resist arrest is not justified unless the law enforcement officer resorts to deadly force when it is not called for.

---

1 克朗诉塔德里和斯蒂芬案（*Crown* v. *Dudly & Stephens*）。
2 这两人最后被判六个月监禁。
3 cannibalism：食人（罪）；同类相食。
4 law enforcement officer：执法人员。

III. Excuses

An excuse, in contrast to a justification, does not claim that the conduct in question is justified by the situation nor that it is moral[1]. Excuses recognized by the law include: (1) duress, (2) age, (3) mistake, (4) involuntary intoxication[2], (5) unconsciousness, (6) provocation, (7) insanity, and (8) diminished responsibility.

a. Duress

Duress has been defined as any unlawful threat or coercion used by a person to induce another to act (or to refrain from acting) in a manner he or she otherwise would not (or would). A person may act under duress if, for example, he or she steals an employer's payroll in order to meet a ransom demand for kidnappers holding the person's children. Should the person later be arrested for larceny or embezzlement[3], the person can claim that he or she felt compelled to commit the crime to help ensure the safety of the children. The defense of duress is sometimes also called coercion. Duress is generally not a useful defense when the crime committed involves serious physical harm, since the harm committed may outweigh the coercive influence in the minds of jurors and judges.

b. Age

Age offers another kind of excuse in the face of a criminal charge, and the defense of "infancy"—as it is sometimes known in legal jargon—has its roots in the ancient belief that children cannot reason logically until around the age of seven[4]. The defense of infancy today has been expanded to include people well beyond the age of seven. Many states set the sixteenth birthday as the age at which a person becomes an adult for purposes of criminal prosecution. Others use the age of 17 and still others

---

1 excuse：可得宽恕。这相当于大陆刑法的"责任阻却"。与正当理由相对应，这种抗辩理由既不主张涉案的行为合法，也不主张其符合道义。
2 involuntary intoxication：非自愿醉态。
3 larceny or embezzlement：盗窃罪或侵占罪。Embezzlement can be defined as the fraudulent conversion of the property of another by one who has lawful possession of the property and whose fraudulent conversion has been made punishable by the statute. —*Criminal Law in a Nutshell* 94 (2nd. ed. 1987).
4 公元6世纪，东罗马《查士丁尼法典》认为孩子因年幼而不会有预谋恶意，这可以被视为西方刑法中"未成年"合法辩护的最早的权威法例。1324年，英国普通法采纳了这种观点，承认因年幼而作为合法辩护的理由。英国法确定7岁以下儿童没有责任能力。7岁这个年龄界限也来源于罗马法。——摘自储槐植著《美国刑法·第二版》，第91页。

Lesson 2

Criminal Law: Types of Defenses to a Criminal Charge

18. When a person below the age required for adult prosecution commits a "crime", it is termed a juvenile offense[1].

c. Mistake

Two types of mistake may serve as a defense. One is mistake of law, and the other is mistake of fact. Rarely is the defense of mistake of law acceptable. Most people realize that it is their responsibility to know the law as it applies to them. "Ignorance of the law is no excuse" is an old dictum still heard today. Mistake of fact is a much more useful form of the "mistaken" defense.

d. Involuntary Intoxication

The claim of involuntary intoxication may form the basis for another excuse defense. Either drugs or alcohol may produce intoxication[2]. Voluntary intoxication itself is rarely a defense to a criminal charge because it is a self-induced condition. Involuntary intoxication, however, is another matter. On occasion a person may be tricked into consuming an intoxicating substance. Secretly "spiked" punch[3], popular aphrodisiacs, or LSD-laced desserts[4] all might be ingested unknowingly. Because the effects and taste of alcohol are so widely known in our society, the defense of involuntary intoxication due to alcohol consumption can be difficult to demonstrate.

e. Unconsciousness

A very rarely used excuse is that of unconsciousness. An individual cannot be held responsible for anything he or she does while unconscious.

---

1 juvenile offense：未成年犯罪。在表示"罪"这一术语时，英文中通常有两个词crime以及offense，但这两个词有一定的区别，offense通常指"违法"，"犯罪（较轻的罪）"；此外，offense还有民法中"违法行为"的意思，与故意侵权基本相同。根据《布莱克法律字典》（第377页）Crime: A social harm that the law makes punishable; the breach of a legal duty treated as the subject-matter of a criminal proceeding. 另外，（第1108—1110页）offense: 1. A violation of the law; a crime, often a minor one. 2. Civil Law. An international unlawful act that causes injury or loss to another and that gives rise to a claim for damages. This sense of offense is essentially the same as the common-law international tort.

2 intoxication：醉态。produce intoxication：引起醉态。

3 secretly "spiked" punch：偷加了酒精的饮料。

4 LSD-laced desserts：加入了迷幻药的甜点。(LSD) lysergic acid diethylamide：麦角酸酰二乙胺（迷幻药的一种）。

f. Provocation

As a rule, the defense of provocation is generally more acceptable in minor offenses than in serious violations of the law.

g. Insanity

It is important to realize that, for purposes of the criminal law, insanity is a legal definition and not a psychiatric one. Legal definitions of insanity often have very little to do with psychological or psychiatric understandings of mental illness. Legal insanity is a concept developed over time to meet the needs of the judicial system in assigning guilt or innocence to particular defendants. The differences between psychiatric and legal conceptualizations of insanity often lead to disagreements among expert witnesses[1] who, in criminal court, may appear to provide conflicting testimony as to the sanity of a defendant.

h. Diminished Capacity

The diminished capacity defense is similar to the defense of insanity in that it depends upon a showing that the defendant's mental state was impaired at the time of the crime. Unlike an insanity defense, however, which can result in a finding of "not guilty", a diminished capacity defense is built upon the recognition that "mental condition, though insufficient to exonerate, may be relevant to specific mental elements of certain crimes or degrees of crime".

IV. Procedural Defenses

Procedural defenses make the claim that defendants were in some manner discriminated against in the justice process or that some important aspect of official procedure was not properly followed and that, as a result, they should be released from any criminal liability. The procedural defenses we shall discuss here are (1) entrapment, (2) double jeopardy, (3) collateral estoppel[2], (4) selective prosecution, (5) denial of a speedy trial, (6) prosecutorial misconduct, and (7) police fraud.

---

1 expert witness：专家证人。A witness qualified by knowledge, skill, experience, training, or education to provide a scientific, technical or other specialized opinion about the evidence or a fact issue. 专家证人所作的"专家证言"叫作"expert testimony"。

2 collateral estoppel：间接再诉禁。An affirmative defense barring a party from re-litigating an issue determined against that party in an earlier action, even if the second action differs significantly from the first one. 又分为defensive collateral estoppel与offensive collateral estoppel两类。

Lesson 2

Criminal Law: Types of Defenses to a Criminal Charge

Glossary

allege 宣称
aphrodisiacs 春药
assault 恐吓；侵犯；殴击
attempt 企图；犯罪未遂
attorney 律师
cannibalism 食人（罪）
castle exception 城堡例外规则
charge 指控
circumscribe 限制
consent 被害人同意
criminal trial 刑事审判
deadly force 致命武力
defense of infancy 未成年辩护
documentation 证据资料
double jeopardy 双重危险；双重追诉
dwelling 住处
embezzlement 侵占罪

excuse 可得宽恕
expert witness 专家证人
fault 过错
inflict 强加于
intoxication 醉态
inviolable 神圣不可侵犯的
involuntary intoxication 非自愿醉态
juvenile offense 未成年犯罪
law enforcement officer 执法人员
mens rea 犯罪意图；犯意
mistake of fact 事实错误
mistake of law 法律错误
necessity 紧急避险
offer 提出；提供
proportionate 成比例的；相成的
recourse 权力的行使
witnesses 证人

EXERCISES

Answer the following questions.

1. List the types of defenses to a criminal charge discussed in the text.
2. What is an alibi? Why alibi is different from all of the other defenses?
3. Explain the castle exception rule.
4. What is the difference between voluntary intoxication and involuntary intoxication?
5. What are the procedural defenses consisting of?
6. Which of the following is not an excuse defense: duress, diminished capacity, consent, or insanity?

II. Translate the following terms into English.

1. 刑法
2. 刑事责任
3. 刑法典
4. 刑事诉讼
5. 犯罪学
6. 虐待儿童
7. 暴力犯罪
8. 犯罪动机
9. 刑事责任能力
10. 刑事管辖权
11. 致命武力
12. 专家证人
13. 财产防卫
14. 执法人员
15. 警察设的圈套
16. 责任减等
17. 刑事审判
18. 辩护律师

III. Translate the following paragraph into Chinese.

Criminal proceedings take place in a series of stages. Usually, the police are responding to a citizen's complaint that a crime has been committed. Once they are called, the police investigate, take statements from witnesses, and prepare a report on their findings. At times, they will arrest people during the course of their investigation. At other times, they will complete their report and submit it to the prosecutor's office for evaluation, and a prosecutor will decide whether charges should be filed against any suspects named in the police report. The exact procedure for how charges are filed varies from jurisdiction to jurisdiction. Some jurisdictions give the police greater discretion in charging defendants with specific crimes, while others place more power with the prosecutor's office.

IV. Translate the following sentences into English.

1. 美国的法律制度通常认可下列四类抗辩事由：一、不在犯罪现场；二、正当理由；三、可得宽恕；四、程序（不正当）。
2. 证人和证据资料是不在犯罪现场的最好支持。
3. 科克说："一个人的家就是他的城堡——如果一个人在其家中都不安全，那在哪里才能安全呢？"
4. 非自愿醉态主张可以形成另一种可得宽恕抗辩的基础。
5. 无意识辩护是一种很少使用的可得宽恕抗辩。

Lesson 2
Criminal Law: Types of Defenses to a Criminal Charge

Supplementary Reading

Entrapment can be defined as an improper or illegal inducement to crime by agents of enforcement, is a defense which limits the enthusiasm with which police officers may enforce the law. Entrapment defenses argue that enforcement agents effectively create a crime where there would otherwise have been none. For entrapment to have occurred, the idea for the criminal activity must have originated with official agents of the criminal justice system. Entrapment can also result when overzealous undercover police officers convince a defendant that the contemplated law-violating behavior is not a crime. In order to avoid claims of entrapment, officers must not engage in activity that would cause a person to commit a crime that he or she would not otherwise commit. Merely providing an opportunity for a willing offender to commit a crime, however, is not entrapment.

The Fifth Amendment to the U.S. Constitution makes it clear that no person may be tried twice for the same offense. People who have been acquitted or found innocent may not be again put in "jeopardy of life or limb" for the same crime. The same is true of those who have been convicted: They cannot be tried again for the same offense. Cases that are dismissed for a lack of evidence also come under the double jeopardy rule and cannot result in a new trial. The U.S. Supreme Court has ruled that "the Double Jeopardy Clause protects against three distinct abuses: a second prosecution for the same offense after acquittal[1]; a second prosecution for the same offense after conviction; and multiple punishments for the same offense."

Collateral estoppel is similar to double jeopardy and applies to facts that have been determined by a "valid and final judgment". Such facts cannot become the object of new litigation. Where a defendant, for example, has been acquitted of a multiple murder charge by virtue of an alibi, it would not be permissible to try that person again for the murder of a second person killed along with the first.

The procedural defense of selective prosecution is based upon the Fourteenth Amendment's guarantee of equal protection of the laws. The defense may be available where two or more individuals are suspected of criminal involvement, but not all are

---

1 acquittal：无罪释放。

actively prosecuted. Selective prosecution based fairly upon the strength of available evidence is not the object of this defense. But when prosecution proceeds unfairly on the basis of some arbitrary and discriminatory attribute[1], such as race, sex, friendship, age, or religious preference, protection may be feasible under it. In 1996, however, in a case that reaffirmed reasonable limits on claims of selective prosecution, the U.S. Supreme Court ruled that for a defendant to successfully "claim that he was singled out for prosecution on the basis of his race, he must make a... showing that the Government declined to prosecute similarly situated suspects of other races."The Sixth Amendment to the Constitution guarantees a right to a speedy trial[2]. The purpose of the guarantee is to prevent unconvicted and potentially innocent people from languishing in jail.

Another procedural defense may be found in prosecutorial misconduct. Generally speaking, prosecutorial misconduct is a term used by legal scholars to describe actions undertaken by prosecutors which give the government an unfair advantage or that prejudice the rights of a defendant or witness. Prosecutors are expected to uphold the highest ethical standards in the performance of their roles. When they knowingly permit false testimony, when they hide, information that would clearly help the defense, or when they make unduly biased statements to the jury in closing arguments, the defense of prosecutorial misconduct may be available to the defendant.

During the 1995 double-murder trial of O. J. Simpson[3], defense attorneys suggested the possibility that evidence against Simpson may have been concocted and even planted by police officers with a personal dislike of the defendant. In particular, defense attorneys

---

1   discriminatory attribute：歧视性因素。
2   speedy trial：快速审理。
3   O. J. Simpson：辛普森。美国六七十年代最杰出的黑人橄榄球运动员，辛普森是黑人青年心目中的英雄和偶像。告别体育场之后，辛普森成为著名电视体育节目主持人。1994年6月，警察发现辛普森前妻尼科尔和她的一位白人男友被人刺杀于她的住宅门前，现场血迹斑斑，惨不忍睹。警方首先确定的凶杀嫌疑犯便是尼科尔的前夫辛普森。从1989年开始辛普森就经常虐待、殴打尼科尔，并威胁要杀死她。1992年3月尼科尔与辛普森离婚。但是此后辛普森对尼科尔的骚扰始终没有停止。警方在案发现场找到了与辛普森血型一样的血迹，接着在对辛氏住所进行的搜查中发现了血迹，并找到了手套、球鞋等与出事现场留下的痕迹相吻合的物证。于是，洛杉矶警察局决定逮捕辛普森。检方出示的证据令人怀疑。用于检验的血样可能受到污染。警方在现场采集的唯一一滴证据说是辛的血液是放置一夜风干后用一张纸包起来的。而辩方复检时，这张纸有一滴鲜血的痕迹，很像有人做了手脚。另外，警方进入辛宅搜查的录像表明卧室床上并无血袜，但后来做记录时却有了。警探弗尔曼肯定干了不可告人的事。即便是那双检方最有力的证据——血手套，辛普森当众费了半天劲才戴上。这也说明，很有可能是警探弗尔曼自己放置在现场和辛普森家中的。辩方认为检方忽略了现场的一串脚印，这既不是受害人的，也不是辛普森的，很可能是凶手的。

Lesson 2
Criminal Law: Types of Defenses to a Criminal Charge

pointed the finger at Los Angeles police department detective Mark Fuhrman[1], suggesting that he may have planted a bloody glove at the Simpson estate and tampered with blood stain evidence taken from the infamous white Ford Bronco Simpson was known to drive[2]. To support allegations that Fuhrman was motivated by racist leanings[3], defense attorneys subpoenaed tapes Fuhrman made over a ten-year period with a North Carolina screenwriter who had been documenting life within the LAPD[4].

---

1 Los Angeles police department detective Mark Fuhrman: 洛杉矶警察局弗尔曼警探。
2 Ford Bronco Simpson was known to drive: 辛普森驾驶的白色福特烈马轿车。
3 racist leanings: 种族主义倾向。
4 LAPD: 洛杉矶警察局。

Lesson 3
Defendant's Rights: Key Aspects of Modern Criminal Procedure[1]

Everyone is equal before the law.

法律面前人人平等。

There are two fundamental aspects of the U.S. criminal justice system[2]—the presumption that the defendant is innocent and the burden on the prosecution[3] to prove guilt beyond a reasonable doubt. But criminal defendants have other rights too. Here we explore some of the other hallmarks of basic criminal procedure.

I. The Defendant's Right to Remain Silent

The Fifth Amendment to the U.S. Constitution provides that a defendant cannot "be compelled in any criminal case to be a witness against himself." In short, the defendant has the right to "sit mute". The prosecutor cannot call the defendant as a witness, nor can a judge or defense attorney force the defendant to testify if the defendant chooses to remain silent. By contrast, a defendant may be called as a

---

1 criminal procedure: 刑事诉讼；刑事程序。规定有关对犯罪的侦查（investigation）、起诉（prosecution）、审理、裁判（adjudication）、刑罚（punishment）等程序的法律规则，其规定中包括对被告人宪法性权利（constitutional rights）的保护。
2 criminal justice system: 刑事司法系统，也称为law-enforcement system。对参与处理对被告人的刑事指控问题的各种机构的总称，通常它包括三个组成部分：①执法部门（law enforcement），包括警察（police）、行政司法官（sheriffs）、执行官（marshals）；②司法程序（judicial process），包括法官（judges）、检察官或自诉人（prosecutors）、辩护律师（defense lawyers）；③矫正程序（corrections），包括狱政官（prison officials）、缓刑官员（probation officers）、假释官员（parole officers）。
3 prosecution: 控诉方；公诉方。指代表政府提起刑事诉讼追究被告人刑事责任的律师。

witness in a civil case.

II. The Defendant's Right to Confront[1] Witnesses

The "confrontation clause"[2] of the Sixth Amendment gives defendants the right to "be confronted by the witnesses against" them. Implicit in this right is the right to cross-examine witnesses—that is, the right to require the witnesses to come to court, "look the defendant in the eye", and subject themselves to questioning by the defense. The Sixth Amendment prevents secret trials, and except for limited exceptions, forbids prosecutors from proving a defendant's guilt with written statements from absent witnesses.

III. Special Confrontation Rules for Child Sexual Assault[3] Cases

In recent years, legislators have been concerned about defendants who escape punishment for sexually molesting young children because the children are afraid to testify in the defendant's presence. To address this problem, many states have enacted special rules that authorize judges—in certain situations—to allow children to testify via closed circuit television. The defendant can see the child on a television monitor, but the child cannot see the defendant. The defense attorney can be personally present where the child is testifying and can cross-examine the child.

IV. The Defendant's Right to a Public Trial[4]

The Sixth Amendment guarantees public trials in criminal cases. This is an important right, because the presence in courtrooms of a defendant's family and

---

1 confront: 使对质；使对证。confrontation: 对质；对证。在刑事诉讼中，指被告人有权与对方证人对质。美国宪法第六条修正案规定的这一被告人权利使被告人能面对证人，能对其证词提出反对意见，或使证人能辨别被告人。对质权的实质不在于使被告人能见到证人，而是保障被告人具有质询对方证人的宪法权利。
2 confrontation clause: 〈美〉对质条款。指美国宪法第六条修正案，该条保障刑事被告人有权直接与控方证人对质，并向该证人进行交叉询问(cross-examination)。
3 sexual assault: 性侵犯，指性交以外的各种非法性行为。例如，以身体伤害相威胁，或以造成恐惧、羞辱或精神痛苦相胁迫，而猥亵妇女、儿童或其他男子的行为。
4 public trial: 公开审判。审判向公众公开，即无所偏颇地准许公众旁听；但有时为了避免人员过于拥挤或秩序混乱，或不至于给证人造成思想压力而不敢当庭作证，可以限制到庭人数。

friends, ordinary citizens and the press can help ensure that the government observes other important rights associated with trials.

In a few situations, normally involving children, the court will close the court to the public. For example, judges can bar the public from attending cases when defendants are charged with sexual assaults against children. Also, the judge may exclude witnesses from the courtroom when it appears that they will coach each other.

V. The Defendant's Right to a Jury Trial[1]

The Sixth Amendment to the U.S. Constitution gives a person accused of a crime the right to be tried by a jury. This right has long been interpreted to mean a 12-person jury that must arrive at a unanimous decision to convict or acquit. (In most states, a lack of unanimity is called a "hung jury[2]", and the defendant will go free unless the prosecutor decides to retry the case. In Oregon and Louisiana, however, juries may convict or acquit on a vote of ten to two.) The potential jurors must be selected randomly from the community, and the actual jury must be selected by a process that allows the judge and lawyers to screen out biased jurors. In addition, a lawyer may eliminate several potential jurors simply because he feels that these people would not be sympathetic to his side—but these decisions (called peremptory challenges[3]) may not be based on the juror's personal characteristics such as race, sex, religion or national origin.

VI. The Defendant's Right to Be Represented by an Attorney

The Sixth Amendment to the U.S. Constitution provides that "in all criminal

---

1 jury trial: 陪审团审判。案件的事实问题由陪审团而非法官来裁决的审判。陪审团制是普通法系中一种独特的法律制度。它在现代社会中的具体含义是：在这一制度下由国家官员召集一定数量的法律外行人士(lay people)协助法庭在庭审到的证据的基础上裁决案件中有争议的事实问题。
2 hung jury: 悬案陪审团。指陪审员意见分歧而无法作出一致裁决或达到法定票数裁断的陪审团。也称"僵局陪审团"(deadlocked jury)。
3 peremptory challenges: 无因回避。指民事诉讼或者刑事诉讼中的当事人可以不说明理由，拒绝或者阻止某人充任本案陪审员，法院即应更换该陪审员并召集另一陪审员。在美国大多数司法区，无因回避权的行使随案件类型而异，并有次数的限制，当事人在其无因回避权用尽之后，再提出回避请求的，必须说明理由。

Lesson 3

Defendant's Rights: Key Aspects of Modern Criminal Procedure

prosecutions[1], the accused shall enjoy the right...to have the assistance of counsel for his defense." A judge must appoint an attorney for indigent defendants[2] (defendants who cannot afford to hire attorneys) at government expense only if the defendants might be actually imprisoned for a period of more than six months for the crime. As a practical matter, judges routinely appoint attorneys for indigents in nearly all cases in which a jail sentence is a possibility. Otherwise, the judge would be locked into giving an unrepresented defendant a non-jail sentence or a shorter sentence than he or she might think appropriate after hearing the evidence.

A judge normally appoints the attorney for an indigent defendant at the defendant's first court appearance. For most defendants, the first court appearance is either an arraignment[3] or a bail hearing[4].

The job of defense counsel at trial is to prepare and offer a vigorous defense on behalf of the accused[5]. A proper defense often involves the presentation of evidence and the examination of witness, all of which requires careful thought and planning. Good attorneys, like quality craftspeople everywhere, may find themselves emotionally committed to the outcome of trials in which they are involved.

VII. Defendant's Right to a Speedy Trial[6]

The Sixth Amendment gives defendants a right to a "speedy trial". However, it does not specify exact time limits. Thus, judges often have to decide on a case-by-case basis whether a defendant's trial has been so delayed that the case should be thrown

---

1 criminal prosecutions: 刑事诉讼，刑事起诉。指为了使被指控的人被定罪并被判处刑罚而在有管辖权的法院提起的诉讼。
2 indigent defendants: 贫穷被告人。指因贫穷而无力聘请律师的被告人。在刑事诉讼中，贫穷被告人可获得法院为其指定的辩护律师的帮助，并免于承担法庭费用。
3 arraignment: 传讯，提讯。
4 bail hearing: 保释听证。hearing, 听审，听证。指可就有争议的问题提供证据，陈述理由，并由有裁判权的个人或机关作出裁决的相对正式的程序。听证的目的在于为争议各方，尤其是可能被剥夺权益的一方，创造陈述意见的机会。
5 the accused: 刑事被告人。
6 speedy trial: 〈美〉迅速审判。指根据法定规则和程序在法定期限内或在无不合理拖延的情况下进行的审判。美国宪法第六条修正案保障刑事被告人有受到迅速审判的权利，根据联邦最高法院的解释，赋予被告人这项权利的目的在于防止被告人在尚未被定罪的情况下受到长期羁押，缩短被告人必须忍受审判开始前的焦虑和公众注意的时间，将由于拖延而给被告人进行辩护的能力造成的损害降至最低限度等。但宪法并未具体确定在多长期限内开始审判方可被认为是迅速。有些州已通过立法确立了具体的时间限制，超过该期限而未审判者将导致指控被驳回。被告人也可以放弃这一权利。

out. In making this decision, judges look at the length of the delay, the reason for the delay and whether the delay has prejudiced (harmed) the defendant's position.

Every jurisdiction has enacted statutes that set time limits for moving cases from the filing of the initial charge to trial. While these statutes are very strict in their wording, most defendants cannot get their convictions reversed on the ground that these statutes were violated.

VIII. The Defendant's Right Not to Be Placed in Double Jeopardy[1]

Among the several clauses of the Fifth Amendment to the U.S. Constitution is this well-known provision: "nor shall any person be subject for the same offense to be twice put in jeopardy of life or limb." This provision, known as the double jeopardy clause[2], protects defendants from harassment by preventing them from being put on trial more than once for the same offense. Double jeopardy problems are unusual, because prosecutors usually want to wrap up all their charges[3] at one time in the same case.

One important exception to the rule against double jeopardy is that defendants can properly be charged for the same conduct by different jurisdictions. For example, a defendant may face charges in both federal and state court for the same conduct if some aspects of that conduct violated federal laws while other elements ran afoul of the laws of the state.

Furthermore, the double jeopardy clause forbids only more than one criminal prosecution growing out of the same conduct. A defendant can be brought once to criminal court (by the government) and once to civil court (by members of the public) for the same crime. For instance, after O.J. Simpson was acquitted of murdering his ex-wife and her friend, their relatives filed a civil suit against him for actual[4] and

---

1 double jeopardy: 双重追诉，双重危险。指对实质上同一的罪行给予两次起诉、审判、定罪或科刑。禁止对当事人的同一罪行进行双重追诉是英美法上一项重要的诉讼原则。
2 double jeopardy clause: 双重追诉条款。
3 charges: 指控，指控的犯罪。指控是通过向法院或其他司法机关提出正式的控告书（complaint）或起诉书（information or indictment）而对犯罪进行的控告。
4 actual damages: 实际损害赔偿。

Lesson 3
Defendant's Rights: Key Aspects of Modern Criminal Procedure

punitive damages[1] caused by the killings. The civil suits raised no double jeopardy issues, even though punitive damages are a type of punishment, and Simpson was held civilly liable for the deaths.

Glossary

actual damages 实际损害赔偿
arraignment 传讯；提讯
bail hearing 保释听证
compensatory damages 补偿性损害赔偿金
confrontation clause 对质条款
confrontation 对质；对证
corrections 矫正
criminal justice system 刑事司法系统
criminal procedure 刑事诉讼；刑事程序
cross-examine 交叉询问
defense lawyers 辩护律师
double jeopardy clause 双重追诉条款
hearing 听审；听证
hung jury 悬案陪审团

indigent defendants 贫穷被告人
investigation 侦查
judicial process 司法程序
jury trial 陪审团审判
law enforcement 执法部门
parole officers 假释官员
police 警察
probation officers 缓刑官员
prosecution 起诉
punishment 处罚
sexual assault 性侵犯
sheriffs 行政司法官
speedy trial〈美〉迅速审判

EXERCISES

I. Answer the following questions.

1. What are the defendant's rights in modern criminal procedure?
2. How do you understand "the defendant's right to remain silent"?
3. What is double jeopardy?
4. What are the two fundamental aspects of U.S. Criminal Justice System?

---

1 punitive damages: 惩罚性损害赔偿（金）。损害赔偿金的一种，与补偿性损害赔偿金(compensatory damages)相对，是指当被告以恶意、故意、欺诈或放任之方式实施行为而致原告受损时，原告可获得的除实际损害赔偿金外的损害赔偿金。

5. What are the procedural rights in the Sixth Amendment?
6. In which amendments does Bill of Rights provide the procedural rights of defendants?

II. Translate the following terms into Chinese.

1. criminal procedure
2. criminal justice system
3. prosecution
4. confrontation
5. confrontation clause
6. sexual assault
7. cross-examination
8. public trial
9. jury trial
10. hung jury
11. peremptory challenge
12. indigent defendants
13. arraignment
14. hearing
15. speedy trial
16. double jeopardy
17. punitive damages

III. Explain the following terms in English.

1. criminal justice system
2. prosecution
3. confrontation clause
4. jury trial
5. double jeopardy
6. punitive damages

IV. Cloze.

Both 1_____ and the 2_____ provide many defenses to crime. Other than having an 3_____ (which is not technically a defense but a denial), there are three main types of defenses: (A) 4_____, (B) 5_____, and (C) procedural defenses. These terms are not easily defined, and the distinction is less than perfect. Justifications refer to situations in which the 6_____ doesn't deny they did it but that they did it for all the right reasons, an appeal to higher loyalty or ideals (as in self-defense) or more important reasons (as in necessity), for instance. Excuses refer to situations in which the defendant also doesn't 7_____ they did it but that they are not 8_____ for it (as in insanity or diminished capacity defenses), typically on grounds of lacking volition over their free will.

Lesson 3

Defendant's Rights: Key Aspects of Modern Criminal Procedure

Sometimes, it's said that Justifications involve denying mens rea（犯罪意图）and Excuses involve denying actus reus（犯罪行为）, but the mind-body connection is complicated in this regard, and this saying can confuse you. Take sleepwalking, for instance, which might be treated as the inability to form mental intent although it's the body (which is asleep). The law also tends to think of "mental" disorder as brain disorder, to avoid metaphysical debates over whether or not it's possible for something invisible like a "mind" to get sick.

Supplementary Reading

Criminal procedure refers to the methods we use to deal with people accused of committing a crime—when they can be searched, when evidence can be seized, when eyewitnesses can be investigated. The core purpose of modern criminal procedure is to bring criminals to account[1] in a manner that: instills confidence that the result is correct and just, and meets constitutional standards of fairness (known as "due process[2]" in legalese).

The word "criminal" reflects our society's belief that certain acts are unacceptable and that people committing these acts should be punished. Because we place a high value on freedom, however, our state and federal constitutions make it very difficult for the government to take that freedom away from us. As a result—and perhaps as a price—the court system often appears to protect the criminal rather than the victim, and to unduly[3] favor defendants who are blessed with clever attorneys. On the other hand, if the system doesn't place a heavy burden on government prosecutors, we risk sending innocent people to jail and we make it easier for our government to slide into totalitarian[4] practices. One thing is sure, no matter what type of system we have for separating the bad citizens from the good, it will always be a matter of great controversy.

Though legislators have relatively unfettered power to decide whether a certain

---

1 bring to account：责问；对……进行清算。
2 due process：正当程序；正当法律程序。due process of law常用的缩略形式。正当程序是个多意的宪法概念，既指法制、法律程序的公正，也指一项基本权利。
3 unduly：过度地，不适当地。
4 totalitarian：极权主义的。

behavior should be a crime, many rules limit the ways in which the state or federal government can prosecute someone for a crime. These restrictions start with the U.S. Constitution's Bill of Rights[1], which provides basic protections for people suspected of and charged with crimes. These include the right to confront witnesses, the right to not testify, the right to an attorney, the right to a jury trial and the right to be free from unreasonable searches and seizures[2], among others. State constitutions may increase (but not take away from) the federal protections. Federal and state legislatures can pass statutes governing how criminal procedures work in their jurisdictions, but these laws cannot reduce the protections offered by the federal and state constitutions.

Criminal Procedure

Both criminal and civil law apply when one person commits a wrongful act that causes injury to another person. Despite this overlapping jurisdiction, however, civil and criminal proceedings are not identical, primarily because each body of law allows for[3] the imposition of different penalties. Suppose, for example, that your neighbor drives his car negligently and that your front lawn and the surrounding fence are damaged as a result. Although the civil-justice system will require your neighbor to pay you for the damage to your property, the neighbor is not likely to be jailed for the offenses.

By contrast, criminal penalties are only imposed for "serious" crimes. Indeed, in some states, people who are convicted of committing serious crimes can be divested of certain civil rights—(for example, the right to vote). If the crime is serious enough, they may even be executed. Because of the significant differences between civil and criminal cases in the United States, different procedures are used for the two kinds of cases.

In light of[4] the seriousness of the penalties for violating a criminal law, both the Constitution and statutory law[5]—federal and state codes—impose strict sets of procedural

---

1 Bill of Rights：〈美〉权利法案。指美国宪法第一至十条修正案。它由詹姆斯麦迪逊（James Madison）起草，1791年生效。内容包括保护言论自由、出版自由等。美国各州宪法均含有权利法案，大部分内容与美国宪法的权利法案的内容相同。
2 seizure：扣留；拘留；逮捕。指对人身自由的限制或剥夺。美国宪法第四条修正案禁止对公民人身进行非法扣留。如果根据当时的情况，一个理性的人会相信自己已经失去了自由，即可认为已构成对其人身的扣留。其形式包括从为调查目的而进行的暂时性的拦截（stop）到正式的逮捕（arrest）等各种形式的限制或剥夺人身自由的情形，但实施扣留的警察或官员必须具有合理的怀疑或可成立的理由（probable cause），否则即为非法扣留。
3 allow for：考虑到；容许。
4 in light of：根据，按照。
5 statutory law：〈美〉立法机关的制定法。指源于制定法（statute），而非宪法或法院判决的法律总称。

Lesson 3
Defendant's Rights: Key Aspects of Modern Criminal Procedure

rules to ensure that persons who are accused of criminal acts are tried fairly and convicted only if guilt has been established beyond a reasonable doubt[1].

The Defendant's Right to Adequate Representation

The U.S. Supreme Court has ruled that both indigent defendants who are represented by appointed counsel and defendants who hire their own attorneys are entitled to adequate representation. However, adequate representation is by no means perfect representation. Here are examples of claims that defendants have made against their attorneys to try to get their guilty verdicts thrown out and that appellate courts have rejected:

- failing to call favorable witnesses at trial
- using cocaine during the time the representation took place
- failing to object to a judge's mistaken instructions to jurors concerning the burden of proof
- eliciting evidence very damaging to the defendant while cross-examining prosecution witnesses
- repeatedly advising a defendant who claimed innocence to plead guilty, and
- representing the defendant while being suspended from the practice of law for failure to pay state bar dues.

On the other hand, circumstances can be sufficiently shocking to justify throwing out a guilty verdict based on an attorney's incompetence. Judges have ruled that the following claims justify a reversal of a guilty verdict: putting a law student intern in charge of the defense and leaving the courtroom while the case was going on during closing arguments, acknowledging that the defendant was guilty of a lesser crime without first securing the defendant's approval of this tactic, and during *voir dire* (questioning of the jury), failing to challenge two potential jurors who said they would be bothered by the defendant's failure to testify.

---

1 reasonable doubt: 合理怀疑。按照案件审理中提出的证据或因缺乏足够的证据，使正常的、谨慎的人对被告人是否有罪产生合乎情理的怀疑。认定刑事被告人有罪，必须达到"排除合理怀疑"的证明程度（beyond a reasonable doubt）。

Lesson 4
The Right to Remain Silent

No one can be forced to incriminate himself.
人们没有义务证明自己有罪。

You've probably heard it lots of times on TV crime shows: "You have the right to remain silent. Anything you say can and will be used against you in a court of law. You have the right to speak to an attorney, and to have an attorney present during any questioning. If you cannot afford a lawyer, one will be provided for you at government expense." That is the Miranda Warning, named after a famous case involving a suspect named Miranda.

All of the statements in the warning are true; however, it is not necessary for a police officer to recite the magic words in order to arrest you. In most situations, the police will give the warning only if you are going to be asked questions; if they interrogate[1] you outside the presence of your lawyer without giving the warning, any answers you give probably cannot be introduced in court as evidence against you. However, the police are allowed to ask routine booking[2] questions such as your name, address, date of birth, and social security[3] number in order to establish

---

1 interrogation: （刑事）讯问。通常指警察通过向被逮捕的或被怀疑有犯罪行为的嫌疑人提问来查明其是否真正犯有罪行的程序。The formal or systematic questioning of a person; esp., intensive questioning by the police, usu. of a person arrested for or suspected of committing a crime.
2 booking:（逮捕）登记。指被逮捕的犯罪嫌疑人(a person arrested)被带到警察局后，要在登记簿（blotter）上记下被逮捕人的姓名、涉嫌犯罪及其他相关事项，必要时还包括被逮捕人的照片、指纹等（usu. including a photograph and a fingerprint）。
3 social security: 社会保障。美国于1935年通过的《社会保障法》（Social Security Act）规定，要建立全国范围内的联邦和州老年资助、老年和遗嘱保险金(old-age and survivors' benefits)、失业保障或补偿以及某些意外补助(incidental benefits)制度。各国都已或正在制定社会保障方面的立法。

your identity, without reading you the Miranda warning. You can also be given a breathalyzer test[1] without the warning. Of course, you always have the right to refuse to answer any questions.

I. The Miranda Decision

In the area of suspect rights, no case is as famous as that of *Miranda* v. *Arizona*, which was decided in 1966. Many people regard Miranda as the centerpiece of Warren Court[2] due process[3] rulings.

The case involved Ernesto Miranda, who was arrested in Phoenix, Arizona, and accused of having kidnapped and raped a young woman. At police headquarters he was identified by the victim. After being interrogated for two hours, Miranda signed a confession which formed the basis of his later conviction on the charges.

Upon eventual appeal to the U.S. Supreme Court, the Court rendered what some regard as the most far-reaching opinion to have impacted criminal justice in the last few decades. The Court ruled that Miranda's conviction was unconstitutional[4] because "The entire aura and atmosphere of police interrogation without notification of rights and an offer of assistance of counsel tends to subjugate the individual to the will of his examiner."

The Court continued, saying that the defendant, "must be warned prior to any questioning that he has the right to remain silent, that anything he says can be used against him in a court of law, that he has the right to the presence of an attorney,

---

1 breathalyzer test: 呼吸测试。对酒后驾车而被扣留者血液中的酒精浓度进行的测试。只要测试的程序合法，其结果可作为证据使用。A device used to measure the blood alcohol content of a person's breath, esp. when the police suspect that the person was driving while intoxicated. Breathalyzer test results are admissible as evidence if the test was properly administered. 也作alcoholometer; drunkometer; intoxilyzer; intoximeter.
2 沃伦法院（Warren Court 1953—1969）。得名于时任美国联邦最高法院的首席大法官厄尔·沃伦。布朗诉教育委员（Brown v. Board of Education of Topeka 1954）是奠定沃伦法院历史地位的最有影响的案件。
3 due process: 正当程序；正当法律程序。"非经正当法律程序，不得剥夺任何人的生命、自由或财产。" The conduct of legal proceedings according to established rules and principles for the protection and enforcement of private rights, including notice and the right to a fair hearing before a tribunal with the power to decide the case.
4 unconstitutional: 违宪的；与宪法相抵触的。Contrary to or in conflict with a constitution, esp. the U.S. Constitution. 此外，Unconstitutional与 non-constitutional 含义不同，后者是指与美国宪法原则之外的某一法律原则有关的、非宪法性原则的。

and that if he cannot afford an attorney one will be appointed for him prior to any questioning if he so desires. Opportunity to exercise these rights must be afforded to him throughout the interrogation. After such warnings have been given, and such opportunity afforded him, the individual may knowingly and intelligently waive these rights and agree to answer the questions or make a statement. But unless and until such warnings and waiver are demonstrated by the prosecution at the trial, no evidence obtained as a result of interrogation can be used against him."

To ensure that proper advice is given to suspects at the time of their arrest, the now-famous Miranda rights are read before any questioning begins. These rights, as they appear on a Miranda warning card commonly used by police agencies. Persons 18 years old or older who are in custody[1] must be given this advice of rights before any questioning:

1. You have the right to remain silent.

2. Anything you say can be used against you in a court of law.

3. You have the right to talk to a lawyer and to have a lawyer present while you are being questioned.

4. If you want a lawyer before or during questioning but cannot afford to hire a lawyer, one will be appointed to represent you at no cost before any questioning.

5. If you answer questions now without a lawyer here, you still have the right to stop answering questions at any time.

II. Waiver[2] of Rights

After reading and explaining the rights of a person in custody, an officer must also ask for a waiver of those rights before any questioning. The following waiver questions must be answered affirmatively, either by express answer or by clear implication. Silence alone is not a waiver.

1. Do you understand each of these rights I have explained to you? (Answer must be YES.)

---

1 custody: 羁押；拘留；拘禁。广义上是指对自由的限制，而不仅仅是指某人实际关押在监狱里。因缓刑、假释或取保、个人具结悔过获得释放的人都处于被监禁状态(in custody)。
2 waiver: 弃权；权利放弃。指故意或自愿抛弃其明知的权利。The voluntary relinquishment or abandonment—express or implied—of a legal right or advantage.

Lesson 4
The Right to Remain Silent

2. Having these rights in mind, do you now wish to answer questions? (Answer must be YES.)

3. Do you now wish to answer questions without a lawyer present? (Answer must be YES.)

For juveniles age 14, 15, 16, and 17, the following question must be asked:

4. Do you now wish to answer questions without your parents, guardians[1], or custodians[2] present? (Answer must be YES.)

Once suspects have been advised of their Miranda rights, they are commonly asked to sign a paper which lists each right, in order to confirm that they were advised of their rights, and that they understand each right. Questioning may then begin, but only if suspect waive their rights not to talk or to have a lawyer present during interrogation.

When the Miranda decision was made, some hailed it as one which ensured the protection of individual rights guaranteed under the Constitution. To guarantee those rights, they suggested, what better agency is available than the police themselves, since the police are present at the initial stages of the criminal justice process. Critics of Miranda, however, have argued that the decision puts police agencies in the uncomfortable and contradictory position of not only enforcing the law, but also of having to offer defendants advice on how potentially to circumvent conviction and punishment. Under Miranda the police partially assume the role of legal advisor to the accused. During the last years of the Reagan administration, for example, then-Attorney General[3] Edwin Meese focused on the Miranda decision as the antithesis of "law and order". He pledged the resources of his office to an assault upon the Miranda rules to eliminate what he saw as the frequent release of guilty parties on the basis of "technicalities". Nonetheless, the Miranda decision survives into the

---

1 guardian: 监护人。One who has the legal authority and duty（依法有权并有责任）to care for another's person or property（人身、财产）, esp. because of the other's infancy, incapacity, or disability.
2 custodian: 监管人；保管人。A person or institution that has charge or custody of property（财产）, papers（有价证券）, or other valuables（其他资产）.
3 Attorney General: 总检察长。联邦政府的首席法律官员（the chief law officer），同时是司法部的首长，由总统任命而产生。其职权主要是应总统、政府各部首长的要求，为他们提供法律咨询意见；在特别重大案件中代表联邦政府在联邦最高法院出庭参加诉讼（litigation）等。

present day virtually unscathed.

III. Waiver of Miranda Rights by Suspects

Suspects in police custody may legally waive their Miranda rights through a voluntary "knowing and intelligent" waiver. A knowing waiver can only be made if a suspect has been advised on his or her rights and was in a condition to understand the advisement. A rights advisement made in English, for example, to a Spanish-speaking defendant, cannot produce a knowing waiver. Likewise, an intelligent waiver of rights requires that the defendant be able to understand the consequences of not invoking the Miranda rights. In the case of *Moran* v. *Burbine* (1968), the Supreme Court defined an intelligent and knowing waiver as one "made with a full awareness both of the nature of the right being abandoned and the consequences of the decision to abandon it." Similarly, in *Colorado* v. *Spring* (1987), the court held that an intelligent and knowing waiver can be made even though a suspect has not been informed of all the alleged offenses about which he or she is about to be questioned.

IV. Is an Arrest Illegal If the Police Neglect to Read the Miranda Rights to the Suspect?

No. These rights are your protection against self-incrimination[1] only, not against being arrested. The only thing the police need before making an arrest is "probable cause"[2]—a sufficient reason, based on facts and observations, to believe you have committed a crime. Police must recite the Miranda rights only when they are about to interrogate a suspect. If they do not, then a judge might later throw out[3] any statements made, though the arrest may still be valid.

---

1 self-incrimination：自证其罪；自我归罪。指在庭审中或在庭审前通过作陈述等表明自己与某一犯罪有关或将使自己受到刑事指控的行为。美国宪法第五条修正案和许多州的宪法和法律都禁止政府强迫某人成为对自己不利的证人或提供对自己不利的证据。

2 probable cause：合理根据；可成立的理由。指极有可能是确实的根据，其可信程度大于怀疑但小于确切无误。从合理调查所获知的明白无误的事实，足以使明智而谨慎的人相信刑事案件的被控人犯有被指控的罪名，或民事案件中存有诉讼根据。

3 throw out：驳回起诉；驳回请求。

Lesson 4
The Right to Remain Silent

V. Public Safety Exceptions to Miranda

In 1984 the U.S. Supreme Court also established what has come to be known as the public safety exception to the Miranda rule. The case *New York v. Quarles* centered upon an alleged rape in which the victim told police her assailant had fled, with a gun, into a nearby A&P supermarket. Two police officers entered the store and apprehended the suspect. One officer immediately noticed that the man wearing an empty shoulder holster and, apparently fearing that a child might find the discarded weapon, quickly asked, "Where's the gun?"

Quarles was convicted of rape, but appealed his conviction, requesting that the weapon be suppressed as evidence because officers had not advised him of his Miranda rights before asking him about it. The Supreme Court disagreed, stating that considerations of public safety were overriding and negated the need for rights advisement prior to limited questioning which focused on the need to prevent further harm.

Glossary

apprehend 逮捕
Attorney General 总检察长
booking （逮捕）登记
breathalyzer test 呼吸测试
circumvent 防止……发生
contradictory 矛盾的；对立的
custody 羁押；拘留；拘禁
due process 正当程序；正当法律程序
guardian 监护人
hail 欢呼；拥立
holster 手枪皮套
interrogation 刑事讯问

negate 取消；使无效
prior to 在前；居先
public safety 公共安全；公众安全
self-incrimination 自证其罪；自我归罪
social security 社会保障
subjugate 使屈服；使服从
throw out 驳回起诉；驳回请求
unconstitutional 违宪的；与宪法相抵触的
unscathed 未受损失的
waiver 弃权；权利放弃
Warren Court 沃伦法院

EXERCISES

I. Answer the following questions.

1. What is the Miranda Warning?
2. If the police neglect to read the Miranda rights to the suspect, can the police arrest him? Why or why not?
3. Can a defendant waive his Miranda rights? Can he waive his rights by silence?
4. When do the police have to read the Miranda rights?
5. Are there any exceptions to Miranda (when a cop doesn't need to advise a suspect of his or her rights)?
6. Why did some people hail the Miranda decision, while some other people criticize it?

II. Translate the following terms into English.

1. 社会保障
2. 呼吸测试
3. 自证其罪
4. 总检察长
5. 正当程序
6. 合理根据
7. 米兰达警告
8. 权利的放弃
9. 公共安全
10. 保持沉默权

III. Translate the following sentences into Chinese.

1. To preserve and protect the rights of victims of crime to justice and due process, victims shall be entitled to be present at all proceedings where the defendant has the right to be present.
2. The defendant has the right to an attorney. If the defendant cannot afford an attorney, and if the court declares the defendant to be indigent, the court will appoint an attorney for that person.
3. The defendant has the right to remain silent. If a statement is made, any statement that is made can be used against him/her.
4. You have the right to remain silent. Anything you say can be used against you in a

Lesson 4
The Right to Remain Silent

court of law.

5. If you want a lawyer before or during questioning but cannot afford to hire a lawyer, one will be appointed to represent you at no cost before any questioning.

IV. Dictation.

Most of the world's legal systems are based on one of the two great historical traditions of Western law. The first is the civil-law tradition, which is based on legal codes or statues that define a society's basic laws on various subjects. The second tradition is common law, whose cornerstone is case law or the accumulation of judicial decisions, as opposed to a comprehensive code. Common law is also known as judge-made law. Civil law is more adaptable—that is, easier to transfer from place to place—than common law. In addition, religion includes various laws which have had and continue to have varying degree of influence upon the legal systems of certain countries.

Supplementary Reading

While the Miranda warnings are considered a cornerstone[1] of our civil liberties, the person after whom they were named was hardly someone most people would consider a hero. In 1963, Ernesto Miranda, an eighth-grade dropout with a criminal record, had been picked up by Phoenix police and accused of raping and kidnapping a mildly retarded 18-year-old woman. After two hours in a police interrogation room[2] Miranda signed a written confession, but he apparently was never told that he had the right to remain silent, to have a lawyer, and to be protected against self-incrimination.

Despite his lawyer's objections, the confession was presented as evidence at Miranda's trial, and he was convicted and sentenced to 20 years. His appeal went all the way to the Supreme Court, where it was joined with three other similar cases. In a landmark ruling issued in 1966, the court established that the accused have the right to remain silent and that prosecutors may not use statements made by defendants while in

---

1 cornerstone 基础；基石。
2 interrogation room 审问室。

police custody unless the police have advised them of their rights.

That ruling offered only temporary reprieve[1] to Miranda. He was retried. The second time round the prosecutors couldn't use the confession, but they did have additional evidence from a former girlfriend of Miranda's who testified that he had told her about the kidnapping and rape. He was convicted again and served 11 years before being paroled in 1972. He was arrested and returned to prison several times after.

Miranda died in 1976 at age 34 after being stabbed during an argument in a bar. The police arrested a suspect who chose to remain silent after being read his rights. The suspect was released and no one was ever charged with the killing.

In 1992 Miranda rights were effectively extended to illegal immigrants[2] living in the United States. In a settlement of a class-action lawsuit reached in Los Angeles with the Immigration and Naturalization Service, U.S. District Court Judge William Byrne, Jr., approved the printing of millions of notices in several languages to be given to those arrested. The approximately 1.5 million illegal aliens arrested each year must be told they may (1) talk with a lawyer, (2) make a phone call, (3) request a list of available legal services, (4) seek a hearing before an immigration judge, (5) possibly obtain release on bond, and (6) contact a diplomatic officer representing their country. This kind of thing was "long overdue," said Roberto Martinez of the American Friends Service Committee's Mexico-U.S. border program. "Up to now, we've had total mistreatment of civil rights of undocumented people."

---

1 reprieve: 缓刑；暂缓执行刑罚。
2 illegal immigrant: 非法移民。

Lesson 5
Property Law

A thing that has no owner naturally belongs to the first taker.
无主物理所当然地属于最初取得该物的人。

Property is a word with high emotional overtones and so many meanings that it has defied attempts at an accurate all-inclusive definition. For the purpose of this chapter, property may be defined as an exclusive right to control an economic good. It is the name for a concept that refers to the rights and obligations, privileges and restrictions, that govern the relations of persons with respect to things of value. What is guaranteed to be one's own is property in a broad sense.

However, property would have little value (and the word would have little meaning) if the law did not define the right to use it, to sell or dispose of it, and to prevent trespass[1] on it.

Property covers a lot of ground. The law treats different kinds of property differently, so it is helpful to sort out the kinds of property that one can own. Perhaps the most basic distinction is between real property and personal property. Real property[2] (sometimes called realty or real estate) consists of the land and the buildings, foliage, and anything else permanently attached to the land. All other property is personal property, or personalty. Attorneys sometimes refer to personal

---

1 trespass：侵入。An unlawful act committed against the person of property of another; esp., wrongful entry on another's real property.在现代法中，trespass有三类：侵害他人财物（trespass to goods）、侵犯他人人身（trespass to the person）及侵入他人土地（trespass to land）。
2 real property, realty, real estate：不动产。从历史角度看，在英格兰法上，real property 是指可用物权诉讼（real action）予以实际返还和救济的物及在物上的权利。现在，越来越多地用来指土地及土地附属物和在它们之上的权利。

property as chattel[1], a term used under the common law to denote all forms of personal property. Personal property can be tangible or intangible. Tangible personal property, such as a TV set or a car, has physical substance. Intangible personal property represents some set of rights and interests but has no real physical existence. Stocks and bonds, patents, and copyrights are examples of intangible personal property. As the subject of property law is so large, we can only hit some highlights here. This chapter just deals with the most important concepts in property law.

I. Ownership of Real Property

Ownership of real property is an abstract concept that cannot exist independently of the legal system. No one can actually possess or hold a piece of land, the air above it, the earth below it, and all the water contained on it. The legal system therefore recognizes certain rights and duties that constitute ownership interests in real property.

a. Ownership in Fee Simple

The most common type of property ownership today is the fee simple[2]. Generally, the term fee simple is used to designate a fee simple absolute, in which the owner has the greatest possible aggregation of rights, privileges, and power. The fee simple is limited absolutely to a person and his or her heirs and is assigned forever without limitation or condition. Furthermore, the owner has the rights of exclusive possession and use of property. A fee simple is potentially infinitely in duration and can be disposed of by deed[3] or by will[4] (by selling or giving away). When there is no will, the fee simple passes to the owner's legal heirs.

The rights that accompany a fee simple include the right to use the land for

---

1 chattel, personal property, personalty：动产，除不动产之外的一切财产。但是，广义的personal property也指"个人财产"，指不用于经营活动滋生收益的财产，包括不动产和动产。本文的personal property 取狭义解释。
2 fee simple：无条件继承之不动产（财产）权，在现代法中，其与fee simple absolute实属同意，是法律所认可的最广的土地（财产）权益。其在保有期限、处分、可世袭性方面无任何限制，保有人有接近于完全所有权的权利，可以立遗嘱自由处分，无遗嘱死亡时则由其法定继承人继承。
3 deed：契据。A written document by which land is conveyed.其记载一项契约或约定（contract or covenant）表示当事人同意转移某项地产权利，或设定某项义务，或确认某项转移地产权利的行为。例如，租约（lease）、抵押证书（mortgage certificate）及财产和解协议（settlement）均属契据。
4 will：遗嘱。A document by which a person directs his or her estate to be distributed upon death.

Lesson 5
Property Law

whatever purpose the owner sees fit. Of course, certain uses of the property may be prohibited by applicable laws, including zoning laws[1], environmental regulations, and laws that prevent the owner from unreasonably interfering with another person's land. Another limitation on the absolute rights of owners in fee simple is the government's power of eminent domain[2].

Ownership in fee simple may also become limited whenever a conveyance[3], or transfer of real property, is made to another party conditionally. When this occurs, the fee simple is known as a fee simple defeasible[4] (the word defeasible means capable of being terminated or annulled). A conveyance "to A and his heirs as long as the land is used for charitable purposes" creates a fee simple defeasible because ownership of the property is conditioned on the land's being used for charitable purposes. The original owner retains a partial ownership interest because if the specified condition does not occur (if the land ceases to be used for charitable purposes), the land reverts, or returns, to the original owner. If the original owner is not living at the time, the land passes to her or his heirs.

b. Life Estate

A life estate is an estate that lasts for the life of some specified individual. A conveyance "to A for his life" creates a life estate. In a life estate, the life tenant[5] has fewer rights of ownership than the holder of a fee simple defeasible because the rights necessarily cease to exist on the life tenant's death.

The life tenant has the right to use the land, provided that he or she commits no waste (injury to the land). In other words, the life tenant cannot use the land in a manner that would adversely affect its value. The life tenant can use the land to harvest crops or, if mines and oil wells are already on the land, can extract minerals

---

1 zoning law：（美）城市区划法。zoning: the legislative division of a region, esp. a municipality, into separate districts with different regulations with the districts for land use, building size, and the like.
2 eminent domain：国家征用权；（国家对一切财产的）支配权。The inherent power of a governmental entity to take privately owned property, esp. land, and covert it to public use, subject to reasonable compensation for the taking.
3 conveyance：财产转让、让与。Transfer or delivery of sth. (such as a right or property) to another.
4 fee simple defeasible：可限定无条件继承之不动产；可废除的非限嗣继承地。即当某特定事件发生或不发生时，即可宣告其无效或予以废除。
5 life tenant：土地等不动产的终身占有人。A person who, until death, is beneficially entitled to land; the holder of a life estate.

and oil from it, but the life tenant cannot exploit the land by creating new wells or mines.

Along with these rights, the life tenant also has some duties—to keep the property in repair and to pay property taxes. In short, the owner of the life estate has the same rights as a fee simple owner except that the life tenant must maintain the value of the property during her or his tenancy, less the decrease in value resulting from the normal use of the property allowed by the life tenancy.

c. Future Interests[1]

When an owner in fee simple absolute conveys the estate conditionally to another (such as with a fee simple defeasible) or for a limited period of time (such as with a life estate), the original owner still retains an interest in the land. The owner retains the right to repossess ownership of the land if the conditions of the fee simple defeasible are not met or when the life of the life estate ends. The interest in the property that the owner retains (or transfer to another) is called future interest because if it arises, it will only arise in the future.

If the owner retains ownership of the future interest, the future interest is described as a reversionary interest[2] because the property will revert to the original owner if the condition specified in a fee simple defeasible fails or when a life tenant dies. If, however, the owner of the future interest transfers ownership rights in that future interest to another, the future interest is described as a remainder[3]. For example, a conveyance "to A for life, then to B" creates a life estate for A and a remainder (future interest) for B.

d. Nonpossessory Interests

In contrast to the types of property interests just described, some interests in land do not include any rights to possess the property. These interests are thus known as nonpossessory interests, including easements, profits, and licenses.

---

1 future interest：未来财产权益。A property interest in which the privilege of possession or of other enjoyment is future and not present. 与现实权益（present interest）相对。
2 reversionary interest：归复权益；将来权益。指某人因土地或其他财产的归复而享有的权益。也指对于目前为他人占有的财产所享有的将来用益的权利。在美国法中，一般指归复权益，并与剩余地产权益（remainder interest）相区别，前者须在期满后将财产归复原所有人，而后者则转让于原所有人以外的人。
3 remainder：剩余地产权；（剩余地产）继受权；剩余继承权。

Lesson 5
Property Law

Easements[1] and Profits[2] An easement is the right of a person to make limited use of another person's real property without taking anything from the property. An easement, for example, can be the right to travel over another's property. In contrast, a profit is the right to go onto land in possession of another and take away some part of the land itself (e.g. sand or gravel) or some product of the land.

Licenses[3] A license is the revocable right of a person to come onto another person's land. It is a personal privilege that arises from the consent of the owner of the land and that can be revoked by the owner. A ticket to attend a movie at a theater is an example of a license. Assume that a Broadway theater owner issues to Carla a ticket to see a play. If Carla is refused to entry into the theater because she is improperly dressed, she has no right to force her way into the theater. The ticket is only a revocable license, not a conveyance of an interest in property.

II. Ownership of Personal Property

Ownership of personal property can also be viewed as a bundle of rights, including the right to possess property and to dispose of it—by sale, lease, or other means. The following ownership of personal property, actually, may also share with real property.

a. Fee Simple

As explained above, a person who holds the entire bundle of rights to property is said to be the owner in fee simple. The owner in fee simple is entitled to use, possess, or dispose of the property as he or she chooses during his or her lifetime, and on this owner's death, the interests in the property descend to his or her heirs.

b. Concurrent Ownership[4]

Persons who share ownership rights simultaneously in a particular piece

---

1. easement: 地役权,为实现自己土地的利益而使用他人土地的权利,最主要的有(在他人土地上的)通行权和用水权等。
2. profit: 用益权,又作"right of common",指某人使用他人的土地并参与分享土地收益或土地出产物的权利。
3. license: 特许权,许可人允许被许可人在其土地上从事某项行为或一系列行为,但被许可人对该土地不具有任何永久性权益,此项许可基于个人信任,不得转让。
4. concurrent ownership: 共同所有权。

of property are said to be concurrent owners. There are two principal types of concurrent ownership: tenancy in common and joint tenancy. Another type of concurrent ownership is tenancy by the entirety.

Tenancy in common[1] The term tenancy in common refers to a form of co-ownership in which each of two or more persons owns an undivided interest in the property. The interest is undivided because each tenant has rights in the whole property. On the death of a tenant in common, that tenant's interest in the property passes to her or his heirs.

Joint tenancy[2] In a joint tenancy, each of two or more persons owns an undivided interest in the property, and a deceased joint tenant's interest passes to the surviving joint tenant or tenants. The rights of a surviving joint tenant to inherit a deceased joint tenant's ownership interest, which are referred to as survivorship rights, distinguish the joint tenancy from the tenancy in common. A joint tenancy can be terminated before a joint tenant's death by gift or by sale; in this situation, the person who receives the property as a gift or who purchases the property becomes a tenant in common, not a joint tenant.

Tenancy by the Entirety[3] Concurrent ownership of property can also take the form of a tenancy by the entirety—a form of co-ownership between a husband and a wife that is similar to a joint tenancy, except that a spouse cannot transfer his or her interest during his or her lifetime without the consent of the other spouse.

III. Acquiring Ownership of Property

The most common way of acquiring property is by purchasing it. Often, property is acquired by will or inheritance. Here we look at additional ways in which ownership of property can be acquired, including acquisition by possession, production, gift, accession, and confusion.

1　tenancy in common：普通共有，与联合共有（joint tenancy）的区别是，普通共有人之间彼此不享有生存者财产权（right of survivorship）。
2　joint tenancy：联合共有，也作"共同保有"。
3　tenancy by the entirety：夫妻共有，实际上是联合共有的一种形式，夫妻关系解除后将使联合共有的财产转变为普通共有财产（tenancy in common）。

Lesson 5
Property Law

a. Possession[1]

One example of acquiring ownership by possession is the capture of wild animals. Wild animals belong to no one in their natural state, and the first person to take possession of a wild animal normally owns it. The killing of a wild animal amounts to assuming ownership of it. Those who find lost or abandoned property also can acquire ownership rights through mere possession of the property.

b. Production

Production—the fruit of labor—is another means of acquiring ownership of personal property. For example, writers, inventors, and manufacturers all produce personal property and thereby acquired title[2] to it. (In some situations, though, as when a researcher is hired to invent a new product or technique, the researcher-producer may not own what is produced.)

c. Gift

A gift is another fairly common means of acquiring and transferring ownership of real and personal property. A gift is essentially a voluntary transfer of property ownership for which no consideration[3] is given. The presence of consideration is what distinguishes a contract from a gift. Certain conditions must exist, however, before a gift will be effective in the eyes of the law. The donor (the one making the gift) must intend to make the gift, the gift must be delivered to the donee (the recipient of the gift), and the donee must accept the gift.

d. Accession[4]

Accession, which means "adding on" to something, occurs when someone adds value to an item of property by labor or materials. When accession is accomplished with the permission of the owner, generally there is no dispute about who owns the

---

1. possession: 占有; 占有权; 先占。The right under which one may exercise control over something to the exclusion of all others.
2. title: 产权; 权利, 资格。The union of all elements constituting the legal right to control and dispose of property.
3. consideration: 对价, 英美法中合同成立的要件之一, 指一方当事人获得的权利、利益、利润或好处, 或另一方当事人所遭受的损失或承担的义务。
4. accession: 添附, 相当于罗马法中的 "accession", 根据罗马法的财产添附原则, 如果某一物得到添附, 无论是自然添附或人工添附, 则原物的所有人有权对添附主张财产权; 但如果由于添附而产生新物, 例如葡萄酿成酒, 小麦制成面包, 则属于加工 (specification), 加工物属于加工人 (species)。

property after the accession occurred. When accession occurs without the permission of the owner, the courts will tend to favor the owner over the improver—the one who improves the property—provided that the accession was wrongful and undertaken in bad faith. In addition, many courts will deny the improver any compensation for the value added: for example, a car thief who puts new tires on the stolen car will obviously not be compensated for the value of the new tires when the rightful owner recovers the car. If the accession is performed in good faith, however, even without the owner's consent, ownership of the improved item most often depends on whether the accession has increased the value of the property or changed its identity.

e. Confusion

Confusion is defined as the commingling (mixing together) of goods so that one person's personal property cannot be distinguished from another's. Confusion frequently occurs when the goods are fungible, meaning that each particle is identical to every other particle, as with grain and oil, and the goods are owned by two or more parties as tenants in common. For example, if two farmers put their Number 2-grade winter wheat into the same storage bin, confusion would occur.

Glossary

accession 添附
aggregation 集合；集合体
chattel 动产
concurrent 同时发生的；并存的
confusion 混合
consideration 对价
conveyance 财产转让；让与
decease 死亡
deed 契据
donee 受赠人
easement（在他人土地上的）通行权；地役权
eminent domain 国家征用权
emotional overtones 感情色彩

fee simple defeasible 可限定无条件继承之不动产
fee simple 无条件继承之不动产（财产）权
fungible 可代替的；可互换的
future interest 未来财产权益
gift 赠与
gravel 砂砾；碎石
inheritance 继承；遗产
intangible 无形的
joint tenancy 联合共有
license 特许权
life estate 终身财产；终身不动产
life tenant 土地等不动产的终身占有人

Lesson 5
Property Law

possession 占有；占有权；先占取得
profit 用益权；利益
real estate 不动产；地产
real property 不动产
realty 不动产；地产
remainder 剩余地产；剩余地产权；剩余继承权
reversionary interest 归复权益；将来权益

spouse 配偶
tangible 有形的
tenancy by the entirety 夫妻共有
tenancy in common 共同共有
title 产权；权利；资格
trespass 侵入
will 遗嘱

EXERCISES

I. Answer the following questions.

1. What is property? How do we classify it generally?
2. Is earning capacity intangible personal property? Why or why not?
3. What is the fee simple absolute? When the owner dies, how will it be disposed of?
4. When does the future interest occur? What's the difference between reversionary interest and remainder?
5. How many types of concurrent ownership are there?
6. When does the accession occur?
7. Compare tenancy in common and joint tenancy.

II. Translate the following terms into English.

1. 动产
2. 不动产
3. 无条件继承之不动产（财产）权
4. 国家征用（权）
5. 终身财产、终身不动产
6. 未来财产权益
7. 归复权益
8. 剩余地产
9. 地役权
10. 普通共有
11. 联合共有
12. 夫妻共有
13. 先占取得
14. 赠与
15. 混合

III. Translate the following sentences into Chinese.

1. The requisite period of possession may also vary with the nature of possession: a good faith possessor ordinarily acquires property rights in a shorter period of time than a bad faith possessor.
2. Co-ownership has been recognized from early times and may arise by application of any of the methods available for the acquisition of property rights.
3. In modern times, the federal government and states have asserted ownership over a variety of things that were previously considered to be without owner, such as running waters and wild animals.
4. Property that is involuntarily left and forgotten is lost property. A finder of the property can claim title to the property against the whole world, except the true owner.
5. Property may be given to a trustee for the benefit of a person or for the accomplishment of certain purposes.

IV. Cloze.

One of the most prevalent modes of 1_____ of property rights is by the contract of sale. A sale involves the 2_____ of a thing in consideration of a sum of money or the promise of a sum of money; if the consideration is a thing other 3_____ money, the transaction is technically designated an 4_____. In common law jurisdictions the contract of sale, upon its completion, transfers the ownership of the things sold as between the 5_____. Insofar, as third persons are 6_____, however, transfer of ownership may depend on 7_____ chattels of recordation of the title of lands. Contracts of sale are 8_____ of any formalities and may be based on verbal agreement; but 9_____ of evidence may exclude the proof of contracts the object of which exceeds a certain value. Moreover, in most jurisdictions, the sale of lands required, 10_____ for its validity against third persons or for the transfer of rights, recordation in public records.

Lesson 5
Property Law

Supplementary Reading

A trust[1] is a division of the bundle of rights in property in an unusual way. First, the management of the property is separated from the benefit of the property. The property is managed by a trustee[2], who usually has the authority to invest the property, collect income, rent, or sell, but who is paid a fee for its services, rather than receiving any income from the property itself. The beneficiary[3] of the trust owns the right to receive the benefit from the property, such as the income it produces. Second, the beneficiary's rights are defined when the trust is established by the grantor[4], the person who gives the property that becomes the principal[5] (or corpus, meaning body) of the trust. The grantor can, for example, specify that the beneficiary can receive the income from the trust but no payments from principal, that one beneficiary receives the income for life and then the principal goes to someone else, or, in the case of charitable trusts[6], that the income should be devoted to seeking a cure for cancer or the care and feeding of stray cats.

As last examples suggest, some trusts are devoted to charitable purposes, but in the context of wills and family purpose, private trusts[7] are more important. Trusts are used for many purposes. Living trusts[8] can be used to keep property out of probate[9], which minimizes publicity and may save fees, although the advantages of living trust have been lessened by recent reforms in probate laws. Trusts either created during the grantor's lifetime (inter vivos trusts[10]) or in a will (testamentary trusts[11]) can protect the property of a person who is unable to manage the property, either because of a legal disability[12] (a minor child, for example) or because of practical inability[13] to do so (someone who is

---

1 trust: 信托。
2 trustee: 托管人，保管人，理事。
3 beneficiary: 受益人。
4 grantor: 授予者，让渡人。
5 principal: （代理关系中的）本人；委托人。
6 charitable trust: 公益信托。
7 private trust: 私人信托。
8 living trust: 生前信托。
9 probate: 遗嘱检验，遗嘱认证。
10 *inter vivos* trust: 生前信托。
11 testamentary trusts: 遗嘱信托。
12 legal disability: 法律上无能力。
13 practical inability: 实际上无能力。

unsophisticated in financial matters). Probably the most prevalent use of trusts is for tax purpose, particularly in estate[1] planning. The federal estate tax law imposes a tax on the amount of an estate above a certain minimum amount. Assume the amount is $700,000 (it varies from year to year). If a wife and husband each owns property worth $650,000, and the wife dies first, leaving all her property to her husband, there is no tax on her estate because it is below the minimum amount. But when the husband dies subsequently, leaving all his and his wife's property to the children, his estate may be above $700,000; adding his and his wife's property together, the portion above that amount will be subject to the federal tax. Using a trust avoids the tax; the wife's will can direct that her property be placed in a trust, with the income and a portion of the principal available to the husband for his life. After he dies, the income is used for the benefit of the children until they are of an age where they are presumed to be mature enough to handle the principal, at which time it is distributed to them.

---

1 estate: All that a person or entity owns, including both real and personal property. 产业，个人的全部资产、地产等所有权。

Lesson 6
Contract Law

Consent makes law.

合意产生法律效力。

I. Definition

A contract has been defined as "an agreement between two or more persons consisting of a promise or mutual promises which the law will enforce or the performance[1] of which the law in some way recognizes as a duty". A contract has also been defined as "a promise or a set of promises for the breach of which the law gives a remedy[2], or the performance of which the law in some way recognizes as a duty".

The essence of a contract is mutuality[3]. A contract requires an agreement between two or more persons. It is impossible for one person to make a contract or for two persons to contract if they have not agreed on the terms of the contract. A common expression of the requirement of mutuality is that there must be a "meeting of minds". This generally recognizes that parties to a contract must come to some understanding that has similar, if not identical, implications in their minds.

Another essential element of a contract is the idea of a bargained exchange[4]. A gratuitous promise[5] is usually not enforceable as a contract. For example, if I promise

---

1 performance:（合同义务的）履行。Fulfillment of one's obligations required by contract.
2 remedy: 法律补救方法。The means to achieve justice in any matter in which legal rights are involved.
3 mutuality: 合意。The quality of a contract under which both parties are bound by obligations.
4 bargained exchange: 利益交换。即下文所指的对价（consideration）的重要组成部分，为英美传统合同法理论中合同成立的要件之一。只有存在对价，允诺才成为法律上可执行的合同。
5 gratuitous: 无偿的，自愿的。Not involving a return benefit, compensation, or consideration; a gratuitous promise.

to give you $500 and you say you'll take it, a contract is not formed. A gratuitous promise does not create a meeting of the minds but merely shows an intention on my part to do something that I may or may not follow through on.

II. Classification

Formal and informal contracts A formal contract is one that is binding because of the form of the contract. Formal contacts include contracts under seal, negotiable instruments[1], and such.

Express and implied Express contracts are formed where the agreement of the parties is in oral or written form. If the agreement of the parties and its terms are inferred from their actions, the contract is said to be implied or implied in fact[2].

Unilateral and bilateral A unilateral contract is a contract in which a promise of one party is exchanged for performance by the other party. A bilateral contract is one in which each party makes a promise to the other.

Executed and executory An executed contract is one in which all parties have performed their obligations under the contract. An executory contract is one in which the performances have not been completed.

Voidable, valid, and void A contract that is voidable is one in which one of the parties has a right to select to avoid[3] or disaffirm[4] his or her obligation, e.g., a contract entered into by a minor. Unless the selection is made, the law will enforce the contractual obligation. A valid contract is one which is neither voidable nor void. A void contract is a nullity from its inception.

---

1 negotiable instrument: 可流通票据。Check, promissory note, bill of exchange, security or any document representing money payable which can be transferred to another by handing it over and/or endorsing it. 指可以通过背书或递交方式转让的权利凭证，包括支票、本票、汇票以及债券等。

2 implied in fact contract: 推定合同或默示合同，亦称"implied contract"。是与express contract(明示合同)相对应的概念。英美法中还有个易混淆的概念即"implied in law contract" (also called "quasi contract")，an obligation that is not created by a contract but that is imposed by law to prevent the unjust enrichment of one party from the acts of another party. 即为了防止产生不当得利，根据法律规定而产生的义务，并非合意约定的义务。虽然被称作"准合同"，但实际上并不是合同。

3 avoid: 使无效，免除。To annul or make void.

4 disaffirm: 否认或驳斥。To deny or contradict.

Lesson 6

Contract Law

III. Offer and Acceptance

a. Offer

Generally, in order for a contract to be formed, one party must take an offer to the other. The party making the offer is called the offeror; the party receiving the offer is called offeree. A statement that purports to be an offer must be definite and certain and must show the intent to make an offer. A statement by an individual to another like "I would like to sell you my car for $100. Do you wish to purchase it?" is a definite and certain offer showing intent. A statement like "I am thinking about selling my car for $100" is not an offer because it lacks certainty as to the offeror's intent to sell.

The intent of the offeror to make an offer is of primary importance. Though it is impossible to know what is happening in the mind of an individual, one can look to circumstances surrounding the transaction to determine the intent of the offeror. Courts use an objective standard to determine intent. If a reasonable person would interpret the statements and circumstances to create an offer, it will be interpreted as such even where the offeror had not intended to make an offer.

Communication[1] is a second important element of an offer. The communication need not be words, but the offeree must be aware of the offer. A person who is not aware of the offer cannot accept it.

Termination of an offer occurs with the occurrence of one of several events: acceptance by the offeree, revocation[2] by the offeror, rejection[3] by the offeree, death or insanity of the offeror or offeree, subsequent illegality of the subject matter of the offer[4], destruction or prior sale of the subject matter, expiration of the time stated in the offer, or expiration of a reasonable period of time.

1　communication: 这里是指信息传达的方式。A means of communicating.
2　revocation: 撤回。Withdrawing an offer before it is accepted. 要约被接受之前，要约人在一定条件下可以撤销要约。英美合同法中，标明是不可撤销或带有承诺期限的要约不可撤销。
3　rejection: 受要约人拒绝接受要约。拒绝的方式可以是明确说明拒绝承诺，也可以是提出反要约。
4　这里是指要约做出时，标的物是合法的、可流通的。但在受要约人接受要约前因为立法或其他原因，标的物变得不合法，即"嗣后不合法"。此时要约终止。

b. Acceptance[1]

The nature of acceptance is strictly defined. An acceptance must conform to the terms of the offer. An acceptance that makes only minor changes will not be considered a rejection. The specific determination of whether a change is a major or minor one is a matter of fact that has to be determined in each situation. An acceptance that adds terms may operate either as an acceptance or a rejection. If the additional terms are major, the acceptance will operate as a rejection of the original offer and become a counteroffer. If the new terms are minor in comparison with the rest of the contract, then the acceptance will be effective.

Communication of acceptance takes various forms. An acceptance creates a contract. In order for an acceptance to take place, it must be communicated to the offeror. The most desirable medium to communicate an acceptance to an offer is the same that was used by the offeror to communicate the offer to the offeree. An acceptance, if communicated in the same manner as the offer, is effective when the acceptance is placed into the channels of communication.

IV. Consideration

If there has been an offer and an acceptance, a contract is normally created. A promise that is unsupported by consideration, however, even if accepted, does not create a contract. If I promise to pay you $500 and you say that you accept my promise, a contract does not result. There is no reason why I should pay you this money, and though I may fulfill my gratuitous promise, it will not be enforced by law. Consideration is giving something that has value to another party (benefit) or giving up something that has value to oneself (detriment[2]). For a contract to exist, consideration must go both ways. Courts recognize that there is a determent to the

---

1　acceptance：承诺。An overt act by the offeree, indicating a positive, unequivocal intention of agreeing to the terms of the offer. An acceptance generally must be communicated to the offeror. In the case of a bilateral contract, the acceptance is in the form of a promise by the offeree to do what was requested by the offeror. In the case of a unilateral contract, the acceptance constitutes the performance by the offeree of the act requested by the offeror. An acceptance can only be made by the offeree.

2　detriment: 损害。A giving up of a thing or mode of conduct to which one is entitled that constitutes consideration for a contract. 英美合同法上，如果一个人放弃了自己的权利，可以视为对价，称之为对自己的"损害"，也称"法定损害"（legal detriment）。

promisors if they agree to do something they are not otherwise obliged to do or agree to refrain from doing something which they have a right to do.

A promise that is so indefinite and uncertain that it cannot be enforced cannot be consideration. Such promises are often referred to as illusory because they appear enforceable when, in fact, they are not.

If a person promises not to do something that he or she has no right to do in the first place, it is not consideration. Consideration is also not present where a person does something that he or she is already legally obligated to do. Where a promise is made to do something as a result of moral obligations, many courts take the position that there is no legal consideration.

V. Deceit[1], Duress[2], and Mistake

Deceit has several subcategories. Where two parties have exchanged what appears to be consideration and entered into what appears to be a contract, there are several defenses that may be raised that will cause the contract to be voidable by one of the parties. The first of the defenses is fraud, which is defined as an intentional misrepresentation of a material fact made for the purpose of inducing another person to rely upon that fact to do something that would not otherwise have been done.

Misrepresentation, a second act that allows a party to a contract to disaffirm the contract, is essentially the same as fraud except that a misrepresentation need not have been made intentionally. Puffing is another aspect to consider. Not every statement that is untrue constitutes deceit. It is important that there be a misstatement of a material fact. An opinion or comments such as are generally recognized as salespersons puffing are not statement of fact and, therefore, would not constitute an act of deceit. Furthermore, if a particular fact is misrepresented but it is not material (i.e., knowledge of the true state of facts would not have caused a person to change

---

1 deceit和fraud都是指利用不诚实的行为获取不公平或不合法的利益。这里作为合同效力瑕疵的抗辩理由，deceit是作为fraud的上位概念，包括故意的与不论故意与否的欺骗性行为（分别指fraud和misrepresentation），本文译为"不实行为"。有人将deceit译为"诈欺"，与译为"欺诈"的fraud相区别。

2 duress: 胁迫。The use of force, false imprisonment or threats to compel someone to act contrary to his/her wishes or interests. If duress is used to get someone to sign an agreement, a court may find the document null and void. 包括各种形式的武力或非武力威胁，是合同无效的依据之一。

his or her conduct), then disaffirmance of the contract would not be allowed. It is also essential for the defense of deceit to prevail that the plaintiff has relied on the statement of the defendant and not on some independent source.

Duress and undue influence comprise a second category of acts that allows one party to a contract to disaffirm the contract. Duress is any action that causes individuals to do something that they would not otherwise have done or to refrain from doing something that they would otherwise do. Undue influence is taking advantage of a difference in the bargaining capacity of parties that results from a special position that is occupied by one of the parties. Undue influence exists where there is a special obligation on the part of the stronger party to protect the interests of the weaker party. This obligation is referred to under law as a fiduciary obligation. It exists in relationships such as attorney-client, doctor-patient, executor-beneficiary (under a will), and trustee-beneficiary (in a trust arrangement).

Mistakes come in several kinds, some of which make the contract voidable. A mistake is different from ignorance or the exercise of poor judgment. If you purchase a piece of property with knowledge of the fact that it has thousands of dollars worth of marketable timber on it and I, the seller, am unaware of this fact, this is a situation of ignorance and poor judgment; there has been no mistake.

VI. Capacity

Despite the presence of an offer and an acceptance, freely given by both parties, and consideration, the law recognizes that contracts are entered into by certain persons shall be voidable by those persons. The two major categories of persons who lack capacity to enter into a contract are minors and persons who have a degree of mental limitation because of insanity or drunkenness. A contract entered into by a person who lacks contractual capacity because of one of the preceding reasons will be voidable by the person who lacks the capacity.

VII. Third Party Beneficiary Contracts

A contract entered into between two individuals specifying that a third individual is to receive certain rights is called a third party beneficiary contract. There are three types of third party beneficiary contracts: creditor beneficiary, donee beneficiary, and incidental beneficiary[1]. These contracts are distinguished by two features. The first is the beneficiary's relationship to the promisor, and the second is the beneficiary's rights with respect to the contract.

VIII. Discharge and Remedies

A discharge of contract is anything that will cause a binding promise to cease to be binding. Discharge may result from performance, breach of contract or disaffirmance, release, discharge of a joint debtor[2], novation[3], material alteration, merger, and such. In addition, certain laws, such as subsequent illegality or bankruptcy or both will also cause a contract to be discharged.

Remedies are alternatives the individual who has been harmed has when a contract has been discharged because of a wrongful act. These alternatives are called remedies and include monetary damages, which can be liquidated, compensatory, or punitive[4]. Damages are computed by taking into consideration what the individual, who is not guilty of the breach, has lost from the other individual's actions. These damages can include wages, and such. Another remedy that may be available is specific performance. Specific performance is a mandate by the court ordering the defendant to perform under the terms of the original agreement. This remedy is appropriate when a specific, unique, and unusual property exists, such as real estate or rare antiques and monetary compensation would be inadequate or inappropriate.

---

1 《美国合同法重述》详细规定了为第三人利益的合同又叫利他合同的保护，并将第三人分为三类：债权受益人（受利益系因受允诺人对其清偿债务），赠与受益人（受利益系因接受允诺人的赠与）与意外受益人。前两者并称为有意受益人，可以依合同取得法律上可强制执行的权利，而意外受益人不能依合同取得任何权利。

2 joint debtor: 共同债务人。The person who owes money.

3 novation: 更新。novate: (agreement of parties to a contract) to substitute a new contract for the old one.

4 liquidated damages: 预先确定数额的损害赔偿。An amount of money agreed upon by both parties to a contract which one will pay to the other upon breaching the agreement or if a lawsuit arises due to the breach.
compensatory damages: 补偿性损害赔偿。Damages recovered in payment for actual injury or economic loss, which does not include punitive damages.
punitive damages: 惩罚性损害赔偿。(also called "exemplary damages"), damages example to others for malicious, evil or awarded in a lawsuit as a punishment and particularly fraudulent acts.

Glossary

avoid 使无效；免除
beneficiary 受益人
detriment 损害
disaffirm 否认或驳斥
discharge 清偿（债务）；履行（义务）；免除；撤销
fraud 欺诈
gratuitous 无偿的；自愿的；无理由的
inception 开始

mandate （法庭的）命令；要求
negotiable instrument 可流通票据
nullity （法律上的）无效；无效行为
performance （合同义务的）履行
puffing （对商品质量的）自我吹嘘；夸大说明；抬价
revocation 撤销；撤回
unequivocal 明确的；不含糊的

EXERCISES

I. Answer the following questions.

1. Who is not eligible to enter into a binding contract?
2. Make a list of causes that may terminate a contract.
3. What are the remedies and what do they include?
4. How many types of contracts are there according to the text?
5. Tell the major difference between fraud and misrepresentation.

II. Translate the following terms into English.

1. （法定）损害
2. 无偿许诺
3. 欺诈
4. 不实陈述
5. 受要约人
6. 票据
7. （合同）履行
8. 胁迫
9. 不当影响
10. 对价
11. 为第三人利益的合同
12. 默示合同
13. 合意
14. 违约
15. （合同）终止

Lesson 6
Contract Law

III. Match the definitions from column B with the words in column A.

A	B
1. breach of contract	a. to bring civil proceedings against
2. damages	b. legal responsibility
3. liability	c. financial compensation awarded in civil case
4. to sue	d. a contract in which a promise of one party is exchanged for performance by the other party.
5. (a) unilateral contract	e. non-performance of contractual obligations

IV. Use the word "as" to complete the following definitions.

1. The person who makes a promise is known...
2. Regarding contractual capacity, drunken persons are treated much the same...
3. Consideration may be defined...
4. Deceit, mistake and undue influence are referred to...

Lesson 7
Tort Law

The thing speaks for itself.

事实不言自明。

I. What Is a Tort?

The word "tort" derives form the Latin tortus, meaning twisted or crooked, and early found its way into the English language as a general synonym for "wrong". Later the word disappeared from common usage, but retained its hold on the law and has a purely technical meaning—a legal wrong[1] for which the law provides a remedy[2].

The law of tort has been used for many centuries to protect personal interests in property. Some of the earliest actions known to Anglo-American law are those concerned with protecting interests in land, including the torts of nuisance[3] and trespass[4] to land. Tort has also been concerned with protecting people from intentional interference, through actions for assault and battery[5] and false

---

1 wrong: 过错。Breach of legal duties; violation of another's legal rights.这里的wrong为法律术语，指违反法定义务的过错行为，与前文出现的wrong意义不同。
2 remedy:（法律上的）救济、补偿。The means to enforce a right or to prevent or obtain redress for a wrong, the relief (as damages, restitution, specific performance, or an injunction) that may be given or ordered by a court or other tribunal for a wrong.
3 nuisance：滋扰、妨碍。An act or failure to act resulting in an interference with the sue of enjoyment of property.
4 trespass: 侵犯。(1) an unlawful act committed against the person or property of another, especially wrongful entry on another's real property, e.g. trespass to land（对土地的侵犯），trespass to chattel （侵犯动产），trespass ab initio（从开始便侵犯）; (2) the common-law form of action for redress of injuries directly caused by such a wrongful act. 如trespass to try title（美国请求损害赔偿并确定所侵占不动产权利归属的诉讼），trespass on the case（间接侵犯行为诉讼）。
5 assault and battery: 威胁与殴打。二者各自独立构成两种侵权类型，如assault and battery连在一起不可分，则是指刑法上的battery（殴打罪）。

Lesson 7
Tort Law

imprisonment, and the reputation, through the torts of libel[1], slander, malicious prosecution[2] and injurious falsehood[3]. When negligence[4] was first officially recognized as a separate tort in early 20th century, negligence has been of central importance. The vast majority of tort claims[5] today are for negligence, and negligence has proved the most appropriate action in modern conditions, especially since the development of the motor car.

Tortious liability arises from the breach of a duty primarily fixed by law; this duty is towards persons generally and its breach is redressable[6] by an action for unliquidated damages[7].

To understand the definition given above, it is necessary to distinguish tort from other branches of the law, and in so doing to discover how the aims of tort differ from the aims of other areas of law such as contract law or criminal law.

a. Tort and Crime

The laws of tort and crime, despite their common origin in revenge and deterrence[8], long ago parted company and assumed distinctly separate functions. A crime is an offence against the State, as representative of the public, which will

---

1　libel: 书面诽谤。A defamatory statement expressed in a fixed medium, especially writing but also a picture, a sign or electronic broadcast.
2　malicious prosecution: 恶意控诉，诬告。The tort of initiating a criminal prosecution or civil suit against another party with malice and without probable cause.
3　injurious falsehood: 诬蔑，诋毁。Disparagement, a false and injurious statement that detracts from the reputation of another's property, product or business. 特点是造谣中伤，以降低他人的商誉或其他名誉。
4　negligence: （侵权法中）过失侵权。[in tort] failure to exercise the degree of care expected of a person of ordinary prudence in like circumstances in protecting others from a foreseeable and unreasonable risk of harm in a particular situation.
5　claim: 请求，主张等。(a) a demand for money or property due. （有权）请求，要求；(b) a right to seek a judicial remedy arising from a wrong or injury suffered. 向法庭请求损害赔偿的请求权；(c) the formal assertion of an existing right. 权利主张。这里是第一个含义。
6　redressable: 可获得救济。Worthwhile redress. 比较常用的是redress *n*. 意为remedy 或relief。
7　unliquidated damages: 未约定数额的损害赔偿金。与liquidated damages相对应。Damages whose amount is agreed upon by the parties to a contract as adequately compensating for loss in the event of a breach. 即合同双方事先约定的合同违约时向对方支付的损失补偿，其数额或是数额具体计算方法是违反合同义务前确定的。unliquidated damages在这里就是指数额或是具体计算方法没有，也不可能在违反义务前确定的损害赔偿。所以需要提起损害赔偿诉讼，请求法官确定赔偿数额。该定义引自Rogers, Winfield & Jolowicz on Tort, 15th ed., 1998, London: Sweet & Maxwell, p. 4.
8　deterrence: 妨碍，阻却。The inhibition of criminal behavior by fear especially of punishment. （通过威慑来）阻却（不法行为）。这是指人类经历了从无限制复仇到同态复仇直至放弃复仇的过程，最终用刑法与侵权法，特别是刑法代替了复仇。由国家代替被害方对侵害人进行惩罚，最根本的目的，是为了防止当事人之间无休止的同态复仇。

vindicate its interests by punishing the offender. A criminal prosecution is not concerned with repairing an injury that may have been done to an individual, but with exacting a penalty[1] in order to protect society as a whole. Tort liability, on the other hand, exists primarily to compensate the victim by compelling the wrongdoer to pay for the damage he has done. The same fact situation, for example, a road accident, may lead both to criminal prosecutions and to tort actions. Tort, as part of civil law, is concerned with actions by private individuals against other individuals or legal persons[2]. Criminal law is concerned with prosecutions brought on behalf of the state for breaches of duties imposed upon individuals for the protection of society.

If I punch you in the face, that is a crime and a civil wrong (both the crime and the tort of battery). The one event gives rise to two legal responses. First, I may be prosecuted by the state for committing the criminal offence and if found guilty by the court, made to pay a fine to the state, sent to prison or punished in some other way. Secondly, I may be sued by you in the civil courts and if found liable, ordered to pay you a sum of money (damages) or to change my behaviour in the future (by an injunction[3]). It is those individuals, not the state, who stand to benefit directly from a court judgment against the defendant. The standard of proof in criminal cases is more stringent than in civil cases and the consequence of a finding of criminal guilt may be regarded as more serious for the individual concerned.

b. Tort and Contract

Many liabilities in tort arise by virtue of the law alone and are not fixed by the parties. The law imposes in tort not to libel people, not to trespass on their land, and so on. The details of these duties are fixed by the law itself and not by the parties. By contrast, the law of contract is based notionally on agreements, the terms of which are fixed by the parties. Therefore, the parties in tort usually have no contact

---

1 penalty: 惩罚。Punishment imposed on a wrongdoer, especially in the form of imprisonment or fine. 这里指刑罚，即触犯了刑法而依据法律规定强加于被告人的各种惩罚。
2 legal person：法人。A body of persons or an entity (as a corporation) considered as having many of the rights and responsibilities of a natural person and especially the capacity to sue and be sued. 是法律拟制的人，依据法律可以享有人的大多数权利（尤其是起诉与被诉权）的人的集合或是法律实体。与"自然人"相对应。
3 injunction: 禁令。An equitable remedy in the form of a court order compelling a party to do or refrain from doing a specified act. 由法庭发出，强制当事人为或不为某种行为，为衡平法上的救济方法。

before the tort is committed. The pedestrian who is injured by a negligent motorist will probably never have met the defendant until the accident which gives rise to the legal action[1]. Of contract, it is often said that the parties will, through negotiation or by every act of contracting, have had some contact and be fully aware of their legal duties before any breach of contract occurs.

The remedy for breach of duty in tort is usually a claim for damages, though equitable remedies[2] are also available in appropriate cases. The main aim of tort is said to be compensation for harm suffered as a result of the breach of a duty fixed by law and deterrence of behaviour which is likely to cause harm. The main aim of contract on the other hand is to support and enforce contractual promises, and to deter breaches of contract.

Since the rise of the tort of negligence, the law of tort places great emphasis on the need to prove fault[3]. The aim here is to compensate for wrongs suffered through the fault of another person. Damages will usually only be awarded in tort if the claimant can establish fault. Contract on the other hand has been less concerned with fault as a basis of liability, and it is unnecessary to prove fault in order to be compensated for a breach of contract.

II. Negligence

Tort liability is customarily divided into intentional, negligent and strict liability torts. What is the central and most important is liability for negligent harm. The elements of this liability are: (a) a duty of care, (b) breach of that duty by negligent conduct (act of commission or omission), (c) causing injury, and (d) subject to the

---

1 action: 诉讼。action, a civil or criminal judicial proceeding. lawsuit一般指非刑事案件。
2 equitable remedies: 衡平性救济。Nonmonetary remedies, such as an injunction of specific performance, obtained when monetary damages cannot adequately redress the injury. 在某些案件中，单凭赔偿金本身还不足以解决争执，这时法庭就会采取衡平性救济，最常见的就是我们所说的禁令（injunction）。例如，某废品处理公司在城镇的水库旁堆放含有有毒化学物质的垃圾，那么该镇除向法院申请损失赔偿金（damages），还可以向法庭申请阻止性禁令（prohibitory injunction）禁止该公司继续堆放垃圾以及强制性禁令（mandatory injunction）强迫该公司移走垃圾。
3 fault:（判断上或行为上的）过错。An error or defect of judgment or of conduct. 与wrong相区别。

defenses of assumption of risk[1] and contributory negligence[2].

a. Duty of Care

"The rule that you are to love your neighbour becomes in law, you must not injure your neighbour and the lawyer's question, 'Who is my neighbour?' receives a restricted reply. You must take reasonable care to avoid acts or omissions which you can reasonably foresee would be likely to injure your neighbour. Who, then, in law is my neighbour? The answer seems to be—persons who are so closely and directly affected by my act that I ought reasonably to have them in contemplation as being so affected when I am directing my mind to the acts or omissions which are called in question."

This is Lord Atkin's "Neighbour Principle"[3], probably the most important 104 words ever spoken by a judge in the world, of which the impact cannot be overstated.

The defendant must be under a duty of care for the benefit of the plaintiff before his carelessness can incur liability. Whether such a duty exists in the particular relationship between the parties is a question of law to be decided by the judge. In the absence of precedent the most important determinant is foreseeability[4] of injury, but legal policy has the last word. One formula lists among the most important factors: the closeness of the connection between the injury and the defendant's conduct, the moral blame attached to the defendant's conduct, the policy of preventing future harm, and the prevalence and availability of insurance.

b. Breach of Duty

Negligence consists in conduct fraught with unreasonable risk of harm, or more

---

1 assumption of risk: 风险自负，人身侵权赔偿诉讼发展得来的一条免责理由。The plaintiff cannot receive compensation for injuries from the defendant because the plaintiff freely and knowingly assumed the risk of injury and relieved the defendant of the obligation to act with reasonable care.
2 contributory negligence: 共同过失或互有过失。指被害人的损害是由被害人和侵权行为人的共同过失所致。这是英美侵权法上近年来几近废弃的一项制度，即如果原告因过失未能对自身安全履行相应的注意义务，且该过失客观上促成了该项损害的发生，则过失侵权人全部免责，原告不能就此项损害向被告要求任何赔偿。
3 这是英国法官阿特金勋爵在 *Donoghue v. Stevenson* 这一著名案例中提出的，该案被认为是英国"过失侵权行为"的源头，也是"危险物责任"和"产品责任"的源头。此案中，Donoghue太太喝完朋友给她买的一瓶姜汁啤酒后，发现在这只不透明的瓶子里居然有一只未完全腐烂的蜗牛。她起诉了制造商，认为他们有责任去发现蜗牛，防止其外壳不进到啤酒里去。英国上议院的简单多数认为，制造商有责任采取合理的注意。
4 foreseeability: 可预见性。判断可预见性一般要问的问题是：一个理性人能否预见被告的行为会造成损害，而并非问该被告是否追求这样的损害。

Lesson 7
Tort Law

simply, in failure to observe the care of a reasonable person[1] in like circumstances. This is preeminently a jury issue. The standard is objective and individual failings do not excuse the actor from liability. There are some exceptions: for example, physical infirmities[2], provided the handicapped person took care to compensate for his disability. Also, children are judged by the standard of reasonable behavior of children of like age, intelligence, and experience except when engaged in adult activities like driving automobiles (*Robinson* v. *Lindsay*[3]).

c. Causation

Actual injury is a necessary element of liability for negligence. There are two aspects. First, was the defendant's conduct a "cause in fact" of the injury? That is to say, the plaintiff must prove that harm would not have occurred 'but for' the negligence of the defendant. The burden of proof ordinarily rests on the plaintiff to establish this relationship on a "balance of probabilities"[4]. Secondly, the negligence must not only be the cause, but the proximate cause of the injury. There is no consensus on how to determine proximity.

d. Defenses

There are two defenses to negligence claims: contributory negligence and voluntary assumption of risk.

Contributory negligence bars a party from recovering for damages if he or she contributed in any way to the injury, but recently has been modified so as merely to

---

1 reasonable person (man): （法律上的）理性人。A reasonable person is a hypothetical individual with an ordinary degree of reason, prudence, care, foresight, or intelligence whose conduct, conclusion, or expectation in relation to a particular circumstance or fact is used as an objective standard by which to measure or determine something (as the existence of negligence). The reasonable man or reasonable person standard is a legal fiction that originated in the development of the common law. The question, "How would a reasonable person act under the circumstances" performs a critical role in legal reasoning. e.g. "We have generally held that a reasonable person would not believe that he or she has been seized when an officer merely approaches that person in a public place and begins to ask questions."
2 infirmity: 身体残疾。A bodily ailment or weakness. 身体极度虚弱，这里是身体残疾的委婉说法。
3 此案中，13岁的被告驾驶一辆雪地摩托，用绳子拖拉坐在轮胎上的原告，将原告的大拇指卷入绳子致残。此案法庭采用成年人的注意义务标准来衡量身为未成年人的被告驾驶机动车时是否违反注意义务。
4 balance of probabilities: 或然性权衡，英美法民事诉讼程序所采用的一种证明标准，即事实存在的可能性高于其不可能性。

reduce damages. Where this reform of "comparative negligence"[1] was carried out, it is mostly conditional on the plaintiff's fault being no greater than the defendant's, and nowadays comparative and contributory negligence are both used as defenses available to mitigate the amount that a defendant may have to pay to a plaintiff for damages.

Voluntary assumption of risk used to play a big role in defeating actions by employees against their employers or co-employees. It is an affirmative defense that a plaintiff is not entitled to compensation if, knowing of a dangerous condition, he voluntarily exposed himself to the risk that resulted in injury. Assumption of risk may be expressed or may be implied from the plaintiff's words and actions. Today it is virtually confined to passengers of drunk drivers and spectators of sporting events like baseball or hockey.

e. Damages

Damages are awarded in lump sums once-and-for-all, not by periodic payments subject to variation. Damages are either pecuniary or non-pecuniary loss, known respectively as special or general damages. The former compensate for medical costs and loss of earnings, past and future. For non-pecuniary damages, called general damages or damages for pain and suffering, juries are given a very free hand, there being no tariffs. Though general damages for emotional distress have been traditionally confined to tort, awards are allowed in certain contract lawsuits as treating "malicious breach" of contract as torts. Punitive or exemplary damages are increasingly assuming major importance. Their purpose is to punish the tortfeasor[2] for atrocious misconduct, not to compensate the plaintiff for his humiliation and anger, which is the function of general damages.

III. Strict Liability

By the middle of the 19th century, an earlier tradition of stricter liability had

---

1 comparative negligence: 相对过失，这是英美侵权法继共同过失之后的一种侵权责任以及损害赔偿认定方式。当损害是部分由于受害人的过错所致，不得以受害人有过错为由驳回其赔偿请求，但他们应得的损害赔偿金应由法官酌情减至公平合理的程度。Negligence and damages are determined by reference to the proportionate fault of the plaintiff and defendant with the negligence of the plaintiff not constituting an absolute bar to recovery from the defendant. 即对原被告的过失行为在程度上加以比较，以确定责任以及赔偿承担比例。

2 tortfeasor: 侵权行为人。One who commits a tort.

Lesson 7
Tort Law

been repudiated in favor of the principle "no liability without fault". 150 years later no-fault liability is again making big strides.

Strict liability makes some persons responsible for damages their actions or products cause, regardless of any "fault" on their part. Shifting the burden of proof, or at least producing evidence, to the defendant under relaxed conditions of res ipsa loquitur[1] is a straddle between negligence and strict liability.

Strict liability is mainly recognized in the following situations:

Abnormally Dangerous Activities Strict liability often applies when people engage in inherently hazardous activities, such as bursting dams, "blowing-out" oil wells, testing rocket motors, or blasting on a construction site. If you are injured by the activities-no matter how careful the doer was—he/she is liable for the injury. Extension of strict liability to automobile driving has been refused as an exception generally allowed for common usage.

Vicarious Liability[2] An employer is liable, regardless of fault either in hiring or supervision, for the torts of its employees committed in the course of their employment. The guilty employee is liable as a joint tortfeasor, though judgment is rarely executed against that party.

Products Liability[3] Strict liability also may apply in the case of certain manufactured products. In strict product liability, typically anyone who is engaged in the stream of commence of the product (from the manufacturer to the wholesaler to the retailer, or all of them) can be held responsible if the product was defective and someone was injured. There is no need to prove negligence but the injured party must prove that the product was defective.

Defective products may be the result of bad manufacturing for the failure to provide adequate instructions for the use of the product. Those engaged in the stream

---

1. res ipsa loquitur：事情不言自明，或称事实自证。The thing speaks for itself. 一般用于过失侵权诉讼中，指事件发生的本身就可以证明过失的存在。Under specified circumstances, this principle allows the judge and/or the jury to draw from circumstantial evidence submitted by the plaintiff the conclusion that the defendant was negligent and is thus liable to the plaintiff.
2. vicarious liability：转承责任。Liability that a supervisory party bears for the actionable conduct of a subordinate because of the relationship between the two parties.
3. Products Liability：产品责任。The liability imposed on a manufacturer or seller for a defective and unreasonably dangerous product. 产品严格责任的认定不要求原告与销售商或是生产商事先具有合同关系。但原告必须证明产品在购买时就具有瑕疵，并且按规定用途进行正当使用。

of commence with respect to products should reasonably foresee that some people will misuse the product and should design the product so that injury does not occur.

IV. Intentional Torts

a. Personal Injuries

Among the historically oldest of the intentional delicts are the trespass torts of assault, battery, and false imprisonment. Assault[1] consists of intentionally putting another in apprehension (not fear) of immediate physical contact and battery[2] consists of inflicting such a contact, which is unlawful, unconsented. Both protect the basic right to one's bodily integrity against physical harm. False imprisonment[3] consists of confining a person or preventing him from leaving the place where he is. Neither actual force nor physical contact is required so long as the plaintiff's will is overborne. Bearing some resemblance is the tort of malicious prosecution, which consists of maliciously and without reasonable and probable causes instituting groundless legal proceedings, especially criminal prosecutions.

b. Property Wrongs

Trespass to the person had its counterpart in trespass to land and chattels[4]. Any direct interference, such as entering land without the occupier's consent or dispossessing him of a book, a hat, or a picture is thus actionable. Proof of actual damages is not required and the interference must have been intended[5]. The action for conversion[6] provides a more comprehensive remedy for interference with possessory

---

1. assault：（侵权法上）威胁。(1)the act of threatening or attempting to inflict immediate offensive physical contact or bodily harm that one has the present ability to inflict and that puts the victim in fear of such harm or contact [in tort law]; or (2)the act of assault accompanied by battery [in criminal law]. 指对他人非法试图施用暴力或恐吓使用暴力，而被威胁者有理由相信其人有现实的能力实现其目的。
2. battery：殴打。An intentional and offensive touching of another without lawful justification.指无正当理由、未经他人同意而故意以武力攻击其身体或造成其身体伤害。这必须有触碰到原告的身体，虽然这种触碰可能是被告间接造成的。例如向原告投掷物体、向原告食物里投毒或违反原告意愿强迫其接受身体检查等，都被视为是英美侵权法上的殴打。assault and battery 是指刑法上battery（殴打罪）。
3. false imprisonment：非法限制人身自由，非法禁锢。The tort of intentionally restraining another by physical force or the threat of physical force without privilege or authority.
4. chattel：动产。Movable or transferable property.
5. 对财产的侵犯一般为故意，如果是过失，则要求有实际损失才能算作侵权。
6. conversion：侵占（动产）。The crime or tort of interfering with the ownership of another's movable or personal property without authorization or justification and especially of depriving the owner of use and possession. 形式多样，不仅限于非法移走，还包括原先合法占有，但拒绝返还，或是将动产转移给非合法所有者，以及否认合法所有者的权利。

Lesson 7
Tort Law

rights in chattels.

c. Defenses

Defenses to intentional misconducts are mistake[1], consent, defense of self and others, defense and recovery of property, necessity and legal authority.

V. Reputation and Privacy

a. Defamation

A communication[2] is defamatory if it tends to harm plaintiff's reputation in the community, either by lowering others' estimation of him, or deterring others from associating or dealing with him. Examples include communications which expose plaintiff to hatred, contempt, or ridicule; which reflect unfavorably on his morality or integrity; or which impair his financial reputation. Written defamation is known as libel, oral defamation as slander. The former is actionable per se[3], the latter only on proof of special damage, that is, pecuniary loss. Communication must be to a third person because defamation is concerned with reputation, not dignity as such. A lone confrontation with the plaintiff or an insult is not actionable.

b. Privacy

Invasion of privacy became recognized as a tort in the 20th century. It may take four different forms: (1) intrusion, like bugging a home; (2) misappropriation of personality, such as commercialization of one's name or face; (3) putting someone in a false light by non-defamatory but embarrassing falsehoods; and (4) publicity of private facts. Publication of contemporary newsworthy matter is privileged.

---

1 一般来讲，错误（包括认识错误或行为错误）不能作为故意侵权的抗辩理由，如你砍倒了别人的树，却以为那是自己的树。你仍需为砍倒的树进行赔偿，以防止不当得利。但是如果警察有合理由相信，确是错误认为某人违反了法律进行而拘捕，错误就可以作为侵权的抗辩理由，因为警察的目的是保护社会治安。
2 communication: The exchange of thoughts, messages, or information, as by speech, signals, writing, or behavior. 这里指意思的表达、观点的交流。
3 actionable per se: 当然诽谤，即便原告无法提供或不予提供任何实际损害的证明，法官仍可推断损害严重性需要进行赔偿。

Glossary

action 诉讼
assumption of risk 自愿承担风险
battery 非法侵犯;殴击罪(刑法)
claim (有权)请求;要求;向法庭请求损害赔偿的请求权
comparative negligence 相对过失;比较过失
contributory negligence 共同过失;互有过失
conversion 侵占(动产)
deterrence (通过威慑来)阻却(不法行为)
equitable remedies 衡平救济
false imprisonment 非法限制人身自由;非法禁锢
forseeability 可预见性
infirmity 身体虚弱
injunction 禁令
injurious falsehood 诬蔑;诋毁
legal person 法人;法律拟制人

libel 书面诽谤
liquidated damages 预定损害赔偿金;违约金
malicious prosecution 恶意控诉;诬告
negligence 过失侵权;过失
nuisance 滋扰;妨碍
penalty 刑罚
Products Liability 产品责任
reasonable person (man) (法律上的)理性人
redressable 可获得救济的
remedy 救济、补偿
res ipsa loquitur 事情不言自明;事实自证
tortfeasor 侵权行为人
trespass on the case 间接侵害行为
trespass to chattel 侵犯动产
trespass to land 对土地的侵犯
wrong 过错行为;不法行为

EXERCISES

I. Answer the following questions.

1. Can tort liabilities and crime arise in the same situation?
2. How do you distinguish tort and crime?
3. What is the assumption of risk?
4. What does "special damages" cover?
5. What is the difference between libel and slander?

II. Translate the following terms into English.

1. 注意义务
2. 损害赔偿金
3. 过失侵权
4. 衡平法上的救济

Lesson 7
Tort Law

5. 言辞诽谤
6. 诽谤（统称）
7. 非法禁锢
8. 威胁
9. 殴打
10. 禁令
11. 因果关系
12. 理性人
13. 故意侵权
14. 侵犯动产
15. 恶意控告

III. Translate the following sentences into Chinese.

1. The claimant must produce evidence which infers a lack of reasonable care on the part of the defendant.
2. If harm is foreseeable but occurs in an unforeseeable way there may still be liability.
3. If the danger of a serious accident outweighs the burden or inconvenience of taking precautions to avoid the accident, the reasonable person would take those precautions.
4. If the defendant has violated a statute, the unexcused violation might be considered negligence per se, create a presumption of negligence, or simply be some evidence of negligence.

IV. Fill the blanks with proper adverbs or prepositions.

Multiple tortfeasors are classified 1_____ either joint or concurrent. The principal example of the first is that of two or more acting 2_____ concert, for example, to engage 3_____ a road race, in which event all are liable regardless 4_____ which one of them caused the injury. Concurrent tortfeasors are those who, acting independently, cause an indivisible injury, for example, by colliding 5_____ each other and harming a passenger. Each is liable in toto (the so-called joint and several liability rule), but the plaintiff may collect 6_____ any one or both any amount until he has recovered 100 percent of his loss. As 7_____ them, they can claim contribution if one has paid more than his appropriate share. But 8_____ practice it will often happen that the "deep pocket" defendant will end up paying most, if not all, the damages.

Supplementary Reading

The issues raised by the road traffic accident described below illustrate some facets of the objectives of tort and its relationship with other systems of compensation.

A, a man aged 27, had consumed five pints of beer in a public house one Sunday lunchtime. He left for home on foot in the early afternoon when road and weather conditions were good. His route took him across a busy main road close to the centre of a city, but as this was a quiet Sunday, he decided to take a chance and cross the road some distance from the traffic lights and adjoining pedestrian crossing. He looked to the right and noticed that the lights were red and that there were two cars just approaching the traffic lights. Then he looked to the left and began to cross the road. As he reached the centre of the first carriageway, he realized that the cars were now approaching at speed and that he might not be able to reach the central reservation. He dithered[1] for a moment and the next thing he knew he was hit by the car driven by B. A was taken to hospital and detained there for 10 weeks suffering from multiple injuries. After leaving hospital, A slowly recovered, but still suffered from mild post-traumatic stress disorder[2] and has pain in his legs which were operated on immediately after the accident. A will always walk with a slight limp and he has numerous scars on his face and arms, and will require cosmetic dental treatment[3] to replace damaged teeth. He is paying for private dental treatment and hopes to recover the cost of this from B. The estimated speed of the car which hit A was 45 mph in a 30 mph limit and he is lucky to have survived at all. B was convicted by magistrates[4] of driving without due care and attention, and was fined £150 and given nine penalty points.

A is now seeking compensation from B by means of tort action. He is still angry about having been injured by B and would like to see B suffer by being brought before a civil

---

1 dither: 不知所措。
2 post-traumatic stress disorder(PTSD): 创伤后遗症。不论是亲身经历灾难的幸存者，协助救灾的救难人员，或经由媒体观看灾难的一般民众，灾难事件可能对他们造成一系列伤害，导致其心理创伤，统称为创伤后遗症。
3 cosmetic dental treatment: 牙科整形治疗。
4 magistrate: （英）治安法官。治安法院（magistrate's court）一般由二三个治安法官组成，主要负责审理轻微刑事案件和有限的民事案件，执行简易程序。

Lesson 7
Tort Law

court because he believes that B "got of much too lightly" in the magistrates' court. A is also hoping to receive a large sum by way of compensation from the pain he has suffered.

A has received a large sum in state benefits[1] during the recovery period. He is surprised to learn that this will be deducted from any award[2] of damages which he will receive. He is also surprised to discover that because he has made such a good recovery he will not receive a particularly high award. A was found at least 25% contributory negligent because he told the doctor that he had drunk five pints of beer just before the accident. Witnesses have stated that they thought he took a chance in trying to cross the road when he did.

In the event, the case never reaches court. A is told that a sum of £10,000 has been paid to court by lawyers acting for B's insurance company. He is advised to accept this because his barrister is concerned that there may be a finding of a high percentage of contributory negligence (up to 40%), which means a lower award made by the judge. The case is finally settled three years after the accident for £12,000.

B is now having to pay much higher motor insurance premiums and is worried about losing his license if he is prosecuted for another driving offence in the near future. A does not know about this.

Apparently, not all the objectives of tort have been met in this situation. To take the picture from A's perspective: the tort system has protected A's interests through the negligence action. However, A does not feel that he has had the revenge, a criminal law matters in any event. He has had the support of the state benefits during the most crucial period of his hospitalization and recovery, but feels that he has had to wait much too long to obtain his tort damages. He is disappointed that he will only receive part of the compensation which he thought he deserved because the case is to be settled out of court, and he had never heard about contributory negligence before this happened to him.

As far as B is concerned, tort has had some deterrent effect because he will now probably drive more carefully, at least for a while, to avoid having to go on paying higher insurance premiums, as these will gradually be reduced if he has no more accidents. He has probably had some sleepless nights worrying about what will happen, but he is

---

1 state benefit: 官方补助。指政府为符合一定条件、具有经济困难的人群提供一定的福利与补助。
2 award: 这里指法院判决。

reassured that the insurance company will pay any compensation.

From the point of view of society as a whole, tort has ensured that A is compensated. The insurance system has to some extent been driven by tort, and B's original insurance cover which provided the compensation was compulsory under the Road Traffic Act. Compulsory insurance for motorists means that all motorists help to pay compensation to people who are injured like A. This has achieved a form of loss distribution. The general deterrent effect of contributory negligence is minimal. A had never even heard of the rule and there are many road users who have not. The law has allowed recovery of the cost of A's financial support form B's insurance company but the state benefit system has proved quicker and more efficient than the tort system in providing medical care and money to A at the very time he needed them.

Lesson 8
Company Law[1]

Where there is a right, there is a remedy.

凡有权利必有救济。

I. Types of Business Entity[2]

There exist a number of business structures that differ greatly in several important aspects. Some of the common trading entities are as follows:

a. Sole Proprietorships[3]

Being a sole proprietorship is the simplest way to run one-person business. The sole trader runs the business, carries all the responsibilities and is entitled[4] to all the profits. The costs of formation are very low and there are fewer formalities required. A sole trader has the benefit of the complete control of his business. However, he is personally responsible for any debts run up by his business, which means he runs the risk of being made bankrupt and losing most of his possessions if the business runs into trouble. Being a sole proprietorship is relatively uncomplicated and consequently is cheap and convenient for many small businesses.

---

1 本文除标题上的"company law"按照使用习惯译成公司法以外,其余出现的company全按照严格法律意义,译成"企业"。因为company一词在美国可以指非法人组织的企业,但是在英国一般来指具独立法律人格、享受有限责任的法人组织。
2 (legal) entity: 法律实体。An organization having under the law rights and responsibilities and esp. the capacity to sue and be sued. 依法可以享有权利承担义务,并能以自己名义起诉应诉的组织。
3 sole proprietorship: (个人)独资企业。A business owned and controlled by one person who is solely liable for its obligations.
4 entitle: 给予权利。To give an enforceable right to claim something. 通常用被动语态。e.g., In any lawsuit that you win, you are entitled to reimbursement for court costs and attorney's fees.

b. Partnerships[1]

In a partnership, two or more people share the risks, costs, and responsibilities of being in business. As with sole traders, partners are also responsible for all the debts incurred by the business. Each partner invests a certain amount (money, assets[2] and/or effort) which establishes an agreed-upon percentage of ownership, and is responsible for all the debts and contracts of the partnership even though another partner created the debt or entered into the contract, has a share in management decisions, and shares in profits and losses according to the percentage of the total investment. There is no need for a partnership to be registered[3] in some countries. Indeed, there is no need even for a written agreement between the partners. A partnership can arise merely by two or more people agreeing to trade together in the hope of making a profit. Although there is slightly more regulation of a partnership than a sole proprietorship, a partnership is still relatively unregulated.

c. Limited Companies

By contrast, limited companies are extensively regulated, and must be registered. The shareholders[4] (members) have limited liabilities and are not generally personally liable for the company's debts, as will be seen in greater detail later.

d. Limited Partnerships[5]

A limited partnership consists of two or more persons, with at least one general partner and one limited partner. It is run by the general partners, who have unlimited liability for its debts. While limited partners are merely investors in the business, and their liability is limited to the amount of their investment in the company. However, if they take any part in the management of the business they lose the benefit of their

---

1 partnership: 没有特指的情况下，指的是普通合伙（general partnership），即所有合伙人均为普通合伙人，对合伙企业债务承担无限连带责任。
2 asset: 资产，有经济价值的东西。Property, including real property (for example, land or buildings) and personal property (for example, cash, stocks or vehicles) that belong to a person, corporation, estate, or other entity; or a resource that has economic value to its owner. 通常用复数。
3 register: 注册，登记。公司成立要件之一，在符合成立条件的情况下，向有关主管部门履行一定手续。一般公司必须注册方能成立。其他类型的企业是否需登记注册，各国法律规定不一。
4 shareholder: 股东。One that owns a share in a fund or property. 在某项财产中拥有份额的人。这里专指公司的股东。后文有详细界定。
5 Limited Partnership: 简称LP，有限合伙制。在普通合伙基础上发展起来的新合伙形式，即合伙企业中存在两种合伙人（普通合伙人和有限合伙人），二者在企业内外的权利义务均不一致。

limited liability altogether. A limited partnership has to be registered, and is especially useful for raising capital since it permits investors to participate financially in the business without incurring personal liability.

e. Limited Liability Partnerships[6]

The limited liability partnership is similar to a limited partnership except that all partners enjoy limited liability, and it is similar to an ordinary partnership in that a number of individuals or limited companies share in the risks, costs, responsibilities and profits of the business. Limited liability partnerships are common among professionals such as attorneys and accountants, who are not allowed to use corporations to limit their liability[7]. Limited liability partnerships offer both pass-through taxation of a partnership and the liability protection of a corporation.

II. Corporations

The corporation is the most common and complicated form of business among large companies. It is a legal entity that is separate and distinct from its owners in the eyes of the law. No shareholder of a corporation is personally liable for the debts, obligations or acts of the corporation. As a separate entity, corporations have several distinguishing characteristics including limited liability, easy transferability of shares, and perpetual existence. Corporations also have centralized management who may be different persons from the actual owners.

a. Types of Corporations

US corporations are generally classified into C Corporations, S Corporations, close corporations[8], professional corporations[9] and non-for-

---

6 Limited Liability Partnership: 简称LLP，有限责任合伙制。是英美法中新近引入的概念，最初出现于美国合伙法。它是一种把公司股东的有限责任与合伙制度固有的经营上的灵活性结合起来，又适用一般合伙法的新型合伙形式。由于具有其适应社会需要的客观必要性与内在的合理性，现在LLP在世界各地流行。
7 这里指的是英国的情况。在美国，如果符合一定要求，律师或会计师等职业可以组建professional corporation。
8 close corporation：封闭公司。A close corporation is a corporation whose shares are held by a small number of individuals (as management) and not freely or publicly traded.
9 professional corporation: 专业公司。A professional corporation is a corporation organized by one or more licensed individuals (as a doctor, accountant or lawyer) to provide professional services and obtain tax advantages. 在美国用来指那些提供专业服务的公司。

profit corporations[1], and in Britain, there are mainly public and private corporations, corporations limited by shares[2] and corporations limited by guarantee[3]. Traditionally, there are holding[4] and subsidiary corporations, single member corporations[5].

b. S Corporations vs. C Corporations[6]

An S Corporation is simply a C Corporation (also known as a standard business corporation) that elects a special tax status with the Internal Revenue Service[7]. The articles of incorporation that are filed with the state are the same whether a corporation is a C Corporation or S Corporation. They both are separate legal entities, and both offer the same limited liability protection, the owners are typically not personally responsible for the debts and liabilities of the business. Both entities are required to follow the same formalities. They must hold annual meeting of shareholders and directors are required each year and meeting minutes must be kept with the corporate records.

However, they differ greatly in certain aspects.

Taxation The S Corporation is a pass-through[8] tax entity—this means that the income or loss generated by the business is reflected on the personal income tax return of the owners, while a C Corporation is a separately taxable entity. The profits and losses are taxed directly to the corporation. This can lead to double taxation on

---

1 non-for-profit corporation：非营利性公司，一般为教育或慈善等目的成立的法人组织，享受特别税收优惠。
2 corporation limited by shares：〈英〉股份有限公司，是跟担保有限公司相对立的一种公司形式。这种公司在成立时股东需缴纳一定的注册资本，但不一定要全额缴纳。
3 corporation limited by guarantee：〈英〉担保有限公司，这种公司成立时并没有注册资本。成员的责任只限于各成员在公司组织大纲上承诺的在公司一旦清算时，所分别分担提供的公司资产的款额。
4 holding corporation: 控股公司。A holding corporation is a corporation whose sole function is to own and control other companies.
5 single member corporation: 一人公司。传统公司法理论不认可仅有一个成员的公司的法人资格，认为其违背了公司法基本理念。但实质上的一人公司无法避免，目前各国的趋势是逐步认可一人公司的法律资格，同时立法加以规范，防止利用法人组织的便利损害他人利益。
6 S公司与C公司是对应的法律概念，它们都是美国联邦税收法典S节和C节中依据双重征税与否的标准，就公司形态所作的划分。S Corporation, called also "subchapter S Corporation", a small business corporation that is treated for federal tax purposes as a partnership.专业公司一般采用S Corporation 的付税方式，如此可免交公司的联邦所得税。相比之下，C corporation公司的法律限制较少，但却是双层征税主体。这种税法上的不同待遇实际上是鼓励支持中小企业的法律手段之一。
7 Internal Revenue Service：美国国内税务署，缩写为IRS。
8 pass-through (taxation)：单层征税。pass-through, the taxation of an entity's owners for the entity's income without taxing the entity itself.税收方式的一种，即不向企业本身征税，与既向企业征税又向企业所有者征税的double taxation相对应。

Lesson 8
Company Law

dividends[1] that are paid out of corporate profits to the owners.

Ownership   The ownership of an S Corporation is restricted; however, the C Corporation does not possess these same limitations. The following are some of the restrictions imposed by the IRS:

• The number of shareholders of a C Corporation is not limited while an S Corporation is restricted to no more than 35 shareholders;

• Non-US residents can be owners of a C Corporation while an S Corporation may not have non-US residents as shareholders; and

• A C Corporation is allowed to have business organizations including corporations as shareholders, while the shareholders of an S Corporation must be individuals or certain estates and trusts.

c. Public Corporations vs. Private Corporations[2]

A public corporation has to satisfy four criteria, which are designed to put potential investors and creditors on notice that the corporation has a minimum level of capital and could potentially, at some stage, offer its share for sale to the public:

Its nature of being a public corporation must be stated in its memorandum; its name must end with the words "public limited corporation" (plc); the nominal value of its issued capital must be at least £50,000, and it must be registered as a public corporation.

Any corporation not a public corporation is a private corporation. Private corporations don't have to comply with certain procedural requirements as public corporations do. It is one of the measures to reduce the procedural burdens on small corporations.

---

1 dividend: 股息，红利。A portion of a company's earnings or profits distributed to its shareholders usually in the form of cash or additional shares.
2 Public Corporation:〈英〉公众公司。In Britain, a Public Corporation is also called a public held corporation, a business corporation whose stocks are publicly traded. 指股份可以公开流通的公司。而在美国，public corporation 是指公益公司，即基于公益的、由政府投资并控制的公司。Private Corporation: a corporation founded by and composed of private individuals principally for nonpublic purpose, such as manufacturing, banking, and railroad corporations. 与public corporation相对，股份一般不公开流通，股东也相对固定。是最常见的一种小型公司，某些重要特征与美国的close corporation相类似。"私人公司"的习惯译法实质不够准确，应为"非公众公司"。

A public corporation may have its shares listed[1]. Floating[2] on the stock exchange is an effective way of raising large amounts of capital for investment in the corporation's business: on flotation the wider public is invited to subscribe for shares in the corporation.

III. The Elements of a Corporation

The people who provide the money to run the business of the corporation are called shareholders or members. They put money into the business by buying shares from the corporation. Their rights and liabilities are governed by the constitution of the corporation contained in the memorandum and articles of association[3]. It is usually (though not universal) for a share to carry voting rights. Many of the decisions necessary for the running of a corporation can be arrived at by a majority vote of the shareholders taken at a meeting. However, it would be cumbersome for the everyday running of the business to be conducted in this way, so the corporation votes that certain people should be 'directors' of the corporation and should take care of the everyday running of the corporation. The meeting of shareholders has the right to appoint and remove directors by majority vote.

a. Nature of Memorandum and Articles

The memorandum of association contains certain important information: the corporation's name, country of registration, objects, amount and division of share capital. The articles comprise the regulations governing the running of the corporation. Together the memorandum and articles form the constitution of the corporation. They bind all the members and are valued as the charter of the corporation.

b. The Interest of the Owners

An essential step in the establishment of a corporation is that the subscribers

---

1 list:（股票）上市。To register (a security) on an exchange so that it may be publicly traded.
2 float:（票据）流通。To issue (a security) for sale on the market.
3 memorandum and articles of association: 美国分别称为设立章程（Certificate of Incorporation; Articles of Incorporation）与附属章程（By-Laws）。前者是用以指导公司与外界关系的，被称为公司的外在宪章（External Constitution），是法定的必须向政府注册机构递交公司设立的必备文件。后者则用以规范公司内部事务，主要规定了公司与股东的关系，被称为公司的内部宪章（Internal Constitution），因此被视为公司与股东之间以及股东之间的合同。

Lesson 8
Company Law

agree to acquire some shares in the corporation (often only one each) by writing their names at the bottom of the memorandum: by doing this they become the initial members of the corporation. In order to raise money, a corporation, once established, will issue shares to the initial members (or to others) for an agreed price. The issue of the share to an applicant makes the applicant a shareholder who thereby becomes party to the statutory contract[4]. The owners do not share property but certain rights. They will have the rights conferred on shareholders by the memorandum and articles, e.g. to vote, to take a dividend, etc. The term 'member' is also used to denote a shareholder.

Although the shareholders do not own the assets of the corporation and do not themselves employ its managers, they have ultimate control over what happens to both (unless the corporation goes into insolvent liquidation[5]): as a body, the shareholders can remove and appoint the directors; and can resolve to wind up the corporation and, after paying off the creditors, distribute its assets among themselves. It is not surprising, given that shareholders had these ultimate powers and that it was the money they had invested in the corporation that the directors are managing, that the directors' duty to act *bona fide*[6] in the interests of the corporation was regarded as meaning that they had to act in the interests of the shareholders collectively. In other words, the interest of other people, e.g. creditors and employees, in the corporation was limited to having their contractual rights fulfilled but the shareholders had an interest in the enterprise as such and the business was run for their benefit and no-one else's.

c. Limited Liability

A shareholder of a corporation has the amount of his liability limited to the amount payable on the shares he holds. When we say that a company is limited

---

4　指公司章程。
5　insolvent liquidation:（因资不抵债）破产清算。
　　insolvent: *adj*. 资产不足以还债的。Insufficient to pay all debts.
　　insolvency: *n*. 资不抵债的状态。The condition of being unable to pay debts as they fall due or in the usual course of business.
　　liquidate:（企业破产或解散时）清算。To ascertain the liabilities and distribute the assets of an entity especially in bankruptcy or dissolution.
6　*bona fide*:〈拉丁语〉善意，诚实。这里指公司董事对公司的忠诚义务。

liability company, this is what we mean—not that in some way the liability of the corporation itself is limited. If the members' shares are fully paid for when the members acquire the shares from the corporation, the members will never have anything further to pay, irrespectively how insolvent the corporation is. Sometimes shares are issued partly paid. In this case, the member is liable to pay what remains unpaid on his shares if the corporation is wound up.

d. Different Classes of Shares

All shares in a corporation do not necessarily have the same rights. A corporation may have different types, known as classes of shares. The share capital of a corporation can be divided into different classes and each class may have differing rights as to voting, dividends and the return of capital on a winding up. Normally these rights will be set out in the corporation's constitution but that is not compulsory.

e. The Directors

The traditional theory is that the shareholders are the owners of the corporation and the role of the directors are to manage the business of the corporation for the benefit of its owners. There are two important aspects of the common law's attempts to provide a control mechanism over the directors' behaviour. Firstly, what are the duties? And the second issue is: who can enforce those duties?

IV. Corporate Personality

The essence of a corporation is that it has a legal personality distinct from the people who create it. This means that even if the people running the corporation are continuously changing, the corporation itself retains its identity and the business need not be stopped and restarted with every change in the managers or members of the business. As a limited liability company, not only is the money owned by the corporation regarded as wholly distinct form the money owned by those running, but also the members of the corporation are not liable for the debts of the corporation (except where the law has made exceptions to this rule in order to prevent fraudulent or unfair practices by those in charge). Members can only be called upon to pay

Lesson 8
Company Law

the full price of their shares. After that a creditor must depend on the corporation's money to satisfy his claim. This means that the corporation's property is its own and its debts are its responsibility, and the shareholders are neither party to the corporation's contracts nor liable for the corporation's debts. It is sometimes said that they are behind the corporate veil[1].

The limitation of liability of the members has led to careful rules being drawn up to attempt to prevent a corporation from wasting its money. It is one of the disadvantages of incorporation[2] that a number of formal rules, designed to protect people doing business with corporations, have to be complied with. A partnership had many fewer formalities to be complied with, as members of a partnership are liable for all the debts incurred by the business they run.

The fundamental importance of the invention of separate personality is vital as it means that it sets the company apart from the individuals who are running it.

The separate personality of a corporation creates a range of problems because although the corporation is regarded as a person in law, it can, of course, only function through the humans who are running the business in which the corporation is involved. The law must regulate the relationships between a corporation and its creators and members or shareholders as well as the relationship between a corporation and outsiders who do business with the corporation.

---

1 corporate veil: 法人面纱。A legal concept through which a corporation's shareholders, who generally are shielded from liability for the corporation's activities, can be held responsible for certain actions. 这是从 "Piercing the Corporate Veil" 理论中抽取的词汇。揭开法人面纱理论认为，当某个法人实体表现为其主要股东的 "工具"（instrumentality）或 "化身"（alter ego, shell）时，应当对该实体的法人人格予以否认，否认有限责任，直接追究法人背后股东的责任。
2 incorporation: 法人组织成立过程。The formation of a legal corporation. incorporate v. 结社、组成法人组织。incorporate, to form a legal corporation. 美国公司名称中比较常见的Inc.就是Incorporated的缩写，表示这是个法人组织。

Glossary

articles of association 社团章程；公司章程
asset 资产
bona fide〈拉丁法谚〉善意；诚实
close corporation 封闭公司
corporate veil 法人面纱
corporation limited by guarantee 担保有限公司（英国公司类型）
corporation limited by shares 股份有限公司（英国公司类型）
creditor 债权人
cumbersome 棘手的；麻烦的
entity 实体
float（票据）流通
fraudulent 欺诈性的
general partnership 普通合伙
holding corporation 控股公司；持股公司
insolvent liquidation（因资不抵债）破产清算
insolvent 支付不能的
Internal Revenue Service (IRS) 美国国内税务署
legal entity 法律实体
Limited Liability Partnership 简称LLP，有限责任合伙制
Limited Partnership 简称LP，有限合伙制
liquidate（企业破产或解散时）清算
list（股票）上市
non-for-profit corporation 非营利性公司
Public Corporation〈英〉公众公司；〈美〉公益公司
register 注册；登记
shareholder 股东
sole proprietorship（个人）独资企业
statutory 法定的

EXERCISES

I. Answer the following questions.

1. Tell the differences between S Corporation and C Corporation?
2. What does "limited liability" mean in the context of company law? In other words, who have the limited liabilities?
3. Why are the "memorandum and articles of association" called "the charter of the corporation"?
4. What rights do shareholders possess as a body of the company?
5. Do Partnerships have any advantages over Corporations? What are they?

Lesson 8
Company Law

II. Translate the following terms into English.

1. 股息
2. 因资不抵债的破产清算
3. 非营利性公司
4. 合伙企业
5. 独资企业
6. 有限合伙企业
7. 有限责任合伙企业
8. 一人公司
9. 单层征税
10. 上市公司
11. 公司章程
12. 控股公司
13. 债权人
14. 善意、诚实〈拉丁法谚〉
15. 法人面纱

III. Translate the following sentences into Chinese.

1. The company owns the business property in its right, and the shareholders own shares, they do not own the assets of the business they have invested in.
2. When a business enterprise wants to carry on a variety of diverse activities, it is sometimes administratively convenient to do so through separate subsidiary companies, each of which substantially manages its own affairs.
3. With a partnership the members share any profits, and by the same toke, are also liable for any losses.
4. If the company has insufficient assets to pay its debts, it is insolvent, and a creditor can put it into liquidation.

IV. Case discussion.

Williams v. Natural Life Health Foods [1998]

Natural Life Health Foods is a small limited liability company running a health food shop in Salisbury. The managing director, Mistlin, who was also the major shareholder, advertised for potential franchisees to run their own health food outlets. His company, the franchisor, would offer advice and assistance to the franchisee and would be paid fees for this.

Williams and a partner decided to take advantage of this business opportunity and open a shop in Rugby. They were sent detailed financial projections for the proposed business. Mistlin, as the managing director of the franchisor had played a prominent part in producing these projections. However, the projections proved to be negligent and over-optimistic. The Rugby shop operated at a loss for eighteen months and then ceased to trade completely. Williams began proceedings against the franchisor, but soon after proceedings had begun, the Salisbury business went into liquidation. For this reason Williams joined the franchisor's former managing director Mistlin in the proceedings as a second co-defendant.

In the trial and in the Court of Appeal, Mistlin was held personally liable to the plaintiffs on the basis that he had assumed responsibility for the negligent conduct of the people who represented Natural Life.

The House of Lords dismissed the Court of Appeal's decision, holding that Mistlin was not personally liable for the negligent advice given by the company.

Instructions: Participants should be assigned into small groups. After reading the case given above, they are required to give opinions on the following questions based on the company law principles they've learned:

1. How do you understand "Corporate Personality"? Give examples on its advantages or disadvantages.
2. As stated in the text, the shareholders or the directors are behind "corporate veil". Do you think it is fair that they are still behind "the veil", if the company is used for certain unlawful purposes or as a sham?
3. Which side are you on? Do you think Mistlin should be held liable for the plaintiff's loss?
4. The House of Lords' judgment reassured the firm place of "Corporate Veil". What do you think are the reasons for the judges to render the judgment?

Lesson 8

Company Law

Supplementary Reading

The principle of separate corporate personality has been established for over a century. In the leading case of *Salomon* v. *Salomon & Co.* [1897][1], the House of Lords held that, regardless of the extent of a particular shareholder's interest in the company, and notwithstanding that such shareholder had sole control of the company's affairs as its governing director, the company's acts were not his acts; nor were its liabilities his liabilities. Thus, the fact that one shareholder controls all, or virtually all, the shares in a company is not a sufficient reason for ignoring the legal personality of the company; on the contrary, the "corporate veil" will not be lifted[2] so as to attribute the rights or liabilities of a company to its shareholders.

The separate personality of the company can have some unexpected and sometimes unwelcome effects. In *Nepture Ltd* v. *Fitzgerald* [1995], the defendant was a sole director of a company who resolved to terminate his own service contract and pay himself over 100,000 in compensation acted in breach of fiduciary duty[3] and had to repay the money to the company. The court had little difficulty in concluding that he had not acted bona fide in the interests of the company but had preferred his own interests to those of the company. And a limited company can be a very powerful weapon in the hands of one determined on

---

1 该案被视为英国公司独立人格确立的里程碑。多年从事皮靴业务的商人Salomon于1892年决定将他拥有的靴店卖给了由他本人组建的公司，以享有限责任的优惠。靴店转让价格为39 000英镑。作为对价，公司近乎将其所有股份发行给Salomon。此外，公司还以其所有资产作担保向Salomon发行了10 000英镑的债券，其余差额用现金支付。但公司很快陷入困境，一年后公司进行清算，其资产若清偿Salomon有担保的债券，则公司的其他无担保债权人总共7 000英镑的债权就一无所获。无担保债权人声称，Salomon和其公司实际上是同一人，因而公司不可能欠他10 000英镑的债，公司资产应该用来偿还这些无担保债权人的债。法院驳回无担保债务案人的主张，确认公司与Salomon各自享有独立法律人格。

2 Lifting Corporate Veil: "刺破公司的面纱"或称"揭开公司的面纱"（Piercing the Corporate Veil），实际上都是对公司法人人格否认制度（Disregard of the Corporate Entity/Personality）的不同说法。一般认为该制度产生于美国法院的判例，指当公司的独立人格被滥用时，就具体法律关系中的特定事实，否定公司的独立法人人格，追及背后的股东或公司的内部人员对公司的相对人直接承担责任。

3 fiduciary duty: a duty obligating a fiduciary (as an agent or trustee) to act with loyalty and honesty and in a manner consistent with the best interests of the beneficiary of the fiduciary relationship. 受托义务或诚信义务，这里指董事必须竭尽忠诚地为公司工作并诚实地履行职责，其理论基础是董事与公司间的信托关系，当公司利益与董事个人利益发生冲突时，基于信托关系的存在，董事必须忠实于公司，公司利益优先。

fraud[1] and on defeating a creditor's rightful claims. Will the courts make no exceptions to the rule that a company is wholly separate from those who manage and control it?

A survey of the case law shows that the courts do contravene[2] the strict principles of the separate personality from time to time. There are certain situations where the English Courts have shown themselves willing to "lift the corporate veil", that is to ignore or set aside the separate legal personality of a company. There is no coherent pattern created by those cases where court has been prepared to go behind the corporate veil. While all instances can be described as being founded upon policy consideration, it is probably best to consider them under a series of headings:

a. where the company is a sham[3] or a party to a fraud;

b. group of companies;

c. where a company is regarded as an agent of another company;

d. enemy ownership or unlawful purpose.

The court will lift the corporate veil where the company is a sham formed for some fraudulent purpose or so that the proprietors of the company can exploit rules of law in an improper manner. The ability to hide behind the corporate veil could be a powerful weapon in the hands of those with fraudulent tendencies. The courts have therefore always reserved the right to ignore a company which is formed or used merely to perpetrate[4] a dishonest scheme. A mere wish to avail oneself of the benefits of limited liability is not of itself to be regarded as fraudulent. A different view was taken of the conduct in *Gilford Motor v. Horne* [1933], where the court refused to allow the defendant to avoid[5] an agreement that he would not compete with former employers. He had attempted to do so by competing with them in the guise of a limited company.

The courts have sometimes to make difficult decisions about the circumstances in which a group of companies is to be regarded as one entity. Different jurisdictions have reached different answers. In UK case law, there is no formal or informal recognition of

---

1 fraud: a knowing misrepresentation of the truth or concealment of a material fact to induce another to act to his or her detriment. 欺诈行为。
2 contravene: to violate. 违犯，与之相抵触。
3 sham: a person who pretends to be something that he or she is not.
4 perpetrate: to be responsible for or to commit (a crime). 实施（犯罪等不当行为）。
5 avoid: to make void, to invalidate. 使无效。一般较多使用void一词，以避免与avoid的通常词义相混淆。

group interests. In many circumstances, statutes dictate where groups should act as if they were enterprises. In the USA it is recognized that dominant shareholders have fiduciary duties towards both the company and other shareholders. Thus, dominant shareholders are distinguished from other shareholders. Transactions between a dominant shareholder and the corporation are valid if (a) the transaction is fair to the corporation when entered into; or (b) the transaction is authorized or ratified by distinguished shareholders, following disclosure concerning the conflict of interest and the transaction, and does not constitute a waste of corporate assets at the time of the shareholder transaction. Conflicting duties of loyalty owed by directors who sits on boards of parents and subsidiaries are also judged on a "fairness" scale: "In the absence of total abstention of an independent negotiating structure, common directors must determine what is best for both parent and subsidiary".

The finding of agency or trust may be a convenient excuse for a refusal to follow separate personality rule. The interests of justice require the court to have regard to the realities behind the situation. A similar motive lies behind the decision in *Daimler* v. *Continental Tyre Co.* [1916], where an English company was held to be an enemy alien because of the nationality of its shareholders.

Lesson 9
Intellectual Property Law

 It is the role of a good judge to enlargeor extend justice.
拓展正义的疆域是一名优秀法官义不容辞的责任。

Intellectual property is any property resulting from intellectual, creative processes—the products of an individual's mind. Although it is an abstract term for an abstract concept, intellectual property is nonetheless wholly familiar to virtually everyone. The information contained in books and computer files is intellectual property. The software you use, the movies you see, and the music you listen to are all forms of intellectual property. In fact, in today's information age, it should come as no surprise that the value of the world's intellectual property now exceeds the value of physical property, such as machines and houses.

The need to protect creative works was voiced by the framers of the U.S. Constitution over two hundred years ago: Article 1, Section 8, of the U.S. Constitution authorized Congress "to promote the Progress of Science and useful Arts, by securing for limited Times to Authors and Inventors the exclusive Right to their respective Writings and Discoveries." Laws protecting patents, trademarks, and copyrights are explicitly designed to protect and reward inventive and artistic creativity. In the subsections that follow, we examine these forms of intellectual property, as well as intellectual property that consists of trade secrets.

I. Trademarks and Related Property

A trademark is a distinctive mark, motto, device, or emblem that a manufacturer stamps, prints, or otherwise affixes to the goods it produces so that they may

Lesson 9
Intellectual Property Law

be identified on the market and their origin vouched for. Statutory protection of trademarks and related property is provided at the federal level by the Lanham Trade-Mark Act of 1946. The Lanham Act was enacted in part to protect manufacturers from losing business to rival companies that use confusingly similar trademarks. The Lanham Act incorporates the common law of trademarks and provides remedies for the owners of trademarks who wish to enforce their claims in federal court. Many states also have trademark statutes.

Trademarks may be registered with the state or with the federal government. To register for protection under federal trademark law, a person[1] must file[2] an application with the U.S. Patent and Trademark Office in Washington, D.C. Under current law, a mark can be registered (1) if it is currently in commerce or (2) if the applicant intends to put the mark into commerce within six months. Whenever a trademark is copied to a substantial degree or used in its entirety by another, intentionally or unintentionally, the trademark has been infringed (used without authorization). When a trademark has been infringed, the owner of the mark has a cause of action[3] against the infringer. A person need not have registered a trademark in order to sue for trademark infringement, but registration does furnish proof of the date of inception of the trademark's use.

A service mark is similar to a trademark but is used to distinguish the services of one person or company from those of another. For example, each airline had a particular mark or symbol associated with its name. Titles and character names used in radio and television are frequently registered as service marks. Other marks protected by law include certification marks[4] and collective marks.[5]

---

1. person: "人"。A human being, or an entity (such as a corporation) that is recognized by law as having the rights and duties of a human being. 英语中"person"不但包含公民个人，还包括被法律上承认的具有权力和义务的法人（legal person）。
2. file: 提交（法律文件）。To deliver a legal document. 通常指作为法律程序中一个步骤，向合法的相关机构或部门提交有关法律文件，以作登记备案。
3. cause of action: 诉因；诉讼理由。A group of operative facts giving rise to one or more bases for suing. 具体指原告起诉寻求司法救济所依据的事实，如侵权行为和损害后果。
4. certification marks: 证明标。A mark (a word, a symbol, or device used on goods or services) to certify the place of origin, material, mode of manufacture, quality, or other characteristic. 用以证明商品或服务的原产地、原料、制造工艺、质量和其他特定品质的标志。
5. collective marks: 集体商标。A trademark or servicemark used by an association, union, or other group either to identify the group's products or services or to signify membership in the group. 以团体、协会或其他组织的名义注册和使用的，用以证明为该组织产品或用来表明商标使用者为该组织成员。

Trademarks apply to products. The term trade name is used to indicate part or all of a corporation. Generally, a trade name is directly related to a business and its goodwill[1]. Trade names may be protected as trademarks if the trade name is the same as the company's trademarked product—for example, Coca-Cola. Unless also used as a trademark or service mark, a trade name cannot be registered with the federal government. Trade names are protected by common law, however. As with trademarks, words must be unusual or fancifully used if they are to be protected as trade names.

II. Patents

A patent is a grant from the government that gives an inventor the exclusive right to make, use, and sell an invention for a period of twenty years from the date of filing the application for a patent. Patents for designs, as opposed to inventions, are given for a fourteen-year period. For either a regular patent or design patent, the applicant must demonstrate to the satisfaction of the U.S. Patent and Trademark Office, that the invention, discovery, process, or design is genuine, novel, useful, and not obvious in light of current technology. A patent holder gives notice to all that an article or design is patented by placing on it the word Patent or Pat plus the patent number.

In contrast to patent law in other countries, in the United States patent protection is given to the first person to invent a product or process, even though someone else may have been the first to file for a patent on that product or process. The distinction is important because people working independently often arrive at essentially the same invention at about the same time. Under the U.S. first-to-invent rule, the inventor who can provide evidence of having invented first (e.g., dated lab note-books) receives the patent. Under the first-to-file rule, the inventor who is able to get the legal wheels turning first receives the patent.

If a firm makes, uses, or sells another's patented design, product, or process

---

1 goodwill: 商誉。A business's reputation, patronage, and other intangible assets that are considered when appraising the business, esp. for purchase. 商事主体引起个体特色、技术水平、可信度、经营位置或随附经营的其他条件，从而吸引顾客或保有固定客户进而获得的声望或公众偏爱，构成无形资产。

without the patent owner's permission, it commits the tort of patent infringement. Patent infringement may exist even though the patent owner has not put the patented product in commerce. Patent infringement may also occur even though not all features or parts of an invention are copied. (With respect to a patented process, however, all steps or their equivalent must be copied for infringement to exist.)

Traditionally, patents have been granted to inventions that are "new and useful processes, machines, manufactures, or compositions of matter, or any new and useful improvements thereof". The U.S. Patent and Trademark Office routinely rejected computer systems and software applications because they were deemed not to be useful processes, machines, articles of manufacture, or compositions of matter. They were simply considered to be mathematical algorithms, abstract ideas, or "methods of doing business". In a landmark 1998 case, however, *State Street Bank & Trust Co. v. Signature Financial Group, Inc.*, the U.S. Court of Appeal for the Federal Circuit ruled that only three categories of subject matter will always remain unpatentable: (1) the laws of nature, (2) natural phenomena, and (3) abstract ideas. This decision meant, among other things, that business processes were patentable.

III. Copyrights

A copyright is an intangible property right granted by federal statute to the author or originator of certain literary or artistic productions. Under the Berne Convention[1], a copyright lasts from the time that the works is fixed to at least fifty years after the author's death. In the U.S., changes in copyright law have led to a complex system of variable copyright terms. Currently, copyrights are governed by the Copyright Act of 1976, as amended. Works created after January 1, 1978, are automatically given statutory copyright protection for the life of the author plus 70 years. For works by more than one author, the copyright expired 70 years after the death of the last surviving author. After the term of a copyright has expired, the work enters the public domain, that is, anyone is free to copy it.

---

1 the Berne Convention:《伯尔尼公约》，全称为 the Berne Convention for the Protection of Literary and Artistic Works《保护文学艺术作品的伯尔尼公约》，本公约于1886年缔结，曾多次修订，是著作权领域第一个世界性多边国际条约。

Works that are copyrightable include books, records, films, artworks, architectural plans, menus, music videos, product packaging, and computer software. To obtain protection under the Copyright Act, a work must be original and fall into one of the following categories: (1) literary works; (2) musical works; (3) dramatic works; (4) pantomimes and choreographic works; (5) pictorial, graphic, and sculptural works; (6) films and other audiovisual works; and (7) sound recording. To be protected, a work must be "fixed in durable medium" from which it can be perceived, reproduced, or communicated. Protection is automatic. Registration is not required.

Whenever the form or expression of an idea is copied, an infringement of copyright occurs. The reproduction does not have to be exactly the same as the original, nor does it have to reproduce the original in its entirety. An exception to liability for copyright infringement is made under the "fair use"[1] doctrine. Fair use, as currently defined, allows one to copy a small portion of a work for education, criticism, or parody. Under current U.S. law there is no right to fair use *per se*; it is merely a legal defense to a claim of copyright infringement. In other words, unauthorized copying for educational and critical purposes is still infringement, but law does not allow the copyright holder to obtain money damages if the infringer can demonstrate fair use.

IV. Trade Secrets

Some business processes and information that are not or cannot be patented, copyrighted, or trademarked are nevertheless protected against appropriation[2] by a competitor as trade secrets. Trade secrets consist of customer lists, plans, research and development, pricing information, marketing techniques, production techniques, and generally anything that makes an individual company unique and that would have value to a competitor.

As long as the secret stays secret, and as long as no one else independently

---

1 fair use：合理使用。A reasonable and limited use of a copyrighted work without the author's permission, it is a defense to an infringement claim. 为衡平法的规则，认为合理使用是对版权侵权的抗辩(defense)，将某些版权侵权行为视为不构成侵权。

2 appropriation：擅用、私用、盗用。The exercise of taking and controlling as one's own. 在侵权法上，指某人为牟利而盗用他人的姓名或名称。

Lesson 9
Intellectual Property Law

figures it out, the holder of a trade secret has an advantage over potential competitors. If someone hacks into a computer system and steals the secret, or if a disgruntled employee spills the beans, trade secret law can be invoked to punish the thief. However, once the secret is out, it is out. Although laws protecting trade secrets do so in perpetuity as long as the secret remains secret, once the secret is disclosed anyone can produce the invention or use the process.

Perhaps the most famous trade secret is the formula for Coca-Cola. By the virtue of its tight security policies, the Coca-Cola Company has been able to maintain the secrecy of its product's formulation since 1886. Had the company sought a patent, its right to the formula would have expired by 1906. The company reportedly goes to extreme measures to protect its secret formula for Coke. The actual recipe is kept in a bank vault in Atlanta, and corporate rules require a resolution of the board of directors[1] to open the vault. Only those very few people who oversee the mixing of Coke syrup are allowed to know the formula.

Recent years, the nature of new computer technology undercuts a business firm's ability to protect its confidential information, including trade secrets. For example, a dishonest employee could e-mail trade secrets in a company's computer to a competitor or a future employer. If e-mail is not an option, the employee might walk out with the information on a computer's disk. Nowadays, companies increasingly seek to protect their trade secrets through nondisclosure contracts[2] or noncompete agreements between employer and employee. The problem is that over-protection of trade secrets may prevent a former employee from making a living.

V. Licensing

One of the ways to make use of another's trademark, copyright, patent, or trade secret, while avoiding litigation, is to obtain a license to do so. A license in this context is essentially an agreement to permit the use of a trademark, copyright, patent, or trade secret for certain purposes. For example, a licensee (the party

---

1 the board of directors: 董事会。The government body of a corporation, elected by the shareholders to establish corporate policy, appoint executive officers and make major business and financial decisions.
2 nondisclosure contract: 公司与员工签订的不披露合同或保密合同，通常会列明保密信息或专有信息的类别，及涉密人员的保密义务等。

obtaining the license) might be allowed to use the trademark of the licensor (the party issuing the license) as part of the name of its company, or as part of its domain name, without otherwise using the mark on any products or services.

Technology transfer arises from agreements to conduct research and development abroad, to provide technical assistance to subsidiary[1] or joint venture[2], or to perform other activities under direct commercial licensing agreements between a manufacturer or intellectual property right owner and a foreign entity. Technology licensing is a contractual arrangement in which the licensor's patents, trademarks, service marks, copyrights or know-how are sold or otherwise made available to licensee for compensation. Such compensation, known as royalties, may consist of a lump sum royalty or a royalty based on volume of production or sales.

Glossary

affix 使固定；附加
algorithm [数]运算法则
appropriation 擅用；私用；盗用
audiovisual 视听的
authorize 授权
cause of action 诉因
certification mark 证明商标
choreographic 舞台舞蹈的
collective mark 集体商标
disgruntled 不满意的；不高兴的
distinctive 有区别的；与众不同的
emblem 象征；标记
equivalent 对等物
fair use 合理使用

fancifully 富于想象力的
feature 特点；特征
file 提交
formula 处方；配方
genuine 真实的；真正的
goodwill 商誉
hack (slang) 闯入；侵入
in entirety 完全
in light of 按照；根据
in part 部分的；有几分
in perpetuity 永远
invoke 援引；调用
joint venture 合资公司
motto 座右铭；题词

---

1 subsidiary：subsidiary corporation的简称，子公司。A corporation in which a parent corporation has a controlling share.
2 joint venture：合资公司。A corporation that has joined with one or more individuals or corporations to accomplish some specified project.

Lesson 9
Intellectual Property Law

nondisclosure contract 不披露合同；保密合同
nonetheless 虽然如此；但是
originator 创作者；发明人
pantomime 哑剧；舞剧
patent 专利
per se〈拉丁语〉自身；本身
pictorial 图画的；用图画表示的
reproduce 再生；复制
sculptural 雕刻的

subsidiary 子公司
surviving 依然健在的
syrup 糖浆
the Berne Convention《伯尔尼公约》
the board of directors 董事会
trademark 商标
undercut 削弱
vault 银行的保险箱；保险柜
vouch 担保

EXERCISES

I. Answer the following questions.

1. What does the United States Constitution say about the protection of intellectual property?
2. What's the requirement for the registration of a trademark according to the text?
3. If two persons arrive at essentially the same invention at about the same time, who will get the patent in U.S.? And what about in other countries?
4. What kinds of subject matter will always remain unpatentable?
5. What is "fair use"? Can copying a small portion of a work for the purpose of education be called "fair use"?

II. Translate the following terms into English.

1. 知识产权
2. 商标
3. 联邦专利商标局
4. 诉因
5. 服务商标
6. 证明商标
7. 集体商标
8. 商誉
9. 发明优先原则
10. 版权
11. 伯尔尼公约
12. 合理使用
13. 商业秘密
14. 不披露合同
15. 使用税

III. Translate the following sentences into Chinese.

1. Generally, intellectual property is intangible and is created by intellectual effort as opposed to physical effort. In the United States, patents, copyrights and trademarks are governed by federal law. Trade secrets are governed by state law.
2. Patent applications are lengthy and complicated. An inventor should hire a patent attorney to assist in obtaining a patent for the invention.
3. The Berne Convention, also known as the International Union for the Protection of Literary and Artistic Works, now has nearly 80 member nations. Participation in the Berne Convention helps protect copyrighted works from international pirates who steal them and then sell the creative accomplishments of others.
4. Trademarks and service marks permit companies to develop "good will" among customers by making them more aware of the firms they patronize.
5. When detecting an infringing use of trademarked, patented, or copyrighted material, a businessperson should consider the merits of selling the infringer a license to use the property rather than resorting to costly litigation.

IV. Dictation.

A patent is a governmental grant of an exclusive monopoly as an incentive and a reward for a new invention. To be patentable, an idea must be novel, useful and nonobvious. In the U. S. A., the owner of a patent controls the right to make, sell and use a product for a period of seventeen years and a design for fourteen years. If one manufactures, sells, or uses a patented invention without authorization of the patent owner, he has probably committed patent infringement. The infringement exists even if the infringer did not know about the patent. Infringers can be liable for damages and may be enjoined from future infringement.

Lesson 9
Intellectual Property Law

Supplementary Reading

In cyberspace, trademarks are sometimes referred to as cyber[1] marks[2]. Trademark-related issues in cyberspace often relate to the rights of a trademark's owner to use the mark as part of a domain name. A domain name[3] is a part of an Internet address, such as "westlaw. com". The top-level domain (TLD) is the part of the name to the right of the period[4] and represents the type of entity that operates the site (for example, "com" is an abbreviation for "commercial"). The second level (the part of the name to the left of the period) is chosen by the business entity or individual registering the domain name. In the real world, one business can often use the same name as another without causing any conflict, particularly if the businesses are small, their goods or services are different, and the areas where they do business are separate. In the online world, however, there is only one area of business—cyberspace. Thus, disputes between parties over which one has the right to use a particular domain name have become common.

Conflicts over rights to domain names emerged during the 1990s as e-commerce expanded on a worldwide scale. Of the TLDs then available (.com, .org., .net, .edu, .int, .mil, and .gov), only one—.com—was typically used by commercial enterprises. As e-commerce expanded, the .com TLD came to be widely used by businesses on the web. Competition among firms with similar names and products for the names preceding the .com TLD led, understandably, to numerous disputes over domain name rights. It also led to a practice known as cybersquatting[5]. Cybersquatting occurs when a person registers a domain name that is the same as, or confusingly similar to, the trademark of another and then offers to sell the domain name back to the trademark owner. During the 1990s, cybersquatting became a contentious issue and led to much litigation. Often in disputes in these cases was whether cybersquatting constituted a commercial use of the mark so as to violate federal trademark law. Although no clear rules emerged from this litigation, many

---

1 cyber: the internet 网络。cyberspace 网络空间。
2 cyber mark：网络标志。
3 domain name：域名。
4 period：句号。
5 cybersquatting：恶意抢注域名。

courts held that cybersquatting violated trademark law.

In 1999, Congress addressed this issue by passing the Anticybersquatting Consumer Protection Act (ACPA), which amended the Lanham Act—the federal law protecting trademarks, as discussed earlier. The ACPA makes it illegal for a person to "register, traffic in[1], or use" a domain name (1) if the name is identical or confusingly similar to the trademark of another and (2) if the one registering, trafficking in, or using the domain name has a "bad faith intent"[2] to profit from that trademark. The act lists several factors that courts can consider in deciding whether bad faith exists. Some of these factors are trademark rights of the other person, whether there is an intent to divert consumers in a way that could harm the goodwill represented by the trademark, whether there is an offer to transfer or sell the domain name to the trademark owner, and whether there is an intent to transfer or sell the domain name to offer goods and services. The ACPA applies to all domain name registrations of trademarks. Successful plaintiffs in suits brought under the act can collect actual damages[3] and profits, or elect to receive statutory damages[4] of from $1,000 to $100,000.

---

1 traffic in: 交易、买卖。traffic *vi.*
2 bad faith intent: 恶意，欺诈的故意。
3 actual damages: 实际损害赔偿金。
4 statutory damages: 法定赔偿金。

Lesson 10
Civil Procedure Law

The judge is the speaking law.

法官是会说话的法律。

I. General Theory of Pleading

The pleadings are the papers by which the litigants first set the case before the court. A thorough study of the art of pleading[1] embraces both procedural and substantive concerns. How you plead is a procedural question, depending on the specific rules of the court in which you are appearing. What you plead is determined by considerations of substantive law[2] and the knowledge of what facts are legally significant in each context.

a. The Complaint

The principal difference between code pleading and Federal Rules pleading concerns the level of detail required. In a code state the plaintiff must plead in his complaint the ultimate facts constituting the elements of a cause of action. If he is too verbose and recites evidentiary detail, his pleading is improper. But today a complaint is rarely dismissed for this defect. Alternatively, if he pleads general and vague legal conclusions, such as the terms "trespass and assault" or "negligence[3]," some

---

1 pleading: 根据联邦民事诉讼规则第7条，诉辩状是指"起诉状、答辩状、对反请求的再答辩状……对交叉请求的答辩状……，第三当事人起诉状……，以及第三当事人答辩状"。因此，本章内容包括在任何民事诉讼中都必须提交的初始诉讼文件，以及律师在提交这些诉辩状及其他的法律文件之前所承担的调查事实与法律的义务。
2 substantive law: 实体法。The part of the law that creates, defines and regulates the rights, duties, and powers of parties.
3 negligence: 过失。The failure to exercise the standard of care that a reasonable prudent person would have exercised in a similar situation; any conduct that falls below the legal standard established to protect others against unreasonable risk of harm, except for conduct that is intentionally, wantonly, or willfully disregardful of other's rights.

states will grant[1] defendant's request for a general demurrer[2] to dismiss plaintiff's complaint. A plaintiff should also include in his complaint a demand for relief. If the demand is for money damages, a specific amount should be stated. Multiple causes of action[3] may be claimed, so long as they are stated in separate counts[4] in the complaint.

The simplest pleading system is found in federal courts and in those states that have adopted the Federal Rules. The troublesome code pleading concepts of "ultimate facts" and "cause of action" were replaced by the notion that the plaintiff need only "give the defendant fair notice of what the plaintiff's claim is and the grounds upon which it rests." The plaintiff can plead inconsistently and alternatively, even within the same count. With a few special matters, however, such as allegations of fraud[5] or mistake, the plaintiff must state the circumstances with particularity. The rationale here is to deter certain frivolous suits that sometimes are filed solely to harass defendants. The plaintiff must also plead special damages with specificity to protect the defendant from surprise. In general, nevertheless, liberalized pleading rules make it easier to sue in federal court and often require the defendant to engage in discovery[6] to obtain enough support to win a dismissal.

b. The Answer

If the defendant challenges the plaintiff's selection of a court or contends that the complaint fails to state a claim upon which relief can be granted, he may either raise these defenses in an answer or a motion to dismiss[7]. Otherwise, a defendant normally

---

1 grant: 同意，允许。To permit or agree to.
2 demurrer: 诉求不充分抗辩。A pleading stating that although the facts alleged in a complaint may be true, they are insufficient for the plaintiff to state a claim for relief and for the defendant to frame an answer. General demurrer is an objection pointing out a substantive defect in an opponent's pleading, such as the insufficiency of the claim or the court's lack subject-matter jurisdiction.
3 cause of action: 诉因，即是规定一方当事人应对另一方承担责任的情形。在美国侵权法中最为常用的诉因就是过失（negligence）。
4 count: 诉讼理由，说明为什么诸种情形综合构成了诉因，以及你寻求什么救济。
5 fraud: 欺诈。民法上的欺诈是指虚伪的陈述（misrepresentation）或骗人的诡计。
6 discovery: 证据开示。关于discovery的中文翻译，目前国内有两种译法，一是译为发现，如白绿铉所著的《美国民事诉讼法》；二是译为开示，如刘荣军所著《美国民事诉讼的证据开示制度及其对中国的影响》。基本含义是：民事诉讼的当事人相互获取对方或者案外第三人持有的与案件有关的信息和证据的方法。
7 motion to dismiss: 撤销案件的请求。A request that the court dismiss the case because of settlement, voluntary withdrawal, or a procedural defect.

Lesson 10
Civil Procedure Law

raises his defenses in the answer.

A defendant may deny some or all of the allegations in plaintiff's complaint, admit some of the allegations (either by specifically acknowledging their truth or by failing to properly deny them), raise new facts for an affirmative defense[1], or add his own claim against the plaintiff[2]. In a code state the defendant must plead the ultimate facts regarding his affirmative defense or counterclaim against the plaintiff. Under the federal system, enough detail "in short and plain terms" to provide general or fair notice is adequate. Affirmative defenses include such matters as accord and satisfaction[3], contributory negligence[4], duress[5], res judicata[6], or statute of limitations[7].

A defendant may select among five different types of denials for his answer. A proper denial places the matter denied in issue for future determination. A denial must be truthful and should not be misleading. For instance, if the complaint in a code state alleges that "defendant owned and operated a fork lift", a defendant who owned but not operated the lift may not make a specific denial that "he did not own and operate the lift". This is an improper conjunctive denial that misleads the plaintiff, which will be deemed an admission on both the issues of ownership and operation. Some federal courts have found that even a simple "deny" can be misleading and is improper.

---

1 affirmative defense: 积极抗辩，是一种表明即使事实上被告负有责任，但由于原告已经实施了某些行为因而导致原告不可能获得胜诉的抗辩。例如，如果原告在损害发生了相当长的时间后才提起诉讼，那么，被告就可以成功主张有关诉讼时效的积极抗辩。
2 add his own claim against the plaintiff: 即counterclaims。指如果被告认为原告的行为反而导致了对被告的损害，那么被告也可以针对原告提出反请求。
3 accord and satisfaction: 和解和清偿协议。以此协议，其中一方当事人原本有权起诉另一方，而另一方则向对方表示愿意向其给予或支付或为对方做一定行为，而对方意接受从而满足他的诉讼请求。
4 contributory negligence: 共同过失。指原告人的疏忽亦导致了其所控诉的伤害或损坏，并构成造成该伤害或损坏的全部原因或部分原因。
5 duress: 胁迫。 用暴力或暴力威胁，强迫他人实施和实际正在强迫他人实施某一特定行为。胁迫可能是对他人人身的实际伤害或人身的威胁，通常采用非法强制或至少是无理强制的恐吓方式，如以解雇相胁迫等。它包括对妻子、父母或子女的威胁。在胁迫下所做的行为在法律上一般是无效的。
6 res judicata: 已决事项不再理。An issue that has been definitively settled by judicial decision. 是指由具有管辖权的法院对案件做出终审判决后，原当事人或其他利益关系的继承人不得就已决事项或已判决的争诉要点再次提起诉讼或提出质疑。
7 statute of limitations: 诉讼时效法。A law that bars claims after a specific period; a statute establishing a time limit for suing in a civil case, based on the date when the claim accrued(as when the injury occurred or was discovered.)

II. Amendments

At common law the pleadings assumed such an important role that no variance was permitted between the pleadings and proof at trial. Code states and the Federal Rules, in contrast, by promoting decision based on the substantive merits rather than on procedural technicalities, freely allow amendments to pleadings.

Under Federal Rule 15(a) the plaintiff may amend his complaint once without applying to the court for permission as long as the defendant has not served his answer. After service the defendant has a similar right to amend his answer for 20 days. Otherwise a party may amend his pleading only by leave of court or by written consent of his adversary; the rule then states that "leave shall be freely given when justice requires so". Rule 15(c) and most states permit the pleading's amendment to relate back to the date of the original pleading so that it will not be precluded by the running of a statute of limitations, but only if the newly stated claim or defense arose out of the conduct, transaction, or occurrence in the original pleading.

If evidence is submitted at trial on an issue not found in the pleadings and no objection is raised, the court will normally conform the pleadings to the proof based on the parties' implied consent. If a party at trial requests an amendment, since the other party has objected to his presentation of evidence, the court will freely allow the amendment if it would promote decision on the merits and the objecting party fails to satisfy the court that he would be unduly prejudiced in maintaining his action or defense. The judge may grant a continuance to enable the objecting party to meet this evidence. Undue prejudice might include the disappearance of documents or the unavailability of a witness. Finally, a party may request amendment even after judgment to conform the pleadings to the proof, usually to clarify a decision for the purpose of res jucdicata.

III. Assuring Truthfulness in Pleading

The two most common methods used to promote truthfulness in pleading and discourage the filing of frivolous claims[1] and defenses are an attorney signature requirement and verification. In many jurisdictions, the attorney is required to sign

---

1 frivolous claim: 轻率诉讼。A claim that has no legal basis or merit, esp. one brought for an unreasonable purpose such as harassment.

Lesson 10
Civil Procedure Law

the pleadings and that signature stands as a certification that the claim or defense is filed in good faith—that there are good grounds to support it and that it is not interposed for purposes of delay. Although these provisions stand as a reminder to attorneys of their obligations to the legal system, they have not been very effective as control devices because, among other things, judges have been reluctant to impose sanctions for violation of the signature requirements unless there is a finding of subjective bad faith—a most difficult element to prove.

Recognizing these enforcement problems, the federal rules were amended in 1983 to provide that the attorney signature is to be affixed only after "a reasonable inquiry" as to whether there are sufficient grounds in law and in fact to support the pleadings. Sanctions for noncompliance were made mandatory. These changes were designed to allow the court to apply objective criteria as to the attorneys' reasonable inquiry and to enlarge the use of the sanction power so as to deter marginal conduct. Considerable litigation involving Rule 11 occurred after its amendment and questions were raised concerning very basic features of the revised requirement, as well as whether the amended rule was achieving its purpose or was breeding a new form of satellite litigation. Thus, there was substantial pressure to revise the rule and 1993 amendments were made to try to respond to some of the criticism.

The revised rule continues to utilize an objective, rather than a subjective, bad faith standard for assessing whether the signer made a reasonable inquiry and concluded that the pleading was well-grounded in fact and law. It also is expanded to cover all written motions and other papers filed in the litigation. Sanctions for violations are now discretionary, however, and a "safe harbor" provision is included by which parties desiring to request sanctions must wait at least 21 days after the paper has been filed and, if the alleged violation is cured in that period, no sanction motion can be filed. Whether the amended rule will achieve the proper balance between deterring frivolous filings and yet allowing attorneys to bring claims and defenses that they believe are meritorious but that may be less well-grounded than others remains to be seen.

IV. Pretrial Conference

Because of the increased liberalization of pleading requirements, the pretrial conference has become the point in time at which the case become crystallized and structured. The conference typically occurs after discovery, when counsel, talking informally with the judge, are able to agree as to what issues are in dispute. They can plan the course of the trial because they know what evidence and witnesses they intend to introduce. In complex litigation, a series of conferences may be used to schedule discovery and to structure the trial.

The judge has discretion to schedule a pretrial conference in both state and federal systems, although some courts have provided by local rules that conferences are mandatory in all cases. The question whether pretrial conferences should be mandatory or discretionary is tied to the perennial debate on their ultimate usefulness. In simple cases, is more time wasted in the conference than is saved at trial or is it really a means of coercing settlement[1]? In complicated cases, are the trials actually simplified and better organized and therefore speedier or does the pretrial conference merely add another hurdle and more time to the case?

In recognition of the frequent complexity of modern litigation and that leaving solely to the attorneys the responsibility to organize and move along their cases has not been satisfactory, the federal courts have been moving toward increased judicial management at the pretrial stage. In 1983, Federal Rule 16 was entirely rewritten to encourage federal judges to manage the cases before them, utilizing the pretrial conference to schedule the pretrial process, including discovery and motions, and thus to keep apprised of the attorneys' progress in the case.

---

1 settlement: 和解。An agreement ending a dispute or lawsuit, the parties reached a settlement the day before trial.

Lesson 10
Civil Procedure Law

Glossary

apprise（正式用语）通知；报告
breed 引起；造成
clarify 澄清；使明白
coerce 强迫某人（服从等）
compliance 顺从；听从；依从
conform 使相似；适应
criterion (pl.criteria) 判断的标准；衡量某事物价值的准则
crystallize（喻：指思想，计划）使变得明确
deter 阻碍做某事
discretion 自由处理；自由决定
evidentiary 证据的；根据证据的
frivolous 不庄重的；不重要的

impose 加（税，义务等）于
interpose 提出（异议，否决等）
mandatory 命令的；强制性的
marginal 边际的
perennial 长久的；持久的
preclude 阻止做某事；使不可能
rationale（某事物的）基本理由；理论基础
reluctant 不愿（做某事）的；勉强的
sanction（为维护或恢复法律或权威的尊严所作的）处罚
satellite 追随者
utility 有用；实用；效用
verbose 啰嗦的；累赘的

EXERCISES

I. Answer the following questions.

1. What does pleading mean?
2. What is the function of "the answer"?
3. What is the principal difference between code pleading and Federal Rules pleading?
4. What are the two most common methods used to promote truthfulness in pleading and discourage the filing of frivolous claims and defenses?
5. What does "safe harbor" provision mean?
6. What is the function of pretrial conference?

II. Translate the following terms into English.

1. 起诉状
2. 答辩状
3. 实体法
4. 诉因
5. 积极抗辩
6. 已决事项不再理原则
7. 和解和清偿协议
8. 胁迫

9. 过失　　　　　　　　　　　10. 审前会议

III. Translate the following sentences into Chinese.

1. A preliminary observation is necessary about the legal concept of "jurisdiction".
2. The obtaining of this type of judgment is known as entering the "default of the defendant".
3. The appellate court agrees with the trial court judgment.
4. An attorney's initial consideration in any lawsuit is to determine whether more than one forum is available to resolve this client's dispute if preliminary efforts to settle it are futile.
5. More than just a question of the proper court, a lawyer should consider the forum that offers his client the best economic and tactical advantages.

IV. Choose the suitable words from the box and fill in the blanks.

> issue　complaint　claim　attach　suffer

A civil action is commenced by plaintiff's filing of a _____ with the court. Thereupon, a summons to opposing parties is _____, directing them to respond to the complaint or _____ a judgment by default. A copy of the complaint must be _____ to the summons, thus notifying the defendant of the terms of the _____. The defendant has a specified period of time in which to respond, usually thirty days.

Supplementary Reading

Code Pleading[1] Following the lead of New York, which adopted the Field Code[2] in

---

1　Code pleading: 法典诉答程序，指依照法典确定的规则而进行的诉答。
2　Field Code: 费尔德法典。David Dudley Field 是19世纪美国杰出的审判律师，因其在最高法院的辩论而一举成名。他最伟大的成就在于法律改革领域。法典编撰的坚定支持者；1846年当选为纽约法律编撰委员会委员；1860—1865年间完成了行政法典、民法典、刑法典的编撰，但只有刑法典于1960年被采纳。几经周折，纽约州还是拒绝采纳民法典。但他编撰的民事程序法典、刑事程序法典被许多州采用。加利福尼亚州采纳了所有五部《费尔德法典》。

Lesson 10
Civil Procedure Law

1848, several states enacted statutes to govern the procedures in their courts. The pleading requirements included in those statutes commonly are referred to as code pleading.

Code pleading abolished the forms of action and eradicated much of the extreme formality and resulting pitfalls of common law pleading. The pleading distinction between cases at law and those in equity[1] were eliminated and a uniform set of pleading rules were adopted for all actions, regardless of the nature of the substantive cause of action. The function of the pleadings was transformed from one of issue formulation to fact revelation[2]. Under code pleading, it is typically said that the plaintiff has only to plead the facts constituting a cause of action; in other words, the plaintiff must plead the facts showing a legal right and wrong. If the allegations fit into some pattern of an established right, the case can continue. This standard is designed to provide notice to the opposing party, as well as to give the court sufficient information to allow it to strike[3] or dismiss legally insufficient claims and avoid useless trials.

The plaintiff can plead alternatively and even inconsistently, at least when the facts are not all within her knowledge, as long as the pleading is in good faith. The only restraint on alternative allegations is that they must be placed in separate counts so as to give adequate notice to the defendant. Multiple causes of action may be alleged, as long as they too are placed in separate counts.

Although the rigid formality of the common law has been abandoned under the codes, fact pleading presents its own problems. First, there has been some difficulty in defining what constitutes a cause of action. Two different views prevail. One, called the primary rights theory[4], defines the cause of action in terms of the nature of the injury allegedly suffered. The focus is on the harm caused rather than the acts that produced the harm or the remedy; the pleader must set forth only all the facts showing each injury. The other view defines a cause of action by the events that give rise to right to relief and requires the pleader set forth the "aggregate of operative facts" for which relief is

---

1 equity: 衡平法。"衡平法"一词首次出现是在十三四世纪的英国，是指通过大法官的司法实践发展起来的旨在对普通法的不足之处进行补救的一整套独立的原则、规范和法院系统。衡平法的发生和发展促进了英国法律体系独特的分类与结构方式。
2 此句的意思是诉辩程序的作用从单一争点陈述转换到事实展示。
3 strike: 法庭的一种行为，在法庭处理争议的过程中，如果表明请求或抗辩不可能存在根据或是中伤性的，法庭将删去一项请求或辩护它们的一部分。
4 the primary rights theory: 主要权利说。

demanded. Difficulty in applying these two views arises because under the primary rights approach courts do not always agree as to what constitutes a single harm, and under the operative facts approach there is no focus provided to determine what facts may be sufficiently related, creating the potential for long and complex pleadings.

Another problem under code pleading is determining the level of detail facts that must be pleaded. It has usually been said that the plaintiff need plead only ultimate facts, not evidentiary facts or legal conclusion. Attempts to delineate the difference between these three terms fill the case reports. In practice, the distinction is primarily one of how much detail is involved. Thus, ultimate facts are those essential to show that the plaintiff has a cause of action. Under a theory of cause of action as the breach of a primary right, the plaintiff must allege a primary right possessed by her, a corresponding duty on the defendant and the facts showing a wrong by the defendant constituting a breach. Any special damages must also be alleged. Evidentiary facts provide greater detail and legal conclusions are necessarily more general and vague. The pleading of evidentiary facts, while improper, is generally harmless and will not result in dismissal[1]. However, a pleading that is filled only with legal conclusions will be fatally defective.

The use of the common counts in some contract cases is also authorized under code pleading, providing an exception to the normal degree of specificity that is required. Under the common counts the pleader need allege only that he is suing for unjust enrichment[2] (money had and received), for labor performed or for goods sold and delivered or services rendered but not paid for . No further facts need be alleged. Thus, in an action based on a common count, there is much less emphasis on the pleadings; indeed, so much so that the common counts[3] remain somewhat anomalous in the code pleading system. The best explanation for the tolerance of this vague pleading standard is that the type of action involved is really one for restitution, premised on a desire to prevent the defendant from being unjustly enriched. Consequently, an action based on the common counts is equitable

---

1 dismissal: 撤销案件。Termination of an action or claim without further hearing, esp. before the trial of the issues involved.
2 unjust enrichment: 不当得利。作为一项普遍原则，不当得利指一方非因赠送或无法律上的依据而从他方获得利益，必须偿还利益，返还原物或弥补他方损失。
3 common counts: 一般款项。在1873年法院法颁布之前，指违约诉讼中原告在诉状中要求债务人支付的款项，包括成交或出售的货物或者出售与交付的货物的价款、借贷的款项、劳务报酬、被告因为原告而收到的款项（不当得利）或所涉账目的应付款项或利息。

in nature and historically did not fall within the common law pleading system.

Federal Pleading

The most liberal pleading system is that utilized in the federal courts and in the many state courts that have adopted the federal rules. Under the federal system, notice pleading prevails with the sole concern being whether the complaint reveals enough information so that the defendant can respond and understand why he is being sued. The standard utilized is that plaintiff must allege a short and plain statement of a claim showing that she is entitled to some relief. Consistent with this liberal approach, the plaintiff can plead alternatively and inconsistently , even with the same count. Similarly, although the plaintiff must include a demand for relief, the court is not bound by the demand in a contested case and can award whatever relief is appropriate. The ad damnum clause[1] limits recovery only in default situations[2]. Finally, the rules require courts to construe the pleading liberally so as to do substantial justice[3]. A good illustration of the simplicity of federal pleading is the official forms produced by the rulemakers.

The only exception to the very liberal pleading requirements of the federal rules is in some very specific types of causes in which, by special rule, more detail is required. For example, in fraud[4] actions it is not enough to allege merely that the defendant committed a fraud. Rather, the pleader must allege the circumstances surrounding the fraud. The same is true in actions for defamation[5]. The different treatment given to these actions undoubtedly reflects, in part, the fact that they are "disfavored" actions. Traditionally, the courts have scrutinized these types of actions rigorously because of their potential as tools of harassment. To discourage frivolous suits in these areas, a higher pleading threshold applies.

The reason for the general de-emphasis on factual revelation in the federal pleading rules was the desire of the rulemakers to eliminate some of the pleading-motion practice

---

1 ad damnum clause: 关于损害赔偿条款。A clause in a prayer for relief stating the amount of damages claimed.
2 default: 缺席判决。指被告因故意、过失或因疏忽没有适当地采取出庭为自己辩护的必要措施的情况下所作的判决，这种情况下所作的判决是合法的。
3 substantial justice: 实质正义；实体公正。Justice fairly administered according to rules of substantive law, regardless of any procedure errors not affecting the litigant's substantive rights.
4 fraud: 诈欺。民法上的欺诈是指虚伪的陈述或骗人的诡计。
5 defamation: 诽谤。一般法律术语，指通过向第三者传播致使他人名誉受到不公正毁损的虚假事实损害他人名誉的不法行为。

that occurs under the code system in which significant amounts of time and money are spent on technicalities prior to reaching the merits of the case. The burden of fact revelation is placed on the discovery process, eliminating what often were definitional squabbles at the pleading stage. Of course, one necessary effect of liberalizing the pleading requirements is to lower the threshold for bringing an action in the federal courts. The notice-giving philosophy of the federal system makes an early dismissal on the pleadings almost impossible to obtain.

Lesson 11
International Law

The laws of nature are unchangeable.
自然法是亘古不变的。

I. Traditional Definition

International law used to be defined as the law that governs relations between states. Under the traditional definition, only states were subjects of international law; that is, only states were deemed to have rights and obligations that international law recognized. Whatever benefits or burdens international law conferred or imposed on other entities or individuals were considered to be purely derivative, flowing to these so-called "objects" of international law by virtue of their relations to or dependence upon a state.

a. States Under International Law

When international lawyers speak of "states", they mean sovereign or nation-states[1]. To qualify as a state under international law, an entity must have a territory, a population, a government and the capacity to engage in diplomatic or foreign relations. States in federal unions[2], provinces or cantons usually lack the last attribute, which is a vital element of sovereignty.

---

1 nation-state: 主权国家。A nation is a group of people bound together by common history, common sentiment and traditions, and, usually by common heritage. A state, on the other hand, is a society of men united under one government. These two forms of society are not necessarily coincident. A single nation may be divided into several states, and conversely a single state may comprise several nations or parts of nations.
2 federal unions: 联邦。联邦是由两个以上成员邦构成的联合体，其存在以联邦国家宪法为根据。世界上有不少国家采取联邦的形式，有的称其成员邦为"州"，如美国；有的称为"省"，如加拿大。在国际法上，联邦是由其成员邦组成的国家，因为联邦政府作为整个联邦的最高权力机关对于成员邦的公民有直接的权力。与联邦不同，邦联是由两个以上的完全主权国家为维持他们对内对外独立的目的，根据他们之间共同缔结的国际条约建立的国家联合体。

b. Modern Subjects

Today intergovernmental international organizations, and even individuals, albeit to a more limited extent, are and can be the subjects of rights and obligations under international law. The United Nations and various specialized international or regional organizations such as, for example, the International Labor Organization[1] and the Council of Europe[2], enjoy the legal capacity to enter into treaty relations, governed by and binding under international law, with states and other international organizations. The direct responsibility of individuals for serious international crimes, such as crimes against humanity[3] and war crimes[4], and the development of the international law on human rights[5], indicate furthermore that, in certain circumstances, individuals have rights and obligations under international law that are not derivative in the traditional sense.

II. Uses of International Law

International law is routinely applied by international tribunals[6]. But

---

1 International Labor Organization: 国际劳工组织。该组织的主要目的是从正义和人道主义出发，改善劳动条件。虽然国际劳工组织是政府间的国家组织，其成员只能是国家，但国家在国际劳工组织并不是单纯由政府来代表的。国际劳工组织在代表结构方面的独一无二的特征就是所谓三方代表制，即：每一会员国的代表团由四人组成，其中有两人代表政府，一名代表工人，一名代表雇主。

2 Council of Europe: 欧洲理事会。1949年由若干欧洲国家为实现成员国间的进一步联合而组建成的一个组织，其宗旨是捍卫和实现属于成员国共同遗产的理想和原则，并通过对各方共同关心的问题的讨论，以及通过在经济、社会、文化、科学、法律和行政方面签订协议和采取共同行动，以及在保持、加速及实现人权和基本自由等方面签订协议并采取共同行动，来促进经济和社会发展。

3 crimes against humanity: 反人类罪。即在战前或战时，对平民施行谋杀、歼灭、奴役、放逐及其他任何非人道行为；或基于政治的、种族的或宗教的理由，而为执行或有关本法庭裁判权之内任何犯罪而做出的迫害行为，至于是否违反犯罪地国国内法，则在所不问。

4 war crimes: 战争罪。即违反战争法规或惯例。此种违反包括为奴役而虐待或放逐占领地平民、谋杀或虐待战俘或海上人员、杀害人质、掠夺公私财产、毁灭城镇或乡村或非基于军事上必要的破坏，但不以此为限。

5 human rights: 人权。是指一个人作为人所享有或应享有的基本权利。人权问题广泛引起国际社会关注，并全面进入国际法领域是第二次世界大战以来的事情。对第二次世界大战的深刻反省成为人权问题受到国际社会普遍关注的基本起因。对人权问题的重视首先表现于战后制定的《联合国宪章》，增加了有关人权条款的规定。《联合国宪章》有关人权条款不仅有着空前的历史意义，也为战后联合国在人权领域的活动奠定了重要的法律基础。在联合国主持制定下缔结的国际人权条约，使最近几十年来新形成起来的国际法部门——国际人权法得到充实和发展。国际人权保护因而也被认为是战后国际法上最为引人注目的发展领域。

6 international tribunals: 国际法庭。国际法庭有权依照国际法管辖国家间的争端并作出裁决。国际法庭有几种类型，有根据条约设立的仲裁法庭，如"阿拉巴马号索赔案"仲裁法庭，还有海牙常设仲裁院、临时仲裁法庭，也有各种混合型委员会，如：联合国利比亚法庭、欧洲共同体法院以及国际法院。其他一些国际机构，如由国际劳工组织设立的调查委员会，对违反国际劳工组织公约的事件可以进行调查并行使司法管辖权。

Lesson 11
International Law

international law is not relevant solely in judicial proceedings[1]. States rely on it in their diplomatic relations, in their negotiations, and in their policymaking. States defend their actions and policies by reference to international law and challenge[2] the conduct of other states in reliance on it. To the extent that international law perceived as "law" by the international community, it imposes restraints on the behavior of states and affects their decision-making process.

a. International Law as Law

The conduct of states is conditioned by many factors; international law is only one of them. Sometimes it is determinative, many times it is not. Yet whoever seeks to understand or predict how states will act in a given situation, or whoever has to counsel states on how they should act in consistent with their national self-interest, needs to take into account applicable principles of international law. A state may be prepared to violate international law in order to achieve a given political objective. But in calculating the short and long-term political costs of such action, the state's policymakers will have to address questions relating to the nature and function of that law, as well as the legal and political consequences of being labeled as a law-breaker.

The dramatic violations of international law, principally those involving the threat or use of force, which attract worldwide attention, should not blind us to the fact that the vast body of international law which regulates international commerce, communication, transportation, and day-to-day diplomatic and consular relations, to mention but a few areas, is applied and observed as routinely as is national law. For lawyers working in these fields, whether as legal advisers to governments, to international organizations or to corporations, or as judges, legislators, policymakers, or arbitrators, international law is law in a very real, practical sense. They have to know how to find and analyze it, in what context to apply it, and where and how to enforce it.

---

1 judicial proceeding: 司法程序。Any proceeding initiated to procedure an order or decree, whether in law or in equity.
2 challenge: 质疑。An act or instance of formally questioning the legality or legal qualifications of a person, action, or thing.

b. Application and Enforcement

As a rule, international courts do not have compulsory or automatic jurisdiction to deal with all international legal disputes that might be ripe for adjudication. The authority of these courts to hear a given dispute depends upon the acceptance of their jurisdiction by the parties to the disputes. There are, as a consequence, many international legal disputes that cannot be adjudicated because one or the other of the parties to the dispute refuses to accept the jurisdiction of a court.

But courts are not the only institutions for the resolution of disputes between states. Many international disputes that cannot be submitted to formal international adjudication, can and have been settled by other methods, such as negotiation, mediation, good offices or arbitration, which all involve the application of international law. Here international law performs a function similar to that which national law performs in the settlement[1] of disputes that do not reach the courts.

Furthermore, numerous methods and organizations exist today, whether of a political, quasi-judicial[2], or diplomatic character—the United Nations, regional organizations, diplomatic conferences, ect.—where international law plays a role, together with other factors, in resolving conflicts and in fashioning solutions to societal problems of all types.

III. Origins of the Modern System

International law or the law of nations, as it used to be called, came into its own as a separate legal system or discipline with the emergence of the modern nation-state in the 16th and 17th centuries. Of course, practices such as the exchange of diplomatic emissaries, the conclusion of peace treaties, etc., and some of the rules applicable to them can be traced back far into antiquity. But it was not until modern times that the rules governing relations between states came to be seen as a distinct body of law. Many of these rules were derived either from Roman Law[3] or Canon

---

1 settlement: 和解。诉讼当事人为解决双方争议和了解诉讼而达成的协议或妥协方案。和解条件可以包括在双方同意且经法院认可的判决之中,还可包括在双方达成的合同之中。
2 quasi-judicial: 准司法性的。意指在实体上或程序上与司法相类似的。准司法性经常用来指那些不是严格意义上司法的、不是法院或法官和团体的职权与行为。
3 Roman Law: 罗马法。在古罗马及后来罗马帝国时期,即自罗马城市建立传统上认为是公元前753—1453年君士坦丁堡陷落,东罗马帝国崩溃这一时期发展起来的法律制度。

Lesson 11
International Law

law[1], which drew heavily on principles of natural law[2]. These two sources of law also formed the basis of much of the national law of the nation-states that came into being in Europe as the medieval period[3] drew to a close with the dawn of the Renaissance. Roman law and Canon law exerted great influence on the European statesmen and legal scholars of the period who created and systematized what became modern international law.

IV. Sources of International Law

Viewed in terms of law-making, international law is primitive legal system. The international community lacks a constitution that can be viewed as a fundamental source of law. There exists no institution comparable to a national legislature with power to promulgate laws of general applicability, nor administrative agencies to produce regulations. Moreover, the International Court of Justice[4](abbreviation for I.C.J) lacks plenary jurisdiction over disputes arising under international law, and the decisions of the Court are legally binding only on the parties to the dispute. They have no precedential value in a formal sense because stare decisis[5] is not a rule of international law.

---

1. Canon law: 宗教法，教会法。由基督教机构为教会的组织和管理制定的一套法律。宗教法规是一种规则、规范或措施。如同世俗社会一样，教会亦发现有必要制定规则为各种场合下的行为设定标准和准则，这些规则的总和就是宗教法。但由于教会的性质和目的，这些规则所处理的事务有别于世俗社会。
2. natural law: 自然法。哲学、法律史和法理中最古老、最永恒的主题之一就是对自然法的信念和自然法理论。通常来说，它表示了对权利或正义制度的信念，这种适用于全人类的权利和正义制度，为宇宙间最高控制力量所厘定，完全不同于任何特定国家或其他组织制定的实在法。所有自然法思想的出发点是"理性"和"人性"。然而对于自然法的具体含义以及它与实在法的关系，自古以来有不同的看法。
3. medieval period: 中世纪。西方法律的中世纪时期是指自公元4世纪东罗马帝国兴起，公元476年西罗马帝国衰弱和最终灭亡时起，直至公元15世纪后期这段时期。公元15世纪，发生了君士坦丁堡陷落，1453年拜占庭帝国或东罗马帝国灭亡，被称为文艺复兴的启蒙运动，宗教改革的开始，罗马法的接受，民族国家的兴起，新的地理大发现及标志近代历史开始的一系列变化。在中世纪，西方各国的发展变化具有某种统一性和一致性，并且在这段时期里发展了深刻地影响近代法律的法律制度和法律思想。
4. International Court of Justice: 国际法院。联合国的主要司法机构，继国际常设法院之后于1946年创建于海牙。国际法院的管辖权限于主权国家之间的民事诉讼案件，只有在征得当事国同意的情况下，国际法院才能对有关的争端进行审理。
5. stare decisis: 遵循先例。在英美审判活动中，创立了遵循先例的原则，或称先例具有约束力的原则，其意思是指法官在对审理的案件进行判决时，不但要考虑先例，即其他法官以前对相同或密切相关的问题所作的判决中所适用的原则，而且在某些情况下，他还要受已有判决观点的约束，接受和遵循特定先例的原则，他个人赞同与否在所不问。这一惯例在英格兰法中由来已久，并不断发展。

How then do we know whether a given rule is international law? This question can be answered only by reference to the sources of international law and analyzing the manner in which international law is made.

a. Primary Sources

Article 38(1) of the I.C.J. Statute is generally considered to be the most authoritative enumeration of the sources of international law. It reads as follows:

The Court, whose function is to decide in accordance with international law such disputes as are submitted to it, shall apply:

a) international conventions, whether general or particular, establishing rules expressly recognized by the contesting states;

b) international custom, as evidence of a general practice accepted as law;

c) the general principles of law recognized by civilized nations;

d) ...judicial decisions and the teachings of the most highly qualified publicists of the various nations, as subsidiary means for the determination of rules of law.

b. Meaning of Article 38 of the I.C.J. Statute

Article 38 was included in the I.C.J. Statute to describe the nature of the international law that the Court was to apply. Article 38 (1) indicates that international law consists of or has its basis in international conventions (treaties), international custom, and general principles of law. It follows that a rule cannot be deemed to be international law unless it is derived from one of these three sources.

"Judicial decisions" and the "teachings" of the publicists are not sources of law as such; they are "subsidiary means" for finding what the law is. International lawyers look to these authorities as evidence to determine whether a given norm can be deemed to have been accepted as a rule of international law.

Article 38 (1) is silent on the question of whether the three primary sources it lists have the same hierarchic value, that is, whether treaties take precedence over custom and custom over general principles of law.

c. Treaties

Treaties are formal agreements between countries, and have legal significance for both domestic and international purposes. Treaties between two governments are called bilateral; those entered into by more than two governments are called multilateral. The initial signatures to a treaty establish the parties' agreement that its text is authentic and definitive, but nations are not bound until they approve the treaty through ratification[1], accession[2], or some certain provisions, or declarations providing their own interpretations of treaty terms. The texts of treaties usually identify the point at which they enter into force, often (in the case of multilateral conventions) when a specified number of nations have indicated their ratification or accession.

d. Custom

Customary international law develops from the practice of states. A practice does not become a rule of customary international law merely because it is widely followed. It must, in addition, be deemed by states to be obligatory as a matter of law. This test will not be satisfied if the practice is followed out of courtesy or if states believe that they are legally free to depart from it at any time. The practice must comply with the "opinio juris"[3] requirement to transform it into customary international law.

V. Character of Modern International Law

The discussion in the preceding sections indicates that modern international law consists principally of conventional and customary international law. The fact that legislative treaties now play an important role in the law-making process is beginning to transform international law into a more dynamic legal system. The development of customary international law is, on the whole, more cumbersome and consequently less suited for the fast pace of modern life. General principles perform an ever more marginal role as a source of law.

---

1 ratification: 批准。在国际法上系指对一个条约或其他国际协议的确认。
2 accession: 加入。根据国际法，系指一个国家无条件地接受其他国家之间缔结的条约。
3 opinio juris: 法律确信。国际习惯有两个因素构成：一是各国的重复类似行为；另一是被各国认为有法律约束力。前者是"常例"，是客观的因素，后者是"法律确信"，是主观的因素。

Glossary

albeit 虽然
attribute 特征
authentic 可信的
authoritative 权威的；有权威的
bilateral 有两面的；双边的
canton 州；行政区（尤指瑞士的州，法国的区）
conclusion 缔结
confer 赠与；把……赠与
consular 领事的
definitive 最后的；确定的；权威性的
derivative 派生的事物
discipline 学科
dynamic 动力的；动力学的；动态的
emissary 使者

enumeration 列举
hierarch 教主；掌权者；高僧
numerous 众多的；许多的；无数的
obligatory 义不容辞的；必须的
observe 遵守
plenary（指权力）无限的；绝对的
precedential（作为）先例的
primitive 粗糙的；简单的
promulgate 发布；公布
publicist 国际法专家
ratification 批准
restraint 抑制；制止；克制
sovereign 独立自主的
subsidiary 辅助的；补充的

EXERCISES

I. Answer the following questions.

1. What is the traditional definition of international law?
2. What are the modern subjects under international law?
3. What are the uses of international law except in judicial proceedings?
4. Do international courts have compulsory or automatic jurisdiction to deal with international legal disputes?
5. What are the main resources of international law?

II. Translate the following terms into English.

1. 战争罪
2. 反人类罪
3. 联邦
4. 国际法院
5. 遵循先例原则
6. 法律确信

Lesson 11
International Law

7. 调停　　　　　　　　8. 斡旋

9. 调解　　　　　　　　10. 难民权利

III. Translate the following paragraph into Chinese.

This brief survey of international law highlights the extent and variety of available sources. With the increasingly global nature of business and legal relationships, and the frequent treatment of transnational legal issues by American courts, international law research is no longer an exotic specialty known only to a few practitioners.

IV. Choose the suitable words from the box and fill in the blanks.

> purpose　economy　discrimination　society　advance

The United Nations is a universal organization both in terms of its membership and the _____, it is designed to _____. It is an organization charged with peacekeeping responsibilities; with the development of friendly relations among nations; with the achievement of international cooperation in solving international problems of an _____, _____, cultural and humanitarian character; and with the promotion of human rights and fundamental freedoms for all human beings without _____.

Supplementary Reading

Public international law is the body of law which governs relations among nations. Although its primary historical functions have been the preservation of peace and regulation of war, international law now governs an ever broader range of transnational activities. It regulates matters from copyright protection[1] to the rights of refugees[2], and agreement such as the Convention on Contracts for the International Sale of Goods

---

1　copyright protection: 著作权保护，版权保护。版权是一种独立的知识产权，版权人有权将其版权中的一项或多项权利内容许可给他人使用。许可使用作品的方式主要有复制、表演、播放、展览、发行、改编、摄制成电影或电视、录像、翻译、网络传播等。
2　rights of refugees: 难民权利。一旦经申请取得难民地位，难民本人及家庭成员便可根据联合国1951年《关于难民地位的公约》在缔约国内享有特定的权利与待遇。

(CISG)[1] have made international law an inherent aspect of commercial activity. Private international law[2] (or conflict of laws) determines where, and by whose law, controversies involving more than one jurisdiction are resolved, as well as how foreign judgments are enforced.

A modern legal practice often requires knowledge of international law. Lawyers representing an American firm investing in another country, for example, must be aware of treaties between the two nations as well as the investment and trade laws of both the United States and the other country. They may also need to examine jurisdictional issues in resolving disputes or in determining the application of one country's rules in the other's courts.

The classic statement of the sources of international law doctrine is found in Article 38 of the Statute of the International Court of Justice. Treaties and international custom are generally considered the two most important sources. If a treaty is relevant to a problem involving its signatories, it is the primary legal authority. International custom consists of the actual conduct of nations, when that conduct is consistent with the rule of law. Custom is not found in a clearly defined collection of sources, but is established instead by evidence of state practices. Other sources include judicial decisions and scholarly writings, although these are subsidiary to treaties and international custom. Judicial decisions are not considered binding precedents[3] in subsequent disputes, but they are evidence of international practice and can aid in treaty interpretation and in the definition of customary law.

Here we describe the methods international law has developed for the peaceful resolution of international disputes. The parties to any dispute, the continuance of which is likely to endanger the maintenance of international peace and security, shall, first of all, seek a solution by negotiation, enquiry, mediation, conciliation, arbitration[4], judicial

---

1 Convention on Contracts for the International Sale of Goods：《国际货物销售合同公约》。它是规定国际贸易合同的订立、执行和解释的最重要的国际公约。
2 private international law：国际私法，又称法律的冲突。国际私法主要解决不同国家对于私人关系的不同法律规定所发生的冲突，包括管辖权的冲突。
3 binding precedent：有约束力的先例。A precedent is a decided case that furnishes a basis for determining an identical or similar case that may arise later. A binding precedent must be followed.
4 arbitration：仲裁，是指争端当事国一致同意把它们之间的争端交给自己选任的仲裁人来裁判并承诺服从其裁决的一种解决争端的方法。

settlement, resort to regional agencies or arrangements[1], or other peaceful means of their own choice.

Non-judicial Methods

The traditional non-judicial methods for the resolution of international disputes are negotiation, inquiry, mediation and conciliation. Depending upon the dispute, its context and the attitude of the parties to it, one or more and sometimes all of these methods may come into play. In short, they are not necessarily distinct or exclusive techniques for the resolution of a conflict. Each of these methods has national institutional counterparts which function in much the same way.

Negotiation[2]

Bilateral and multilateral negotiation to resolve differences between two or more states or between groups of states may be carried out by diplomatic correspondence, or by face-to-face encounters between permanent diplomatic envoys[3] or specially designated negotiators. Negotiation is the traditional and most commonly employed method. It tends to be the first stage in a process that may require resort to other, more formal, dispute-resolution methods. Prior negotiation is often also required as a condition precedent to the exercise of jurisdiction[4] by international courts.

Inquiry[5]

The reference of a dispute to a process of inquiry involves the designation of a group of individuals or an institution to act as an impartial fact-finding or investigatory body. This method can be extremely effective under certain circumstances. An inquiry undertaken with the consent of the parties that results in an unambiguous finding of fact is more likely than not to lead to the resolution of the dispute when the disagreement between the parties involves only issues of fact.

---

1   judicial settlement: 司法解决，是一种和平解决国际争端的法律方法，争端当事国把争端提交给一个已事先成立的、由独立法官组成的国际法院或国际法庭，根据国际法对争端当事国作出具有法律约束力的判决。
2   negotiation: 谈判，是争端当事国就其争端进行交涉、交换意见以求解决的方式。谈判是解决国际争端的最基本方式。
3   envoy: messenger, esp. one sent on a special mission; diplomatic agent next in rank below an ambassador. 使者；特使；公使。
4   jurisdiction: 管辖权。A court's power to decide a case.
5   inquiry: 查询。又称调查（investigation）或查明事实（factfinding），是指在涉及事实性问题争端中，有关当事方同意将有关事实真相的调查交由第三方进行，以解决争端。

Mediation[1] or Good Offices[2]

This technique consists of third-party efforts to assist the parties to a dispute to resolve their disagreements through negotiation. The role of mediator is to bring the parties together, to serve as intermediary between them, to propose solutions and to explore opportunities for settlement. Today these techniques take on many different forms. Mediators may serve as a bridge between contending states whose representative may or may not speak to each other—the Middle East shuttle diplomacy provides a good example. Mediators may sit in on negotiations, chair meetings, suggest solutions, cajole, etc.

Conciliation[3]

This is a more formal process than the other dispute resolution techniques described above. It requires an agreement by the parties to the dispute referring the controversy to a group of individuals or to an institution which will receive the views of the parties and then issue a report containing recommendations for resolution of the disputes. The parties do not obligate themselves to accept the recommendations, but the existence of a report tends to make it more difficult for the parties to disregard it or to reject the recommendations, particularly if they wish to avoid the appearance of acting in an arbitrary manner.

---

1 mediation: 调停，是指第三方以调停人的身份，就争端的解决提出方案，并直接参加或主持谈判，以协助争端解决。
2 good office: 斡旋，是指争端以外的第三方为促成当事国进行谈判或争端解决，采取和提供某些协助活动。
3 conciliation: 调解。在国际法中，指通过把某一争端提交一个委员会解决的一种程序。该委员会的任务是阐明事实和提出一个包含争端解决建议案的报告，该报告并不是具有像仲裁裁决或判决那样的约束力。

Lesson 12
WTO and International Economic Law

 Scarcely any law can be made which is beneficial to all; but if it benefits the majority it is useful.

法律难顾及全民，于大多数人有利足矣。

The massive growth in international trade and the explosion of information technology are leading towards a world trading market and economic interdependence of the various nations. Perhaps this will eventually lead to a world government of sorts, with international trade being an arm of government. In the meantime, there is a complex myriad of treaties, laws, rules, and guidelines for those involved with international trade to decipher. The importance of an understanding of the laws governing international trade transactions to a corporate and commercial legal practitioner cannot be understated.

Briefly, international economic law refers to that normative[1] framework which governs mainly the international economic relations between states, and indirectly and consequentially those between individuals. International economic law is not derived from a single source or even several sources of law; it has its genesis in many. National, regional, and international law (public and private), policy and customary practices are all components of international economic law. International economic law encompasses a wide spectrum of subjects including trade in goods and services, financial law, economic integration, development law[2], business regulation

---

1 normative：标准的，规范的。e.g., normative decrees 规范性法令，normative functions（法律的）规范作用。
2 development law：发展法。International development organizations aim to promote social and economic development through programs and financial assistance to developing countries. 发展法是国际组织为发展中国家的社会和经济发展所制定的法律和财政援助项目的统称。

and intellectual property. In particular, at the core of these economic relations rest international development, investment, monetary and trade issues. These core aspects of international economic relations have been the focus of the international community, through what are known as the Bretton Woods[1] (and post) institutions viz., the International Monetary Fund (IMF), the World Bank Group and the World Trade Organization (WTO). Among all the international organizations, the World Trade Organization, undoubtedly, is the most powerful legislative and judicial body. In view of the significant role it plays and the complexity of the international economic law, this chapter just highlights the brief introduction of the WTO.

THE WTO IN BRIEF

I. History: The Multilateral Trading System—Past, Present and Future

The World Trade Organization came into being in 1995. One of the youngest of the international organizations, the WTO is the successor to the General Agreement on Tariffs and Trade (GATT)[2] established in the wake of the Second World War.

So while the WTO is still young, the multilateral trading system that was originally set up under GATT is well over 50 years old.

The past 50 years have seen an exceptional growth in world trade. Merchandise exports grew on average by 6% annually. Total trade in 2000 was 22-times the level of 1950. GATT and the WTO have helped to create a strong and prosperous trading system contributing to unprecedented growth.

The system was developed through a series of trade negotiations, or rounds,

---

1 Bretton Woods: 布雷顿森林，是美国东部新罕不什尔（New Hampshire）一个风景优美的地区。1944年世界货币会议在此召开。会议成立了国际货币基金组织（International Monetary Fund, IMF）和国际复兴与开发银行（the International Bank for Reconstruction and Development, IBRD, 简称世界银行），并拟成立国际贸易组织（ITO）。拟由这三个组织组成的体系因会议召开地点而被称为布雷顿森林体系（Bretton Woods System）。
2 GATT（关税与贸易总协定）是世界贸易组织（英文缩写WTO）成立之前，唯一协调和处理国家和地区间关税与贸易政策的多边协定。关税与贸易总协定的宗旨是通过彼此削减关税及其他贸易壁垒，消除国际贸易上的歧视待遇，以便充分利用世界资源，扩大商品生产和交换，保证充分就业以及实际收入和有效需求的增加。关税与贸易总协定自1948年开始临时实施至1995年1月1日世界贸易组织正式成立，拥有47年的历史，截至1994年年底，关税与贸易总协定共有128个缔约方。

Lesson 12
WTO and International Economic Law

held under GATT. The first rounds dealt mainly with tariff reductions but later negotiations included other areas such as anti-dumping and non-tariff measures. The last round—the 1986—1994 Uruguay Round[1]—led to the WTO's creation.

The negotiations did not end there. Some continued after the end of the Uruguay Round. In February 1997 agreement was reached on telecommunication services, with 69 governments agreeing to wide-ranging liberalization measures that went beyond those agreed in the Uruguay Round.

In the same year 40 governments successfully concluded negotiations for tariff-free trade in information technology products, and 70 members concluded a financial services deal covering more than 95% of trade in banking, insurance, securities[2] and financial information.

In 2000, new talks started on agriculture and services. These have now been incorporated into a broader agenda launched at the fourth WTO Ministerial Conference in Doha, Qatar, in November 2001.

The work programme, the Doha Development Agenda (DDA)[3], adds negotiations and other work on non-agricultural tariffs, trade and environment, WTO rules such as anti-dumping[4] and subsidies[5], investment, competition policy, trade facilitation, transparency in government procurement[6], intellectual property, and a range of issues raised by developing countries as difficulties they face in implementing the present WTO agreements.

---

1 Round: 轮，指不同地区的很多国家就自由贸易展开的多边谈判。在谈判中，每个国家都有自己的贸易目标。每轮谈判最终都会出台一个将所有协议汇总的"单一协议"。关贸总协定曾经主持七轮多边贸易谈判。Uruguay Round，乌拉圭回合是在1986—1994年间举行的第七轮全球贸易自由化谈判。这轮谈判的成果之一是成立了世贸组织。
2 security: 有价证券；如股票证书或债券等。An instrument that evidences the holder's ownership in a firm (e.g., a stock), the holder's creditor relationship with a firm or government (e.g., a bond), or the holder's rights (e.g., an option).
3 Doha Development Agenda：缩写为DDA（多哈发展议程），是指多哈世界贸易组织第四次部长级会议上启动的新一轮全球贸易谈判议程。DDA实际上是一个具有开拓性的谈判，世界贸易组织将在经济增长、就业、消除贫困以及促进可持续性发展方面进行谈判，并将发挥更大的作用。
4 anti-dumping: 反倾销的。Intended to discourage importation and sale of foreign-made goods at prices substantially below domestic prices for the same items. 由于进口的和外国制造的商品价格大大低于同类本国商品的价格而意图对其实行限制的（政策和法规）。
5 subsidies：补助金、补贴。Monetary assistance granted by a government to a person or group in support of an enterprise regarded as being in the public interest. 政府为支持有益于公众的企业而给予个人或团体的资助。这里指出口国政府或其他任何公共机构提供的并为接收者（通常为出口企业）带来任何利益的财政资助及任何形式的收入或者价格支持。
6 government procurement：政府采购，国家使用财政性资金采购货物工程和服务的行为。

(The deadline for the negotiations is 1 January, 2005.)

II. The Organization

The WTO's overriding objective is to help trade flow smoothly, freely, fairly and predictably. It does this by:

- Administering trade agreements
- Acting as a forum for trade negotiations
- Settling trade disputes
- Reviewing national trade policies
- Assisting developing countries in trade policy issues through technical assistance and training programmes
- Cooperating with other international organizations

Structure

The WTO has nearly 150 members, accounting for over 97% of world trade. Around 30 others are negotiating membership.

Decisions are made by the entire membership. This is typically by consensus[1]. A majority vote is also possible but it has never been used in the WTO, and was extremely rare under the WTO's predecessor, GATT. The WTO's agreements have been ratified in all members' parliaments.

The WTO's top level decision-making body is the Ministerial Conference which meets at least once every two years.

Below this is the General Council (normally ambassadors and heads of delegation in Geneva, but sometimes officials sent from members' capitals) which meets several times a year in the Geneva headquarters. The General Council also meets as the Trade Policy Review Body and the Dispute Settlement Body.

At the next level, the Goods Council, Services Council and Intellectual Property (TRIPS) Council[2] report to the General Council.

---

1 consensus: 全体一致同意。From Latin, an agreement of parties to the same thing; a meeting of minds.
2 货物贸易理事会、服务贸易理事会和与贸易有关的知识产权理事会，这三个理事会都根据总理事会的总体指导运作，分别履行货物贸易多边协议、服务贸易总协定和与贸易有关的知识产权协定和总理事会制定的职能。

Numerous specialized committees, working groups and working parties[1] deal with the individual agreements and other areas such as the environment, development, membership applications and regional trade agreements.

III. The WTO Agreements

How can you ensure that trade is as fair as possible, and as free as is practical? By negotiating rules and abiding by them.

The WTO's rules—the agreements—are the result of negotiations between the members. The current set was the outcome of the 1986—1994 Uruguay Round negotiations which included a major revision of the original General Agreement on Tariffs and Trade (GATT).

GATT is now the WTO's principal rule-book for trade in goods. The Uruguay Round also created new rules for dealing with trade in services, relevant aspects of intellectual property, dispute settlement, and trade policy reviews. The complete set runs to some 30,000 pages consisting of about 30 agreements and separate commitments (called schedules) made by individual members in specific areas such as lower customs duty rates and services market-opening.

Through these agreements, WTO members operate a non-discriminatory[2] trading system that spells out their rights and their obligations. Each country receives guarantees that its exports will be treated fairly and consistently in other countries' markets. Each promises to do the same for imports into its own market. The system also gives developing countries some flexibility in implementing their commitments.

a. Goods

It all began with trade in goods. From 1947 to 1994, GATT was the forum for negotiating lower customs duty rates and other trade barriers; the text of the General Agreement spelt out important rules, particularly non-discrimination.

Since 1995, the updated GATT has become the WTO's umbrella agreement[3] for

---

1 working party:（执行特定任务的）工作组，工作班子；专题调查委员会。
2 non-discriminatory: 非歧视性的。Of not giving differential treatment; esp., relating to treat all persons equally when no reasonable distinction can be found between those favored and those not favored.
3 umbrella agreement: an agreement covering rules of several aspects. 总括协定，指WTO货物贸易多边协议，该协议项下包括协议的总体解释说明，1994年的关贸总协定，农业协议，纺织品与服装协议等许多方面。

trade in goods. It has annexes dealing with specific sectors such as agriculture and textiles, and with specific issues such as state trading, product standards, subsidies and actions taken against dumping.

b. Services

Banks, insurance firms, telecommunication companies, tour operators, hotel chains and transport companies looking to do business abroad can now enjoy the same principles of freer and fairer trade that originally only applied to trade in goods.

These principles appear in the new General Agreement on Trade in Services (GATS)[1]. WTO members have also made individual commitments under GATS stating which of their services sectors they are willing to open to foreign competition, and how open those markets are.

c. Intellectual Property

The WTO's intellectual property agreement amounts to rules for trade and investment in ideas and creativity. The rules state how copyrights, patents, trademarks, geographical names used to identify products, industrial designs, integrated circuit layout-designs and undisclosed information such as trade secrets—"intellectual property"—should be protected when trade is involved.

d. Dispute Settlement

The WTO's procedure for resolving trade quarrels under the Dispute Settlement Understanding is vital for enforcing the rules and therefore for ensuring that trade flows smoothly. Countries bring disputes to the WTO if they think their rights under the agreements are being infringed. Judgements by specially-appointed independent experts are based on interpretations of the agreements and individual countries' commitments.

The system encourages countries to settle their differences through consultation. Failing that, they can follow a carefully mapped out, stage-by-stage procedure that

---

1 关贸总协定第八轮回合多边贸易谈判结束，达成了第一部管理国际服务贸易的法律文件——服务贸易总协定（General Agreement on Trade in Service，简称GATS），才形成了权威性和指导性的解释。GATS对服务贸易做出了明确的定义，"Trade in Service"是指以下四种服务提供的方式，即cross boarder supply（跨境交付）、consumption abroad（境外消费）、commercial presence（商业存在），还有movement of natural persons（自然人流动）。

includes the possibility of a ruling by a panel of experts, and the chance to appeal the ruling on legal grounds. Confidence in the system is borne out by the number of cases brought to the WTO—around 300 cases in eight years compared to the 300 disputes dealt with during the entire life of GATT (1947—1994).

e. Policy Review

The Trade Policy Review Mechanism's purpose is to improve transparency, to create a greater understanding of the policies that countries are adopting, and to assess their impact. Many members also see the reviews as constructive feedback on their policies.

All WTO members must undergo periodic scrutiny, each review containing reports by the country concerned and the WTO Secretariat[1].

IV. Developing Countries

a. Development and Trade

Over three quarters of WTO members are developing or least-developed countries. All WTO agreements contain special provision for them, including longer time periods to implement agreements and commitments, measures to increase their trading opportunities and support to help them build the infrastructure for WTO work, handle disputes, and implement technical standards.

The 2001 Ministerial Conference in Doha set out tasks, including negotiations, for a wide range of issues concerning developing countries. Some people call the new negotiations the Doha Development Round.

Before that, in 1997, a high-level meeting on trade initiatives and technical assistance for least-developed countries resulted in an "integrated framework" involving six intergovernmental agencies, to help least-developed countries increase their ability to trade, and some additional preferential market access[2] agreements.

---

1 the WTO Secretariat: 秘书处，是WTO的职能机构，主要职责是：为WTO的代表机构（如理事会、委员会、工作组、谈判组等）进行谈判和执行协议，提供行政和技术支持；为发展中国家，特别是不发达国家提供技术援助；在贸易争端解决过程中，由法律雇员提供有关规则和先例解释方面的法律帮助；处理新成员加入的谈判，为准备加入的国家提供咨询。
2 market access: 市场准入，指政府向外国商品（包括服务）和外国资本开放国内市场，以便利用国际贸易和国际投资。市场准入是WTO多边贸易框架下致力推动的主要目标之一，主要体现一个时间的过渡。

A WTO committee on trade and development, assisted by a sub-committee on least-developed countries, looks at developing countries' special needs. Its responsibility includes implementation of the agreements, technical cooperation, and the increased participation of developing countries in the global trading system.

b. Technical assistance and training

The WTO organizes around 100 technical cooperation missions to developing countries annually. It holds on average three trade policy courses each year in Geneva for government officials. Regional seminars are held regularly in all regions of the world with a special emphasis on African countries. Training courses are also organized in Geneva for officials from countries in transition from central planning to market economies.

The WTO set up reference centres in over 100 trade ministries and regional organizations in capitals of developing and least-developed countries, providing computers and Internet access to enable ministry officials to keep abreast of events in the WTO in Geneva through online access to the WTO's immense database of official documents and other material. Efforts are also being made to help countries that do not have permanent representatives in Geneva.

Glossary

annexes 文件的附件
anti-dumping 反倾销的
bear out 证实
centre in 集中于
consensus 全体一致同意
development law 发展法
Doha Development Agenda（缩写为DDA）多哈发展议程
economic integration 经济整合
GATT 关税与贸易总协定
General Agreement on Trade in Service 简称

GATS，服务贸易总协定
government procurement 政府采购
in the wake of 直接随着……
map out 计划；设计
market access 市场准入
merchandise 商品；货物
non-discriminatory 非歧视性的
normative 标准的；规范的
of sorts（口语）暗指名实不符
on the grounds of 因为；根据
scrutiny 详细审查

Lesson 12
WTO and International Economic Law

security 有价证券
spectrum 光谱；比喻广阔的范围、领域或系列
state trading 国营贸易
subsidies 补贴
tariff-free 免关税；零关税

the WTO Secretariat 秘书处
umbrella agreement 总括协定
unprecedented 空前的；史无前例的；无比的
working party 工作组；工作班子；专题调查委员会

EXERCISES

I. Answer the following questions.

1. What's the difference between GATT and WTO?
2. What implication did Uruguay Round have to international trade?
3. How does WTO work to help trade flow smoothly, freely, fairly and predictably?
4. What is umbrella agreement? How many parts does it conclude?
5. What's the aim of Trade Policy Review Mechanism?
6. Most WTO agreements require governments to fully disclose import policies and practice publicly including formally notifying the WTO of any changes. Is it right to say so?

II. Translate the following terms into English.

1. 国际货币基金组织
2. 关税与贸易总协定
3. 乌拉圭回合
4. 反倾销
5. 证券
6. 部长级会议
7. 关税壁垒
8. 政府采购
9. 技术协助
10. 总理事会
11. 政策审查
12. 专业委员会
13. 非歧视性
14. 伞形协议
15. 服务贸易总协议
16. 专家组
17. 基础设施
18. 市场准入

III. Translate the following sentences into Chinese.

1. Membership in GATT gave countries access to foreign markets but imposed upon them the obligation to keep their own markets open and to reduce trade barriers through the multilateral GATT negotiation.

2. The WTO, for the first time, offers an internationally accepted neutral and non-confrontational venue for countries to negotiate on a multi-lateral basis for trade activities.

3. The dispute settlement services offered by the WTO to member countries offers, in theory, an opportunity for disputes to be adjudicated in an open, fair and objective manner therefore allowing countries to conclude disputes in a peaceful and reasonable fashion.

4. By opening its country to trade China has created closer links with the rest of the world, creating personal as well as business relationships between Chinese and people overseas.

5. Under the WTO agreements, countries cannot normally discriminate between their trading partners. Grant someone a special favour (such as a lower customs duty rate for one of their products) and you have to do the same for all other WTO members.

IV. Word Derivation.

1. The postwar GATT has led to the _____ (establish) of a permanent international institution known as the World Trade Oragnization.

2. The _____ (initiate) aim of GATT was to expand free trade through the reduction of tariffs worldwide.

3. National regulatory agencies need to balance potential health, safety, and environmental concerns with the nation's _____ (oblige).

4. Before enacting any countervailing measures, the countries that has been victimized must seek WTO permission through the WTO dispute _____ (resolve) process.

5. Antidumping duties to be imposed only if goods are sold for export at a price below which they are sold for domestic _____ (consume).

6. The WTO agreements are _____ (long) and complex because they are legal texts covering a wide range of activities.

Supplementary Reading

The member of countries of the WTO have agreed that if they believe that another member country has violated trade rules, they will use the WTO system of resolving disputes instead of taking unilateral action[1]. The WTO Dispute Settlement Understanding (DSU)[2], enacted in 1994, provides for the prompt handling of international trade disputes. Its procedures for settling disputes provide fixed time periods for prompt resolution; in urgent cases, the rules provide for a final decision within three months. In cases that use the maximum time periods and that are appealed, the dispute resolution process should not take more than 15 months. The settlement system provides the following maximum time periods: 60 days for consultation and mediation; 45 days for the appointment of the Dispute Panel[3]; 6 months for the Panel to issue the decision and report; 3 weeks for the submission of the report to WTO members; 60 days for the Dispute Settlement Body to adopt the report. In case of an appeal the appeals court has 90 days to issue its report and the Dispute Settlement Body has 30 days to adopt the appeals report[4].

The Dispute Settlement Body is the sole authority for appointing the panel of experts to decide cases. Before taking any formal action the disputing countries must consult with each other in attempt to settle the dispute. They can also ask the WTO director-general[5] to mediate the dispute. Upon the failure of consultation, the complaining country[6] can request that a panel be established to hear the dispute. WTO Panels are like tribunals[7],

---

1 unilateral action: an act in which there is only one party whose will operates. 单边行为，这里指采取单方面的报复行为。unilateral, *adj.* one-sided; relating to only one of two or more persons or things. 单边的。与此相对，bilateral, 双边的；multi-lateral, 多边的。
2 DSU: WTO争端解决谅解书，全称Understanding on Rules and Procedures Governing the Settlement of Dispute, DSU《关于争端解决规则和程序谅解书》。
3 60天之内磋商和调停，如果没有解决争端，（申诉方）申请在45天之内任命专家组。
4 对于上诉案件，上诉机构（法院）在90天之内发布裁定报告，争端解决机构在30天内采纳上诉机构的报告。
5 director-general：总干事。
6 complaining country：申诉国、申诉方。
7 tribunal: the seat, bench, or place where a judge sits. 法官席或审判员席。

usually consisting three, sometimes five, experts. The two countries usually agree on the panel members. If they cannot agree, then the director-general will appoint the panelists. The activities of the panel are confidential. Before the hearing[1] each side prepares its case in writing. At the first hearing, both parties present, along with any other country that voices an interest in the case. At a second hearing, both parties submit written rebuttals[2] and present oral arguments. The panel may also consult experts or appoint an advisory group of experts to prepare a report.

The panel prepares a first draft report and submits it to both parties for comments. It then submits an interim report[3] consisting of its findings and conclusions, allowing either party one week in order to request a review. If a review is requested the panel has two weeks to hold additional meetings with the parties. The panel then submits a final report, which becomes the ruling of the Dispute Settlement Body unless it is rejected. However, the final report can only be rejected by a unanimous vote of the DBS. The losing party then must prepare and submit a proposal to implement the ruling within a reasonable period of time,In cases where the losing party fails to implement the ruling within a reasonable period of time,the parties must negotiate compensation pending a full implementation[4]. If the parties do not agree on compensation, then the Dispute Settlement Body will authorize measures of retaliation for the winning country[5]. These sanctions usually entail withholding or suspending tariff concessions previously mandated under GATT.

---

1 hearing: a judicial session, usu. open to the public, held for the purpose of deciding issues of fact or of law, sometimes with witnesses testifying. 听证。
2 rebuttal: in-court contradiction of an adverse party's evidence. 辩驳、反对意见。
3 interim report：临时报告; final report：最终报告。
4 如果败诉方在合理的期限内没能执行裁决，双方当事人必须在完全履行之前对赔偿问题进行磋商。
5 如果双方未能对赔偿达成一致，那么争端解决机构将对授权胜诉方采取单边报复措施。

Appendix I
Text Translation & Key to Exercises (Part One)

附录一 课文译文及练习答案（上篇）

上篇 各课译文

第一课 法的概念及其分类

一、法的概念

现在已经有，而且今后还会有很多关于法的不同的定义。亚里士多德视法为行为的准则。柏拉图认为法是一种社会控制的形式。西塞罗则主张法是自然与理性的统一，是正义与非正义之间的界限。英国法学家布莱克斯通将法描述为"国家最高权力规定的市民行动准则，它规定正确的事，禁止做违法的事"。在美国，杰出的法学家奥利弗·温德尔·霍姆斯主张，法是允许人们去预测法院将如何解决某一特定纠纷的一整套准则："对于法院在事实上将如何处理的预测，而绝非其他更虚饰的东西，便是我所谓的法"。

尽管这些定义在细节上有所不同，不过，所有这些关于法的定义都是建立在下面这一概括判断之上的。即：法由调整个人与个人、以及个人与社会之间关系的强制性规则所组成。这个对法所下的宽泛的定义包含下列意思：

- 要有法就必须有制定成文的规则，例如宪法、制定法（法律）、行政机关规章以及司法判决等。
- 这些规则必须是可强制执行的，换言之，法律和命令在一司法体系内都有执行力。
- 这些规则必须制定一些被认可的行为，个人可依此与他人交往或参与社会活动。

国内法由国会制定，国会作为立法部门由众议院和参议院组成。国会可以就各种事务立法，例如在高速公路上设置时速限制，或制定规则调整饮用水中氡的含量。每一届国会中，参议员和众议员们会提出大量议案。议案由国会通过后，经总统签署成为法律。

二、法的分类

法的分类按照适用的不同标准或特征可分为若干不同的种类。首先是要区分公法与私法。刑事法律同民事法律之间也存在重要的区别。其他分类包括大陆法与普通法，实体法与程序法。本课主要考察这几种重要的法律分类。

（一）公法与私法

法律可划分为两大部门：一公法，二私法。公法是调整个人与政府间关系的法律，同时还是关于政府框架本身及其运作的法律；公法包括宪法、刑法和行政法。私法是调整个人、个人财产以及相互之间关系的法律。根据涉及的法律权利与义务，私法可以分为六大部门。这些部门是合同与商法，侵权行为法，财产法，继承法，家庭法，以及公司法。

（二）刑事法律与民事法律

刑事法律总体上阐述的是违反社会的义务。通过称为检察官（例如，地区检察官）的政府官员，社会对违法者提起诉讼。如果你被发现犯有某种罪行，例如盗窃罪，你可能会被处以监禁刑或罚金刑。支付的罚金通常属于国库，而不属于犯罪的受害者。

民事法律确立个人（包括公司）之间的个人责任。例如，我们有义务履行自己做出的合同承诺。侵权行为法界定人们互负的众多义务。其中一个最为常见的义务是要对他人尽合理注意义务。不能够尽到合理注意义务会导致过失侵权。

违反民事义务的诉讼只能由不法行为的受害人提起。通常，法院并不去惩罚不法行为人，而是通过叫作"损害赔偿金"的金钱给予使受不法侵害方得到补偿。例如，如果某人不小心开车撞倒了你的车子，则他的行为构成过失民事不法行为（侵权行为）。如果你的下肢因此受到损伤，你可以从该驾驶人（或其保险公司）处获得损害赔偿金。这一损害赔偿金的数额应足以维修你的汽车、支付你的药费、误工费、以及其他任何如致跛等永久性残疾的补偿。你也有可能得到"痛苦与创伤"精神损害赔偿金。

尽管民事法律通常并不旨在做出惩罚，但是也有例外。如果侵权人的行为十分过分，可要求行为人支付惩罚性损害赔偿金（也称为"惩戒性损害赔偿金"）。与刑事案件中支付的罚金不同，惩罚性损害赔偿金归受损害方所有。

有时，同一行为会既违反民事法律也违反刑事法律。比如说，醉酒人的驾车行为导致他人死亡，他可能会既面对国家对其提起的刑事诉讼，又面对尚存者的损害赔偿金民事诉讼。如果这两种诉讼均成功，驾驶人就要以罚金或监禁刑向社会偿还造成的损害，而且还要以金钱损害赔偿金向尚存者做出补偿。

参考下表所列刑事法律同民事法律之对照，以期对刑事案件与民事案件能有一个大概的比较。

	刑事案件	民事案件
构成要件	故意或过失违反制定法	给他人或他人财产带来损害（侵权行为）或违反合同
参与者	检察官　诉　被告人 （政府）　　（刑事被告人）	原告　诉　被告 （受不法侵害方）　（不法侵害方）
惩罚	罚金刑，监禁刑，死刑等。	被告可能须向原告支付补偿性损害赔偿金或惩罚性损害赔偿金。

（三）大陆法与普通法

我们已经了解法律体系可以分为两大类：刑事法律与非刑事法律（或民事法律）。但是，尽管"非刑事"的确是"civil law"这一术语的一个意思，但是这个意思不是我们

Appendix I

Text Translation & Key to Exercises (Part One)

这里所讨论的。大陆法是一特定法律体系的名称，世界上许多国家都效仿并确立了这一法系。简单地讲，我们可以说大陆法系是建立在详细规定社会基本法律之法典（或制定法）上的法律体系，这些基本法律的立法主题广泛，如构成犯罪的行为、纳税义务、以及拥有和转让财产的规则等。

"大陆法"这一术语以及法律的基本原则均来自古罗马法——市民法。随着时间推移，古罗马法被改写进大量的法典之中。"黑暗世纪"之后，查士丁尼（公元483—565年）的法典复兴，并成为意大利、德意志帝国、荷兰、法国、西班牙以及上述国家的殖民地地区现代法的基础。路易斯安那州同样有着大陆法传统。今天，大多数西欧国家都属于大陆法系国家，拉丁美洲国家、大多数非洲国家、日本、泰国以及土耳其也属于大陆法系国家。

除了美国和英国，普通法法系国家还包括澳大利亚、缅甸、加拿大、印度、伊拉克、利比里亚、马来西亚、新西兰、新加坡以及大英帝国前非洲殖民地，例如，加纳和尼日利亚。普通法的基础不是包罗万象的法典，普通法系的基本组成部分是判例法，判例法由审理一个个案件的法官所传下来的裁决所组成。因为每一司法意见都充当后来裁决的先例，所以，普通法有时也被称为"法官造法"。普通法法官在适用先前的司法裁决和解释制定法方面有着很大的权力。

大陆法与普通法之间最明显的区别是，大陆法属于成文法，但普通法并非通过立法途径创立，它主要是建立在判例法之上。普通法的审判原则，即先前的司法判例——通常是上级法院已经做出的判决，在后来的相似案件中应当得到遵守，即先例应该得到尊重。这一原则就是著名的"遵循先例"原则。普通法由判例法所建立这一判断并不完全正确，因为普通法在很大一部分上还建立在制定法之上，因此普通法法官同大陆法法官一样适用、解释这些制定法（例如1979年的《英国货物买卖法》和《统一商法典》）。

（四）实体法与程序法

法律体系还可以分为实体法和程序法两大类。

程序法确立规则以及指导方针，即程序，法律根据这些程序运行。例如，在我们的法律之中，程序法明确规定提起诉讼的诉讼时效长度。程序法可以分为刑事诉讼法，例如警方在讯问前必须向犯罪嫌疑人告知他享有的一系列权利；以及民事诉讼法，例如民事诉状——诉讼双方当事人对将在审判中的阐述的立场之书面说明。有些诉讼程序在刑事诉讼法与民事诉讼法中是通用的。

实体法包括权利、义务或在各种情形下适用于个人、企业的限制。实体法可建立在美国宪法、立法机关颁布的制定法、或法官发展的判例法之上。在刑法中，例如，对构成犯罪的行为之实际界定为实体法。在合同法中，实体法包括合同一方在违反契约条款时，（另一方享有的）权利及救济方式。

三、法律女神什么样

正义的象征通常是一位手持天平、眼睛蒙着布的女神。正义女神的起源可以追溯到很久以前。古埃及的正义女神称为玛特，玛特的样子通常被描述为手持宝剑、头带一支鸵鸟羽毛（但无天平）用来象征真理和正义。"治安法官"这一术语来自"玛特"，因为她通过称量死者的心脏帮助奥西里斯神审判死者。

古希腊人认为的正义女神是西弥斯，她最初是"人类共同事务特别是公民大会"

的组织者。她能够预见将来的事，这使她成为德尔菲的一个神喻（德尔菲，古希腊宗教中心，阿波罗神庙是这里的一个主要建筑），这反过来使她的"神圣正义女神"的地位得以确立。西弥斯的经典象征是，她并未带蒙眼布（因为她具有预见能力，没有必要蒙眼），也不持宝剑（因为她象征着同意，而非压制）。

罗马的正义女神叫作"宙斯提提亚"。她通常被描述为：左手持一平衡的天平，右手持长剑，眼睛蒙着布。有时，她也被描述为一手持权杖（绑在斧头周围的象征司法权力的一捆棍杖），而另一只手持着象征真理的火焰。

第二课　法的渊源

尽管美利坚合众国宪法是美国最高法律，但它只是美国法律众渊源之一。除了宪法，美国法律还包括普通法、制定法、以及行政法规和规章等。

一、宪法（宪法性法律）

各州宪法以及联邦政府宪法是国家最高的法律并且是比其他法律渊源更为重要的法律渊源。美国宪法创立联邦政府，宪法的修正案保证美国公民最基本的权利及自由。

各州宪法同样规定州一级政府的总体组织结构，分为立法、行政、以及司法部门，实现各部门间的牵制与平衡，并对各部门的权力与职能作出限定。与联邦宪法一样，州宪法也保证各种权利以及自由。

如果你的宪法性权利被侵犯，违反宪法的法律则无效（即这些法律对你不产生法律效力）。

解释美国宪法并保证宪法权利得以实现的法律被称为宪法性法律。政府的司法部门有权审查联邦和州政府的宪法以及其他法律。这就是著名的"司法审查"原则。司法审查权确立于"马伯里诉麦迪逊"一案（收集在美国案例汇编第5卷（克兰奇汇编1卷），第137页，1803年形成审判意见），在该案中，联邦最高法院确立了政府司法部门审查行政、立法部门的行为与判决的权力，并且司法部门有权确定这些行为的合宪性。法院审查这些政府部门行为的能力是美国法律体系的核心，而且对于法律的发展至关重要。

二、普通法（判例法）

法官创造普通法。通常，法院从先前已经确定的案例（先例）入手，然后再将这些规则适用于手头的案件，继而宣布由特定事实形成的案件之规则。在形成这一新的规则之前，法院会使用手头案件的事实与其他案件的事实进行比较，以发现案件间的异同。依照遵循先例原则，法院通过这种方法对类似的案件作出类似的判决。

根据遵循先例原则（"让判决持久"），法院一旦确立适用于特定种类事实的某种法律原则，当事实相同或相似时，法官将会在今后的案件中遵循这一原则。这一原则确定了美国法律制度的稳定、一致，如果没有遵循先例原则，法律制度将会混乱且变得任意。但是这点十分重要——遵循先例原则并非永恒不变。随着判例法的发展与变化，有些判决由于变化的社会价值观、或者制定法、宪法的修正案而失去了其控制性作用。

三、制定法（立法）

制定法（正式的成文法律）是最为重要的法律渊源之一。立法部门通过的，以调整

Appendix I

Text Translation & Key to Exercises (Part One)

公民行为的法律称为制定法。在美国法律体系中的联邦层面，国会通过由美国总统签署的制定法。各州可以经各自州立法部门通过各州州长签署的法律。立法部门所通过的法律必须同美国宪法及州宪法相一致，否则司法部门有可能会宣布它们无效。

各级政府均设有立法机关，不仅包括联邦国会，还包括州议会、市政会、以及其他通过或颁布法律的地方政府机构。市、镇颁布的法律通常称为"条例"，它也是一种形式的制定法。广义上的立法还包括政府行政机构所签订的、参议院批准的条约。各级政府的立法编纂称为"法典"。例如，我们有地方交通法典，它涵盖诸如最高车速限定等事项；州法律如《统一商法典》，该法涵盖了商事交易中的各个方面。联邦政府的制定法均编入了《美国法典》。

（一）立法的统一

因为国会、50个州立法机构、以及众多的地方政府均颁布制定法和条例，所以需要考虑法律缺少统一性这一问题。如果法律缺少了统一性，它会降低商事行为以及社会整体秩序所必需的确定性。

立法者可以通过下列两种方法实现法律的统一：
- 国会可颁布单独法律，并使其优先于其他诸州法律。
- 全体州立法机构在某一特定领域可采用某一统一法律。

后一种方法已经被"统一州法全国委员会"这一立法起草团体多次运用，这些委员们通过起草"模范法案"致力于推动法律的统一。在全国会议批准之后，提议的统一法案再被推荐到州立法部门以期通过。

起草并提到各州立法机构的大约有100多部统一法，（这些法调整的内容）大多与商业活动有关。各州在通过上述提案法律的态度上不尽相同。只有极少数统一法为全部州所采用。有时，有的州只在原则上采用统一法，但对一些条文要作修改以满足当地的需要。针对商业活动制定的最为重要的统一法是《统一商法典》（UCC）。

（二）立法的解释

立法的语言通常是概括性术语。法律准确的意思常常不是很清楚。在美国法律中，司法机关决定立法机关所颁布的法律中概括性语言的意思、并将之适用于案件的特定事实之中。法院解释制定法或条例的意图在于确定制定法在制定时立法者的本意。这一过程称为"制定法的解释"。

四、行政规章（行政法）

行政机关是指有权制定规则、规范行为、并且审判违反行政机关规则和规章等行为的政府实体。行政规章的特殊之处在于，作为联邦以及州政府权力授予的结果，行政机关同时履行政府三个部门的许多职能：行政机关可以通过制定规则和规章来立法；行政机关可以通过行使行政权力监督规章是否被遵守；行政机关还可以同法院一样通过裁决做出判决。

由于行政机关的权力在早期的发展阶段实际上未受制约，国会于1946年通过了一部叫作《行政程序法》的制定法，该法分为四大领域，即《情报自由法》《隐私权法》《阳光下的政府法》，以及《管理弹性法案》。根据《行政程序法》，行政机关依照与联邦宪法相一致原则，管理和监督联邦行政机关如"联邦环境保护局"、"联邦航空管理局"等联邦机构的活动。

第三课　美国的法院体系

不同于世界上大多数国家，美国实际上存在五十二个法院体系——五十个州每州一个，哥伦比亚地区一个，再加上一个联邦体系——它们都富于相似性。州法院体系是根据各州的宪法建立起来的。联邦法院并不高于州法院，它们只是根据美国宪法第二条第三款建立起来的一个独立的法院体系。尽管各州法院系统有所不同，表3-1还是阐明了许多州法院系统的基本组织结构特征。这个图表还表明了联邦法院系统是如何构成的。

一、州法院体系

典型的州法院体系包括几个层级，或者说几个审级的法院。州法院可能包括：（1）具有有限管辖权的初审法院，（2）具有一般管辖权的初审法院，（3）上诉法院，（4）州最高法院。通常来说，案件的任何一方当事人都有获得在初审法院进行案件审判的权利，如果他/她败诉，至少可以上诉到上一级上诉法院。最后需要指出，如果州最高法院的判决涉及联邦法律或者联邦宪法问题，那么此项判决将能继续上诉至联邦最高法院。

（一）初审法院

初审法院就像其名称所表明的那样，是举行审判和采纳证词的法院。州初审法院或者具有一般管辖权，或者具有有限管辖权。具有一般对事管辖权的初审法院还可以被称作郡（县）法院、地方法院、高级法院或者巡回法院。这些法院的管辖权通常是由法院所在郡（县）的大小来决定的。具有一般管辖权的州初审法院对各种事由都存在管辖权，既包括民事纠纷又包括刑事诉讼。在一些案件中，一般管辖权的初审法院可以审理从有限管辖权法院来的上诉案件。

一些具有有限管辖权的法院被称为特殊低级法院或次级司法法院。小额索赔法院便是这样的低级初审法院——它只审理不足一定数额索赔的民事案件，如五千美元以下（每个州各不相同）。起诉到小额索赔法院的案件通常进行非正式审理，在大多数情况下甚至不允许律师代表出庭。低级初审法院的另一个例子就是主要审理交通案件的地方市镇法院。小额索赔法院和市镇法院的判决可以被上诉到具有一般管辖权的州初审法院。

其他具有有限对事管辖权的初审法院还包括家事法庭（该法院仅仅处理离婚诉讼、子女监护权案件）和遗嘱检验法庭。

（二）上诉法院

每个州至少有一个上诉法院（上诉审法院或复审法院），该法院可能是中级上诉法院，也可能是该州的最高法院。大约有四分之三的州设有中级上诉法院。通常来说，上诉法院不审理新案子，新案件通常要求提交证据，以及讯问证人。相反地，上诉法院中由三到四名法官组成的合议庭审查的是上诉案件的记录，包括初审程序的副本，以此来判定初审法院是否犯了错误。

通常情况下，上诉法院不看事实问题（比如一个当事人实际上是否实施了某一行为，如烧国旗），而是关注于法律问题（比如烧国旗行为是否为宪法第一修正案所保护的言论的一种形式）。只有法官——而不是陪审团，能对法律问题做出裁决。正常情况下上诉法院会遵从初审法院对事实问题的认定，因为初审法院的法官和陪审团在庭审期

Appendix I

Text Translation & Key to Exercises (Part One)

间通过直接观察证人的言行举止和非语言行为，能更好地评价证人证言。在上诉法院这一级，法官只审查初审笔录，其中并不包括这些非语言行为的内容。

只有当初审法院的事实认定明显错误（即事实认定与呈递到法院的证据相反），或者认定没有证据支持时，上诉法院才会对该事实认定提出质疑。如果陪审团断定生产商的产品伤害了原告但又没有证据呈递到法院支持该结论，那么上诉法院将认定初审法院的判决错误。

（三）州最高法院

州最高级的上诉法院通常被称作最高法院，但是也可能叫作其他名字。举例来说，纽约州和马里兰州的州最高法院都叫作上诉法院。每个州最高法院对所有该州法律问题所作的判决为终审判决。只有当涉及联邦法律问题时，州最高法院的判决才有可能被联邦最高法院推翻。

二、联邦法院体系

联邦法院体系基本上是三级（审判）模式，包括：（1）联邦地区法院（具有一般管辖权的初审法院）和各种具有有限管辖权的法院，（2）联邦上诉法院（中级上诉法院），（3）联邦最高法院。

不同于州法院法官通常由选举产生，联邦法院的法官，包括最高法院的大法官，都是由美国议会通过并由总统任命产生。所有的联邦法官都是终身制的（根据宪法第三条，法官廉洁奉公，品行良好而终身任职）。

（一）联邦地区法院

地区法院在联邦法律体系下相当于具有一般管辖权的州初审法院。每个州至少有一个联邦地区法院。联邦法院司法辖区的数量随着时间而变化，主要是根据人口数量和待审案件的数量而变化。目前共有九十四个联邦司法辖区。

联邦地区法院审理涉及联邦问题的案件，像联邦犯罪和执行联邦法律所产生的案件。大多数联邦犯罪涉及反政府罪和因侵害联邦财产产生的犯罪。举例来说，绑架罪就是一种联邦犯罪，尽管此罪不一定涉及联邦几个州的土地辖区。绑架罪的联邦管辖权是以受害人被跨州或跨国绑架的假设为基础，联邦法律规定，如果绑架发生后二十四小时内未释放人质，便产生了一种可予反驳的推定——人质已被转运到其他州或被贩到外国。

除此之外，当原告和被告人来自于不同的州或国家时，尽管可以根据州法律来主张权利，到联邦法院起诉也是可能的。当原告是一个州的居民而被告是另一个州的居民，或者一方当事人是一个外国国家或一个外国的居民而另一方是美国居民时，多元管辖权就产生了。多元管辖权案件中主张索赔的金额至少必须达到七万五千美元。

另外，还有其他法院具有初审管辖权——但是这些管辖权都是特别的或有限的，比如联邦破产法院和在表3-1中列出的其他法院。

（二）联邦上诉法院

联邦法院体系中共有十三个联邦上诉法院——也被称作联邦巡回上诉法院。联邦上诉法院有十二个巡回区，包括哥伦比亚地区，这些法院负责审理位于各自巡回审判区内的联邦地区法院的上诉案件。第十三巡回审判区的上诉法院叫作联邦巡回法院，该法院对某些类型的案件——诸如专利权案件和美国联邦政府作为被告的案件——具有国家的上诉管辖权。另外这一法院还审理特别法院（比如联邦索赔法院和联邦国际贸易法院）的上诉案和由联邦政府机构的决定所引发的索赔案。

（三）联邦最高法院

联邦司法体系三级（审判）模式的最高级就是联邦最高法院。根据美国宪法第三条的所述，只有一个国家最高法院，联邦体系内的其他法院都被认为是"低级的"。国会认为必要时有权创建其他低级法院，包括三级模式中的第二级——联邦上诉法院，也包括地方法院和其他有具有有限或特殊管辖权的法院。

联邦最高法院由九名大法官组成。虽然最高法院对极少数案件具有初审管辖权（例如，法律纠纷的一方当事人是一个州、两个州之间的案件、涉及大使的案件），但它的主要工作还是担任上诉法院。最高法院可以审查任何联邦上诉法院判决的案件，并且有权审理由某些州法院判决的上诉案件。

最高法院上诉 要把案件上诉到最高法院，一方当事人要求法院发布调案复审令。调案复审令是最高法院向下级法院发布的命令，要求下级法院呈递案件的记录来加以审查。最高法院一般不会发布调案复审令，除非九名大法官中的四位同意这样做，这被称作四人规则。法院是否发布调案复审令是完全属于其自由裁量范围的。最高法院不是必须发布调案令的，大多数要求复审的请求都被拒绝了。（每年有几千件案件充斥着最高法院，然而受理的平均不到一百件。）拒绝不是断定案件没有价值，也不是表明同意下级法院的观点。最高法院拒绝复审时，实际的结果就是同意了下级法院的判决，该判决将继续约束当事人各方。

第四课 陪审团

英美陪审团制度是非常著名的政治制度。陪审团从广泛的人群中随机征募12个非法律专业人士，在审理某一特定案件时将这些人召集起来，授予他们极大的决断权，允许他们进行秘密审议，并允许他们在最后公布裁决结果的时候无须说明理由。陪审团履行完对国家的短暂服务后即行解散，陪审员们重新返回到各自的生活中去。

陪审团制度可追溯到9世纪的法国，之后被威廉一世（即征服者威廉）引入到英格兰。在早期，陪审团由被告人的邻居组成，在其知晓的范围内回答问题。当时的陪审员既是事实见证人同时也是事实审判者。后来，陪审团的审判权利得到了权利法案和美国宪法以及各州宪法的保障。

今天，在英国王室法院的审判中，只要被告人做无罪答辩，且这一辩称不被控方接受，被告人就要接受陪审团的审理。与之对照，在美国，任何联邦法院初审案件，如果可能判处6个月以上刑罚，而且案中被告人是成年人，被告人均有权获得陪审团审判。在英国，民事案件的陪审制度已经废除；在美国，民事案件的陪审制度正面临着被废除的压力。

一、陪审团的作用

陪审团在审判中的作用在于其对案件的事实进行判断。陪审团成员都是非法律专业人士，不具备法律专业知识，但他们却可以提出法律上的观点。他们必须依据常识对被告人以及证明其有罪的证据进行判断以做出裁决。法官的职责之一便是向陪审团解释

Appendix I

Text Translation & Key to Exercises (Part One)

法律，陪审团在对法官所作的法律解释理解的基础上做出裁决。法官与陪审团之间的关系至关重要。法官主持审讯，对审讯中出现的任何法律问题作出裁判，并控制由陪审团听审的证据。如果证据不充分，法官可以指示陪审团作出被告人无罪的裁决。在证据展示完毕时，法官会在陪审团休庭准备做出判决之前就审理的案件为陪审团作出总结。此后法官就无法继续干预了。法官可以在总结中向陪审团指明唯一合理的裁断就是有罪裁决。但法官实际上并没有指示对被告人作出有罪判决的司法权。如果陪审团的裁决不当，法官也无能为力，只能接受。如果陪审团作出无罪裁决，法庭不得拒绝该裁决的有效性。对于王室法院作出的无罪判决不能上诉，并且一旦被告人被宣判无罪，就不能再对其以相同理由再行起诉。

二、陪审团成员的选定

任何18岁到70岁的注册选民都有合法资格担任陪审员。而不具备该资格的人包括司法人员以及审判制度其他相关人员，如出庭律师和事务律师，神职人员以及心智有缺陷的人。

（一）陪审员审查

陪审员全体成员是随机选出的，诉讼任何一方都可以对其进行审查，从而选出陪审员。作为一种剔除随意性的机制，陪审员审查程序通过对陪审员背景的调查来决定候选人是否适合履行陪审职责。

（二）对陪审员资格提出异议

诉讼双方有权基于以下三个理由要求某一陪审员回避：
（1）该陪审员在事实上不合格；
（2）该陪审员存在偏见（主要指并非针对被告人本身的偏见）；
（3）有合理的理由怀疑该陪审员对被告人存在偏见。

法院召集而来的陪审员在法院集合，组成一个陪审员候选人小组，从该小组中再分入某个特定的刑事或民事审判案件。各方律师和/或法官向其提问，提问内容包括他们的背景、经验以及其对自己是否能对证据作出公正客观的判断。这一程序称为voir dire，这是个是诺尔曼时期英国所用的法语词汇，意为"照实陈述"。

在美国，可要求回避的陪审员数量没有限制。而在英国，只有辩护方有机会针对陪审员候选人提出无因回避请求，即不必解释理由便可拒绝一定数量的候选陪审员。控方有权要求陪审员一位留作备用，备用陪审员仅于所有陪审员都已用尽的情况下才能进入陪审团。

三、陪审团审判

陪审团审判是指民事或刑事的诉讼案件提交给陪审团审理，由其审理案件事实和做出最终裁判结果。陪审团审判与法官审判不同在于后者由法官审理事实问题以及法律问题，并做出最终裁判结果。

早期的陪审团经常就事实问题或事实与法律的混合问题进行裁判。近代陪审团做总体裁决时，在判断事实性问题之外还可以处理法律问题，但联邦陪审团通常仅限于处理事实问题。

美国的法律体系中有三种陪审团审判形式，各自在联邦法院中受到美国宪法的保障,并且为各州所使用:刑事小陪审团、民事小陪审团和大陪审团。

四、大陪审团

大陪审团作为一项制度在美国先辈的传统中就已稳固地建立起来了,甚至在权利法案中也有体现。美国宪法第五修正案一部分就规定"非经大陪审团提起公诉,任何人不受死罪或其他辱罪之审判——"

联邦大陪审团的权力和作用与普通陪审团(又称小陪审团)不同。小陪审团就刑事审判中控辩双方提供的证据进行听审(如其选择提供证据的话),并作出罪与非罪的裁决。而大陪审团并不就罪与非罪作出裁决,而仅就是否存在犯罪发生以及某特定的人是否实施过该犯罪的合理依据进行判断。如果大陪审团发现存在合理依据,则会签署书面公诉书。此后,被告人就会受到审判。

大陪审团通常仅听取欲证明有犯罪发生的检察官提交的证据。大陪审团必须根据这些证据并且在不审查被告人提交证据的情况下决定此被告人是否犯了严重的联邦罪行,也就是权利法案所指的"辱罪"。辱罪是指可判处一年以上监禁的罪行。一般情况下,除非大陪审团裁决经其审理的证据确实证明有严重犯罪发生,否则任何人不得被控诉犯有严重罪行。这样,大陪审团既是"矛"——授权政府起诉犯罪嫌疑人,同时也是"盾",保护公民免受无根据的或不正当的指控。不过一个人也可以放弃大陪审团审理的要求,自愿接受由检察官签署起诉书发起的控诉。

大陪审团宣誓后,主审法官会告知大陪审团其应负义务以及如何最佳履行职责,这一程序称为对大陪审团的指示。进行该指示必须审慎小心,因为法官指示以及其他说明包括大陪审团在其存续期间必须遵守的规则和指令。

16人是由23人组成的大陪审团法定最少人数。如果少于16人,即便是暂时的,陪审团的审议也必须停止。大陪审团的多数时间都花在听审证人的证词和对文件及其他证据的审查上,其目的就在于确定这些证据能否支持控告。

证人按要求顺序分别出庭作证。证人宣誓后,陪审团会向其提问。一般来说,检察官会首先向证人发问,接着陪审团主席提问,然后轮到其他陪审团成员。在回答问题之前,证人可能会离开大陪审团所在的房间与其律师进行协商。大陪审团审判案件中的证人可以援引第五修正案赋予的不自证其罪的权利拒绝回答任何问题。此种情形下,大陪审团可能将此提交给法庭,由法庭裁决是否要求强制回答提问。强制回答的方式之一就是准许证人免受起诉,以换取其证言。

陪审团听取了对被告人不利的证据后,必须决定该证据能否支持将由大陪审团签署的"公诉书",即大陪审团发出的正式刑事控告书。公诉书一经由法庭签发,被起诉的人要么认罪,要么进行无罪申诉,或者受审。

如果证据不能说服大陪审团,不能让大陪审团有合理依据相信被指控的人实施了犯罪,大陪审团会表决决定不起诉,出现这种情况时,就不要求该嫌疑人为刑事指控辩护,也没有必要进行审判。

大陪审团获取指控的所有证据后,所有陪审团成员之外的人必须离开陪审团所在的房间以便陪审团进行审议。大陪审团进行审议或表决时,任何陪审员以外的其他人在场都可能导致针对指控所作的公诉书无效。

大陪审团每个团员都有表达其对讼争事实意见的权利,且应在做出决定前听取其他陪审团成员的评论。只有在每个陪审员都有机会让其他人听取其意见后才能进行表决。陪审团就公诉书表决时须至少有16个陪审员出席，并且至少12个成员表决支持方能签署公诉书。

如果一项公诉成立，大陪审团会就此在公开法庭上向法官或司法官报告。它也可以以同样的方式报告指控不成立，或决定不提起公诉。不起诉的决定必须立即有大陪审团主席以书面形式报告给法庭，以便被指控的人可以立即从监狱获得释放或保释。

法律规定每个大陪审团成员有严格的保密义务。陪审员的宣誓和法官对陪审团的指示进一步强调了这一义务。出于众多因素考虑，保密传统直到今天仍然是大陪审团制度至关重要的组成部分。它保护陪审员免受来自成为大陪审团调查对象及其关系人的压力，防止可能卷入公诉的人逃跑；它鼓励证人为大陪审团提供完整真实的有关犯罪的信息；保密制度还可以预防证人在作证之前免受贿赂或胁迫；最后保密制度还将防止对大陪审团调查无果而终的披露，避免某人因成为大陪审团调查的对象而背负污名。

陪审员所负有的保密义务也是保护他们自己的主要措施。此外，对于陪审员的言论和所作的表决，非经法庭命令也不受。法律赋予陪审团成员对其权利范围内的行为享有广泛的豁免权，所有的陪审员都应以最高的责任感履行其义务。

第五课　主要法理学流派

法学（法理学）一词来源拉丁语juris prudentia，意思是"法律研究、法律知识或法律科学"。在美国，法学通常指法哲学（法律哲学）。法律哲学包括很多方面，但是最为普遍的有四个方面。第一种也是最为普通的一种法律哲学形式寻求对整个法律体系进行分析、解释、分类以及批评。法学院的教科书以及法律大百科全书属于这一类型。第二种类型的法律哲学将法律与其他学科如文学、经济学、宗教以及社会科学进行比较与对照。第三种类型的法律哲学寻求体现某一特定法律概念的历史、道德、以及文化基础。第四种法律哲学关心的主要是寻找抽象问题如"法是什么？"、"法官如何（适当）判定案件？"等问题的答案。

除不同类型的法学之外，还有不同流派的法学。实证法学与自然法学流派思想之间就法律的适当渊源问题有一场经典的辩论。实证主义者认为，法与道德之间并无联系，法的唯一渊源是政府实体或法院所明确制定的规则。自然主义者，或是自然法的支持者则坚持认为政府制定的规则并非是法的唯一渊源。他们主张道德哲学、宗教、人类理性、以及个人良心同样是法的不可缺少的组成部分。

不同法学流派之间并无明显的界限。某一法学家的法律哲学可能由法律思想众多流派中某些种类思想结合而成。有些法学家认为将法理学视为一个连续统一体可能更为合适。

上面提及的法学思想流派只是美国多彩法学图卷中的一个部分。还有很多卓著的法学思想流派存在。

一、自然法学派

自然法学派是最古老、最重要的法理学流派之一。坚持自然法学派思想的人认为政府及法律制度应该反映人类本质中固有的普遍的道德及伦理原则。

自然法概念的起源可追溯到古希腊。希腊哲学家亚里士多德（公元前384—322年）对自然法与常规法（又叫实证法，或成文法）作出了区别。在亚里士多德看来，"自然法在任何地方都有同样的效力……"因此，自然法是人类社会中普遍存在的道德法则。另一方面，常规法反映的是某一特定时期特定社会中被人们接受了的价值观和道德观。例如，在我们这个时代，法律规定选举权或饮酒的最低年龄，这并非是神意的产物，而只是反映这一特定时期特定社会中的主流观点。再如，法律禁止谋杀，这反映的并非是某一特定时期某一特定社会所认定的价值观，而是建立在一个举世公认的认识——即谋杀即错误的判断之上的。谋杀由此便是对自然法的侵犯。

因为自然法是普遍的，所以它比实证法或常规法具有更高的权威。自然法观念鼓励人们在认为实证法与自然法相冲突的情况时不去遵循常规法或成文法。例如，在越南战争（1964—1973）期间，抗议美国卷入战争的人民就将自然法作为他们反对成文法的依据。

托马斯·阿奎那（1225—1274），中世纪著名的神学家，他试图将亚里士多德自然法哲学与基督教教义结合起来。阿奎那认为，法有四种类型（1）永恒法是上帝统治整个宇宙的法律；（2）自然法是人们凭靠自身的理性能力所认识的永恒法中的某些方面；（3）神法是上帝通过《圣经》给人类的直接的启示。最后，（4）人法是人们针对特定问题或特定情况所创制出的特别的规则。

阿奎那认为由人类所创制的特定法律会常常受到人的恶性如自私、无知等的影响。因此，人法绝对不可以与自然法相冲突。事实上，阿奎那认为，人们不应该服从那些与自然法相违背的人法。这种不服从行为支持了自然法至上的思想。

自然法中基本的概念是所有的人均享有天赋权利。英国历史上重要的政治哲学家约翰·洛克在1689年指出，没有人生来就有义务来服从统治者。他声称所有的个人都生而平等、自由、独立，他们具有普遍的自然权利，包括生命、自由和财产权。政府的目的是确保这些权利。

我们这个时代的朗·富勒（Lon Fuller）也试图将自然法原则运用到法律制度的分析之中。在《法的道德性》（1964年版）一书中，富勒为理解法律制度的"内在道德性"考察了我们的法律制度。他列举出具有内在道德的法律制度应具备的一些要求。

- 法律制度应该包括具有理性的、清楚的、所有公民提前便知道的一般性原则。
- 这些原则不应该具有溯及既往力——换言之，这些原则不该被适用到它们制定以前的情况中。
- 法律应该避免自相矛盾，不应该要求人们去做无法做到的事情。
- 法律应该保持稳定，并以一种一致的方式来实施。

尽管富勒的自然法表述与亚里士多德不同，但富勒也试图确定一种构建任何法律制度基础的不变的道德性原则。

二、实证主义法学派

法的一端是自然法学派，另一端是实证法学派（或分析法学）。坚持这一学派的人坚信没有什么法可以高于一国的实证法——也就是说某一特定社会在某一特定时间创设的法。

英国哲学家托马斯·霍布斯（1588—1679）被人们认为是对法律作实证探索的奠基

Appendix I

Text Translation & Key to Exercises (Part One)

人。霍布斯认为在原始的自然状态之中，人类并不比在香蕉树上相互残杀以争食寥寥无几的几个香蕉的猴子强多少，他总结说对于稳定与和平而言，主权权力是必要的，事实上对生存而言也是如此。个人并没有什么"天赋"的权利；他们拥有的只是作为可强制执行法律的结果所要求的权利。这与某一特定法律是善法还是恶法并无关系。某一特定法是优是劣是可以被讨论的，法律可以通过合法的立法程序以合适的方式加以变更。但是只要法律存在一天，人们就必须遵守它。

约翰·奥斯丁（1790—1859）是法律实证主义传统中一位极其重要的思想家，他赞同道德在法的形成中确实应该起某种作用。但是奥斯丁像其他实证主义法学家一样，他认为在确定真正意义上的法这个问题上，道德理论是不起作用的。"恶法"与"善法"一样是法。"法的存在是一回事，"他写道，"它的优点或缺点是另一回事"。

对于奥斯丁而言，法律与意见的区别在于：法律是在惩罚的痛苦基础之上必须得以服从的。因此，法律是由"最高统治者"发布的"命令"。奥斯丁认为，"命令"由两部分组成。第一部分是希望某人去做或不去做某件事情的表达；第二部分是针对倘若别人没有按照上述希望行事的威胁或默示的威胁。

同时"最高统治者"必须是"一位不受命的下命令者"——即，某个人或机构"并没有养成习惯性的服从"于别人以及"在那个社会里习惯性地被大多数人服从。"此外，最高统治者又必须是"明确的"，换言之，它必须由一些特定个人或机构组成。

另一位法律实证主义者，英国人H.L.A.哈特，生于1907，他强调了"有义务"（being obligated）做某事与"被强迫"（being obliged）做某事的区别。

根据哈特，成熟的法律制度同样包括两种规则，即首要规则和次要规则。

此外，哈特提出，有三种次要规则。审判规则告诉人们如何解决纠纷；变更规则解释如何才可以改变法律制度；认可规则也是一种规则，它是某一特定法律是否有效的标准。但是，关于"有效问题"，哈特并不指道义上有效。像奥斯丁一样，哈特是实证主义者，他认为尽管道德可能也应该影响法律，但它并不能帮助人们确定什么是有效的法律。

三、社会法学

社会法学表明法律及其司法解释都应考虑将社会学的调查研究结合进去。布朗诉教育委员会一案（1954年）具有典型意义，这则著名的案例中最高法院宣布了公学中的种族隔离政策违法。在解释其判决时，法院援引了植根于社会学家著作之中的信息，它表明黑人儿童在统一的学校里要比隔离的学校里更容易学到知识。当法院将这些调查结果提出并作为理由禁止在公学里的隔离政策时，它的推理恰恰是社会法学的一个例子。

美国社会法学最具代表的人物是罗斯科·庞德（1870—1964）。庞德认为文明国家的法律制度是建立在特定的同样的设想或预期之上的，在这样的文明国家里我们有这样的设想：

- 没有人会故意伤害别人；
- 财产权、不动产、动产以及如专利权、著作权等知识产权都会受到人们的尊重；
- 任何签署了合同的人都会遵守合同；
- 人们会尽量避免对他人不必要的伤害；
- 人们仅会在不给公众造成威胁的情况下才使用危险材料。

四、法现实主义

现实主义法学派在20世纪20年代、30年代特别流行，它对美国法理学产生过重大影响。法现实主义者对法官无偏袒、合乎逻辑、统一地适用法律的这种假设提出了质疑。他们认为，假如这是事实的话，那么所有涉及类似情形及问题的案件都应具有相类似的结果。但是涉及相同事实的问题往往在不同法院、甚至在运用同一法律原则时会有不同的审判结果。为什么会这样呢？根据法现实主义者的解释，这种不同的结果是缘自法官都是具有独特品格、价值体系及智力的人。因此，要求两名法官在评价同样案件时作出同样的推理过程是不可能的。换言之，要让法律完全公平地、合乎逻辑地、以统一的形式去得以运用是不可能的。从法现实主义者的观点看来，法学家的任务是承认这一事实并且要尽可能客观地意识到、认清在特定案件的分析方法上会受到他们个人偏见及价值的影响。

美国最高法院大法官奥利弗·温德尔·霍姆斯（1841—1935）是现实主义法学派一名最有影响的倡导者。在他的一部著名著作《普通法》中，霍姆斯强调了法的实用性："法的生命不在逻辑，而在经验。"这一思想学派的另一位倡导者是卡尔·卢维林（1893—1962），主要以起草《统一商法典》而著名。卢维林认为法官的判决会受到法官的价值判断以及他们对以前案件结果的解释的影响。

第六课　遵循先例原则

一、遵循先例的概念

大陆法系与普通法法系间最显而易见的区别是，大陆法系属于成文法体系，而普通法并非通过立法方式来创设，普通法主要建立在判例法基础之上。有一条原则应该坚持——先前的司法判例，通常是上级法院已经做出的相似判例，在后来的案件中应当得到遵守，即先例应该得到尊重。这一原则就是著名的"遵循先例"原则——它从未通过立法得以确立，但是被法院认为具有拘束力。在遵循先例（拉丁语"遵守已判决案例"或让判例持久之意）原则下，普通法某一案例中形成的某一法律原则充当今后相同或相类似案件的有约束力的法律依据。

遵循先例制度于13世纪在英格兰形成，它是普通法法系的"心脏"。爱德华一世统治时期，普通法法院开始保存先前案例的纪录以指导法官审理当前的案件。这一做法使得普通法更为客观，更具可预见性。与制定法一样，先前的案例成为非法行为或侵权行为的警告形式。如果你想对某人提起诉讼，你可以通过检索先前相似的诉讼案件来估算胜诉的概率。同样道理，如果有人指控你，你也可以由此确定何种抗辩理由最适合你。

与普通法不同，判例法在大陆法系并无效力。遵循先例原则并不适用于大陆法系国家的法院，所以法院判决对下级法院在后来的案件判决上并无约束力，这些判例在同一法院也无约束力，因而在相似案件中得出相反的结论在这些法院中并不罕见。大陆法系中，法院并不创制法律，而只是适用及解释法律。但是，在实践中，高等法院的判决当然对低等法院的判决有一定的影响，因为低等法院的法官通常会考虑这一风险——即如果他们与高等法院的判决相违背，则他们所做出的判决有可能被撤销。法官通常会尽力避免高等法院撤销他们的判决，因为如果他们的判决多数被撤销，则他们的升职会受到不利影响。因此，即便判例法在大陆法系中并无约束效力，通常法院也会对先前的判例做出考虑。

遵循先例原则中包含有先例这一概念。先例是指为今后具有类似事实或问题的案件提供基础的已决案例。判例意见经收集发表成册，称为"判例汇编"，这些判决意见书成为后来相似案件的先例用来处理类似的事实与法律问题。

遵循先例在同司法管辖区内的上下级法院间起作用。同一司法管辖区内高等法院中所形成的法律原则对低等法院有约束力。地位相同的高等法院各分庭做出的裁决被互认为是有说服力的法律依据。判决属于有约束力的判决还是属于有说服力的判决取决于法院判决的来源。有约束力的先例法院必须遵循，而有说服力的先例法院不必遵循。马萨诸塞州最高法院就一特定法律问题的判决在该州所有的下级法院中都会有约束力。但是，缅因州或其他任何州就任何未决法律问题的判决在马赛诸塞州法院只是有说服力的判决。例外的是，联邦最高法院的判决在所有州法院及联邦法院中均属于有约束力判决。先例在确定将什么法律适用于当事人问题中充当着一个法律向导的作用。它在我们的社会中确立标准，保证法院判决很大程度上的公正。

二、遵循先例制度的优、缺点

要想查找先例，了解先例出处的卷宗号十分有帮助。例如，某一案件的法官意见出处的卷宗号是313 N.W.2d 601（1982），则该意见可从《西北汇编》第313卷，第二版，第601页处找到。美国法律制度对司法判例的广泛依赖有优点，也不乏缺点。

优点

遵循先例制度的诞生是法院、社会寻求法律的确定性及可预见性的结果。此外，遵循先例有其他优点。通过先例，普通法解决了许多法律问题并使法律的许多部门，例如合同法，具有了稳定性。

缺点

首先，尽管普通法的产生是寻求法律确定性的结果，今后也会照此创造法律，但是普通法也制造出法律中许多的不确定面。先例的检索可能会花上大量的时间。此外，互相冲突的先例经常得以发现。

第二，在许多案件中，通过查找案例并不能够找到合适的法律。

第三，先例与不必要的法官意见书之间有十分重要的区别。法院经常做出与达成的判决并无必然关联的评论，这种评论称为"法官的个人意见（附带意见）"，它不具司法解决的效力。严格地讲，它们并不属于遵循先例规则中要求法院去遵守的先例。但是，如果附带意见合理、公正，则它们可被遵循，经反复重复的附带意见常常具有先例的效力。

第四，判例法体系不确定的一个重要原因是先例可能会被更改或推翻。既然判例法容易被改变，因此对它的绝对遵循是不可能的。

三、遵循先例原则的条件

遵循先例原则有四个重要的条件。

第一，如果后来的案件同产生法律原则的先前案件在案件事实上有重大区别，则遵循先例原则不适用。因此，如果法官可以"识别"出先前案件的事实与后来的案件事实不一样，则该判例不可援用作先例。

第二，如果法律的状况发生改变，则遵循先例原则不适用。因此后来的立法可以宣布普通法裁定无效，该判例在这之后不再具有先例的作用。

第三，只有法院裁定的核心部分（称为判决理由）才具有先例的作用。出现在判例中对事实或法律无关的说明（附带理由）对后来的法院并不具有约束力。

最后，当严格的遵循先例会导致某一特定案件的不公正，或不当地限制法的健康发展时，遵循先例的现代观点允许法院脱离先前的裁定。不过，这点只是在最不寻常的情形下才适用，因为遵循司法先例的真正理由就是要使法律具有确定性。

遵循先例原则在宪法性案件中受到的限制最大。宪法处于判例法以及制定法之上，处于支配地位。有时，一条宪法修正案改变先前案例所遵循的规则。（例如，美国内战时期修正案有效地推翻了德雷德·斯哥特裁定，该判例曾否认黑人奴隶的公民身份权利。）有时，不同的法官对宪法的解释会有所不同并作出异议。在任何时候，法官都受宪法的约束，而不是受解释宪法的先前判例限制。

第七课　当今世界两大主要法系

一、什么是民法法系的传统？

当我们用一些熟悉的名称如，"罗马法学家"，"罗马—日耳曼法系"，或者"民法法系"来描述世界上的某些法律体系时，我们可以注意到这样一个现象，即尽管它们和其他法系有相似之处，尽管适用国家之间也存在差异，但是它们都共同继承了独具特色的传统。民法法系传统的特征，体现在它的早期形成阶段，是罗马法、日耳曼法、地方习惯和教会法之间特殊的相互作用的结果；到后来，则体现为对封建制度灭亡和国家兴起的非同一般的响应；此外，对于法律科学所起到的独特的重要作用也是民法法系传统特征的一个方面。

二、罗马法

用罗马法这个词来形容从《十二铜表法》（公元前450年）到《查士丁尼民法大全》（公元534年）将近一千年的罗马法律成果就如同用"普通法"一词来形容从公元1066年至今英国的法律思想成果一样有意义。罗马法学研究者把古罗马法分成了不同的时期。早在公元前三世纪的共和时期，出现了以法律为专职的人，被称为法学家（精通法律之人）。到公元前一世纪的罗马共和国后期，法学家基本垄断了法律技术信息和法律经验。对于一些复杂的案件，非专业法官开始向这些法律专家求教。凭借这种咨询作用，法学家始终和司法实践保持紧密联系，并且总能接触到实际发生的争议。他们是世界上最早的职业律师（与像西塞罗一样的演说家不同，后者的主要才能在修辞和政治方面）。我们现在所知的罗马法就是从他们对一个个案件的意见和观点累积进化而来的。最终，法学家所发展的法律原则被以独具特色的文字和风格写成论著并加以传授和解释说明。

罗马法起初相当正式和刻板，后来，它在固定的规则里加入了富有弹性的准则，从而使罗马法从具体实际向较为抽象的思想类型过渡。罗马法的特征是注重实际应用的细节，并且采纳那些广为流传的专门术语。古典时期（从大约公元117年开始到大约公元

Appendix I
Text Translation & Key to Exercises (Part One)

235年出现政治混乱、外来入侵、祸患及内战时结束）的法律代表了古罗马法的最高发展成就。乌尔比安、盖尤斯及帕皮尼安是这个时期最为著名的法学家。在其全盛时期，古典罗马法形成了世界上从没有过的现实理性体系。因此，在西罗马帝国败落后，它又引起了拜占庭法学家的极大兴趣，也正是通过这些法学家，罗马法极大地影响了民法法系的发展。

几个世纪以后，当欧洲从中世纪走向崛起时，学者们"重新发现"了罗马法，并把它称为"成文的理性"。但是，在西方社会愿意接受法律，并让它在各种规范人们行为的准则中发挥主导作用时，他们所"发现"的罗马法已经不再是古典时期的罗马法的原始形态了。大多数古典法律的渊源已经消失。幸存的只是依据公元六世纪拜占庭时期的皇帝查士丁尼的指示编撰的罗马法汇编。到那时为止，西罗马帝国已经败落一个多世纪了，其标志是公元410年罗马城的沦陷。拜占庭时期的法学家在保存罗马法遗产方面所做工作的重要性是不可估量的。从查士丁尼时期到现在，"罗马法"这一术语，除对法学家以外，通常就意味着在出现在公元六世纪的《查士丁尼民法大全》。

《民法大全》包括四个部分：《法学阶梯》《学说汇纂》《查士丁尼法典》和《新律》。从对民法法系传统的影响来看，《学说汇纂》的影响最为深远，尤其是在主体资格、侵权、不当得利、合同和法律救济方面。《学说汇纂》是根据查士丁尼时期的法学家们的判断，从以往各个时期最有价值的法学著述中挑选出来的论著的汇集。由于法学家们编撰《学说汇纂》时所依据的所有书籍都已丢失，《学说汇纂》本身也就成了人们认识早期罗马法状况的主要渊源。《法学阶梯》只是一个为学生们作简要介绍的教科书，《法典》是对罗马立法的系统汇编，《新律》则是《查士丁尼法典》和《学说汇纂》完成之后的罗马帝国的新的立法。《学说汇纂》和《查士丁尼法典》合起来被认为是罗马法的完整、权威的重述。

拜占庭时期的罗马法学家并不只是抄录以前各个时期的法律。《民法大全》是一个经过仔细摒弃和挑选之后的成果。不论是从总体上看，还是从细节上看，它都与古典时期的法律不同。它沿袭了不拘泥于形式的立法趋势，但是这种趋势也伴随了立法技术上的倒退。衡平，这一在古典时期被认为是赋予整个法律以生命的正义的基本原则，已退化为对细枝末节的盲目追求。在查士丁尼王国之后，随着伦巴第人和阿拉伯人的入侵，罗马法被战火硝烟湮灭了几个世纪之久。

三、罗马法在中世纪习惯法中幸存下来

在中世纪，罗马法虽然因其得以产生的生活方式的瓦解而陷入困境，但这并不意味着罗马法学家的法律影响也随之消失。当然，罗马帝国分裂后，在法律和政治均陷入混乱的情况下，罗马法并没有能维持几个世纪以来所形成的精致和完善的法律技术。在罗马帝国衰落后的五个世纪中，接踵而来的入侵者和殖民者占领了原来属于罗马的土地。由于没有强大中央集权式的政权，各个王国兴衰不定。人们的生活状况是地方自治式的，当地的习惯取代了规范的法律。几个世纪后法律学者们才能够再次应用古典时期的罗马和拜占庭法学家们遗留下来的法律技术。到了十一世纪，人们对罗马法的兴趣被重新唤醒，《民法大全》再次引起注意，这一过程被称为罗马法的"复兴"。

然而，在五到十世纪盛行的各式各样的习惯法中，"残存"了大量的罗马法。这是因为，罗马征服者的足迹曾经遍及欧洲，那些推翻先前帝国统治的日耳曼殖民者、罗马

军团士兵以及外来移民都已经在某种程度上被"罗马化"了。作为征服者，在被征服的土地上，日耳曼统治者用罗马法来统辖罗马臣民，而对本民族的臣民则适用他们自己的法律。但是，随着时间的流逝，这种地域间的差别逐渐消失。到了十世纪后期，对特定领土上的所有人都适用相同的规则。原始的罗马法规则和日耳曼入侵者的习惯法已在不同程度上相互融合，因此，历史学家称这个时期的法律为"罗马化的习惯法"或"蛮族化的罗马法"。这样，尽管罗马法律科学和古典时期的罗马法在中世纪的混乱、割据和地方自治中消失，罗马法的要素却幸存下来，它们使罗马法得以存续，并且成为罗马法普遍化的潜在因素，也就是我们今天所说的民法法系的传统。

最早于公元五世纪开始被书面记载下来并且广为传播的日耳曼习惯法（连同当地的习惯），也构成民法法系传统的一部分，尤其影响了婚姻财产法和继承法。现代民法法系的财产法和商法中设计最精巧和最实用的法律制度不是源自罗马法，而是中世纪的习惯法，这也提示我们中世纪繁杂的法律不仅只是支离破碎、无序的状态，也有多产和富于创造性的一面。日耳曼法在中世纪逐渐发展，从部落法演变为领地法，直至开始形成一种完全不同于罗马法的法律科学和新的法律文化。但是，它的进一步发展却受到了限制，部分是由于它残酷的审判程序，（比如神明裁判），部分是由于它不适应封建社会转型时所产生的社会和经济上的变化。

四、教会法

随着庞大的罗马政权的瓦解，教会接管了政府的部分职能。实际上，从罗马帝国衰落到十一世纪罗马法复兴这一时期，在民法法系多种多样的地域化的法律渊源中，教会法是唯一最重要的，也是最普遍的渊源。但是，教会法本身是各类法的混合体。在罗马帝国接受了基督教以后，教会法是基督教义和罗马法相互作用的产物，这一过程在康斯坦丁（逝于公元337年）王朝时尤为突出。公元六世纪查士丁尼的《民法大全》尤其受到了基督教思想的影响，但是，对于教会来说，也从古罗马法的体系、原则及具体规则中借鉴颇多。而且，正像是日耳曼习惯法、当地习惯及被贬低的罗马法的融合一样，教会法也渗透到由日耳曼统治者予以颁布的法典当中，并且后来成为神圣罗马帝国的立法。在中世纪，教会对婚姻事由、刑法和个人财产继承的某些方面谋求并且获得了独立裁判权。它在这些方面发展出的许多规则和程序在教会丧失了民事裁判权后的很长时间内都被非宗教法庭所采纳。

第八课 美国的法律教育

一、历史简述

1865年之前，美国法律职业培训思想根源主要是受英国的影响。在19世纪，大多数美国律师都是通过英国学徒式途径学习法律的。威廉·布莱克斯通（1723—1780）为学生和法律从业者专门设立了场所，并以他所著的四卷本《英国法释义》作为教材，该著作在美国的版本得到了广泛的使用，并为《美国法释义》所效仿。

第一批法律学校是从接收学徒来赚钱的律师事务所演变而来的。比起从事法律实务来说，一些律师则更热衷于指导学徒，并通过教学来博取名声。里奇菲尔德法律学院

Appendix I

Text Translation & Key to Exercises (Part One)

（从1784年到1833年间吸引了来自数个州的学生）以及其他20多个按照这一模式而成立的法律事务所式的学校都带有明显的英国痕迹。

成立于1817年的哈佛法学院在创立之初是按照里奇菲尔德法律学院模式建立起来的一所普通的法律学校，但它最后却成为法律院校中的泰山北斗，这主要归功于它在1869年任命查尔斯·艾略特（1834—1906）担任校长职务和在1870年聘克里斯托弗·哥伦布·朗德尔（1826—1906）担任新设立的法学院院长。这两个人中，艾略特所起的作用更为重要，他积极倡导并支持对整个大学进行改革。朗德尔平生最重要的创新则是引进了一种教学方法，这种方法使用苏格拉底式的对话来讨论上诉法院判决的案例。

美国法学院中的学生数量1870年为1650人，到1900年，这一数量上升至12500人；同时，法律院校由31所上升为102所。20世纪之初，有四分之三的法律院校附属于各个大学。但是为了满足城市民众的需求，还设立了20所法律夜校，同大学法律院校相比，这些学校更注重强调当地法律，而且更加注重实践。律师中一些精英分子对那些经过夜校培训而大量出现的外来律师及其水准开始表示担忧。州律师协会于是开始对资格考试进行严格把关。1900年，法律院校自身成立了美国法律院校协会（简称AALS），该协会同美国律师协会（简称ABA）一起负责法律水平资格认证的业务。美国法律院校协会最初吸收了32所学院作为其创始成员。没有进入资格认证榜的学院在招收学生时处于极大的劣势。

二、美国法律教育的特征

1. 美国法律教育的基础是普通法。

而普通法系与民法法系之间最主要的区别是，前者所依赖的是先例具有束约力这一英国法原则。因而，今天法院对案件所做的判决必须同以前对类似案件的判决相一致，即使此案件已经非常古老。其主要理念是法官在以前案件所作的推理必须适用于现在的案件，因此使法律具有可预测性。即便如此，普通法依然是非常灵活的，因为法官能够运用以前的法律推理在类似的案件中得出不同但不失公平的结果。

2. 美国的法律教育是全面性教育而非专业性教育。

每一所法律院校在第一年所开设的课程大致相同，有侵权行为法、合同法、财产法、刑法、民事诉讼法、宪法和法律研究与写作。在第二年和第三年，由学生自己选修课程，但是大部分人会选修其他常见的课程如行政法、贸易与商法、诉讼法、家庭法、知识产权和技术法、国际法与比较法等。这样等学习期满毕业时，每名学生对各种法律学科均有接触，即使他们日后可能会专攻某个专门领域。

3. 美国法律制度的发展受到了律师们所接受教育的影响；而法律教育反过来又反映了该国法律制度的多样性。

美国法律教育的多样性主要体现在以下几个方面：首先，美国有许多私立大学法律院校。实际上，所有的州都有一个公立大学，甚至在一些比较大的州里有好几所公立大学。但是没有一届联邦政府的教育部规定法律课程、教师薪水或者研究计划。私立法律院校的存在与竞争是造成了法律教育多样性的最根本原因。其次，法律院校发展的历史模式奠定了不同的法律院校享有不同等级的声誉，这使竞争变得更加白热化。再次，学生和教师群体的构成从白人男性群体占多数转变为更加可以代表美国人口多样性的群体。

三、教学方法

1. 案例教学法

法律教育中的案例教学法是随着系主任朗德尔的判例教科书《契约法案例》的出版以及它于1871年在哈佛大学的应用而开始的。该判例教科书使用的是上诉法院的判决，并对其进行了编排，目的是揭示出案件所蕴含的法律原则。朗德尔认为这些原则要胜过当地的法律，并可以揭露出在具体案例中司法推理的不完善之处。而使用判例教科书的老师则成为苏格拉底式的导师，他向学生们提出那些揭示出上诉法院裁决意见中所包含的概念。教授们以案例教学法或苏格拉底式教学法来替代了传统的讲演教学法，而且苏格拉底式教学还要求学生在上课前深入研究案例。这种方法按照由特殊到一般，由抽象到具体的顺序再现了辩证的普通法方法本身。

朗德尔当年所创新的教学方法所遗留下来的部分在如今可能描述为讨论法。判例教科书中包括成文法令、法庭规则、条例、从期刊以及课本（其中甚至包括从法律以外的学科）中所摘录的部分和其他如契约或诉状等其他法律材料。讨论法的纯粹问答形式对学习必修课的一年级学生是最有效的。他们在具有分析推理能力的律师里面尚属于新手，所以更愿意参加这门课程。

2. 讲演教学法

传统的讲演教学法重新受到青睐，特别是针对越来越细化的课程。教授们试图以此讲授复杂的当代美国法学素材及其在多变的社会环境下的适用。同互联网相连并配有电脑显示的新型电教室使讲演教学法可视化的特点更加容易地体现了出来。另一个因素是为了削弱案例法或讨论教学法固有的是非相对性因素，受此影响，学生们总是试图为自己支持的一方寻找辩论理由。如美国法律实用主义鼓吹的，学生们相信，赢得案件的关键是诡辩而不一定是正义。讲演教学法为学生们就美国法律方面一致观点的形成提供了途径。

3. 问题讨论法

一些人数较少的高级课程或研修班则注重强调对当前问题的解决方法。学生对例如环境、商业组织或侵犯人权等复杂的情况进行研究，并试图通过运用法律规则和制度对此提出解决方法。这些课程为法律素材与非法律素材的有机地结合起来而提供了一个方便的机会。例如，密西根的一个研讨会，议题是全球化和劳动权。会议会探讨结社自由，集体谈判，就业歧视和童工问题。它还质疑美国对侵犯劳动权的国家经济制裁的使用，及公司法人权实验的有效性问题。

4. 专业技能训练（模拟）和诊所式法律教学法

20世纪60年代的学生们抱怨法律教育太过于理论化，不能够提供足够的法律实践经验。自从人们对学徒式方式不感兴趣那时起，这个问题便被提了出来。但这次有更多的教授听从了希望加强法律教育实用性的呼吁。福特基金会专门设立了经费以此鼓励法律院校进行诊所式教学方法的尝试。一些律师委员会讨论设立例如审判辩护等特定实践课程的要求。

如今，实践教育采用了多种方式，但是划分起来只有两种形式：课堂上模拟练习和真实的当事人参加行政和司法诉讼过程，以此来获得实战经验。为了事后的讨论和评估，学生们的表现有时要录制下来。其主要思想是再现出执业律师在实践中的角色与职责。学生们首先做好准备诉状、观点以及向法院提出动议。他们提出口头辩论意见；试着与当事人会面并交流看法；询问证人并同其他律师进行协商。他们还起草文件。这些练习可能出现在逼真的模拟情景中，也可能出现在诊所式法律教育课中，或者出现在房地产法或福利法等迥然不同的课程之中。

5. 校外实习

一些法律院校允许高年级的学生利用一个学期的时间担任州法官或联邦法官的法律助理，或在政府部门、公益律师事务所或者非营利组织中任职。法官或律师对学生们的活动进行监督。

四、律师职业考试

在联邦体制下，各州各自负责各州的法律职业准入及管理等事务。除了八个州（其中加利福尼亚是最主要的）以外的所有州都要求法律职业准入申请人从美国律师协会所认可的学校毕业，满足职业道德委员会所制定的标准，并且通过为期二到三天的书面考试。除了三个州以外所有的州都使用标准化的多州律师联考作为考试过程的一部分。因为每个州剩下的是对当地法律的考核，所以法律职业准入申请人一般花费四到六周的时间集中学习律师职业科目。全国考试的人中，大约75%的初次参加考试者可通过考试。

在另一个州做执业律师通常必须参加该州的律师资格考试，或者他（她）执业已满五年，并向该州提起执业申请。大约有30个州允许后一种方式。律师职业准入许可包括在联邦法院提起诉讼的权力。为了响应法律行业全球化的趋势，有23个州允许外国律师参加他们的律师资格考试（有时也会要求他们具有美国的法学硕士学位），通过考试后成为该州的律师。纽约州主导着这种趋势，有977名外国的律师通过了资格考试，占外国律师总人数的43%。

第九课　美国宪法

美国宪法是公民的一种自发性协议。它规定国家的统治规则，表明司法的根本性原则。它还列明人民不可剥夺的权利，这些权利约束人们相互合作以谋取共同福祉。美国宪法起草于1787年，不到4 400个字，分为七个简短的部分，称作条。1791年增补了权利法案（宪法的前十个修正案），此后的两个多世纪，仅增加了十七条修正案。它是世界上至今仍在使用的最古老的成文宪法。

如今我们提到宪法常指的是基本法或者国家的最高法律。宪法特指的宪法性原则包括：（1）联邦制，（2）权力分立，（3）司法审查，（4）公民权利与自由。这四大特殊分类囊括了宪法法中最广为人知和最令人激动的原则。

一、联邦制

美国在1787年的时候基本上没有中央政府。每个州都声称拥有主权，马萨诸塞州和佛蒙特州之间甚至进行了一场战争。1781年起草的《邦联条例》旨在创设一个主权州之间松散的联盟，并由一个脆弱的一元立法机构领导，据此，中央政府不能够强迫各州及其居民遵守法律或行政规章。尽管可以缔结条约，但中央政府却无权强迫实施，也不能解决各州之间的冲突。比如，如果纽约州限制使用纽约港，邦联政府不能为了相邻各州的利益和国家的经济而干涉此事。相反，宪法所规定的联邦制确保了新政府有权实施这样的行为。

联邦制可以定义为，由两级或两级以上政府为特定地域特定公民提供各种服务的政治架构。举例来说，爱荷华州居民不但有国家政府和州政府为其服务，还有各种地方政府机构为其服务。

学者们估计，美国大概存在80 000多个州及地方政府，每个政府都致力于满足这个复杂的技术驱动型社会的需要和要求。联邦制使得各州管理纯粹的地方性事务的权力和其原有的从整体上保护公众健康、安全和社会福利的权力得以调和。宪法授权各州建立地方政府，进行选举，管理州内商业，并且保留没有明确授予给联邦政府的所有权力。作为回报，宪法特别列举了一些权力给联邦政府，使其有权管理国家经济发展与稳定、国家安全及外交事宜。按宪法规定，联邦政府有权缔结条约，宣布战争，管理州际和国际商业活动，铸造货币，以及供养陆军和海军。除此之外，联邦政府还拥有某种固有或隐含的权力，这些权力虽宪法中并未提到，但对其行使职责来讲必不可少（比如，控制军火买卖的权力）。

另外，州和联邦政府还共享某些并存的权力——只要不相互冲突，这些权力可以由两级政府行使。比如两级政府都有权征税、管理商业活动、禁止住房和就业歧视。由于广义解释的联邦政府权力包含了对影响国家利益的地方活动管理权，州与联邦政府的司法管辖权也相互重合。然而，国会却不能单以公共利益为名义，像各州那样管理国内事务。国会对内管理必须有宪法授权。尽管在管辖权上存在不可避免的混淆和冲突，政府的联邦体制还是有利于公民保有真正的政治权利，在承认地区差异、促进发展的同时，使得一个强有力的中央政府提供国防保障，并对共同关心的领域进行管理。

二、权力分立

权力分立是我们宪法这一课不可缺少的组成部分。宪法根据不同职责来分配政府权力。职能部门包括立法（法律的制定）、行政（法律的实施）和司法（判决）三个部门。对立法部门（包括众议院和参议院）的规定体现在宪法第一条，对行政部门（包括总统、副总统和各部门）的规定体现在第二条，对司法部门（包括联邦法院和最高法院）的规定体现在第三条。

分权使得权力在三个政府部门之间得以有效平衡。不同政府官员拥有独特的和具体的权力，各部门又在不同人的领导下运转，每个部门都能阻止另外两个部门非法获得权力和非法行使权力。这种制度结构抑制了人类个人权力扩张的自然倾向。在避免可能出现的专制（即暴虐的滥用权力）的同时，分权使政府官员能忠实履行宪法所赋予的权力。

宪法的权力分立学说阐明了政府不同部门的相互关系。实际上每个部门都被授予了排他性的职权（比如，税收的提案必须始于众议院），然而涉及的大部分工作都被政府三个部门分担了。

国会可以通过一项议案，总统可以签署也可以否决，而国会又可以使否决权无效并颁布法律。最高法院可以以违宪为由取消该法令。如有必要，国会可能发起修宪运动来达到立法目的。而更有可能的是，国会也许会通过一部符合宪法的新法令。还要注意的是，（在参议院的提议和同意下）总统可能会任命那些同情他（政治）观点的人作为最高法院的新成员。

Appendix I
Text Translation & Key to Exercises (Part One)

然而，所有这些制衡带来效率低下。但这都是经过设计的，并非偶然产生。通过强迫各部门对其他部门负责，没有一个部门能够攫取足够的权力而取得支配地位。

三、司法审查

司法审查是美国联邦最高法院的一项既定权利和义务，当联邦政府和州政府的条例或法令违反美国宪法时，由联邦最高法院宣布其无效。美国人民已习惯于司法审查制度，以至于把它看作是政府机构中自然的、不可或缺的、甚至是必要的组成部分。总统、国会、州立法机构、地方长官、州法院、各州和联邦行政机构、公务员，以及所有的普通居民都服从九名大法官对宪法问题的指挥。

值得注意的是，宪法本身并没有将司法审查权授予联邦最高法院。第三条规定，"合众国的司法权，属于联邦最高法院和国会不时规定和设立的下级法院"，而且它还将权力延伸至"由于本宪法而产生的一切普通法和衡平法案件"，以及其他种类的案件。这些条文属于组织性、司法管辖权性的规定。它们创立了联邦最高法院，但是，最高的意思只代表至高，指明了它（最高法院）在法院层级中的位置，但是并没有授予它权力来行使宪法性的审查权。

尽管没有宪法第三条的特别授权，宪法的制定者还是大概预想出了司法审查的某种形式。依照亚历山大·汉密尔顿所言，联邦最高法院是最不危险的部门，因为它掌控的既不是利剑也不是钱袋。他声称应该由联邦最高法院——而不是国会和总统——作为宪法的管理人。他更进一步指出："作为法院公平正义的媒介，联邦最高法院的责任应当是宣布所有与宪法明示旨意相反的法案无效。如果没有这种权力，联邦最高法院保留的所有特别权力或特权将等于零。"

然而，直到1803年，在马伯里诉麦迪逊一案中，司法审查的意思才被清晰阐明。这个案子不仅确认了对立法机构及行政机构的法案和命令的司法审查。马歇尔大法官还阐明了联邦最高法院的一个主要权力，承认联邦最高法院是宪法唯一的解释者和管理者，从而排除了总统和国会的相应权力。与此声明相随，联邦最高法院从此承担起一项令人敬畏的责任——定义宪法的意思是什么、不是什么。

尽管这些年来排他性的司法审查权引起极大争议，但对这个正在成长并不断变化的社会来说，它还是一直作为一种稳定力量而存在。随着国家经济、社会和政治条件的变化，人们的态度和观念也产生了相应的变化。这种变化体现在人民选举的政府领导人上，还体现在任命的联邦最高法院大法官身上。因此联邦最高法院一些长期存在的判决也产生了变化。一度裁决为合宪的事情其后被宣布违宪。比如，二十世纪初，由Plessy诉Ferguson案确立的"隔离但平等"规则使得学校的种族隔离制得到承认甚至认可。然而，1954年，这一规则在布朗诉托皮卡教育委员会的案件中被推翻。

四、民权法案

在采纳宪法的论战中，反对者不断指责宪法草案会给中央政府的专制开一个口子。在革命战争之前和战争期间英国人侵害人权的记忆在他们脑海中还未抹去。他们需要一个"权利法案"来明确指出公民个体不再受到这样的侵害。几个州在正式批准宪法的大会上都要求做这样的修改，而其他州认为将来会出现这样的补充，就直接对宪法进行了修改。

因此，1789年9月25日，美国的第一届国会向各州的立法机构提出对宪法的十二条补充修正案，以此来应对不断要求改进宪法的论辩。前两个提议的修正案是关于每个众议院议员的选民人数和国会议员报酬的，没有被批准。然而第三至十二条以州议会的四分之三多数得到批准，这便组成了宪法的前十条修正案，称为《权利法案》（见补充阅读）。权利法案对政府规定了一些特殊和一般的限制，以此来保护所有的人免遭联邦官员的独裁和善变。因而，权利法案起初仅仅是用来限制联邦政府的，对各州政府来说，只有当本州宪法作出规定时，其权力才受到公民权利规定的制约。

内战之后，又有几条修正案被加入美国宪法，以此保护和帮助那些刚刚获得自由的奴隶。1865年第十三条修正案正式宣布奴隶制度为非法。在此之前，尽管有独立宣言上的相反表述和第五修正案"非经正当法律程序，不得剥夺任何人的生命、自由或财产"的规定，大多数非裔美国人的自由权利还是未得到承认。三年之后，1868年，第十四条修正案重申了所有人的自由并扩大了保护范围，以下面这些文字来约束所有的州和地方政府：

任何一州，都不得制定或实施限制合众国公民的特权或豁免权的任何法律；不经正当法律程序，不得剥夺任何人的生命、自由或财产；在州管辖范围内，也不得拒绝给予任何人以平等法律保护。

保证法律的正当程序和平等保护的条款在十四条修正案增加时没有进行定义，它的定义工作和对其具体应用留给了司法部门。最终，将由美国最高法院——作为宪法的解释者——定义出宪法保证的权利及其界限。

第十课 行　政　法

一、行政法的概念

行政法的学习可以视为对行政机关权力和行为限制的分析。这些限制附加在方方面面，由于政府对行政机关行政决定的审核，它们可能被追加或更换。我们要详尽论述的一种法律限制是复审法院要求行政机关适用的程序。另一种是国会制定的具体规则，即《行政程序法》。然而，首先要解决的问题是立法机关最初授予行政机关的立法和司法权限。

二、权力分配

通过近现代的行政法规，行政机关被赋予宽泛的权力。一些权力是在产业化的基础上设立的，如赋予联邦通讯委员会，核能管理委员会，海事委员会的权力。其他一些行政机构承担着执行经济领域行为准则的职责。这些机构包括联邦商业委员会，它1914年推行了"不正当竞争"的禁令，到新近的健康和安全调节机构，如环境保护署和职业安全和健康委员会。

使授权更加不寻常的是这些行政机关运用的权力具有政府三个主要职能部门的特征。许多行政机关被立法赋予立法权，可以制定规则限制私人行为，对违反者施加民事或刑事的惩罚；赋予行政权以调查潜在的违规事件继而起诉违法者；赋予司法权以裁定个人或公司是否违背了管理要求。

如证券交易委员会制定规章说明公开的信息要制成证券说明书；这些规章和立法机关通过的法律有同等的效力。最终，证券交易公司要作为法官和陪审团决定规章是否真正被违反；举行裁判听审决定罪行和给予惩罚。另外，行政机关通常独立于这三个政府部门（行政，立法和司法）。尽管证券交易委员会的委员——机关成员是总统任命，并经由参议院同意，证券委员会仍是一个独立的机构，它不附属于国会，也不是行政部门的一部分。

如此授予权力引起了关于宪法在政府体系中权力分配问题的思考。联邦宪法，及大多数州宪法都以分权原则为基础。通常来说，制定法律的权力被赋予立法机关，执行法律的权力被赋予行政机关，法律决定权被赋予司法机关。以这种形式的权力划分，理论上说来，每一部门在行使权力时都与另外两个部门保持制约与平衡。行政机关被视为"第四部门"，看起来，至少在形式上与政府的三权分立范例相矛盾。

三、宽泛授权的理由

对行政机关宽泛授权的理由可以从行政机关制度上的优点上体现出来。尤其是面对新颖和不断变化的活动领域，立法机关很难具体说明各种行为规则。一个机关有灵活的政策决定程序，并且对特定领域负有持续的责任，便能够制订合理和连续的政策。此外，有效地发展和推行规章政策需要同时运用这三种权力。一项法律原则或者决策，如果没有合理的调查和起诉，或者法院的判决没有支持和理解调整性规章政策目的，那么它在实践中很快就会失去效力。如果规范项目的主体事项具有技术性或者复杂性，或被规范产业的具体知识对制定合理政策必不可少，行政机关可以运用它的出色经验和专业知识。一致性和可预见性在许多经济规章的制订中都是很重要的。交易运转和投资计划需要确定性，因此基础规则不能突然改变或间断性地适用——如果政策决定权在政府三个部门之间分散，那么就会产生问题。

还需要注意的是，仍有相当数量的立法者、法官、评论员没有被这些说法所说服。他们认为持续的授权和将起诉权、立法权和司法权合并分配缺少真实理由。这样就有压力要分离职权，建立行政法院，或者限制授予行政机关广泛的职权。

四、美国行政法的起源

美国行政法起源于英国普通法法院。简而言之，行政法由普通法发展而来，普通法对美国行政法有巨大和深远的影响。

刑事法院的警官，如法警和执行官，应当负有损害责任，如（1）受到侵害的公民能初步证明警官犯有普通法上的某项过错，如侵权或殴打，及（2）警官不能援引法规和上级命令证实无过错。在常规法院政府官员对损害案件负有责任这一原则是英国律师"法律规则"概念中的基本要素。但是普通法规定的损害赔偿救济通常不充分。在普通法诉讼形式中很难觅到对应的政府官员行为的诉讼形式。另外，法院设立了基于自由裁量权的行政人员特权原则，以满足行政行为的灵活性需求。即使原告胜诉，被告人政府官员也不会自掏腰包满足判决，或赔偿金也不可能提供充分的救济。

为了应付这种局限性，普通法法院从17世纪开始重新制作古令状并且发展了一些限制官方行为的特殊令状。如训令令状要求官员赋予或恢复市民权利。诉讼中止令状是排除没有管辖权的行政权力。法院重新制作了调卷令状对某些行政主体的裁定进行复审，使一些无法律依据或超出"管辖权"的决定无效。

这些令状被普通律师用来限制日益膨胀的行政职能，包括地方政府对贫民实施救济的责任，授予将沼泽和湿地变为农田的权力，及对牛津和剑桥大学的管理权。对行政行为的司法审查也适用于行政官员诉诸法院要求强制执行其命令的情况。衡平法院的大法官发展了一种指令性的补偿以限制由于官员不法行为造成的不可挽救的损失。然而，在限制官员权力方面，普通法法院继续发挥着领导作用。

五、限制行政行为的方法

然而，现代政府需要一个限制行政权力的机构，单单依靠独立的司法机构——包括负担过度的立法机构和总统——是不够的。一些国家，如意大利和法国，还依靠设立在行政官僚机构内部由高级公务员组成的高素质的特殊化法庭，以限制政府官员的行为。其实，在英国的十六七世纪都铎和斯图亚特王朝国王就基于宣称的皇室特权，设立了行政法庭来控制下级官员和市民的关系。这些部门如星座法院，高级委员会法庭，现已演变为官方所称的行政司法部门，与法国最高行政机构相类似。在英国这种历史进程被1688年爆发的光荣革命所大大缩短，议会政府的胜利及对独立司法权的建立都是对行政权力有效的制约。

上篇　各课练习答案

第　一　课

一、根据课文回答下列问题。

（略）。

二、将下列术语译成英语。

1. Congress
2. Senate
3. House of representatives
4. prosecutor
5. precedent
6. pleadings
7. Goddess of Justice
8. procedural law
9. substantive law
10. inheritance law or law of succession

三、将下列句子译成汉语。

1. "普通法"这一术语还用来区分盎格鲁-美利坚法中称为"衡平法"的另一部分。今天，这两组术语用来指两种不同的法律原则。

2. 当一方为自然人、组织、公司或是政府部门对另一方提起诉讼以获得伤害救济时，这类案件属于民事案件，其结果可能是金钱损害赔偿救济，或是要求完成某一行为或禁止某一行为。

3. 公法定义的是个人同政府的权利与义务关系。公法还规定政府的组成结构及其各自的权力。

4. 大多数国家都有成文宪法，英国是个例外。英国宪法是不成文宪法。

5. 大陆法与普通法之间最明显的区别是，大陆法属于成文法，但普通法并非通过立法途径创立，它主要是建立在判例法之上。

四、听写。

（略）。

Appendix I

Text Translation & Key to Exercises (Part One)

第 二 课

一、根据课文回答下列问题。

（略）。

二、将下列句子译成汉语。

1. 法院不仅有权力介入个人和机关所提起的诉讼，而且还有权审查国会、州及其地区所通过的法律是否与宪法相一致。司法审查权已被普遍认为是制约国会与总统的一个必要的制约。

2. 国会以及州立法机构可以将它们的部分立法权授权给某一政府机关。

3. "普通法"这一术语起源于英国。诺曼人于1066年征服了英国，征服者威廉和他的追随者在统一国家过程中使用的其中一项主要的措施就是，将皇家法官派至不同地方进行巡回审判。

4. 如果你的宪法性权利被侵犯，则违反这些权利的法律无效。

5. 许多针对政府规章的限定都包含在《权利法案》（美国宪法的前十条修正案）之中。这些修正案保证人民的某些权利，包括耳熟能详的言论自由权、宗教自由权以及不受无理的搜查和扣押的权利。

三、完型填空。

1. common law
2. judge-made
3. precedent
4. decisions
5. civil law
6. Roman law
7. civil code
8. effect
9. dispute
10. Code

四、听写。

（略）。

第 三 课

一、根据课文回答下列问题。

（略）。

二、将下列术语译成英语。

1. trial court
2. limited jurisdiction
3. general jurisdiction
4. subject matter
5. civil dispute
6. criminal prosecution.
7. Small claims court
8. municipal court
9. child-custody
10. court of appeals/appellate court
11. district court
12. diversity jurisdiction
13. circuit court
14. writ of certiorari
15. rule of four

三、将下列句子译成汉语。

1. 古时候，人们利用像特尔斐神庙一样的寺庙来帮助他们作出公正的判决。

2. 美国的司法体系具有双重的结构：包括联邦法院和州法院。两重政府（州政府和联邦政府）的共存使得法院体系相互分离。

3. 司法权是授予法院审理特定案件并发布具有约束力判决的权力。

4. 下级联邦法院对联邦问题的判决对州法院没有约束力。

5. 只要美国政府成为一方当事人，那么案件就会在联邦法院体系中进行审判。当政府提起诉讼或被列为被告人时，便成了一方当事人。

四、完型填空。

1. elected
3. life
5. independence
7. jurisdiction
9. judges

2. fixed
4. decisions
6. trial
8. challenges
10. presides

第 四 课

一、根据课文回答下列问题。

（略）。

二、将下列术语译成英语。

1. indictment
3. Charge to the Grand Jury
5. testimony
7. verdict
9. foreperson
11. the petite jury
13. probable cause
15. Bill of Rights

2. information
4. self-incrimination
6. deliberation
8. acquittal
10. the Grand Jury
12. voir dire
14. peremptory challenge

三、将下列句子译成汉语。

1. 大陪审团得到指示以后，被带到大陪审团室，在那里听取并考虑检察官呈送上来的关于本案的证人证言和书面证据。

2. 因为被告人一旦到大陪审团面前作证，将会引起一系列复杂的法律问题，所以如果大陪审团希望要求或准许被告人前来作证的话，必须先跟检察官进行协商。

3. 大陪审团的主席必须对每个正式起诉书的裁决过程中陪审员的人数进行记录，并将记录交给法庭书记员。

4. 不得要求陪审团、也不允许陪审团向法庭报告他们的判断依据。陪审团只需向法庭提交裁决结果。

Appendix I

Text Translation & Key to Exercises (Part One)

四、讨论

（略）。

第 五 课

一、根据课文回答下列问题。

（略）。

二、将下列术语译成英语。

1. schools of jurisprudence
2. natural law
3. sociological jurisprudence
4. natural rights
5. philosophy of law
6. positive law
7. racial segregation
8. divine law
9. human law
10. eternal law

三、将下列句子译成汉语。

1. 自然法学派起源于古希腊，它强调道德和法的绝对要素：只有与自然法相符合的法律——即绝对的道德价值，才被认为是有效的法律。

2. 与高等的道德规范相冲突的法律根本不是法。与自然法相对，常规法反映某一社会在某一时期接受的价值观。

3. 坚持自然法学派思想的人认为政府及法律制度应该反映人类本质中固有的普遍的道德及伦理原则。

4. 自然法概念起源于希腊，自然法的思想受到了斯多葛学派的很大影响。

5. 自然权利的现代理念源自古代以及中世纪时期自然法原则，该原则认为人民作为自然和上帝的创造物，应该依据自然或上帝所形成的规则和训令生活、组织社会。

四、完型填空。

1. natural law
2. sociology
3. jurisprudence
4. judges
5. proponents
6. moral
7. courts
8. jury

第 六 课

一、根据课文回答下列问题。

（略）。

二、将下列术语译成英语。

1. precedent
2. the doctrine of stare decisis/the doctrine of precedent
3. abide by the decided cases
4. binding authority/binding precedent
5. persuasive authority/persuasive precedent

6. reporter
7. citation
8. dicta
9. predictability
10. dissent/ dissenting opinion

三、将下列句子译成汉语。

1. 使用先例来指导法院日后案件判决的原则称为遵循先例原则（拉丁语：遵循已决案例）。

2. 刑事律师在准备案件时所花的大部分时间都用来寻找可以支持其主张的司法先例。反过来，案件的成功结果很大程度上依赖于律师在这一过程中努力的成功。

3. 遵循先例原则有助于实现法的可预见性。进入现代法院的被告人有获得在先例以及程序方面训练有素的律师代理的机会。

4. 遵循先例原则并不适用于大陆法系国家的法院，所以（在这些国家的法院）法院判决对下级法院在后来的案件判决上并无约束力，这些判决在同一法院也无约束力，因而在相似案件中得出相反的结论在这些法院中并不罕见。

5. 除了司法先例制度之外，普通法的其他特征还有陪审团审判以及法律至上原则。

四、完型填空。

1. procedural
2. guidelines
3. steps/procedures
4. lawsuit
5. criminal
6. obligations
7. Substantive
8. court

第 七 课

一、根据课文回答下列问题。
（略）。

二、将下列术语译成英语。

1. the civil law
2. trial by ordeal
3. the canon law
4. Romanist
5. Twelve Tables
6. inheritance law
7. lay judges
8. Holy Roman Empire
9. common law
10. commercial law
11. Classical period
12. personal status
13. tort
14. unjust enrichment
15. the property law

三、将下列段落译成汉语。

罗马法不仅仅是历史上最广为人知的，发展最完善的，最有影响力的法律体系，而且罗马法完整不间断的历史可以从早先的原始时期，一直追溯到法学家手中的精致阐述，这一点除了英国法律之外，也是独一无二的。

Appendix I

Text Translation & Key to Exercises (Part One)

四、用适当词或词组填空。

1. comparisons
2. comparative
3. advance
4. expectation
5. claim

第 八 课

一、根据课文回答下列问题。
（略）。

二、将下列段落译成汉语。

各州负责组织本州律师协会的司法考试笔试。然而，几乎所有的州都采用"多州律师联考"。那些成功通过考试的申请者就可直接成为所在州律师协会的成员，而无须经过任何见习期。联邦法院的执业许可规则依法院的不同而有所差异，但一般而言，有资格在各州最高法院执业的人就可以执业于联邦法院。

三、选择适当的词填空。

1. solicitors
2. assisted
3. associated
4. dominant
5. advisory
6. distinction
7. abolished
8. despite
9. gained
10. occurred

四、将A栏的词同B栏的释义连接起来。

1. j 2. g 3. b 4. c 5. i
6. a 7. d 8. e 9. f 10. h

第 九 课

一、根据课文回答下列问题。
（略）。

二、将下列术语译成英语。

1. fundamental law
2. federalism
3. Articles of Confederation
4. Separation of Powers
5. House of Representatives
6. veto
7. judicial review
8. Bill of Rights
9. due process of law
10. equal protection of the laws

三、将下列句子译成汉语。

1. 由宪法制定者所创设的权力分立原则主要目的是为了避免多数人的铁拳统治。基于其自身的经验，制定者避免将太多权力赋予新政府中的任一部门。

2. 总统也许会因叛国、受贿及其他重罪或轻罪而受到国会弹劾，但其政治行为却不受弹劾。

3. 宪法的草拟和修订反映出了一种越来越普遍的共同看法：联邦政府的权力需要加强。

4. 如今，由权利法案所保障的个人权利已成为对州政府和联邦政府权力的限制。

5. 宪法不断发展以适应不断增长的社会需求，然而宪法的精神和措词还是保持不变。

四、完型填空。

1. power
2. laws
3. Constitution
4. check
5. Supreme
6. extend
7. delegates
8. review
9. acts
10. branches

第 十 课

一、根据课文回答下列问题。

（略）。

二、将下列术语译成英语。

1. reviewing court
2. legislative power
3. judicial power
4. executive power
5. checks and balance
6. self-incrimination
7. writ
8. hearing
9. trespass
10. battery

三、将下列段落译成汉语。

行政法体系不仅仅依赖程序管理以保障政府官员合理的履行职责。它还依赖立法、行政和司法部门来监督行政机关行为的根据。例如，总统指定政府官员并选择行政部门的总体目标。国会主持勘漏听审，必要时，改写授权法规。法院依靠法律规定对行政机关的决策施加外在限制。

四、用下列词的适当形式填空。

1. practice
2. applied
3. reviewing
4. challenge
5. acquaintance
6. agency
7. mission
8. congress
9. discharge
10. diagnoses

Appendix II
Text Translation & Key to Exercises (Part Two)

附录二 课文译文及练习答案（下篇）

下篇 各课译文

第一课 刑法概述

一、犯罪

刑法概念中最根本的是这样一种假设：犯罪行为伤害的不仅是个人，还损害整体社会。因此，我们可以给刑法下一个定义：刑法是现代法律中的一个分支，是惩治对社会、社会成员、财产以及社会秩序造成危害的犯罪行为的法律。刑法在英语中有两个术语，一个是criminal law，另一个是penal law。那么，犯罪行为与民事过错行为（例如民事侵权行为或违反合同行为）有什么区别呢？

首先，刑法与侵权行为法或合同法不同，刑法属于公法。换言之，尽管犯罪行为的直接受害者通常是个人（例如被抢劫、殴击或绑架），且其他个人也可能间接受到伤害（例如直接受害者的配偶），但犯罪牵涉的远非是个人伤害，犯罪还会导致"社会损害"。由于这一原因，犯罪由代表社会的公诉人提起公诉，而非由私人聘用的律师提起诉讼。

在古老的英国，罪犯犯罪被认为是违反"国王的宁静"。他们不仅危害了受害人，而且违反了君主统治下所确立的安定秩序。出于这一原因，国家作为刑事案件中受害一方负责将罪犯诉至法院这一程序。即便受害人死亡而没有人代表他（她）陈述，司法机关也会调查犯罪，并对罪犯提起诉讼。因为犯罪损害了社会的组织，所以国家而非受害者个人成为刑事诉讼中的原告。

当事实调查人（通常是陪审团）确定某人犯有某罪时，最终的有罪判决是社会义愤填膺之表达。但是，不可认为道德上有过错的行为都是犯罪行为。在重视个人自由的社会中，刑法充当着一个最基本的角色：它只确定并调整带来重大社会危害的不法行为；刑法并不寻求"净化人心、完美人性"。"净化人心、完美人性"是宗教、家庭以及其他私人机构等的责任。举例说明，说谎可能是一个性格缺陷，但是刑法只惩罚造成严重后果的谎言，例如，司法程序中，在宣誓后作重大的虚假表述（作伪证）。

英国的普通法将犯罪划分为两大类：重罪和轻罪。重罪"包括普通法中每种引起没收土地以及货物的罪"。所有的普通法重罪都可处死刑刑罚。重罪的种类并不很多，包括重罪杀人（后来依制定法划分为谋杀罪与非预谋杀人罪）、纵火罪、重伤罪、强奸罪、抢劫罪、偷盗罪、夜盗罪、逃狱罪以及（也许有）反自然性行为罪。除此之外所有的刑事犯罪均是轻罪。

在现代刑法典中，区别重罪与轻罪的界限与过去并不相同。一般而言，可处死刑或州监狱监禁刑的属于重罪；最高可处罚金刑、当地监狱关押刑或最高可并处上述两种刑罚的犯罪属于轻罪。出于宣判目的，《模范刑法典》以及众多司法管辖区的制定法方案中均把重罪划分为了若干等级。

违反刑法会导致刑罚。在刑事案件中实施刑罚主要出于一个简单原因，表达社会对进攻性行为的根本不满，并使罪犯对其行为负责。

二、刑事责任原则

如前所述，刑法的目的是震慑和惩罚威胁社会安全与秩序的犯罪行为。这个概念的关键点在于犯罪的构成离不开行为人从事禁止行为，只有不良想法，或只有作为或者不作为（有义务行为而没有做出该行为），这两种情形都不属于犯罪。法律要求不良行为（犯罪行为）和不良心理状态（犯罪意图）同时存在作为承担刑事责任的基础。要注意犯罪的构成还需要其他两个条件。第一，行为人的行为必须引起有害的结果。第二，州法律或联邦法律必须规定该行为属于犯罪行为。

（一）犯罪行为

《模范刑法典》中讲"行为人行为并不构成犯罪除非他的责任基于下列行为（1）自愿行为，或（2）事实上可以行为，而懈怠的不作为。"换言之，被告人必须做出非法的事或者没有完成法律要求完成的事。我们要求违法行为，或犯罪行为，因为如果不这样，刑事司法制度惩罚的依据只能变成人们的意图。因此，不能把学生射杀考试打低分成绩教授的想法当作是犯罪。

不作为 在一些情形之下，不作为可能构成犯罪行为要件。决定性因素是是否存在作为的法定义务，而不是道义上的义务。在大多数情形下，人们并不负有法定义务警告他人伤害可能降至他们面前。例如，有人无意中听到谋杀威胁，但他并无法定义务去警告可能的受害人。但是，个人有法定义务去完成纳税申报，因此，个人负有完成这一任务的法定义务，即便他们不能亲自来完成。

替代责任 替代责任是一种无过错责任，它并不要求行为人犯罪行为这一要件。在替代责任中，被告人对他人的不正当行为承担责任。与在民法中一样，被代理人（本人）对代理人在其代理权限范围内的不当行为承担责任。这一问题常出现在雇佣情形下。

（二）精神要件

犯罪故意，或犯罪意图，是指行为人的心理状态。它不同于加害人的行为动机。《模范刑法典》中规定了适用于犯罪的四种心理状态：（1）故意实施行为或故意引起结果；（2）明知行为的性质或结果；（3）疏忽大意；（4）过失。

严格责任在某些情形下，并不需要犯罪意图这一要件。因此，如果立法机关已经规定某种行为属于犯罪，即便不能证明过错，被告人还是要承担刑事责任，这就是严格责任。但是，对于这些犯罪的刑罚通常并没有对要求有犯罪意图的犯罪之刑罚严厉。注意严格责任与替代责任并不相同。

Appendix II

Text Translation & Key to Exercises (Part Two)

三、排除合理怀疑的证明

在刑事案件中，我们处理的是被告人的生命和自由，也包括伴随定罪而来的不好的名声。考虑到这一事实，法律在给嫌疑人定罪这一国家权力上做出了许多严格的限制。

刑事被告人是被推定无罪的。国家要想推翻这一无罪推定，必须通过证明被告人被控犯罪的每一构成要件都排除合理怀疑，从而让所有陪审员满意。这就是美国法律中降低将无罪的人判罪这一风险的最主要的方法。

国家证明案件必须在程序（设计旨在保护被告人）有保障的框架内进行。国家如果不能证明案件中的任何重要要件，则被告人只能是被无罪释放或宣告无罪，尽管他（她）可能在事实上犯了被指控的罪行。

第二课　刑事指控辩护类型

当人们被指控犯有某罪时，他（她）通常要提出某种抗辩。抗辩包括由被告及其代理人（律师）出示的、证明为何被告不应负被指控的刑事责任的证据和理由。美国的法律制度通常认可下列四类抗辩事由：一、不在犯罪现场；二、正当理由；三、可得宽恕；四、程序（不正当）。

一、不在犯罪现场

有一部现行的刑事审判律师指导书这样写道："不在犯罪现场与其他任何抗辩理由均有所不同……因为……它建立在被告真正无罪的假设之上。"不在犯罪现场抗辩理由否定被告实施了可疑的犯罪行为。我们所要讨论的其他所有类型的抗辩理由都是假定被告实施了犯罪行为，但是这些抗辩理由否定被告（他或她）应负刑事责任。

证人和证据资料是不在犯罪现场的最好支持。被指控犯罪的人可以运用"不在犯罪现场"抗辩事由来表明，当所提及的犯罪行为发生时，他们并不在犯罪现场。宾馆的发票、目击者证明以及参加社交活动的事实均可以用来证明（某人）不在犯罪现场。

二、正当理由

当人们发现自己处于"两害相权取其轻"这种情形时，可能会提出正当理由抗辩。正当理由这类抗辩事由包括：第一、自我防卫；第二、他我防卫；第三、家庭与财产防卫；第四、紧急避险；第五、同意；第六、抗拒非法逮捕。

第一、自我防卫

自我防卫可能是最为著名的正当理由。这一辩护战略主张，为了确保自己免受即将发生的伤害或死的危险而给他人带来一定伤害是必然的。行为人若伤害了进攻者，他通常可以运用这一抗辩。但是，法院判定若受进攻对象有"退路"时，要选择退路。换言之，自我防卫最保险的运用时间是（受进攻对象）被"逼到绝路"，无路可退的时候。

防守所使用的武力程度必须与行为人所防守的武力程度或所觉察到的威胁程度相称。因此，"合理的武力"是指在特定情况下没有超过必要限度的力量程度。合理的武力也可被认为是在面临实际危险时，为保护自己、自己的财产、第三人或他人财产而使用的必要的、最低限度的武力。致命武力是最高程度的武力，人们认为，只有在生命受到立即的威胁或身体受到巨大伤害时，致命武力才会被认为是合理的（武力）。致命武力不可用于对付非致命武力。

自我防卫这一语境下使用的"武力"这个术语指身体上的武力，并不延展到对感情的、心理的、经济的、灵魂或其他形式的胁迫。例如，在一抢劫未遂案件中，某人将桌子砸向抢劫人，并殴击抢劫人，他可以主张自我防卫，但是，若某商人殴击其商业竞争对手，来达到阻止其夺取他的公司便不可享有这样的抗辩权。

第二、他我防卫

他我防卫，有时也称为"第三人防卫"，在一些司法管辖区域内受到"他我规则"的限制。仅为帮助朋友或家庭成员而参与非法斗殴的个人并不可以主张他我防卫。根据法律，第三人防卫通常要求防卫人无过错，且他（她）是对无辜的人在遭受侵害时给予帮助。适用于自我防卫的限制同样也适用于第三人防卫。因此，防卫人只有符合下列条件才可以实施防卫，即必须是他人面临即将发生的威胁，对付非致命武力不能使用致命武力，并且必须只能在程度上运用反抗进攻所需要的武力程度。

第三、家庭与财产防卫

在大多数司法管辖区内，财产所有人可以正当使用合理的、非致命的武力来阻止他人非法占用或损坏财产。但是，作为一个一般原则，性命的保存要胜过对财产的保护，并且使用致命武力来保护财产并不正当，除非非法行为的实施者蓄意对他人或正在对他人实施暴力行为。举例说明，行为人枪击手无寸铁的侵害人，不可以主张"财产防卫"以摆脱刑事责任。不过，行为人如果在被抢劫过程中射杀的是武装抢劫人，则他可以（主张"财产防卫"）。

使用机械设施来保护财产是法律中的一块特殊领域。一般来讲，因为在财产防卫中不允许使用致命武力，所以一般不允许使用陷阱设置如伏击枪、电网、爆炸性装置等来保护无人看管、无人占用的财产。

另一方面来讲，平常会被视为刑事犯罪的行为，如果行为人是用来保护自己的家，则行为人可能并不需要承担刑事责任。出于该法的目的，一个人的"家"是他的住处，而不论是拥有所有权的、租住的或只是"借来的"。宾馆的房间、船舶上的房间以及在属于他人房子中租来的房间，处于该法的目的，均被认为是人们的"住处"。前文提及的撤退原则要求受到进攻的人在运用致命武力前尽可能撤退，但这一原则在此受到称作"城堡例外规则"的限制。城堡例外规则可以追溯到16世纪英国法学家科克（Coke）的著作，科克说："一个人的家就是他的城堡——如果一个人在其家中都不安全，那在哪里才能安全呢？"城堡例外规则通常认为，人在自己的家中享有基本权利，同时认为家是人们可撤退的最后的、神圣不可侵犯的地方（换言之，家应该是一个人所能后退到不能再后退的地方）。因此，当行为人面临直接的威胁时，他不必要撤离家，便可以运用致使武力保护自己的家即便在他使用致命武力之前有撤退的可能。很多法院的判决已将城堡例外原则延伸到了某人的经营地，例如商店或办公室。

第四、紧急避险

紧急避险，或是为了避免一个更大的伤害而需要采取某种非法行为的主张，是不涉及严重身体伤害案件中一种有用的抗辩。这一抗辩最著名的运用是在19世纪晚期"克朗诉塔德里和斯蒂芬"（*Crown v. Dudly & Stephens*）一案。该案涉及的是三名水手和一名船舱服务生，在海船失事之后，同乘一艘救生艇漂流。经过在海上漂泊几天没有食物供

Appendix II

Text Translation & Key to Exercises (Part Two)

给之后,两名水手(塔德里和斯帝芬)决定杀死船舱服务生并将其吃掉。在初审法院,他们辩称那样做是必要的,否则他们四人将无一生还。但是法院认为服务生并不是他们生存的直接威胁,因而拒绝了他们的抗辩。他们被认定犯有谋杀罪并被判处死刑,最后由于皇室的干涉免于死刑。

尽管食人罪通常违反法律,但是法院有时承认在某些生死存亡的关键时刻吃人肉的必要性。不过,这些案件中有关的"受害者"通常已由于自然原因死亡。

第五、(被害人)同意

被害人同意抗辩主张,已经发生的无论什么样的损害,所争论的行为均是得到受害人允许后才做出的。

第六、抗拒非法逮捕

所有的司法管辖区都认为面临非法逮捕时做出的抗拒是正当的。有些司法管辖区有制定法,该法对实施抵抗加以详细限制,对使用该抗辩的条件作了规定。这种法律通常说明人们可以使用合理限度的武力,但不是致命武力,去抵抗执法人员的非法逮捕或是非法搜查,如果执法人员使用或企图使用超过必要的武力进行逮捕或搜查。使用致命武力来抵抗逮捕是不合法的,除非执法人员在不需要使用致命武力时使用了致命武力。

三、可得宽恕

与正当理由相比,可得宽恕并不主张行为合法,也不主张其符合道义。法律认可的可得宽恕包括:第一、强迫;第二、年龄;第三、错误;第四、非自愿醉态;第五、无意识;第六、激怒(挑拨);第七、精神病;第八、责任减等。

第一、强迫

强迫的定义是,某人引诱他人实施(或阻碍他人实施)某一相反行为而使用的任何不法威胁或胁迫。例如,某人为了向绑架其小孩的绑架者支付赎金,而偷盗雇主的薪水总额,此人可能是出于强迫。此行为人如因此以盗窃罪或侵占罪而被逮捕,则他(她)可以主张实施犯罪该行为是为了确保孩子的安全而逼不得已。强迫抗辩有时也称为胁迫。当犯罪行为涉及严重身体伤害时,强迫这一抗辩理由并不十分有用,因为在陪审团以及法官的意识里,犯罪行为带来的伤害可能要远远超过胁迫的影响。

第二、年龄

面临刑事指控时,年龄提供另一种可得宽恕,"未成年"辩护起源于古老的信念——人们认为儿童大约在7岁之后才具有合乎逻辑的推理能力。今天的未成年辩护已扩展到包括大于七岁的人群。出于刑事指控的目的,许多州规定16周岁为成年人的年龄。其他州则规定为17岁,还有一些州18岁。当低于规定成年人指控年龄的人犯"罪"时,人们使用"未成年犯罪"这一术语。

第三、错误

两种类型的错误可以用作抗辩。一种是法律错误,另一种是事实错误。法律错误抗辩很少能被接受。大多数人意识到了解法律是他们的义务,因为法律要适用于他们。"不知法不免罪"是时至今日仍可听到的一句古老格言。事实错误是一种更为有用的"错误"抗辩类型。

第四、非自愿醉态

非自愿醉态主张可以形成另一种可得宽恕抗辩的基础。毒品或酒精都可以引起醉态。自愿醉态很难成为刑事指控的抗辩，因为它属于自我引起的情形。但是，非自愿醉态则是另一回事。有时，人们可能会被哄骗而使用致醉性物质。偷加了酒精的饮料、常用的春药，或是加入了迷幻药的甜点都可能在不知情的情况下使用。因为酒精的效果和味道为人们所周知，所以因使用酒精而做出的非自愿醉态抗辩很难成功实现。

第五、无意识

无意识辩护是一种很少使用的可得宽恕。个人对其在无意识状态下做出的任何事情应该不用负责。

第六、激怒（挑拨）

作为一个原则，激怒抗辩通常在较轻的犯罪案件中比在严重的违法案件中更为容易被接受。

第七、精神病

这一点必须要意识到，精神病出于刑法的目的是一个法律概念，而非精神病学概念。精神病的法律定义通常与精神疾病的心理学上或精神病学上的理解没有关系。法律上的精神失常这一概念经长时间发展，是为满足司法制度中确定特定被告有罪或无罪的需要而形成的。精神病学上与法律上对精神病的理解差异常导致专家证人在刑事法庭上意见的不一致——对于同一被告的精神病问题，他们可能出庭提供互相冲突的证词。

第八、责任减等

责任减等抗辩同精神病抗辩有一点相似，即它同样依靠证明被告的智力状态在犯罪时并不健全。与精神病抗辩不同的是，精神病抗辩可以得出"无罪"的判决结果，而责任减等是建立在"虽不足以证明无罪，但该智力状态可能与一定犯罪行为的智力要件或犯罪的轻重有关"这一认知之上的。

四、程序抗辩

程序抗辩主张被告人在司法程序中在某种程度上受到了歧视待遇，或者是某些正式程序的重要环节没有得到遵守，所以他们应该从任何可能的刑事责任中解放出来。我们在此讨论的程序抗辩主要包括：第一、警察设圈套；第二、双重危险；第三、间接的禁止翻供的事实；第四、选择起诉；第五、否定速审；第六、公诉错误；第七、警察欺诈。

第三课　现代刑事诉讼中的几个主要方面：被告人的权利

美国的刑事司法制度中有两个基本方面：一是推定被告人无罪；二是检察机关负有举证责任，排除合理怀疑证明被告人有罪。但是刑事诉讼中被告人还有其他一些权利。在此我们来探究一下刑事诉讼的一些重要方面。

一、被告人保持沉默的权利

美国宪法第五条修正案规定被告人在任何刑事案件中都不能被迫做不利于自己的证人（自证其罪）。简单地说，也就是被告人有权保持沉默。如果被告人选择了保持沉默，检察官不能要求其作为证人，法官和辩护律师也不能强迫被告人提供证词。与此不同的是，在民事案件中被告可以作为证人。

二、被告人对质证人的权利

美国宪法第六条修正案中的"对质条款"赋予了被告人有与对自己不利的证人对质的权利。这一权利中暗含了交叉询问证人的权利，即有权要求证人出庭，使证人"亲眼看到被告人"并且接受辩护律师的提问。第六条修正案的规定防止了秘密审判，除了极少数例外情形外，它可还禁止检察官在证人不出现的情况下仅凭书面供述即证明被告人有罪。

三、儿童性侵犯案件中的特殊对质原则

近年来，立法者注意到，在对儿童进行性侵犯的案件中，由于儿童在被告人面前不敢指证，有些被告人逃避了惩罚。为了解决这个问题，许多州制定了特殊的对质规则：在特定情况下，这些规则授权法官可以允许儿童通过闭路电视提供证词。被告人可以通过电视监视器看到儿童，而儿童看不到被告人。被告人的律师在儿童提供证词时可以在场并可以对儿童进行交叉询问。

四、被告人获有公开审判的权利

美国宪法第六条修正案保证了被告人在刑事案件公开审判中的权利。该权利十分重要，因为被告人的家人、朋友及普通民众和新闻界的出席对于确保政府遵守与审判相关的其他重要权利有很大的作用。

在少数情况下，通常是涉及儿童时，法庭会向公众封闭。例如，当被告人涉及对儿童进行性侵犯时，法官可以拒绝公众旁听案件审判。此外，当证人在法庭上会互相指导时，法官也可以拒绝证人到庭。

五、被告人获有陪审团审判的权利

美国宪法第六条修正案规定被告人有权获得由陪审团审判。这一权利一直被解释为：由12人组成的陪审团一致作出决定，判定被告人有罪或宣告无罪。（在大部分州，如果陪审团达不成全体一致的意见，则称为悬案陪审团，被告人因而会被释放，除非检察官决定再审。但是，在俄勒冈州和路易斯安那州，当陪审团的表决是10比2时也可以判定有罪或宣告无罪。）可能的陪审团成员须从社区中随机选择，确定最终的陪审团成员时，必须允许法官和律师剔出可能有偏袒的陪审员。此外，律师如果觉得备选的某些陪审团成员不会同情自己一方时，也可以将其剔出（被称为"无因回避"）。但做出这些决定不得基于陪审团人员的个人特征如种族、性别、宗教信仰或国籍。

六、被告人有获得律师辩护权

美国宪法第六条修正案规定"在一切刑事诉讼中，被告人享有从律师处获得帮助为自己辩护的权利"。如果被告人的罪名可能被判六个月以上监禁，法官必须为贫困被告人指派一名律师（如果被告人无力聘请律师的话），费用由政府负担。在实践中，被告人可能被判处监禁刑的所有案件中，法官几乎都会例行公事地为贫困被告人指派一名律师。否则，法官将须判处这一没有代理律师的被告人以非监禁刑刑罚，或者如果经审理，可能的刑罚本应比实际刑期长。

通常法官都是在经济困难的被告人首次出庭时即为其指派律师。对大部分被告人而言，首次出庭是传讯或保释听证。

在审判中，辩护律师的职责是代表刑事被告人准备并不遗余力地提供抗辩。恰当的辩护通常包括证据的出示和对证人的询问，所有这些都要求细心的考虑和设计。好的律师，就像技术精湛的工匠一样，在其代理的案件中，对审判的结果是倾注了感情的。

七、被告人享有迅速审判的权利

美国宪法第六条修正案规定被告人有受到"迅速审判"的权利。但宪法并未具体确定在多长期限内开始审判被认为是迅速。因此，法官通常是在个案基础上决定被告人的审判是否被拖延从而驳回起诉。在作出此决定之时，法官要考虑拖延的长短，拖延的原因以及是否给被告人造成不利。

每个司法管辖区域都颁布有制定法，对案件从开始提起诉讼到审判这一时间段做出了限定。这些制定法的用语都非常严格，一般情况下不会由于违反制定法的时限规定而撤销对被告人的有罪判决。

八、被告人享有不受双重追诉的权利

美国宪法第五条修正案有一款规定了一项重要的诉讼原则："当事人的生命或肢体不受同一罪行的两次追诉"。这一规定就是双重追诉条款，该条款保护被告人不因同一罪行受到一次以上的审判。双重追诉的问题并不常见，因为检察机关通常愿意在同一案件中一次性收集全部指控。

双重追诉的一个例外是被告人的同一罪行可受不同的管辖区域提出两次以上指控。例如，如果被告人行为在某些方面触犯了联邦法，某些方面违反了州法律，那么他有可能受到联邦法院和州法院的双重指控。

此外，双重追诉条款禁止的只是基于同一行为而提起的刑事指控（起诉）。被告人可能会因同一行为而同时被起诉至刑事法院（政府起诉）和民事法院（社会成员起诉）。例如，辛普森在涉嫌谋杀其前妻及前妻的好友被宣告无罪后，她们的亲属对他提起了民事诉讼以获得由杀人行为而引起的实际损害赔偿与惩罚性损害赔偿。民事诉讼并不引起双重追诉问题，尽管惩罚性损害赔偿属于一种刑罚，而且辛普森最终对死亡负有民事责任。

第四课 沉 默 权

也许你在电视上的犯罪节目中不止一次的听到过下面这段话："你有权保持沉默。你所作的任何陈述将可能成为对你不利的证据。你有权和律师谈话并有权在讯问过程中要求律师在场。如果你无力聘请律师，将由政府承担费用为你指派一名律师。"这就是米兰达警告，由一起犯罪嫌疑人叫米兰达的著名案例而得名。

警示原则说的一点不错，可是，警官并没有必要为了逮捕你而把这些神奇的话全背下来。在大多数情况下，警察只有在讯问时才会告知该警示；如果他们在你的律师不在场的情况下进行讯问，而且没有告知该警示原则的话，你所作的回答就不可以成为法庭上对你不利的证据。但是，警察可以在不宣读米兰达警告的情况下问一些例行的问题，如你的姓名、住址、出生日期及社会安全号码，以便确认你的身份。在没有警告的情况下，你也有可能要接受呼吸测试。当然，你随时都有权拒绝回答任何问题。

Appendix II

Text Translation & Key to Exercises (Part Two)

一、米兰达裁决

在犯罪嫌疑人的权利这一块，最著名的案件当属"米兰达诉亚利桑那州"案，一个1966年的判例。许多人视米兰达案为沃伦法院（联邦最高法院）正当程序判决中最为核心的一个案件。

该案涉及恩纳斯托·米兰达，他因涉嫌绑架并强奸一名年轻女子而在亚利桑那州的菲尼克斯市被捕。在警察局总部被害人指认他犯了罪。经过两个小时的讯问，米兰达承认了被指控罪行并签了字，法院后来据此给他定了罪。

在最终的上诉中，联邦最高法院作出的司法意见对之后几十年的刑事司法产生了深远的影响。法院判定对米兰达的定罪是违宪的，因为"整个警察讯问的氛围和气氛是在犯罪嫌疑人没有被告知其权利和提供律师帮助的情况下进行的，这样就可能使犯罪嫌疑人屈从于讯问者的意志"。

法院进一步说，被告人"在任何讯问前必须被告知有权保持沉默，其所作的任何陈述可能成为对其不利的证据；他有权要求律师在场；如无力聘请律师而又有此要求时，得于讯问前为其指派律师。犯罪嫌疑人必须在讯问的全过程中都享有该权利。在被告知这些警示和权利后，犯罪嫌疑人可以在知情并理智的情况下放弃这些权利，同意回答问题或作供述。但是，除非并只有在警示和弃权在审判中由公诉人出示，否则任何讯问的结果都不能作为对其不利的证据。"

为了保证犯罪嫌疑人在被捕时得到适当的建议，如今著名的米兰达权利是在讯问前便宣读的。这些权利写在米兰达警示卡上，警察局广泛使用。在讯问18岁及以上的被羁押人之前，必须告知其以下权利：

1. 你有权保持沉默。
2. 你所作的任何陈述在法庭上可能成为对你不利的证据。
3. 你有权和律师谈话，并有权在讯问过程中要求律师在场。
4. 如果你想在讯问前或讯问过程中有律师在场但无力聘请时，法庭将会在讯问前免费为你指派一名律师。
5. 如果你愿意在现在没有律师的情况下回答问题，你仍有权随时停止回答提问。

二、权利的放弃

在宣读和解释完被羁押人的权利之后，司法人员在讯问前还必须询问权利的放弃。下列这些弃权问题必须得到肯定地回答，明确回答或清楚的暗示，但沉默本身不能视为是对权利的放弃。

1. 你都明白我所解释的每项权利吗？（回答必须是"是的"）
2. 你已知道了这些权利，现在你愿意回答问题吗？（回答必须是"是的"）
3. 现在你愿意在律师不在场的情况下回答问题吗？（回答必须是"是的"）

对于14、15、16、17岁的青少年，必须问下面这个问题：

4. 你愿意在你的父母或监护人不在场的情况下回答问题吗？（回答必须是"是的"）

一旦犯罪嫌疑人被告知其米兰达权利之后，通常要在列清每项权利的文件上签字，以确认自己被告知了每项权利并了解其内容。但只有犯罪嫌疑人放弃同律师谈话或放弃在讯问过程中有律师在场的权利后，讯问方可开始。

米兰达判例作出后，有些人很拥护，认为它与宪法中规定一样可以保障个人权利。为了保证这些权利，他们认为，没有任何机构比警察要好，因为警察参与刑事司法程序的最初阶段。然而，对米兰达原则持批评态度的人则认为，这一裁决将警察置于了既不舒服而又使其感到矛盾的位置当中，一方面他们要执法，而另一方面他们又要给犯罪嫌疑人以建议，使其知道如何去防止定罪和处罚。在米兰达原则下，警察部分地承担着被告人的法律顾问的角色。在里根政府最后几年里，当时的美国司法部长爱德文·密斯认为米兰达裁决与"法律和秩序"是相对立的。他利用其职位资源，对米兰达原则表示反对和攻击，目的在于消除他所见到的有罪当事人常常由于依据"技术性细节"而被释放这一现象。不过，米兰达裁决直至今日仍在适用。

三、犯罪嫌疑人对米兰达权利的放弃

羁押中的犯罪嫌疑人可以基于自愿"知晓并理解"地放弃他们的米兰达权利。"知晓的权力放弃"是犯罪嫌疑人被告知其权利并理解这种建议的情形下才成立的。比如说，用英语告知的权利对于一个说西班牙语的被告人来说，就不产生"知晓的权力放弃" 这种情况。同样，所谓"理解的权力放弃"要求被告人能理解放弃米兰达权利所产生的后果。在"莫兰诉博柏"（1968）一案中，最高法院将"知晓并理解"定义为："做出的决定是基于充分理解弃权之本质和弃权之结果的。"与之相类似的是，在"科罗拉多州诉斯普林"（1987）一案中，法院判定，即便是在犯罪嫌疑人并没有获悉自己将会被讯问的指控的罪名的情况下，也可以视为"知晓并理解"。

四、如果警察没有对犯罪嫌疑人宣读米兰达权利，该逮捕是否非法？

否。这些权利仅用于保护你不受自证其罪，但不能对抗逮捕。警察在逮捕前只需要"合理的依据"——基于事实和观察的充分理由，相信你犯了罪。警察只有在要讯问犯罪嫌疑人时才必须宣读米兰达权利。否则，法官后来可以驳回已作出的任何陈述，不过逮捕可以依然有效。

五、米兰达原则的公共安全例外

1984年联邦最高法院也制定出了米兰达原则的公共安全例外。在"纽约诉夸尔斯"一案中，宣称遭强奸的受害人告诉警察，攻击她的人带着枪跑进了附近一家大洋超市。两名警官进入超市并逮捕了犯罪嫌疑人。其中一名警官马上注意到这名男子肩上的手枪皮套是空的，显然警官是害怕这把丢弃的枪被小孩子找到，于是立刻问道："枪在哪里？"

Quarles被判强奸罪，但他对这一定罪提出上诉，要求不把武器作为证据，因为警察在问话前并没有告知其米兰达权利。最高法院没有支持其理由，认为，对公共安全的考虑高于一切，为防止进一步的危害，在有限的讯问之前可以不告知米兰达权利。

第五课 财 产 法

财产这个单词具有浓厚的感情色彩和多种意思，很难给出一个精确而完整的定义。为了本章论述的目的，财产可以定义为一种控制经济利益的排他性权利。这个概念指的是一种权利与义务、特权与限制——它管理着人们之间涉及有价物所形成的各种关系。

Appendix II

Text Translation & Key to Exercises (Part Two)

从广义上来说，保证是一个人自己的东西就是财产。

然而，如果法律不能赋予其使用、出卖或处置和防止侵害的权利，财产便几乎没有价值（这个单词也没有任何意义）。

财产包含许多方面。法律对不同种财产的规定有所不同，所以将一个人能够拥有的财产加以分类是很有用的，也许最基本的分类就是不动产和动产的划分。不动产包括土地及建筑物、植被和其他任何永久性的地上附着物。而所有的其他财产便是动产。有时候律师们把动产称作"动产"（chattel），这个单词在普通法上指所有形式的动产。动产可能是有形的或无形的。像电视机和汽车这样有形的动产都有确确实实的物质形态，无形动产代表某种权利和利益，没有实际的物体存在。像股票、债券、专利及版权都是无形动产。由于财产法的题目范围太大，我们这里只能论及一些主要方面，这一章仅涉及财产法中最重要的概念。

一、不动产所有权

不动产所有权是一个抽象概念，不能独立存在于法律体系中。没有人能够拥有或者控制一块土地，包括它上面的空气，底下的土壤和里面所包含的所有水分。因此法律体系只承认那些构成不动产所有权权益的某些权利与义务。

（一）无条件继承之不动产（财产）权

现今最普通的一种财产所有权是无条件继承之不动产权。通常来说该术语用来指绝对无条件继承之不动产，这种不动产的所有人具有一切可能的权利、特权及能力。无条件继承之不动产权，只限于个人或其继承人，而且其转让永远没有任何限制和条件。进一步来说，所有权人对该财产具有排他性的占有和使用的权利。无条件继承之不动产权的存续期限可能是无期限的，这样便可立契或遗嘱处置（出售或赠送）。如果没有遗嘱，这种不动产权将由权利人的法定继承人继承。

无条件继承之不动产权项下的权利，包括土地的使用权，可以以所有权人认为适当的任何目的而使用。当然，财产的某种使用可能被现行法律所禁止，这些法律包括城市区划法、环境法规和那些禁止所有权人非法侵入他人土地的法律。另一个对无条件继承之不动产所有人绝对权利的限制是政府的征用权。

当不动产被有条件的让与或转移给另一方当事人时，无条件继承之不动产权也可能受到限制。这种情况下，该不动产被认为是可限定无条件继承之不动产（defeasible这个单词的意思是能终止或取消的）。"只要土地用于慈善目的，财产便转让给A和他的继承人"，由于保有财产所有权以土地用于慈善目的为条件，这种转让就形成一个可限定无条件继承之不动产。原所有人保留财产所有权部分权益，因为如果指定条件没有发生（如果土地不再用于慈善目的），土地将回复或者归还给原所有人。如果那时原所有人已不在世，土地将归还给她或他的继承人。

（二）终身不动产

终身不动产是为某些指定个体终身拥有的不动产。当财产移转时写明"为A终身拥有"时，便创设了一种终身不动产。不动产的终身占有人比可限定无条件继承之不动产的产权人所拥有的权利更少，因为当终身占有人死亡时，权利必须终止。

如果终身不动产占有人不浪费（伤害土地），那么他或她有权使用土地。换句话说，终身不动产占有人不能滥用土地，损害其价值。占有人可以耕种土地收获农作物，如果地上存在矿井或油井，占有人还可以从中开采矿石和石油，但却不能开掘新的油井或矿区来开发土地。

除了这些权利，终身不动产占有人还有相应义务——维护财产和交付税款。简而言之，终身不动产占有人在占有期间必须保持财产价值，减少财产正当使用造成的价值损耗，除了这些之外，该占有人与无条件继承之不动产权人拥有相同的权利。

（三）未来财产权益

当绝对无条件继承之不动产权利人将不动产有条件转让（比如可限定无条件继承之不动产），或在限定的期间内转让（比如终身不动产），原所有人仍然保有该土地的权益。如果可限定无条件继承之不动产的条件没有达到，或终身不动产占有人死亡，那么原所有人仍有权收回土地。这种原所有人保留的（或转移给其他人的）财产权益被称作未来权益，因为它如果发生，只发生在将来。

如果原所有人保有未来财产权益，那么当限定无条件继承之不动产规定的条件没有达到，或终身不动产占有人死亡时，财产将被归还给原所有人，这种未来权益被称为归复权益。然而，如果未来财产权益所有人将未来财产权益转移给其他人，这时未来权益被称作（剩余地产）继受权。例如，财产移转"给A终身所有，然后给B"，这就给A创设了终身不动产权，给B创设了（剩余地产）继受权。

（四）非占有性权益

相对于前述几种财产权益，还存在一些并不实际占有的土地权益，这就是我们所了解的非占有性权益——地役权、用益权和特许权。

地役权、用益权　地役权是指在有限范围内使用他人不动产的权利，这种使用不能从该财产上取得任何东西。比如从他人的不动产经过的权利就是一种地役权。与此相对照，用益权则是可以走进他人所有之土地，并将土地的某些部分（如沙土或碎石）或地上的产物取走的权利。

特许权　这是一种允许进入他人土地的可撤销权利。这种特权源自土地所有权人同意，同样也可被所有权人撤销。一张到电影院看电影的电影票便是一种特许权。假设百老汇剧院的所有人发给卡拉一张观看戏剧的入场券，如果卡拉因为穿着不当而被拒绝进入，她则没有强行入内的权利。入场券只是一种可撤销的特许权，而不是财产权益的转让。

二、动产所有权

动产所有权仍然可以视为一组权利，包括占有权和买卖、租赁和其他方式的处置权。实际上，下列动产所有权的分类也可用于不动产。

（一）无条件继承之财产

正如上文所述，当某人拥有一组完整的财产权时，就被称作无条件继承之财产的所有人。该所有人在有生之年有权按其意愿占有、使用及处置其财产，死后，其财产权益转移给继承人所有。

（二）共同所有权

同时对一项财产具有所有权的人被叫作共有权人。共有权主要有两种类型：共同共有和联合共有。另外一种共同所有权是夫妻共有。

共同共有　该术语指的是两人或两人以上共同拥有所有权的一种形式，其中每个人都对财产拥有不可分割的权益。权益不可分割是因为每个所有权人都拥有完整的财产权。当一个共同共有人死亡,该共有人的财产权益由其继承人继承。

联合共有 联合共有是两人或两人以上拥有一项不可分割的财产权益,当一个共有人死亡时他的财产权益转移给其他在世的共有人。在世的共有人继承死去共有人财产权益的权利被称作生者取得权,这一点是共同共有和联合共有的区别。联合共有权也可能在共有人死前由于共有人的赠与或出卖行为而终止,在这种情况下,获赠人或财产买受人就变为共同共有人,而不是联合共有人。

夫妻共有 财产的共同共有也可以采取夫妻共有的形式。这是一种丈夫和妻子共同所有的形式,与联合共有具有相似性,但是夫妻一方在世时不能未经对方同意将自己的财产权益转移。

三、财产所有权的取得

获得财产的最普通的方式就是购买。财产通常还可以通过遗嘱或继承而取得。这里我们看看其他取得财产的方式,包括先占取得、生产、赠与、添附和混合。

(一)先占

通过先占而取得所有权的一个例子就是捕获野生动物。自然状态下的野生动物不属于任何人,第一个占有野生动物的人便正式拥有。猎杀野生动物也视为取得其所有权。那些发现被遗失或丢弃的财产的人也可以仅凭先占而取得所有权。

(二)生产

生产——取得劳动果实——是另外一种取得动产权的方式。举例来说,作家、发明家以及制造商都是生产出动产从而取得其所有权的。尽管在某些情况下,当研究人员因受雇佣而发明一种新产品或新技术时,生产出的东西可能不能由研究生产者所拥有。

(三)赠与

赠与是另一种相当普遍的获得和转移动产及不动产所有权的方式。从本质上来说,赠与是一种自愿转移财产所有权行为,没有相应的对价。是否存在对价是合同与赠与的区别所在。然而,从法律的角度来判断,赠与行为生效必须有某些条件存在。赠与人(实施赠与一方)必须有赠与的意思,赠与物必须移交给受赠人(赠与的接受者),受赠人还必须接受赠与。

(四)添附

添附的意思是在某物上增添某种东西,添附发生于某人用劳动力或材料为一项财产增添了价值。通常来说,如果添附的发生经所有权人同意,那么当添附行为完成后,对谁拥有所有权就不会产生争议。如果添附没有经过所有权人同意,而这种添附又是不正当的、恶意的行为,那么法院往往都会支持所有权人而不是添附人。此外,许多法院还会拒绝添附人对增添价值给予赔偿的请求。比如,当真正车主的车失而复得时,一个偷车贼显然不能为给偷来的车换新轮胎而得到补偿。但是,如果添附行为是善意的,即使未经所有权人同意,被添附部分的所有权还是往往取决于添附行为是否增加了财产价值或改变了财产性质。

(五)混合

混合是指物品被混合在一起,以至于一个人的动产和另一个人的动产不能相互区分。混合经常发生在物品能相互替代的情况下,就是说当每个粒子和其他粒子都相同时才能发生——就像谷粒和油。混合发生后，混合物就被两个或两个以上的人共同所有。比如，如果两个农民把他们各自的二级冬小麦放到一个储藏库中，混合便会发生。

第六课 合 同 法

一、定义

合同被定义为"在两人或多人之间达成的包括一个或双方允诺的协议，法律将强制其履行或以某种方式认定其履行为一项义务"。它还有一个另外的定义，即"一项或一系列允诺，若该允诺被违反，法律将给与救济，或者法律将对该允诺的履行认定为义务。"

合同的要件是合意。合同要求两人或两人以上之间达成协议。一个人不可能成立一个合同，两个人若没有就合同条款达成一致也不可能成立一个合同。合意要件的一个通用的表述就是必须有"意思表示的一致"。这一点也就是说合同各方必须达成一项在其内心有相同，或者即使不完全相同也是近似意思的理解。

合同的另一个要件是利益的交换。无偿允诺在法律上通常都不具有合同的可执行性。比如，如果我允诺给你500美元，而且你说你接受，合同并没有成立。无偿允诺并没有形成一个意思表示的一致，而只是表明我有意去做某件我可能完成也可能不完成的事情。

二、分类

正式合同和非正式合同 正式合同是指满足合同的形式要求从而具有约束力的合同。正式合同包括盖章的合同，可流通票据等。

明示或默示 以口头或书面的形式达成的协议是明示的合同。如果协议的当事人及其条款是由行为推定出来的，这个合同就是默示的或称事实上的默示。

单方合同和双方合同 单方合同是指以一方承诺交换另一方履行的合同。双方合同是双方都向对方做出承诺的合同。

已履行的合同和待履行的合同 已履行的合同是指合同项下的义务已经履行完毕的合同。待履行的合同是指履行还未完成的合同。

可撤销，有效和无效 可撤销的合同是指合同一方有权选择使其义务无效或否认其义务（如未成年人订立的合同）的合同。除非该种选择做出，否则法律将执行合同义务。有效合同是指既非可撤销又非无效的合同。无效的合同是指自始即无法律上效力的合同。

三、要约与承诺

（一）要约

一般来说，要成立合同，一方必须向另一方发出要约。发出要约的一方称为要约方；接受要约的一方称为受要约方。一项旨在成立要约的表述必须明确、肯定且有做出要约的意思。一个人对另一个人做出的如"我想以100美元的价格把我的车卖给你。你愿意买吗？"的表述就是一个明确的、肯定的、表明意图的要约。而"我在考虑把我的车以100美元卖给你"这个表述则不是一个要约，因为它没有要约方确定出卖的意思。

要约方具有要约的意图是至关重要的。尽管不可能知道个人内心的所思所想，人们也可以通过对交易相关的事实情况分析来确定要约人的意思。法院运用客观标准来对此进行判断，如果一个理性的人会将某个表述或事实情况认定为要约存在，那么即使要约人没有要约的意思也会被照此认定。

要约的通知方式是要约的第二个重要的要件。通知不必采取言词形式，但受要约人必须知道有人向自己要约。不知道有要约存在的人不能接受该要约。

要约的终止在以下几种情形下发生：受要约人接受，要约人撤销，受要约人拒绝，要约人或受要约人死亡或丧失行为能力，要约标的物嗣后不合法，要约标的物毁损或被优先购走，要约人声明的有效期到期，或者合理的期限届满。

（二）承诺

对承诺性质的界定十分严格。承诺必须与要约的条件一致。对要约作微小修改的承诺不能视为拒绝。判断一项修改是构成微小修改还是重大修改应该依个案的实际情况来决定。一个增加条件的承诺既可能是一项承诺，也可能是要约的拒绝。如果添加的条件是重大变动，承诺将构成对原要约的拒绝而成为一个反要约。如果新条件与合同的其他条款相比只是微小的变动，则承诺有效。

承诺的通知也可以多种形式作出。合同一经承诺即成立。为使承诺生效，承诺通知必须向受要约人做出。受要约人向要约人作出承诺的最适当方式就是采取与要约人向受要约人发出要约通知相同的方式。承诺若以与发出要约方式相同的方式作出，则自其进入通知过程即为生效。

四、对价

一般情况下，若要约与承诺已经存在，则合同正式成立。但没有对价支持的允诺即使已被接受，合同也不能成立。如果我承诺付给你500美元，而你答应接受我的承诺，这种情况下并没有合同存在。因为我没有付给你500美元的理由，而且即使我履行了我的无偿承诺，它也不是被法律强制执行的。对价是指给予一方的价值（利益）或使一方放弃对其有价值的事物（损害）。一个合同要成立，对价必须是双向的。要约人若同意做其没有义务去做的事情或者同意不做其有权做的事情，法院就会认定该要约人受损。

如果承诺不明确、不肯定，则不能被强制执行，这样的承诺不具有对价。而且这种承诺通常是虚假的，因为它们表面上是可执行的，而实际上不可执行。

如果某人承诺不去做其原本就无权做的事情，那就不是对价。某人完成其本就有义务去做的事情的情况下，对价也不存在。对于一项出于道德义务而做某事的承诺，很多法院的立场也是不认可其为法律上的对价的。

五、不实行为，胁迫，误解

不实行为包括几种。双方交换表面上成立的对价并订立表面上成立的合同时，一方可提出数种抗辩理由，主张合同可撤销。第一个抗辩理由是欺诈。欺诈也就是为引诱他人基于对某重大事实的信赖去做某事而对该事实故意做出的虚假陈述。

第二个允许合同一方撤销合同的抗辩理由是不真实陈述，它其实和欺诈是相同的，只是它不要求不真实陈述行为是故意做出的。这里面有个需要考虑的内容是吹嘘。并非所有不真实的陈述都构成不实行为。不真实陈述需是对重大事实的不真实陈述，这一点至关重要。有些意见或评论在一般情况下会被认定为销售人员的吹嘘行为，这种吹嘘行为并非是对事实的陈述,因此,它不构成不实行为。而且如果对某一特定事实的陈述是虚假的但却不是实质性的(比如对事实状况的知晓并不会引起此人改变其行为),那么法律就不会允许撤销合同。不实行为的抗辩还要求原告的信赖是建立在被告陈述基础上的,而不是建立在其他某些独立的信息来源基础上。

胁迫和不当影响构成第二类允许合同一方撤销合同的抗辩。胁迫是指任何使某人做其本不愿做的事或不做其本愿意做的事的行为。不当影响是指当事人利用因其所具有的特殊地位,导致谈判地位产生差别,从而产生的谈判优势的行为。当强势一方负有保护弱势一方的特殊义务时,就可以适用不当影响这个抗辩理由。这一义务在法律上称为诚信义务,它存在于代理人与客户,医生与病人,(遗嘱执行中的)执行人与受益人,以及(信托关系中的)托管人与受益人之间的关系中。

误解也有几种情形,其中有些能使合同被撤销。误解与不知情或者错误判断不同。如果你购买一份地产,并知晓该地产有价值数千美元的树木,而我作为卖方,并不知晓此事,那么这种情形就是不知情或者判断错误,而不是误解。

六、缔约能力

尽管具备了双方自由做出的要约和承诺以及对价,法律也还会确认某些主体订立的合同可以由这些人撤销。欠缺订约能力的人主要包括两类,即未成年人和因精神错乱和醉酒使其心智能力受到限制的人。具备上述原因而其订约能力因此受到限制的人所订立的合同,可由该欠缺能力的人撤销。

七、为第三人利益的合同

由两方当事人订立的,规定第三人有权获得某种权利的合同称为第三人利益的合同。它分为三类:债权受益人、赠与受益人和意外受益人。此类合同有两个特点,其一是受益人与要约人的关系,其二是受益人享有的合同的权利。

八、合同的终止和救济

合同的终止是指一个有约束力的允诺不再具有约束力。合同可能因为履行、违约或撤销、免除、共同债务的终止、合同更新、实质性变更以及合并等事项而终止。此外,有些法律规定,如嗣后丧失合法性或破产,或者两者同时发生都会引起合同终止。

救济是指合同终止时因不当行为而遭受损害的个人所能采取的措施。这些措施称为救济手段,其中包括损害赔偿金。损害赔偿金可以是预先确定的,或是补偿性的,也可以是惩罚性的,它根据非违约方因违约一方的行为而遭受的损失来计算,可以包括工资等费用。另一种救济方式还可以是实际履行,这种救济方式适用于特定的、独特的以及非同寻常的财产,比如房地产或是稀有文物,这种情况下用金钱补偿就不够充分或不够恰当。

第七课 侵权行为法

一、侵权行为概念

侵权行为"tort"来源于拉丁语"tortus",本意是扭曲的、歪斜的。英语中最初使

Appendix II

Text Translation & Key to Exercises (Part Two)

用这个词时，与"错误"（wrong）一词同义。后来这个词就从普通民众眼界中消失了，仅在法言法语中保留一席之地。这时tort成为专门术语，意思仅为"依据法律规定应当给予救济的法定过错行为"。

几个世纪以来，侵权行为法一直用来保护个人财产权益。英美法早期著名案例中有一些涉及土地权益的保护，包括对土地滋扰和侵犯的诉讼。侵权法还通过包括威胁、殴打以及非法禁锢等在内的诉讼保护人们免受他人故意干扰，并且确立文字诽谤、言辞诽谤、恶意控诉以及诬蔑等侵权行为来保护个人名誉。自二十世纪初，过失首次正式被确立为独立的侵权行为以来，过失侵权在侵权行为法中处于核心地位。如今大部分侵权赔偿请求都是以过失侵权为标的，现代生活条件下，尤其在机动车辆迅猛发展的今天，过失侵权是最为恰当的诉讼类型。

"侵权责任产生于对法定义务的违反；这个法定义务通常是针对他人的，对该法定义务的违反将通过诉讼请求确定损害赔偿数额来进行救济。"

为理解上述定义，有必要把侵权和其他违法行为加以区分。这样就可以发现侵权法的目的与其他部门法律（如合同法、刑法）目的的不同之处。

（一）侵权法与刑法

尽管侵权法与刑法同是源于对违法行为的报复以及阻却，但二者早就彼此分离，各自起着截然不同的作用。犯罪行为是针对国家的，国家作为公众利益的代表，通过惩罚罪犯来维护自己的利益。刑事控诉以保护社会整体利益为目的而实施刑罚，并不关心对个人可能造成的侵害的救济问题。另外，侵权责任存在的目的主要是弥补受害人的损失，方法是强制过错行为人对自己造成的损害进行赔偿。例如，交通事故这一同样的事实及情况，既可以是刑事诉讼，也可以是侵权行为。作为民法的组成部分，侵权法主要解决个人针对他人（包括法人）提起的诉讼。刑法解决的是以国家名义就个人违反保护整个社会的义务而提起的控诉。

如果我掴你的耳光，这个行为既违反了刑法同时也构成民事过错行为（殴打罪和殴打侵权行为）。同一事件引起两种法律后果。首先，我可能因实施犯罪行为而受到国家的控诉，如果法庭认定我有罪，我将不得不接受向国家缴纳罚金、坐牢或是其他惩罚；其次，你可能在民事法庭上对我提出控告，如果法庭认为我有责任，就会命令我向你支付一定数额金钱（损害赔偿金）或是（下禁令）命令我改变行为方式。正是这些个人，而不是国家，直接从不利于被告的法庭裁判中直接受益。刑事案件的证明责任比民事案件的证明责任严格得多，而且就个人来讲，刑事犯罪成立的后果也要比民事侵权责任后果严重得多。

（二）侵权法与合同法

许多侵权责任直接产生于法律规定本身，并非由当事人规定的。侵权法强制规定不许诽谤他人、不许侵犯他人土地等。这些义务的具体要求都是由法律而不是当事各方规定的。与之相反的是，合同法理论上的基础是协议，协议的具体条款由当事各方共同拟定。因此说，侵权行为发生前，各方当事人通常并无接触。被粗心大意的汽车驾驶员撞伤了的行人在这件引发诉讼的事故发生以前可能从未见过他的被告。而合同法中通常是当事各方通过谈判或是其他各种立约行为，早在违反合同义务之前就有所接触，并且充分了解自己的法律义务。

违反义务造成侵权的救济手段通常是请求损害赔偿金，然而有些案件中也会给予衡平法上的救济。侵权法的主要目的是对违反法定义务造成的损害进行弥补，并且阻却可能造成伤害的行为。而合同法的目的在于维护合同承诺，并使之兑现，同时阻却违反合同的行为。

自从过失侵权问世以来，侵权法侧重于对过错的证明。目的在于弥补他人基于过错造成的损害。通常只有在原告证明被告存在过错时法庭才会判给原告侵权损害赔偿金。

而另一方面，合同很少考虑过错作为责任的基础，对违背合同的行为进行赔偿时，没必要证明过错。

二、过失侵权

侵权责任通常分为故意侵权、过失侵权和严格责任侵权。最主要也是最重要的就是过失损害责任。过失侵权责任主要构成如下：（1）注意义务；（2）过失行为（包括作为或不作为）违反注意义务；（3）过失行为造成损害；（4）是否具有风险自负以及共同过失等抗辩理由等。

（一）注意义务

"你要爱你的邻居"这一规则在法律中应解释为，你不能伤害你的邻居。律师随之要面对的问题是：'谁是我的邻居？'这个问题的答案有严格的界定。你必须采取合理注意避免那些你可合理预见到会对你的邻居造成伤害的作为或不作为。那么法律上，谁是我的邻居呢？答案是：那些能够受到我的行为紧密而直接的影响的人，这个影响如此紧密直接，所以我在决意要实施或是不实施这些有疑义的行为时，必须合理考虑这些可能受到这种影响的人们。

这就是阿特金勋爵的"邻居原则"，可以说是有史以来法官所说的最重要的一段话，其深远影响如何评价也不过分。

被告在其疏忽大意造成侵权之前，必须负有对原告的注意义务。该义务是否存在于当事双方特别关系中，这是一个由法官来决定的法律问题。在没有前例可循的情况下，最重要的决定因素是伤害的可预见性，但法律政策起最终决定作用。下面列出一些最重要的因素：伤害与被告人行为的关联性，被告人行为所应受到的道德谴责，防止可能发生的伤害的措施，以及保险在社会中的流行程度和可行性。

（二）对义务的违反

过失侵权存在于充满不合理伤害危险的行为当中，简而言之，就是未能履行理性人在相同情况下的注意义务。这显然是陪审团决定事项。这一标准比较客观，个体缺陷不能作为行为人逃脱责任的借口。但也有例外情况：例如身体残疾，不能允许残疾人因为自己的伤残承担赔偿责任。同样，儿童的义务标准是智力发育以及经验相类似的同龄儿童的合理行为，但驾驶机动车等成年人行为不包括在内。

（三）因果关系

实际伤害是构成过失侵权的要件之一。这包括两方面。首先，被告人行为是否为此伤害的"实际成因"。也就是说，原告必须证明如果没有被告的过失行为则不会发生损害。举证责任通常由原告承担，来证明事实之间的"或然性权衡"关系。其次，该过失行为不仅是损害的成因，还必须为造成损害的直接原因。如何定义"直接原因"，法律界尚未达成共识。

Appendix II
Text Translation & Key to Exercises (Part Two)

（四）抗辩理由

过失侵权赔偿诉讼有两大抗辩理由：共同过失以及风险自负。

如果原告客观促成了损害的发生，那么他具有的共同过失使之无法获得损害赔偿。但最近共同过失理论得到修正，具有共同过失仅产生降低所得损害赔偿金数额的后果。"相对过失"改革成功的司法管辖内，损害赔偿金判予与否取决于原告过错是否大于被告过错。如今相对过失和共同过失都作为抗辩理由，用来降低被告支付给原告的损害赔偿金数额。

风险自负曾经在雇员起诉雇主或其他雇员的诉讼中，为驳回原告请求发挥了极其重要的作用。如果原告了解情况的危险性，并自愿暴露于最终导致伤害的危险当中，那么原告无权得到任何赔偿，风险自负的抗辩理由成立。风险自负可为明示，或是默示，即通过原告的语言或行动表达出来。如今这项抗辩理由实际上仅限于针对乘坐酒醉司机驾驶的汽车的乘客以及棒球和曲棍球等体育比赛的观众。

（五）损害赔偿金

损害赔偿金要一次性全部给付，不得因各种原因分期支付。损害赔偿既包括金钱损失也包括非金钱损失，分别称作特殊损害赔偿和一般损害赔偿。特殊损害赔偿包括医药费用、收入的损失，包括已发生的和将要发生的。对于称作一般损害赔偿或精神损害赔偿的非金钱损失，陪审团拥有很大自由度，而且这种赔偿金不必纳税。尽管传统上精神痛苦的损害赔偿金仅限于侵权责任，但由于将"恶意违反合同"行为视作侵权，某些合同诉讼中也会判予一般损害赔偿金。惩戒性损害赔偿金逐渐占据重要地位。这种损害赔偿的目的是惩罚侵权行为人的恶劣行径，而不是补偿原告的屈辱和愤怒，因为那是一般损害赔偿的作用。

三、严格责任

十九世纪中期，严格责任的早期适用就遭到了"无过错无责任"原则的支持者们的批判。一百五十年过去了，无过错责任制度仍然在大步向前迈进。

严格责任制度下，不论当事人是否有过错，他们都要为自己的行为或产品造成的损害负责。在非严格的事实自证情况下，举证责任倒置或仅仅是将提供证据义务加于被告，是过失侵权向严格责任迈进的一大步。

严格责任主要成立于下列情形当中：

高度危险行为　人们进行极端危险的活动时适用严格责任。如炸毁大坝、油井喷发、火箭测试或是建筑爆破。如果这些活动伤害到你，则不论行为人有多么小心谨慎，都要为该伤害承担责任。但是严格责任向机动车驾驶的延伸适用得到了限制，因为机动车驾驶已经因其广泛应用而被排除在此类行为之外。

转承责任　不论是在雇用或是管理过程的过错，雇主都要为其雇员在工作过程中实施的侵权行为承担侵权责任。该雇员作为共同侵权人也应承担责任，但是法庭判决很少有向雇员强制执行的。

产品责任　严格责任也适用于某些制造产品案件中。严格产品责任制度下，如果产品存在缺陷，并对他人造成损害，该产品生产流通过程上游经手人（从生产商、批发商到零售商）都要承担责任。受害人不必证明有过失存在，但必须证明产品有缺陷。

瑕疵产品可能是生产的问题，没能为正确使用产品提供适当说明。这些产品生产流通过程上游经手人应当合理预见有人会错误使用该产品，应当重新设计产品消除发生损害的可能性。

四、故意侵权

（一）人身伤害

历史上最古老的故意不法行为类型包括威胁、殴打、非法禁锢等侵害行为。威胁就是故意使他人对即将发生的身体接触产生焦虑心理（不一定是恐惧），而殴打是在未得到对方许可的情况下，非法施加这种身体接触。二者目的都是保护人的身体完整权免受侵害。非法禁锢是限制他人行动自由，或是阻碍他人离开其所在场所。当场使用暴力或身体接触与否不影响非法禁锢的成立，只要原告的意愿遭到违背。与此相类似的是恶意控告，即恶意的、无合理或可能的理由而发起毫无根据的法律程序，特别是刑事检控程序。

（二）财产侵权

与人身侵犯相对应的就是对土地和动产的侵犯。任何直接妨碍都可引发诉讼，如未经占有者同意进入其领地，拿走他人书籍、帽子或画等。构成财产侵权并不需要证明实际损害，但侵犯必须为故意。挪用他人财产的诉讼中，对侵犯他人动产所有权益的救济方式较为全面。

（三）抗辩理由

故意侵权的抗辩理由有错误认识、原告同意、自卫与防卫他人、保卫财产或取回财产、紧急避险以及法律授权。

五、侵犯名誉权与隐私权

（一）诽谤

任何意思表达，不论以何种方式（如降低他人对原告的评价、阻碍他人与原告交往等），只要有破坏原告的社会声誉之倾向便被认定为诽谤。此类意思表达包括让原告遭到仇恨、藐视或奚落；对原告的道德或正直产生负面评价；或损害原告经济信誉。书面形式的诽谤称为文字诽谤，口头形式的称为言辞诽谤。前者为当然诽谤，后者只需要证明特殊损害的存在，即金钱损失。意思表达必须到达第三人，因为诽谤关注的是原告的声誉而非尊严。仅仅与原告当面对峙或侮辱原告不构成诽谤。

（二）隐私

二十世纪以后，对隐私的侵犯开始被认定为侵权行为。主要表现为四种形式：（1）侵扰，如监听他人住宅；（2）滥用他人形象，如将他人的名字或容貌用于商业用途；（3）制造假象，手段是利用令人难堪但不一定带有侮辱性的虚假信息；以及（4）公开隐私。具有当代新闻价值的公开不在此列。

第八课　公　司　法

一、商业交易主体

英美国家中存在若干种商业组织类型，它们在某些重要方面有着显著区别。下面介绍一些比较常见的商业交易主体。

（一）独资企业

独资企业是经营一人企业的最简便方式。企业主一个人经营管理企业运作、自己承担所有责任，同时独享所有利润。独资企业设立成本很低，手续也相对简便。独资企业的一大好处就是企业主对企业享有完全掌控权。然而，企业主须以个人财产对所有企业运作所产生的债务承担责任，这就意味着企业主承担着一旦企业陷入困境自己便将破产或是丧失大部分个人财产的风险。独资企业运营相对简单，因此对很多小型企业来说，经营独资企业成本低而且便于操作。

（二）合伙企业

合伙企业中，两个或两个以上合伙人共同负担运营企业所产生的风险、共同分担成本并共同承担责任。与独资企业主相一致的是，合伙人也须以个人财产对企业运营产生的债务承担责任。每个合伙人向企业注入一定数额的货币、资产或是劳务，按照出资的比例享有所有权益。每个合伙人均须对企业的债务以及以企业名义签订的合同承担责任，即便该债务以及合同均因其他合伙人产生。各个合伙人按照出资比例分享利润、承担损失。在一些国家中，合伙企业不需要注册。实际上合伙人之间甚至连书面的合伙协议都不需要。两个或两个以上的人以营利为目的、愿意共同进行经营的行为就可以产生合伙企业。尽管与独资企业相比，对合伙企业的法律规制稍微多一些。但总体比较而言，法律对合伙企业几乎不进行规制。

（三）有限责任企业

相比较之下，法律对有限责任企业规制较全面。有限责任企业必须注册方能成立。股东（又称"成员"）对企业所承担的责任是有限度的，一般情况下不以个人财产对企业的债务承担责任。这在后文将作详细介绍。

（四）有限合伙企业

有限合伙企业由两个或两个以上的合伙人组成，其中普通合伙人和有限合伙人至少各一名。企业由对企业债务承担无限责任的普通合伙人经营。有限合伙人只能做企业的投资人，责任范围只限于其对企业的投资数额。但如果有限合伙人参与企业经营，则其完全丧失有限责任的保护。有限合伙企业的成立须经注册。由于有限合伙允许投资者仅以资金注入企业而不必承担无限责任，该企业类型特别适用于满足扩大资本的需要。

（五）有限责任合伙企业

有限责任合伙与有限合伙相类似，但不同点在于有限责任合伙企业的合伙人全部享有有限责任。与普通合伙相同的是，各个合伙人（包括个人以及有限责任企业）共同承担企业的经营风险与责任、共同分摊运作成本并且共同分享利润。有限责任合伙常见于律师以及会计等行业，因为法律不允许这些专业人士成立法人组织来限定自己的责任。有限责任合伙在保障单层税收的同时为合伙人提供法人组织式的责任保护。

二、公司[1]

公司是大型企业中最为常见也是最为复杂的一种商业组织形式。在法律视角中，公

---

[1] 本节所用"公司"一词，为严格法律意义上的含义，即具有独立法律人格的商业组织，为"corporation"的严格对应。汉语中"公司"一词最初引入中国是作为英国和荷兰的东印度公司的专有称呼来使用的，含义仅限于具有独立人格、享受有限责任的法人组织。"公司"严格法律含义是按照一定程序设立的、以营利为目的的商业性法人组织，中国现行公司法采用这个含义。但目前由于中国允许非法人组织在字号上使用"公司"字样，公司在法律界之外的含义已日趋模糊，因此日常生活中很多公司并不具备法人人格，应归入"企业"范畴。

司是一个与其所有者相分离的、独立的法律实体。公司的股东并不以个人财产对公司的债务、义务以及行为负责。作为独立的主体,公司具有如下几个显著特征:责任的有限性、股权的易转让性以及永久存续性。公司同时具有集中式的管理体制,管理者可以是实际所有者以外的人担任。

(一)公司的类型

美国的公司一般分为C公司、S公司、封闭公司、专业公司以及非营利性公司。英国主要为公众公司和私人公司,股份有限公司和担保有限公司。传统上还有母公司(控股公司)和子公司、一人公司等形态分类。

(二)S公司和C公司

S公司与被称作标准公司的C公司基本类似,不同之处在于S公司选择向国内税务署付税的方式比较特别。S公司与C公司向州政府上交的公司章程没有区别。二者都是独立的法律实体,都具有有限责任的保护,股东们通常不必以个人财产为公司的债务承担责任。二者都需要符合一定的要件。每年必须召开一次股东大会,并选举出董事,会议记录必须存入公司备案。

然而,两种公司在某些方面也有显著区别。

纳税方式　S公司为单层纳税主体,即公司运作所产生的损益通过股东个人所得纳税。C公司是一个独立纳税主体。税务主管部门直接向公司就其损益进行征税。这就造成从公司所得中分配给股东的红利被双重征税的结果。

股东限制　S公司对股东有一定限制,而C公司却没有。下面是国内税务署规定的一些限制条件:

● C公司的股东人数任意,而S公司的股东人数不得超过35;

● C公司的股东可以是非美国公民,但S公司的股东必须都是美国公民;

● C公司的股东可以是包括公司在内的商业组织,而S公司的股东必须为个人、特定不动产或托管财产。

(三)公众公司和私人公司

公众公司必须符合如下四个条件,目的是能使公司潜在的投资者和债权人了解该公司保有最低资本,而且有可能在将来某个时期向公众出售公司股份:

公司性质——"公众公司"必须在公司组织大纲中表明;公司名称结尾必须有"公众有限公司"(缩写"plc")字样;公司发行资本的票面价值至少为五万英镑,而且必须以公众公司名义注册。

除了公众公司以外都是私人公司。私人公司不必符合公众公司的那些程序性要求。这是减轻小公司程序性负担的措施之一。

公众公司可以将股份上市。公司股份在股票交易市场上公开流通,是募集大量资金对公司运作进行投资的有效途径。因为股票一旦上市,便可引来广大公众认购公司股份。

三、公司基本原理

为公司运作提供资金的人被称作"股东"或是"成员"。这些人通过向公司购买股份而把资金注入公司。股东的权利义务由公司章程(包括公司组织大纲和组织章程)决定。通常所有股份都拥有表决权,但不能一概而论。众多关于公司运作方面的决定都是在股东会议上以多数表决权通过的。但如果日常企业内部运作都通过这种方式进行那就未免过于繁琐了，因此公司表决选举出一些人担任公司"董事"，由他们来负责公司日常运作。股东大会有权通过多数表决权任命或开除董事职务。

（一）公司章程的性质

公司组织大纲包括公司名称、注册国、公司目的、股本总额及比例等重要信息。组织章程包括规范公司运作的规定。两种文件共同构成了公司章程，对所有成员具有约束力，被称为"公司的宪章"。

（二）所有者权益

成立公司必不可少的一个步骤就是认购人在公司组织大纲末尾签名，作出认购公司部分股份（通常每人一股）的承诺。这些认购人就此成为公司的原始股东。公司一旦成立，为了募集资金，公司将以议定的价格向原始股东或其他人发行股份。向申请人发行股份，该申请人便成为股东，成为"法定契约"的当事人。股东依据股份所分享的不是公司财产而是特定权利。他们拥有公司章程所赋予股东的权利，如表决权、股息收取权等。"成员"一词也用来指公司的股东。

尽管股东对公司财产并无所有权，也不是自己直接聘用管理人员，但股东们对公司财产的使用以及管理人员的去留拥有最终决定权，除非公司进入破产清算程序。股东全体作为一个公司机关，有权开除或任命董事，有权做出公司解散的决定，在对所有债权人清偿完毕以后，股东们还有权对公司财产进行分配。倘若股东拥有这些最终决定权，而且董事们经营管理的是股东们作为资本投入公司的财产，那么董事们的职责就是："为公司权益而善意行事"，也就是说董事们必须为股东的共同利益行事，这样理解也不足为奇。换句话说就是，公司运作过程中其他人（如公司债权人或员工）的权益仅限于实现其合同权利，但是股东们拥有上述权利，因此企业的成立、存续与运作完全是为了实现股东而不是其他人的利益。

（三）有限责任

公司的股东对公司的责任限于支付其所持股份的应缴款额。当我们说某个企业是有限责任公司时，指的就是这个意思，根本不是说公司本身的责任有限与否。如果成员购入股份时全部缴足了股份，则不论公司资不抵债状况有多糟，股东也不必再支付任何费用。有时候公司发行的是未缴足股份。这种情况下，在公司进行清算的时候，成员有义务支付其所持股份未缴款额。

（四）股份类别

公司的所有股份不一定拥有同样的权利。公司可以发行不同种股份，即不同"类别"的股份。公司的股本可以划分为多个类别，每个类别的股份拥有不同权利，如表决权、股息权以及清算时分配剩余资产的权利。通常这些权利内容由公司章程加以规定，但权利内容的规定并非公司强制性义务。

（五）公司董事

公司法传统理论认为股东是公司的所有者，而董事则为了公司所有者利益而经营公司业务。普通法上为建立董事行为控制机制的努力主要包括两大方面：一是董事职责范围如何？二是由谁来强制董事履行职责？

四、公司的法人人格

公司的精髓在于公司具有与创办公司的人相独立的法律人格。这就意味着，即便经营公司的人不断变换，公司还是保有其独立身份，公司的业务也不必因公司成员或管理者的任何人事变化而中止或再启。作为有限责任企业，不仅公司拥有的财产与经营者个人财产相分离，公司的成员对公司的任何债务也不必承担责任，除非符合法律规定的例外情形，目的是为防止掌控公司之人实施任何欺诈性或不当行为。成员只能应要求支付其所持股份的全价。其后，债权人只能就公司的财产来满足其债权主张。这就意味着公司财产归公司自己所有，公司自行承担债务，股东们既不是公司对外签订的合同的当事人，也不必为公司的债务承担责任。因此时常有人说，股东们隐藏在"法人面纱"之后。

由于公司实行有限责任，法律制定了详细的规则以防止公司浪费自己的资产。为保护与公司进行交易的人的利益，法律为公司设置了大量规则，这也成为设立公司的一大不利条件。合伙经营法律要件较少，因为合伙人需要对经营的合伙企业产生的任何债务承担无限责任。

公司独立人格这一发明具有极其重要的地位，因为它将企业与经营企业的人彼此独立开来。

公司的独立人格制度也引来一系列法律问题。尽管公司在法律上被视作独立的人，然而公司活动只能通过经营公司业务的人来进行。法律必须对公司与其创办者、成员（股东）的关系以及公司与和公司有业务往来的"外部人"之间的关系进行强行规制。

第九课　知识产权法

知识产权是源于智力的、创造性过程的财产，是个人智力的产物。尽管知识产权是一个抽象概念的抽象术语，然而实际上它还是为大家所熟知。包含在书里或是计算机文件里的信息为知识产权。你所使用的软件、所看的电影以及所听的音乐都是各种形式的知识产权。实际上，在今天的信息时代，世界上知识产权的价值超过了诸如机器和房屋这样有形财产的价值，这是毋庸惊奇的。

美国宪法的制定者早在两百多年前就提出保护创造性作品的要求。美国宪法第一条第八款授权国会"促进科学和有用的工艺的进步，在一定期限内保护作者和发明者对各自作品和发明的排他性权利。"法律对专利、商标和版权的保护明显的是为了保护和奖励发明创造和艺术创作。在下文各部分，我们将讲述这些形式的知识产权，以及包含商业秘密的知识产权。

一、商标和相关知识产权

商标是生产商为了使其生产的商品在市场上能够得以辨认，产品来源能够得以证明，而压印、印刷或附着到其产品上的一种明显标识、箴言、图案或特殊标志。联邦一级对商标和相关知识产权的立法保护主要规定于1946年通过的《兰海姆商标法》。《兰海姆商标法》颁行的部分原因是为了保护厂商避免因对手使用让人感到混淆的相似商标而破产。《兰海姆商标法》运用了普通法中出现的商标保护原则，还规定了对在联邦法院要求执行索赔的商标所有人的救济措施。许多州也已制定了商标法。

Appendix II

Text Translation & Key to Exercises (Part Two)

商标可以在州政府或联邦政府登记。为了得到联邦商标法的保护，个人（或法人）必须向位于华盛顿特区的联邦专利商标局提出申请并备案登记。目前法律规定，能够注册登记的商标必须：（1）目前用于商业领域，或者（2）申请人打算六个月内将商标用于商业。一旦商标在很大程度上被别人模仿或被他人完全使用——不论是故意还是并非故意——都产生商标侵权（未经授权而使用）。如果出现商标侵权，商标所有者便对侵权人产生一个诉因。起诉商标侵权不一定需要已经进行商标登记，但是登记确实能够作为证据证明最初使用该商标。

服务商标和一般商标相似，但是是用于区别某一个人或公司与其他个人或公司的服务。举例来说，每个航空公司都有一个特殊的与其名称相关联的标记或象征。广播和电视所使用的名称和字符也常作为服务商标而登记。其他被法律保护的标记还包括证明商标和集体商标。

商标用于产品。商号这个术语则被用来表示企业名称的部分或全部。通常来说，商号直接关系到企业及其商誉。如果商号和该企业的商标产品相同，比如可口可乐，那么商号就可以作为商标加以保护。同样，除非商号作为一般商标或服务商标使用，否则商号不能在联邦政府登记。但是，商号可以由普通法保护。和商标一样，商号若想获得保护，其用词必须是与众不同的或富有想象力的。

二、专利

专利是政府授予发明人在申请专利备案之日起二十年内制造、使用、销售一项发明的排他性权利。和发明不同，设计专利被给予十四年的保护期。不论是通常的专利还是设计专利，申请人都必须向联邦专利商标局证明，根据当前的技术判断，该发明、发现、工艺或设计是名副其实的、新颖的、有益的，并且不是那么显而易见的。专利持有人将"专利"的字眼和专利号写到一项物品或设计上，以此向所有的人证明该物品或设计是获得专利的。

与其他国家的专利法规定相反，美国的专利保护给予第一个发明产品或工艺的人，而不是第一个将产品或工艺申请备案的人。这个区别非常重要，因为在人们独立工作的情况下，常常在大约同一时间得到实际上相同的发明。按照美国发明优先的原则，是能够提出证据证明发明在先的发明者获得专利（比如，注明日期的实验室笔记）。按照申请优先的原则，则是能够让法律的车轮第一个运转起来的发明者获得专利。

如果一个公司未经专利所有人的同意而制造、使用或销售他人拥有专利权的设计、产品或工艺，那它就实施了专利侵权。即使专利持有人未将专利产品投入商业运转，专利侵权也可能存在。即使被模仿的并非为发明的全部特征，或者仅部分发明被模仿，那也可能出现专利侵权。（而对于获得专利的工艺来说，只有当全部的步骤或流程被模仿时，才存在侵权。）

传统上，被授予专利的发明都是"新型实用的工艺、机器、产品、物质合成或者是对前述几项任何新颖和有益的改进"。联邦专利商标局按常规拒绝了计算机系统和软件的申请，因为这些并不被认为是实用工艺、机器、产品项目或物质合成。它们仅仅被当成数学运算法则、抽象概念或"商业运行方法"。然而，在1998年划时代的State Street Bank & Trust Co.诉Signature Financial Group一案中，美国联邦巡回上诉法院裁决仅有三类物品永远不能授予专利：（1）自然法则；（2）自然现象；（3）抽象概念。这个裁决表明，商业流程也可以像其他发明那样获得专利。

三、版权

版权是联邦法律授予文学或艺术作品作者和创造者的一种无形财产权利。《伯尔尼公约》规定，版权从作品被固定之日起产生，至少持续到作者死后五十年。美国版权法的变化使版权期限有不同规定，从而产生一个复杂的体系。目前实施的是经修订的《1976年版权法案》。1978年1月1日以后创作的作品法律自动给予版权保护，保护期限是作者有生之年至死后七十年。如果作者超过一人，作品版权保护期截止到最后死亡的作者死后七十年。版权保护到期之后，作品就进入公共领域，那就是说，任何人都可自由复制。

可获得版权的作品包括书、唱片、电影、美术作品、建筑方案、菜单、音乐录影、产品包装和计算机软件。要获得《版权法》的保护，作品必须是原创的，并且要归入下列类别中的一类：（1）文学作品；（2）音乐作品；（3）戏剧作品；（4）舞剧和舞蹈作品；（5）图画、图表和雕塑作品；（6）电影和其他视听作品；（7）录音制品。要获得保护的作品还必须"被固定在持久的媒介上"，这样才能被感知、复制和交流。版权保护是自动产生的，登记不是必须的。

当一种思想的表达形式或表述方法被复制时，版权侵权就产生了。这种情况下，复制品不必完完全全的和原作相同，也不一定是整个复制原作。对版权侵权责任的例外规定体现在"合理使用"条款。如目前的定义所述，合理使用是允许以教育、批评或讽刺模仿为目的来复制一小部分作品。现行的美国法律并没有规定合理使用权本身，它仅仅是对版权侵权的一种法律抗辩。换句话来说，那些以教育和批评为目的而未经授权的复制仍然属于侵权，但是如果侵权人能证明是合理使用，那么法律将不准版权所有人获得赔偿金。

四、商业秘密

对于那些没有或是不能授予专利、版权和商标的交易过程和信息，为避免竞争者的盗用，仍作为商业秘密而加以保护。商业秘密包括客户列表、（公司）计划、研发报告、定价信息、营销手段、生产技术，以及任何使一个公司具有独特性并对于其竞争者有价值的东西。

只要秘密还是秘密，只要还没有他人将其独立开发出来，那么商业秘密的持有人就比潜在的竞争对手具有优势。如果有人侵入计算机系统窃取秘密，或是哪个不满的雇员说漏了嘴，就可以调用商业秘密法来惩罚窃贼。然而，一旦秘密泄露，它就泄露出去了。只要商业秘密还是处于秘密状态，就受到法律的永久保护。而一旦其被泄露，任何人都能够生产此发明产品或使用该工艺。

也许最有名的商业秘密就是可口可乐的配方了。由于严格的安全保密政策，可口可乐公司得以从1886年一直将产品配方保密。如果该公司当时以专利保护的话，配方权利早在1906年就已到期了。据说该公司一直采取一些极端的措施来保护可乐的秘方，真正的配方保存在亚特兰大的银行保险库中，并且公司规定必须要有董事会决议才能打开保险库。只有为数极少的看过可乐原浆混合的人才被允许知道配方。

最近几年，计算机技术发展的新特点使得商业企业不能够保护自己包括商业秘密在内的机密信息。比如,一位不忠实员工可能用公司电脑将商业秘密寄给公司的竞争对手或其未来的顾主。如果不用电子邮件的话,该雇员还可以带着装有秘密信息的电脑硬盘出走。现在公司越来越愿意通过顾主与雇员签订保密合同和竞业禁止协议来寻求对商业秘密的保护。商业秘密的过度保护也产生了限制前雇员谋生的问题。

五、许可协议

既能够利用他人的商标、版权和商业秘密,而又不被起诉,其中一种方法就是获得许可。在这种情况下,许可的意思就是允许他人为某种目的而使用商标、版权、专利和商业秘密。比如说,被许可人(获得许可的一方)可以被允许使用许可人(实施许可的一方)的商标作为其公司名称的一部分,或是把其当作自己域名的一部分;而不是将其标志用于产品和服务。

技术转让是为履行海外研发合同、为子公司和合资企业提供技术帮助,或为了履行制造商或知识产权所有者与外国实体的直接商业许可协议而产生。技术许可是这样一种合同安排:许可人将专利、商标、服务标志、版权或专有技术卖给被许可人,或者允许被许可人有偿使用。这种补偿被称作使用税,可能是一次付清,也可能是按照产品和销售的数额来计算。

第十课 民事诉讼法

一、诉辩状的基本理论

诉辩状是当事人向法院提交的初始诉讼文件。诉辩技巧的深入研究包括程序和实体领域。诉辩方式是一个程序性的问题,取决于所选择法院的具体规则。诉辩的内容则由实体法以及有法律意义的事实所决定。

(一)起诉状

各州法典和联邦诉讼规则关于诉辩状的规定的主要区别在于它们对细节要求的程度不同。如果适用法典,原告在起诉状中应当列明构成诉因要素的基本事实。如果原告使用的文字过于啰嗦并且陈述了证据方面的详细情况,那么她的起诉状便是不适当的。但是现在,由于此种缺陷而被撤销的起诉状已很罕见。另一种可能是,原告提出一个内容概括、模糊的法律结论,比如"侵犯和威胁"或者是"过失",一些州便会允许被告做出诉求不充分抗辩并驳回原告的起诉状。原告在起诉状中应写明救济的要求。如果是要求支付损害赔偿金,就应写明具体数额。原告可基于多种诉因提出权利主张,只要在起诉状中分别对其做出阐述。

联邦法院及那些适用联邦诉讼规则的州采用的诉辩规则最为简明。它把繁琐的法典诉讼中的概念,如"主要事实"和"诉因"替换为这样一种表述,即只要原告"给予被告关于诉讼请求内容及依据的合理通知"就可以了。原告提出的主张可以是有选择性的,也可是不连贯的,甚至在同一诉因之内也可以。对于一些特殊事项,如所有关于欺诈或错误的主张,应详细地陈述构成欺诈或错误的情节。这样做的理由是防止那些只是为骚扰被告而提出的轻率诉讼。原告还必须写明具体的损害赔偿金额以防止被告对此准备不充分。从总体上说,自由化的诉讼规则使得在联邦法院的诉讼更为简单,这就要求被告在证据发现过程中获得足够的证据才能够让法院驳回原告起诉。

(二) 答辩状

如果被告对原告选择的法院提出异议，或者主张起诉状中没有说明产生救济的诉讼请求，他既可以在答辩状中提出抗辩，也可以请求法院驳回原告的起诉。然而，被告通常只在答辩状中提出他的抗辩。

被告可能否认原告在起诉状中提出的全部或部分主张，或者承认部分主张（明确承认其真实性或者不能正当地否定原告的主张），或者提出新的事实作为积极抗辩，或者提出自己对原告的反请求。在适用法典诉讼的情况下，被告必须为自己提出的积极抗辩或者针对原告的反请求提供主要的事实依据。在联邦诉讼规则体系下，只要有"简短明确的语言"给原告合理的通知便足够了。积极抗辩包括的事项有和解和清偿协议，互有过失，胁迫，已决事项不再理，或诉讼时效等。

被告在答辩状中有五种否认形式可供选择。适当的否认使被否认的争点留到日后裁判。否认必须诚实而不能构成误导。例如，如果在适用法典诉讼的州，一份起诉状诉称"被告拥有并经营一辆叉车"。事实上被告拥有但并未经营叉车，他就不能做出这样一个明确否认，即"他并不拥有或经营叉车"。这样一个不适当的有关联作用的否认会使原告产生误解，将被认为是对所有权和经营权事项的确认。一些联邦法院认为，甚至一个简单的"否认"也会构成误导并被认为不适当。

二、修改（诉辩状）

在普通法中，诉辩状非常重要，通常同庭审证据之间不允许有任何不符。与此相反，通过鼓励基于实体事实而不是基于程序技巧的判决，法典和联邦诉讼规则允许对诉辩状进行自由修改。

联邦诉讼规则15（a）规定，原告可以在被告提交答辩状之前的任何时间，对其起诉状作一次修改，而无须申请法院的许可。类似的，被告也可以在提交答辩状后的20日内对其答辩状予以修改。否则，当事人只有在取得法院许可或者对方当事人书面同意的情况下才能修改诉辩状，但规则同时规定"只有出于公正的考虑，此种许可才不受限制"。为了避免受到诉讼时效的影响，规则15（c）及大多数州都允许修改后的诉辩状仍然使用其最早提交时的日期，但要求在修改后的诉辩状中所提出的请求或者抗辩仍源于早先提交的诉辩状所陈述的行为、交易或事件。

如果一方当事人提交的证据是有关诉辩状中没有涉及的问题，而对方当事人对此又没有提出异议，法院通常会基于默示同意的原则，默认诉辩状与证据的一致性。如果由于对方当事人对其出示证据提出异议，一方当事人在庭审时要求修改，法院会允许此种修改，只要它有助于使判决更有依据，而且异议方不能向法院证实这会对维持他的诉讼请求或者抗辩构成不当影响。法官可能准许异议方在一定时间内提供他的证据。不当影响可能包括文件消失或者再找不到证人。即使在判决作出之后，当事人也可以要求修改诉辩状使其与证据相一致，通常是为了基于已决事项不再理的原则去确认一个判决。

三、确保诉辩的真实性

提高诉辩真实性及减少轻率索赔和抗辩的两种最常用方法是要求有律师签名和诉辩状结尾的举证声明。许多地方都要求律师在诉辩状上签名，他的签名被当作善意索赔和

Appendix II
Text Translation & Key to Exercises (Part Two)

抗辩的证明，即索赔和抗辩有充分的理由支持而不是为拖延案件故意提出的。尽管此种规定表明律师需承担此项义务，但是它们并没有成为一个有效的控制措施，原因是，和其他一些事情类似，法官很难对违反签字要求的律师作出处罚，除非能够证明他们存在主观恶意，而那又是最难证明的。

由于认识到操作上存在问题，联邦规则在1983年作出修改，规定律师只有对诉辩状中用以支持诉辩的法律和事实问题进行了"合理调查"才能在其上签字。不遵守规定要受到强制性处罚。这些改变目的是为了使法院可以采用客观的标准判断律师是否进行了"合理调查"，并且扩大处罚权的适用以阻止边缘行为。但是在规则11修改后，出现了大量的诉讼，提出了许多关于修改后的规则的基本要求的问题，以及修改后的规则是否完成了它的目的或正在引起新形式的相关诉讼。这样一来，产生了要求再次修改规则的巨大压力，1993年的修改正是对此种指责的回应。

再次修改的规则继续使用客观的而不是主观恶意的标准来评判签署者是否进行了合理调查并得出诉讼是基于充分的事实和法律依据的结论。规则扩展适用于所有的书面申请和诉讼中提交的文件。违反规则的处罚的尺度由法官裁量，然而，一个"安全港"条款被加入进来，根据该条款，要求做出处罚的一方必须等到文件提交后至少21天才能提出要求，而如果被诉的违规行为在这个期间内得以改正，就不允许再提出处罚申请。修改后的条款是否能在阻止轻率诉讼和允许在律师看来是有价值的，而相对来说可能依据不是很充分的索赔和抗辩之间找到平衡还有待于实践的检验。

四、审前会议

由于对诉辩状要求的逐渐放宽，审前会议已经成为一个使案件明确化和条理化的时候。审前会议通常在证据开示后进行，律师和法官通过非正式交谈以确定争点。他们可以制定庭审计划因为他们知道将要出示的证据和证人。对于复杂的诉讼，将会召开一系列的会议来确定证据开示和审判日程。

尽管有些法院通过地方性规则规定所有案件都必须召开审前会议，但无论在地方还是联邦体制中，法官对审前会议的安排都有自由决定权。审前会议应该是强制性的还是任意性的取决于人们对它的根本作用长期争论的结果。在简单的案件中，审前会议浪费的时间是否要多于在审判中节省的时间？或者它确实是一种促使当事人和解的好方法。在复杂的案件中，审前会议是否能使审判程序真正简化、得到更好的组织从而提高效率，还是只为案件另外设置了障碍，拖延了时间呢？

鉴于现代诉讼的复杂性，单单依靠律师组织和推动诉讼的进程是不够的，联邦法院加大了对审前阶段的司法管制力度。1983年，联邦法院彻底修改了联邦诉讼规则第16条，鼓励联邦法官通过召开审前会议安排审前程序，包括证据开示和审前动议，来处置案件，从而获知律师推动案件进展的情况。

第十一课 国 际 法

一、传统定义

国际法曾经被定义为以国家之间的关系为调整对象的法律。在传统的定义下，只有国家是国际法的主体。也就是说，只有国家享有和承担国际法下的权利和义务。其他组织和个人由于与国家之间的各种关系或附属于国家，享有和承担国际法下的权利和义务被认为是纯粹派生性的，常被视为国际法所谓的"客体"。

（一）国际法下的国家

国际法律师们所指的国家是独立的或是单一主权国家。国际法中，国家的构成需要满足如下要素，确定的领土，定居的居民，独立的政府和具备处理对外事务的能力。联合体中的成员（联邦中的州，省，郡）缺少最后一个要素，而那又是国家主权中非常重要的因素。

（二）现代国际法下的主体

尽管是在有限的范围内，今天政府间的国际组织甚至个人也可以成为国际法下的主体，承受国际法下的权利和义务。联合国和各种各样的专业性的国际和地区组织，如国际劳工组织，欧洲理事会，在国际法的约束下，都可以和国家及其他国际组织缔结条约。个人由于国际犯罪行为，如反人类罪和战争犯罪，在国际法上受到直接的惩处，及国际人权法的发展都进一步说明了在特定条件下，个人享有并承担国际法下的权利和义务，而不再是传统意义上派生的产物。

二、国际法的应用

国际法通常是国际法庭所适用的法律。但是国际法不仅仅和司法审判程序相关。无论是在对外交往、谈判还是政策制定，国家都要依据国际法。国家在为自己的行为和政策辩护时引用国际法，在对其他国家的行为提出质疑的时候仍然依赖国际法。在这个意义上，国际法被国际社会认定为法律，它对国家的行为产生法律约束而且影响国家的政策制定。

（一）国际法作为法律

国家行为受多种因素影响；国际法只是其中之一。有时它是决定性的因素，有时它并不具有决定性。然而，不论谁试图理解和预测国家在特定条件下的政治走向，或者就与国家自身利益保持一致的行为提出建议，都需要考虑到国际法适用的原则。一个国家为了达到既定的政治目标可能会违背国际法。但是在考虑这样的行为所带来的短期和长期的政治影响时，这个国家的政策制定者会注意到国际法的性质和作用的问题，以及被认定为违法者的法律和政治上的后果。

对国际法的违反，如引起全球注意的威胁和诉诸武力不应该使我们忽视国际法在国家之间像国内法一样广泛适用，如规范国际商事、交流、交通，及每日发生的外交和领事关系等。对于在这些领域工作的法律工作者，不论是政府的法律顾问，国际组织或是公司的法律顾问，或者是法官，立法者，政策制定者或是仲裁员，国际法是一门真实的，有实际意义的法律。他们应当知道如何去查询和分析它，在何种情况下去适用它，及在哪里和怎样去执行它。

（二）国际法的适用和执行

作为一个原则，国际法庭对于适于司法解决的国际争端没有强制性的和自动的管辖权。法院审理特定案件的权利取决于争端方是否接受国际法院的管辖权。结果是，许多国际争端不能被司法解决，因为一方或其他方拒绝接受国际法院的管辖权。

但是，法院并不是唯一能解决国家间争端的机构。许多没有采用正式司法解决的国际争端可以而且已经用许多其他方法解决，如，谈判，调停，斡旋或者仲裁，这些方法都运用了国际法。这里，国际法起到的作用与国内法处理庭外调解案件时起到的作用类似。

而且，现今社会存在大量的国际组织和解决争端的方法，不论是政治性的、准司法性的还是外交性的，如联合国、地区性组织、外交会议等，这些组织与国际法一起，对国际冲突和各种各样社会问题的解决发挥了重要的作用。

三、现代国际法体系的来源

国际法或者是过去被称作的万国法，成为独立的法律体系是随着十六七世纪主权国家的兴起为标志的。当然，一些国际法惯例，如交换外交使节、签订和平条约等，及国际法适用的原则都可以追溯到古代。但是，直到现代约束国家间关系的原则才被称作一个独立的法律体系。这些原则中的大部分是来源于罗马法或者是教会法规，而它们在很大程度上借鉴了自然法原则。在中世纪即将结束，文艺复兴刚刚开始的时候，这两大法律渊源也形成了欧洲刚兴起的主权国家国内法的基础。罗马法和教会法规对这个时期欧洲的政治家和法学家影响很大，而正是他们创立了现代国际法，并使之形成体系。

四、国际法的渊源

从法律的制定来看，国际法是一个简单的法律体系。国际社会缺少一个可以作为法的基本来源的组织。和国内法相比，国际法没有立法机关去颁布普遍适用的法律，也没有行政机关制定规章。国际法院对国际法下的争端没有绝对的管辖权，法院的判决也只对争端方有法律约束力。在正式意义上法院判决没有先例价值，因为国际法没有遵循先例的原则。

我们如何知道一个特定的原则是否是国际法呢？这个问题可以借助国际法的渊源及分析它的形成方式来回答。

（一）主要渊源

《国际法院规约》第38条最具权威性地列举了国际法的渊源。全文如下：

法院对于陈述的各项争端应依据国际法裁判，裁判是应适用：

a. 确立诉讼的当事国明示承认的，不论是普通或是特别的国际条约。

b. 作为通例并被接受为法律的国际习惯。

c. 为文明各国接受的一般法律原则。

d. 司法判决和各国最具权威的公法学家的学说作为确立法律原则的补充资料。

（二）《国际法院规约》第38条的含义

《国际法院规约》第38条规定了国际法院在裁判案件时所适用的法律。第38条说明了国际法包括或者说以国际条约，国际习惯和一般法律原则为基础。也就是说，一项原则被称为国际法的内容，它必须是这三种渊源之一。

"司法判决"和公法学家的"学说"不是法律渊源。它们是确定法律的"补充资料"。国际法工作者以这些权威说明为根据，确定特定的内容是否是国际法的原则。

第38条没有涉及这三种渊源的层次问题，也就是说，是否条约居于首位，习惯次之，再次是一般法律原则。

（三）条约

条约是国家之间的正式协议，它对国家的国内和国际发展都有重要的法律意义。两国政府间的条约是双边条约；两个以上国家参加的是多边条约。条约最初的签署是签署方对条约内容真实性、确定性的认同，但是国家不受其约束直到对条约批准、加入或者其他的程序。缔约方可以对条约的某些条款做出保留，或者是对条约的用词做出自己的解释。条约需要确认何时生效，通常（尤其是多边条约）是在一定数目的缔约方交存批准书和加入书后生效。

（四）习惯

国际习惯法是从国家的实践发展而来的。一种实践不能只因为它被广泛地遵循而就成为国际习惯法的一项原则。而且，它必须被国家认为有法律强制力。如果一个国家遵循一个实践只是出于礼貌或是认为可以随时放弃这一实践而不负法律责任，这一条件就不能满足。一项实践必须满足法律确信的要求才能称为国际习惯法。

五、现代国际法的特点

以上所作的论述说明现代国际法主要包括国际条约法和国际习惯法。立法性的条约如今在国际法的形成中起到了重要的作用这一事实逐渐使国际法成为一个更有生命力的法律体系。国际习惯法的形成过程，总体上说，需要很长时间，导致它很难适应现代生活的快节奏。一般法律原则作为法律渊源起到的作用越来越有限。

第十二课 WTO与国际经济法

国际贸易的巨大增长和信息技术的爆炸导致了世界性贸易市场的产生和各国经济的相互依存。国际贸易渐渐变成政府的左膀右臂，这种趋势最终可能会产生一个所谓"世界政府"。与此同时，世界上存在着对国际贸易进行解释的无数复杂条约、法律、规则和指导方针。对一个社团和商业法律从业人员来说，明白这些调整国际贸易的法律是很重要的，这种重要性不可轻视。

简要地说，国际经济法指的是一种规范体系，主要规定国家之间的经济关系，也间接地必然涉及个人之间的关系。国际经济法并非来自单一的或者是几个法律渊源，它源自许多法律。各国的法律、地区法律和国际法（包括公法和私法），还有政策和惯例，所有这些都是国际经济法的组成要素。国际经济法所包含的学科具有很大范围，包括货物和服务贸易、金融法律、经济一体化、发展法、商业规则和知识产权。其中国际发展、投资、货币和贸易问题尤其是经济关系的核心。通过我们所熟知的布雷顿森林体系，即国际货币基金组织，世界银行和世界贸易组织，这些国际经济关系问题的核心方面已成为国际社会的焦点。在所有这些国际组织当中，世界贸易组织，无疑是最有影响力的立法和司法机构。鉴于它的重要作用和国际经济法的复杂性，这一章仅将世界贸易组织作以简要介绍。

世界贸易组织（WTO）基本知识

一、历史：多边贸易体制的过去、现在与未来

世界贸易组织（WTO）成立于1995年。作为最新设立的国际组织之一，WTO的前身是第二次世界大战结束后即成立的关税与贸易总协定（GATT）。

因此，虽然WTO尚属年幼，但建立在原先关贸总协定下的多边贸易体系却有五十多年的历史了。

世界贸易在过去五十年当中增长异常迅速。商品出口以每年百分之六的速度递增。2000年的总贸易额是1950年的22倍。GATT和WTO对创立一个强有力的繁荣贸易体系，助其空前增长产生很大帮助。

这个体系是在GATT下举行的一系列或者说一轮轮贸易谈判而发展起来的。最初的几轮谈判大部分涉及关税减让，但是后来的谈判包含了其他领域的问题，比如反倾销和非关税措施。最后一轮谈判——即1986年到1994年的乌拉圭回合，为WTO诞生铺平了道路。

谈判并没有到此结束，在乌拉圭回合结束之后一些谈判仍在继续。1997年2月，69个国家或地区的政府对电信服务达成协议，同意宽领域的自由措施，这超出了乌拉圭回合协议中达成的范围。

同年，40个政府成功地完成了信息技术产品零关税贸易谈判，并且有70个成员国缔结了金融服务协定，涵盖95%以上的银行、保险、证券以及金融信息贸易。

2000年，农业和服务领域的新谈判开始进行。这些现在已经纳入了2001年11月在卡塔尔多哈举行的第四次WTO部长级会议的广泛议程。

多哈议程增加的谈判和其他工作内容包括非农业关税问题、贸易与环境问题、反倾销与政府补贴、投资、竞争政策、贸易促进、政府采购之透明度、知识产权等WTO规则，以及发展中国家提出的他们在实施目前WTO协议中所面临的一系列问题。

谈判的最终期限是2005年1月。

二、组织机构

WTO最重要的目标是促进贸易流通的平稳、自由、公正和具有预测性。它通过如下方式来工作：
- 实施贸易协定
- 担当贸易谈判的论坛
- 解决贸易争端
- 审查成员国贸易政策
- 通过技术协助和培训计划帮助发展中国家解决贸易政策问题
- 与其他国际组织合作

组织结构

WTO有将近140个成员国，占97%以上的世界贸易。还有大约30个国家具有谈判员资格。

WTO框架内的决议由全体成员国作出，这是典型的全体一致决议的做法。多数投票决定也可以，但这种方法还从未在WTO内采用，在WTO的前身关贸总协定中也是非常罕见的。WTO相关协议已经得到所有成员国议会的批准。

WTO最高级别的决策机构是部长级会议，该会议至少每两年举行一次。

在此之下的是在总理事会（通常由驻日内瓦的大使和代表团团长组成，但有时也由从成员国首都派来的官员参加），每年在日内瓦总部召开几次会议。总理事会同时担任贸易政策审查机构和争端解决机构。

再下一级是货物贸易理事会、服务贸易理事会和知识产权理事会。它们都负责向总理事会报告工作。

许多专业委员会，工作小组和工作班子负责处理单个协议以及其他如环境、发展、成员申请和地区贸易协定等工作。

三、WTO协定

如何才能确保贸易尽可能公平，确保贸易自由切实可行？——通过谈判产生规则并且遵行这些规则。

WTO规则——WTO协定，是成员国之间的谈判成果。目前的协议是1986年到1994年乌拉圭回合谈判的成果，包括对最初关税与贸易总协定进行的重大修订。

更换"如今的WTO货物贸易规则主要以关贸总协定为蓝本"。乌拉圭回合还创造了一些新的规则来处理服务贸易、知识产权相关领域、争端解决以及贸易政策审查。整套协议大约有3万页，包括大约30份协议和各个成员国在一些特殊领域分别作出的承担义务的说明（称作"时间表"），比如降低关税税率和开放服务贸易市场。

WTO成员国通过这些协议使一个非歧视性的贸易体系得以运转，这个体系清楚地说明了它们的权利与义务。每个国家都得到保证，该国的出口商品在其他国家的市场上会得到公平且始终如一的对待。每个国家都承诺对进口到自己国内市场的产品采取相同的政策。该体系还给予了发展中国家在实施其承诺时的一定弹性。

（一）货物

整个WTO最初都是为解决货物贸易问题而产生的。从1947年到1994年，关贸总协定成为协商降低关税税率和减少其他贸易壁垒的论坛，总协定的文本阐明了重要规则，尤其是非歧视性原则。

从1995年开始，升级后的关贸总协定成为WTO货物贸易的总括协定（umbrella agreement）。它附加了处理农业和纺织品等特殊领域，还包括国营贸易、产品标准、补贴及反倾销等特殊问题。

（二）服务

希望在国外做生意的银行、保险公司、电信公司、旅行社、连锁酒店和运输公司现在可以同样享受到更加自由，更加公平的贸易原则，这些原则刚开始仅应用于货物贸易。

这些原则出现在新的《服务贸易总协定》中，WTO成员还依据《服务贸易总协定》对愿意对外开放竞争的服务部门以及开放程度单独做出承诺。

（三）知识产权

WTO知识产权协议是对思想和创造力交易与投资做出的规定。规定了涉及贸易的知识产权——包括版权、专利、商标、用来识别商品的地理名称、工业设计、集成电路板设计以及像商业秘密这样的未披露信息等，应该如何保护。

（四）争端解决

争端解决谅解书中规定的WTO贸易争端解决程序对施行规则，并以此确保贸易自由流动至关重要。如果成员国认为其协议项下的权利受到侵害，它们就会把争议拿到WTO中解决。由特别任命的具有独立性的专家对争议作出裁决，裁决的基础是对协议的解释和各个成员国所作出的承诺。

该体系鼓励成员国通过磋商解决彼此的纷争。如果协商不成，它们可以遵循一套精

Appendix II

Text Translation & Key to Exercises (Part Two)

心制定的逐级进行的程序来解决纠纷。这些程序可能包括由专家组进行的裁决，还可能包含对法律问题的上诉。从提交到WTO中解决的案件的数量判断，各国对该体系的信心不断增强——8年当中已大约提交300个案子，而1947年到1994年整个关贸总协定存续期间，只有300个争端得以解决。

（五）政策审查

贸易政策审查机制的目的就是为了提高透明度，为了对各国现在采用的政策有更好的理解，也是为了评估这些政策的影响。许多成员国也把审查结果当作是对自己政策的建设性的反馈意见。

所有WTO成员都必须经历定期的详细审查，每次审查的内容包括相关国家和WTO秘书处的报告。

四、发展中国家

（一）发展与贸易

WTO成员当中有超过四分之三的发展中国家和最不发达国家。所有的WTO协议都包含对这些国家的特殊规定，包括给予它们更长的期限来贯彻协议和其作出的承诺，推出一些措施来提高它们的贸易机会，帮助它们修建基础设施以实现WTO工作、处理争端以及实施技术标准。

2001年在多哈举行的部长级会议提出了几项任务，包括对涉及发展中国家的广泛问题进行磋商。一些人称这轮新谈判为"多哈发展回合"。

在此之前，1997年举行了一次关于对最不发达国家贸易发起和技术帮助问题的高层会议。会议产生了一个包括六个政府间机构的"完整框架"，从而帮助最不发达国家提高开展贸易的能力，会议还通过了一些附加的优惠的市场准入协议。

WTO贸易和发展委员会通过其下属委员会来帮助最不发达国家，着眼于发展中国家的特殊需要。它的责任包括协议的执行、技术合作以及促进发展中国家对全球贸易体制的参与。

（二）技术协助和培训

WTO每年组织大约100个技术合作代表团到发展中国家，还在日内瓦为发展中国家的政府官员平均每年举行三次贸易政策讲座。并且在世界所有地区尤其是非洲国家，定期举行地区研讨会。在日内瓦还为来自从计划经济向市场经济转型国家的官员举办培训讲座。

WTO集中对位于发展中国家和最不发达国家首都100多个政府的贸易部门和地区组织提供参考资料。WTO为这些政府官员提供计算机和网络，以使他们能够进入包含无数官方文件和其他资料的WTO数据库，从而使他们及时了解在日内瓦总部所发生的事情。WTO还作了一些努力来帮助那些在日内瓦没有常驻代表的国家。

下篇　各课练习答案

第 一 课

一、根据课文回答下列问题。

（略）。

二、将下列术语译成英语。

1. (crime of) perjury
2. felonious homicide
3. second-degree murder
4. Model Penal Code
5. actus reus; guilty act
6. *mens rea*
7. (crime of) arson
8. manslaughter
9. imprisonment
10. misdemeanor

三、将下列句子译成汉语。

1. 在美国，有三种法的基本形式：宪法、制定法以及司法法。此外，政府分为三级，每级政府包括三个部门，而且各级政府均制定法律。

2. 所以，我们的社会有许多法律渊源：联邦宪法以及各州宪法、立法机关制订的法案、司法判例以及行政命令。制定法是指由国会或州立法部门颁布的法律。条例是指地方一级政府颁布的法律。

3. 判例法与制定法不同，它由联邦一级法院判决与州一级法院判决共同构成。行政命令是一种并不太常见的法的形式，它是依据总统的宪法性权力或某特定制定法（而颁布）的命令。

4. 在现代刑法典中，区别重罪与轻罪的界限与过去并不相同。一般而言，可处死刑或州监狱监禁刑的属于重罪。

5. 行为人行为并不构成犯罪，除非他的责任基于下列行为：（1）自愿行为，或（2）事实上可以行为，而懈怠的不作为。

四、用适当的词或词组填空。

1. criminal intent
2. capacity; responsible
3. commit; excluded
4. Murder
5. assault; Robery
6. Robbery; perpetrator
7. criminal law; felony
8. Misdemeanors; injury; false
9. Treason
10. *actus reus*

第 二 课

一、根据课文回答下列问题。

（略）。

二、将下列术语译成英语。

1. Criminal Law
2. criminal liability
3. Penal Code/Criminal Law Code
4. criminal action

Appendix II
Text Translation & Key to Exercises (Part Two)

5. criminology
6. cruelty to children
7. crime of violence
8. criminal motive
9. criminal capacity
10. criminal jurisdiction
11. deadly force
12. expert witness
13. defense of property
14. law enforcement officer
15. entrapment
16. diminished capacity
17. criminal trial
18. defense attorney/lawyer

三、将下列段落译成汉语。

刑事诉讼程序的进行分很多步。通常，警察局负责接受公民的报案。一旦有人报警，警察即展开调查，采集证人证词，并准备报告他们的调查结果。有时，他们会在调查过程中执行逮捕；有时，他们须完成报告并将之递交检察院审批，然后由检察官决定是否对警察局报告中所指的犯罪嫌疑人提出指控。提起刑事指控的具体程序因司法管区而异。有些管辖区在指控被告犯有特定罪行方面给警察以较大的自由裁量权；而有些管辖区则赋予检察院更大的权力。

四、将下列句子译成英语。

1. American legal system generally recognizes four broad categories of defenses: (1) alibi; (2) justifications; (3) excuses; and (4) procedural defenses.
2. Alibi is best supported by witnesses and documentation.
3. Coke said, "A man's house is his castle—for where shall a man be safe if it be not in his house?"
4. The claim of involuntary intoxication may form the basis for another excuse defense.
5. A very rarely used excuse is that of unconsciousness.

第 三 课

一、根据课文回答下列问题。
（略）。

二、将下列术语译成汉语。

1. 刑事诉讼
2. 刑事司法系统
3. 公诉方；控诉方
4. 对质
5. 对质条款
6. 性侵犯
7. 交叉询问
8. 公开审判
9. 陪审团审判
10. 悬案陪审团
11. 无因回避
12. 贫困被告人
13. 传讯
14. 听审，听证
15. 迅速审判
16. 双重追诉
17. 惩罚性损害赔偿

三、用英语解释下列术语。

1. The collective institutions through which an accused offender passes until the accusations have been disposed of or the assessed punishment concluded.

2. A criminal proceeding in which an accused person is tried.

3. The Sixth Amendment provision guaranteeing a criminal defendant's right to directly confront an accusing witness and to cross-examine that witness.

4. A trial in which the factual issues are determined by a jury, not by the judge.

5. The fact of being prosecuted twice for substantially the same offense. Double jeopardy is prohibited by the Fifth Amendment.

6. Damages awarded in addition to actual damages when the defendant acted with recklessness, malice, or deceit.

四、完型填空。

1. statutory law
2. common law
3. alibi
4. justifications
5. excuses
6. defendant
7. deny
8. responsible

第 四 课

一、根据课文回答下列问题。

（略）。

二、将下列术语译成英语。

1. social security
2. breathalyzer test
3. self-incrimination
4. Attorney General
5. due process
6. probable cause
7. Miranda Warning
8. waiver of rights
9. public safety
10. the right to remain silent

三、将下列句子译成汉语。

1.为维护及保护刑事被害人司法及正当程序权利，被害人应当享有参加一切被告人有权到场的诉讼程序的权利。

2. 被告人享有获得律师辩护的权利。如果被告人无力聘请律师，同时如果法院认定其为贫困被告人，则法院将为此人指派一名律师。

3. 被告人有保持沉默权。如果做出陈述，则任何做出的陈述都有可能对被告人不利。

4. 你有权保持沉默。你所作的任何陈述在法庭上都可能成为对你不利的证据。

5. 如果你想在讯问前或讯问过程中有律师在场但无力聘请时，法庭将会在讯问前免费为你指派一名律师。

四、听写。

（略）。

Appendix II

Text Translation & Key to Exercises (Part Two)

第 五 课

一、根据课文回答下列问题。

（略）。

二、将下列术语译成英语。

1. personal property (personalty or chattel)
2. real property (realty or real estate)
3. fee simple
4. eminent domain
5. life estate
6. future interest
7. reversionary interest
8. remainder
9. easement
10. tenancy in common
11. joint tenancy
12. tenancy by the entirety
13. possession
14. gift
15. confusion

三、将下列句子译成中文。

1. 占有的必要期间也可能因占有的性质不同而有所不同：善意占有人通常比恶意占有人在更短的时间内取得财产权利。

2. 很早以前就承认有共同所有权，并且任何取得财产权的方式都可能产生这种财产所有权形式。

3. 现今时代，联邦政府和各州都声称对各种东西拥有所有权——而这些东西原先被认为是无主物，比如流水和野生动物。

4. 并非故意落下或遗忘的财产属于遗失财产。拾得财产的人可以向除真正所有人之外的任何人主张财产权利。

5. 可以为了个人的利益或为完成某种目的将财产授予受托人。

四、完型填空。

1. acquisition
2. transfer
3. than
4. exchange
5. parties
6. concerned
7. delivery
8. free
9. rules
10. either

第 六 课

一、根据课文回答下列问题。

（略）。

二、将下列术语译成英语。

1. (legal) detriment
2. a gratuitous promise
3. fraud
4. misrepresentation
5. offeree
6. negotiable instruments

7. performance
9. undue influence
11. the third party beneficiary contract
13. mutuality (or meeting of minds)
15. discharge

8. duress
10. consideration
12. implied contract
14. breach of contract

三、将A栏的词同B栏的释义连接起来。

1. e   2. c   3. b   4. a   5. d

四、完成句子

1. ...as the promisor/offeror.

2. ...as mentally disordered persons.

3. ...as giving something that has value to another party（benefit）or giving up something that has value to oneself.

4. ...as defenses to avoid a contract by one party.

第 七 课

一、根据课文回答下列问题。

（略）。

二、将下列术语译成英语。

1. duty of care
3. negligence
5. slander
7. false imprisonment
9. battery
11. causation
13. intentional torts
15. malicious prosecution

2. damages
4. equitable remedy
6. defamation
8. assault
10. injunction
12. reasonable man/person
14. trespass to chattels

三、将下列句子译成汉语。

1. 原告必须提供得以断定被告未尽合理注意义务的证据。

2. 如果损害结果是可以预见的，即便损害发生方式是不可预见的，同样构成侵权责任。

3. 如果危险事件产生的危害大于采取预防措施所带来的负担或不便，理性人便会采取预防措施。

4. 如果被告实施了违法行为，且无可推脱，则该违法行为会被视为不言自明的过失，构成推定过失或只是过失行为存在的证明。

四、用适当的介词或副词填空。

1. as
3. in

2. in
4. of

Appendix II
Text Translation & Key to Exercises (Part Two)

5. with
7. between
6. from
8. in

第 八 课

一、根据课文回答下列问题。

（略）。

二、将下列术语译成英语。

1. dividend
2. insolvent liquidation
3. non-for-profit corporation
4. partnership
5. sole proprietorship
6. limited partnership
7. limited liability partnership
8. single member corporation
9. pass-through taxation
10. listed corporation
11. memorandum and articles of association/Certificate of Incorporation; Articles of Incorporation and By-Laws
12. holding corporation
13. creditor
14. bona fide
15. corporate veil

三、将下列句子译成汉语。

1. 公司独立拥有公司财产，股东仅拥有股份，他们对已经投入公司的资产不再享有所有权。

2. 如果企业想进入多领域进行经营活动，设立具有独立地位的子公司在管理上是很方便的。各个子公司对本公司的经营管理享有充分的控制权。

3. 合伙人共同分享一切利润，同时也共同对一切损失承担责任。

4. 如果公司无资产可用来还债，则陷入资不抵债，公司债权人有权申请其进入破产程序。

四、案例讨论。

The cause of action brought into focus the vexed question of whether a director or employee should be personally responsible for losses sustained by a third party in consequence of reliance upon representations or advice given to him by a company through the medium of its personnel. At stake are the policy considerations which led to the recognition of limited liability corporations in the first place.

The House of Lords set out in *Williams* v. *Natural Life Health Foods* the principles upon which the personal liability of directors should be assessed:

(i) Firstly, there must be an assumption of responsibility such that a third party suffering loss has a special relationship with the director in question. This is an objective test and does not depend upon the state of mind of the director in question. In short, the question is: did the director convey directly or indirectly to the third party that he was assuming a personal responsibility towards him?

(ii) Secondly, there must be reliance by the third party on the assumption of responsibility on the part of the director. In other words, the question is: can the third party reasonably rely on an assumption of personal responsibility by the director or other individual who performed the services on behalf of the company?

Applying these principles to the facts, the Court held that Mistlin had not assumed any such personal responsibility to Williams.

It was inevitable that in a small one-man company the managing director would play a prominent role, as outlined in the company's brochure, but by itself that fact did not convey to third parties that Mistlin was willing to be answerable to them personally. There were no personal dealings or exchanges which could have conveyed to Williams that Mistlin was willing to assume a personal responsibility towards him. There was not even any evidence that Williams believed that Mistlin was undertaking such a responsibility. Therefore it was not reasonable for Williams to look to Mistlin for indemnification of any loss.

第 九 课

一、根据课文回答下列问题。

（略）。

二、将下列术语译成英语。

1. intellectual property
2. trademark
3. the U.S. Patent and Trademark Office
4. cause of action
5. service mark
6. certification mark
7. collective mark
8. goodwill
9. first-to-invent rule
10. copyright
11. Berne Convention
12. fair use
13. trade secret
14. nondisclosure contract
15. royalties

三、将下列句子译成汉语。

1. 一般来说，知识产权是无形的，并且是由相对于体力劳动的智力劳动创造的。在美国，专利权、版权和商标权是由联邦法管辖的，而商业秘密是由州法律管辖的。

2. 专利申请漫长而复杂，发明人应该雇一名专利律师来帮助获得发明专利。

3. 伯尔尼公约，又叫作保护文学与艺术作品国际联盟，现在已有将近80个成员国。参加伯尔尼公约有助于保护正版作品不被国际盗版者盗用，阻止其将他人的创造性劳动成果出售。

4. 商标和服务商标使顾客对自己惠顾的公司有更加充分的认识，以此在顾客中建立起"商誉"。

5. 一旦发现对商标、专利和著作权产品的侵权使用，商业人员应当考虑将许可证出售给侵权人，而不是采取昂贵的诉讼方式。

Appendix II

Text Translation & Key to Exercises (Part Two)

四、听写。

（略）。

第 十 课

一、根据课文回答下列问题。

（略）。

二、将下列术语译成英语。

1. complaint
2. answer
3. substantive law
4. cause of action
5. affirmative defense
6. res judicata
7. accord and satisfaction
8. duress
9. negligence
10. pretrial conference

三、将下列句子译成汉语。

1. 对"管辖权"做些初步的评论是必要的。
2. 获得的这种判决就是人们所熟知的对被告不应诉判决。
3. 上诉法院同意审理法院的判决。
4. 如果对庭外和解的努力无效的话，律师最先会考虑是否会有不止一个便利法庭可以解决当事人的争议。
5. 不只是合适法庭的问题，律师还要考虑审判地是否可以给当事人提供最好的经济和战术上的优势。

四、用词的适当形式填空。

1. complaint
2. issued
3. suffer
4. attached
5. claim

第 十 一 课

一、根据课文回答下列问题。

（略）。

二、将下列术语译成英语。

1. war crimes
2. crimes against humanity
3. federal unions
4. international court of justice
5. stare decisis
6. opinio juris
7. mediation
8. good office
9. conciliation
10. rights of refugees

三、将下列段落翻译成中文。

对国际法的简单分析明确了国际法的适用范围和各种各样的渊源。随着日益全球化

. 331 .

的商业性质和法律关系，及美国法庭对跨国案件的频繁涉及，国际法的研究不再是只为少数从业者知晓的奇异专业知识。

四、选择适当的词填空。

1. purposes
2. advance
3. economic
4. social
5. discrimination

第 十 二 课

一、根据课文回答下列问题。

（略）。

二、将下列术语译成英语。

1. International Monetary Fund (IMF)
2. General Agreement on Tariffs and Trade (GATT)
3. the Uruguay Round
4. anti-dumping
5. securities
6. the Ministerial Conference
7. tariff barrier
8. government procurement
9. technical assistance
10. the General Council
11. policy review
12. specialized committees
13. non-discriminatory
14. umbrella agreement
15. General Agreement on Trade in Services (GATS)
16. a panel of experts
17. infrastructure
18. market access

三、将下列句子译成汉语。

1. 成为关贸总协定的成员国，各国便能够进入外国市场，但是这些国家也有义务开放本国市场并通过关贸总协定的多边贸易谈判来减少贸易壁垒。

2. 世界贸易组织首次为各国磋商多边贸易活动提供了一个得到国际认可的中立的而非对立性质的舞台。

3. 从理论上来说，世界贸易组织给成员国提供的解决争议的服务为公开、公平和客观的裁决提供了机会，这样使得各国以和平、合理的方式解决纠纷。

4. 通过开放贸易，中国与世界其他国家建立了更加紧密的联系，使中国人和外国人建立了个人以及商业上的联系。

5. 世界贸易组织协议规定，通常情况下，各国不能歧视其贸易伙伴。给予一方特殊优惠（比如给予一种产品较低的关税税率），你就必须给予所有其他的世界贸易组织成员同样的优惠。

四、词形转换。

1. establishment
2. initial
3. obligations
4. resolution
5. consumption
6. lengthy

Appendix III
Common Terms Used in Criminal Law

附录三 常用刑事法律英语术语

abused child 受虐待的儿童
A child who has been physically, sexually, or mentally abused. Most states also consider a child who is forced into delinquent activity by a parent or guardian to be abused.

acquittal 宣告无罪
The judgment of a court, based on a verdict of a jury or a judicial officer, that the defendant is not guilty of the offense or offenses for which he or she was tried.

actus reus 犯罪行为
An act in violation of the law. Also, a guilty act.

adjudication 审判；裁判
The process by which a court arrives at a decision regarding a case. Also, the resultant decision.

adjudicatory hearing 裁决性听证
The fact-finding process wherein the juvenile court determines whether there is sufficient evidence to sustain the allegations in a petition.

adult 成年人
A person who is within the original jurisdiction of a criminal court, rather than a juvenile court, because his or her age at the time of an alleged criminal act was above a statutorily specified limit.

adversarial system 对抗制
The two-sided structure under which American criminal trial courts operate that pits the prosecution against the defense. In theory, justice is done when the most effective adversary is able to convince the judge or jury that his or her perspective on the case is the correct one.

aggravated assault (UCR) 加重的企图伤害罪
The unlawful, intentional inflicting, or attempted or threatened inflicting, of serious injury upon the person of another. While aggravated assault and simple assault are standard terms for reporting purposes, most state penal codes use labels like first-degree and second-degree to make such distinctions.

aggravating circumstances 加重情节
Circumstances relating to the commission of a crime that make it more grave than the average instance of the given type of offense. See also mitigating circumstances.

alias 化名
Any name used for an official purpose that is different from a person's legal name.

alibi 不在犯罪现场（抗辩）
A statement or contention by an individual charged with a crime that he or she was so distant when the crime was committed, or so engaged in other provable activities, that his or her participation in the commission of that crime was impossible.

alter ego rule 他我原则
In some jurisdictions, a rule of law that holds that a person can only defend a third party under circumstances and only to the degree that the third party could act on his or her own behalf.

alternative sanctions 选择性制裁
See intermediate sanctions.

Antiterrorism Act 《反恐怖主义法》
See USA PATRIOT Act of 2001.

appeal 上诉

Generally, the request that a court with appellate jurisdiction review the judgment, decision, or order of a lower court and set it aside (reverse it) or modify it.

appearance (court) 出庭；应诉

The act of coming into a court and submitting to its authority.

appellant 上诉人

The person who contests the correctness of a court order, judgment, or other decision and who seeks review and relief in a court having appellate jurisdiction. Also, the person in whose behalf this is done.

appellate court 上诉法院

A court whose primary function is to review the judgments of other courts and of administrative agencies.

appellate jurisdiction 上诉管辖权

The lawful authority of a court to review a decision made by a lower court.

arraignment 传讯

Strictly, the hearing before a court having jurisdiction in a criminal case, in which the identity of the defendant is established, the defendant is informed of the charge and of his or her rights, and the defendant is required to enter a plea. Also, in some usages, any appearance in criminal court prior to trial.

arrest 逮捕

The act of taking an adult or juvenile into physical custody by authority of law for the purpose of charging the person with a criminal offense, a delinquent act, or a status offense, terminating with the recording of a specific offense. Technically, an arrest occurs whenever a law enforcement officer curtails a person's freedom to leave.

arrest rate 逮捕率

The number of arrests reported for each unit of population.

arrest warrant 逮捕证

A document issued by a judicial officer which directs a law enforcement officer to arrest an identified person who has been accused of a specific offense.

arson 纵火罪

The burning or attempted burning of property, with or without the intent to defraud. Some instances of arson result from malicious mischief, some involve attempts to claim insurance money, and some are committed in an effort to disguise other crimes, such as murder, burglary, or larceny.

assault 企图伤害罪；殴击

An unlawful attack by one person upon another. Historically, assault meant only the attempt to inflict injury on another person; a completed act constituted the separate offense of battery. Under modern statistical usage, however, attempted and completed acts are grouped together under the generic term assault.

assault on a law enforcement officer 殴打执法人员罪

A simple or aggravated assault, in which the victim is a law enforcement officer engaged in the performance of his or her duties.

attendant circumstances 事实相关情况

The facts surrounding an event.

attorney 律师

A person trained in the law, admitted to practice before the bar of a given jurisdiction, and authorized to advise, represent, and act for others in legal proceedings. Also called lawyer; legal counsel.

Auburn system 奥本监狱制度

A form of imprisonment developed in New York State around 1820 that depended on mass prisons, where prisoners were held in congregate fashion requiring silence. This style of imprisonment was a primary competitor with the Pennsylvania system.

backlog (court) （法院）积压案件

The number of cases awaiting disposition in a court which exceeds the court's capacity for

Appendix III
Common Terms Used in Criminal Law

disposing of them within the period of time considered appropriate.

bail 保释
The money or property pledged to the court or actually deposited with the court to effect the release of a person from legal custody.

bail bond 保释保证书
A document guaranteeing the appearance of a defendant in court as required and recording the pledge of money or property to be paid to the court if he or she does not appear, which is signed by the person to be released and anyone else acting in his or her behalf.

bailiff 法庭事务官
The court officer whose duties are to keep order in the courtroom and to maintain physical custody of the jury.

bail revocation 撤销保释
The court decision withdrawing the status of release on bail which was previously conferred upon a defendant.

balancing test 平衡原则
A principle, developed by the courts and applied to the corrections arena by Pell v. Procunier (1974), which attempts to weigh the rights of an individual, as guaranteed by the Constitution, against the authority of states to make laws or to otherwise restrict a person's freedom in order to protect the state's interests and its citizens.

battered women's syndrome (BWS) 受虐妇女综合征
1. A series of common characteristics that appear in women who are abused physically and psychologically over an extended period of time by the dominant male figure in their lives. 2. A pattern of psychological symptoms that develops after somebody has lived in a battering relationship. 3. A pattern of responses and perceptions presumed to be characteristic of women who have been subjected to continuous physical abuse by their mates.

bench warrant 法院传票
A document issued by a court directing that a law enforcement officer bring a specified person before the court. A bench warrant is usually issued for a person who has failed to obey a court order or a notice to appear.

bias crime 偏见犯罪
See hate crime.

Bill of Rights 《权利法案》
The popular name given to the first ten amendments to the U.S. Constitution, which are considered especially important in the processing of criminal defendants.

bind over 责令出庭应诉；责令守法
To require by judicial authority that a person promise to appear for trial, appear in court as a witness, or keep the peace. Also, the decision by a court of limited jurisdiction requiring that a person charged with a felony appear for trial on that charge in a court of general jurisdiction, as the result of a finding of probable cause at a preliminary hearing held in the court of limited jurisdiction.

biocrime 生物犯罪
A criminal offense perpetrated through the use of biologically active substances, including chemicals and toxins, disease-causing organisms, altered genetic material, and organic tissues and organs. Biocrimes unlawfully affect the metabolic, biochemical, genetic, physiological, or anatomical status of living organisms.

Biological School 生物学派
A perspective on criminological thought that holds that criminal behavior has a physiological basis.

biological weapon 生物武器
A biological agent used to threaten human life (for example, anthrax, smallpox, or any infectious disease).

biometrics 生物测定学
The science of recognizing people by physical characteristics and personal traits.

bobbies 警察
The popular British name given to members of Sir Robert (Bob) Peel's Metropolitan Police

Force.

booking 登记

A law enforcement or correctional administrative process officially recording an entry into detention after arrest and identifying the person, the place, the time, the reason for the arrest, and the arresting authority.

Bureau of Justice Statistics (BJS) 司法统计局

A U.S. Department of Justice agency responsible for the collection of criminal justice data, including the annual National Crime Victimization Survey.

burglary 夜盗罪

By the narrowest and oldest definition, trespassory breaking and entering the dwelling house of another in the nighttime with the intent to commit a felony.

capacity (legal) （法律）能力；行为能力；责任能力

The legal ability of a person to commit a criminal act. Also, the mental and physical ability to act with purpose and to be aware of the certain, probable, or possible results of one's conduct.

capital offense 死刑；极刑

A criminal offense punishable by death.

capital punishment 死刑

The death penalty. Capital punishment is the most extreme of all sentencing options.

career criminal 职业罪犯；惯犯

In prosecutorial and law enforcement usage, a person who has a past record of multiple arrests or convictions for serious crimes or who has an unusually large number of arrests or convictions for crimes of varying degrees of seriousness. Also called professional criminal.

carnal knowledge 性交

Sexual intercourse, coitus, sexual copulation. Carnal knowledge is accomplished "if there is the slightest penetration of the sexual organ of the female by the sexual organ of the male".

case law 判例法

The body of judicial precedent, historically built on legal reasoning and past interpretations of statutory laws, that serves as a guide to decision making, especially in the courts.

certiorari 调卷令

See writ of certiorari.

chain of command 命令链条

The unbroken line of authority that extends through all levels of an organization, from the highest to the lowest.

change of venue 变更审判地

The movement of a trial or lawsuit from one jurisdiction to another or from one location to another within the same jurisdiction. A change of venue may be made in a criminal case to ensure that the defendant receives a fair trial.

charge 起诉

An allegation that a specified person has committed a specific offense, recorded in a functional document such as a record of an arrest, a complaint, an information or indictment, or a judgment of conviction. Also called count.

Chicago School 芝加哥学派

A sociological approach that emphasizes demographics (the characteristics of population groups) and geographics (the mapped location of such groups relative to one another) and that sees the social disorganization that characterizes delinquency areas as a major cause of criminality and victimization.

child abuse 虐待儿童

The illegal physical, emotional, or sexual mistreatment of a child by his or her parent or guardian.

child neglect 疏忽儿童

The illegal failure by a parent or guardian to provide proper nourishment or care to a child.

Appendix III
Common Terms Used in Criminal Law

circumstantial evidence 间接证据；情况证据

Evidence that requires interpretation or that requires a judge or jury to reach a conclusion based on what the evidence indicates. From the close proximity of the defendant to a smoking gun, for example, the jury might conclude that she pulled the trigger.

citation (to appear) 法院传票

A written order issued by a law enforcement officer directing an alleged offender to appear in a specific court at a specified time to answer a criminal charge, and not permitting forfeit of bail as an alternative to court appearance.

citizen's arrest 公民逮捕

The taking of a person into physical custody by a witness to a crime other than a law enforcement officer for the purpose of delivering him or her to the physical custody of a law enforcement officer or agency.

civil death 民事死亡；宣告民事权利丧失

The legal status of prisoners in some jurisdictions who are denied the opportunity to vote, hold public office, marry, or enter into contracts by virtue of their status as incarcerated felons. While civil death is primarily of historical interest, some jurisdictions still limit the contractual opportunities available to inmates.

civil liability 民事责任

Potential responsibility for payment of damages or other court-ordered enforcement as a result of a ruling in a lawsuit. Civil liability is not the same as criminal liability, which means "open to punishment for a crime."

class-action lawsuit 集团诉讼；集体诉讼

A lawsuit filed by one or more people on behalf of themselves and a larger group of people "who are similarly situated".

Classical School 经典学派

An eighteenth-century approach to crime causation and criminal responsibility that grew out of the Enlightenment and that emphasized the role of free will and reasonable punishments. Classical thinkers believed that punishment, if it is to be an effective deterrent, has to outweigh the potential pleasure derived from criminal behavior.

classification system 监狱分类制度

A system used by prison administrators to assign inmates to custody levels based on offense history, assessed dangerousness, perceived risk of escape, and other factors.

clemency 宽恕；豁免

An executive or legislative action in which the severity of punishment of a single person or a group of people is reduced, the punishment is stopped, or the person or group is exempted from prosecution for certain actions.

closing argument 总结陈述；终结辩论

An oral summation of a case presented to a judge, or to a judge and jury, by the prosecution or by the defense in a criminal trial.

codification 法典化

The act or process of rendering laws in written form.

common law 普通法

Law originating from usage and custom rather than from written statutes. The term refers to an unwritten body of judicial opinion, originally developed by English courts, that is based on nonstatutory customs, traditions, and precedents that help guide judicial decision making.

community corrections 社区矫正；社区改造

The use of a variety of officially ordered program-based sanctions that permit convicted offenders to remain in the community under conditional supervision as an alternative to an active prison sentence. Also called community-based corrections.

community court 社区法院

A low-level court that focuses on quality-of-life crimes that erode a neighborhood's morale, that emphasizes problem solving rather than punishment, and that builds on restorative principles like community service and restitution.

community service 社区服务
A sentencing alternative that requires offenders to spend at least part of their time working for a community agency.

comparative criminologist 比较刑事学家
One who studies crime and criminal justice on a cross-national level.

compensatory damages 补偿性损害赔偿金
Damages recovered in payment for an actual injury or economic loss.

competent to stand trial 被告人的受审能力
A finding by a court, when the defendant's sanity at the time of trial is at issue, that the defendant has sufficient present ability to consult with his or her attorney with a reasonable degree of rational understanding and that the defendant has a rational as well as factual understanding of the proceedings against him or her.

complaint 刑事控告书
Generally, any accusation that a person has committed an offense, received by or originating from a law enforcement or prosecutorial agency or received by a court. Also, in judicial process usage, a formal document submitted to the court by a prosecutor, law enforcement officer, or other person, alleging that a specified person has committed a specific offense and requesting prosecution.

computer crime 计算机犯罪
Any crime perpetrated through the use of computer technology. Also, any violation of a federal or state computer-crime statute. Also called cybercrime.

concurrent sentence 合并判决
One of two or more sentences imposed at the same time, after conviction for more than one offense, and served at the same time. Also, a new sentence for a new conviction, imposed upon a person already under sentence for a previous offense, served at the same time as the previous sentence.

concurring opinion （判决中的）多数意见；同意意见
An opinion written by a judge who agrees with the conclusion reached by the majority of judges hearing a case but whose reasons for reaching that conclusion differ. Concurring opinions, which typically stem from an appellate review, are written to identify issues of precedent, logic, or emphasis that are important to the concurring judge but that were not identified by the court's majority opinion.

conditional release 附条件释放；假释
The release by executive decision of a prisoner from a federal or state correctional facility who has not served his or her full sentence and whose freedom is contingent on obeying specified rules of behavior.

conditions of parole (probation) 假释（缓刑）条件
The general and special limits imposed on an offender who is released on parole (or probation). General conditions tend to be fixed by state statute, while special conditions are mandated by the sentencing authority (court or board) and take into consideration the background of the offender and the circumstances of the offense.

confinement 监禁；关押
In corrections terminology, the physical restriction of a person to a clearly defined area from which he or she is lawfully forbidden to depart and from which departure is usually constrained by architectural barriers, guards or other custodians, or both.

consecutive sentence 连续判决
One of two or more sentences imposed at the same time, after conviction for more than one offense, and served in sequence with the other sentence. Also, a new sentence for a new conviction, imposed upon a person already under sentence for a previous offense, which is added to the previous sentence, thus increasing the maximum time the offender may be confined or under supervision.

contempt of court 蔑视法庭
Intentionally obstructing a court in the administration of justice, acting in a way calculated to lessen the court's authority or dignity, or failing to obey the court's lawful orders.

Appendix III
Common Terms Used in Criminal Law

controlled substance 法律管制药物
A specifically defined bioactive or psychoactive chemical substance proscribed by law.

Controlled Substances Act (CSA) 《管制物品法》
Title II of the Comprehensive Drug Abuse Prevention and Control Act of 1970, which established schedules classifying psychoactive drugs according to their degree of psychoactivity.

conviction 定罪
The judgment of a court, based on the verdict of a jury or judicial officer or on the guilty plea or nolo contendere plea of the defendant, that the defendant is guilty of the offense with which he or she has been charged.

corporate crime 法人犯罪；公司犯罪
A violation of a criminal statute by a corporate entity or by its executives, employees, or agents acting on behalf of and for the benefit of the corporation, partnership, or other forms of business entity.

corpus delicti 犯罪事实
The facts that show that a crime has occurred. The term literally means "the body of the crime".

correctional agency 矫正机构
A federal, state, or local criminal or juvenile justice agency, under a single administrative authority, whose principal functions are the intake screening, supervision, custody, confinement, treatment, or pre-sentencing or predisposition investigation of alleged or adjudicated adult offenders, youthful offenders, delinquents, or status offenders.

corrections 矫正；改造
A generic term that includes all government agencies, facilities, programs, procedures, personnel, and techniques concerned with the intake, custody, confinement, supervision, treatment, and presentencing and predisposition investigation of alleged or adjudicated adult offenders, youthful offenders, delinquents, and status offenders.

corruption 腐败；徇私舞弊
See police corruption.

Cosa Nostra 黑手党
A secret criminal organization of Sicilian origin. Also called Mafia.

counsel (legal) 法律顾问
See attorney.

count (offense) 罪项；罪状
See charge.

court 法院；法庭
An agency or unit of the judicial branch of government, authorized or established by statute or constitution and consisting of one or more judicial officers, which has the authority to decide cases, controversies in law, and disputed matters of fact brought before it.

court calendar 法庭审理案件日程表
The court schedule; the list of events comprising the daily or weekly work of a court, including the assignment of the time and place for each hearing or other item of business or the list of matters which will be taken up in a given court term. Also called docket.

court clerk 法庭书记员
An elected or appointed court officer responsible for maintaining the written records of the court and for supervising or performing the clerical tasks necessary for conducting judicial business. Also, any employee of a court whose principal duties are to assist the court clerk in performing the clerical tasks necessary for conducting judicial business.

court of last resort 终审法院
The court authorized by law to hear the final appeal on a matter.

court of record 存卷法院
A court in which a complete and permanent record of all proceedings or specified types of proceedings is kept.

court order 法院命令
A mandate, command, or direction issued by

a judicial officer in the exercise of his or her judicial authority.

court reporter 法院记录员

A person present during judicial proceedings who records all testimony and other oral statements made during the proceedings.

credit card fraud 信用卡诈骗

The use or attempted use of a credit card to obtain goods or services with the intent to avoid payment.

crime 犯罪

Conduct in violation of the criminal laws of a state, the federal government, or a local jurisdiction, for which there is no legally acceptable justification or excuse.

Crime Index 犯罪数量

An inclusive measure of the violent and property crime categories, or Part I offenses, of the Uniform Crime Reports. The Crime Index has been a useful tool for geographic (state-to-state) and historical (year-to-year) comparisons because it employs the concept of a crime rate (the number of crimes per unit of population). However, the addition of arson as an eighth index offense and the new requirements with regard to the gathering of hate-crime statistics could result in new Crime Index measurements that provide less-than-ideal comparisons.

crime rate 犯罪率

The number of Crime Index offenses reported for each unit of population.

crime scene 犯罪现场

The physical area in which a crime is thought to have occurred and in which evidence of the crime is thought to reside.

crime-scene investigator 犯罪现场侦查人员

An expert trained in the use of forensic techniques, such as gathering DNA evidence, collecting fingerprints, photography, sketching, and interviewing witnesses.

criminal homicide 杀人罪

The act of causing the death of another person without legal justification or excuse.

criminal investigation 刑事侦查

The process of discovering, collecting, preparing, identifying, and presenting evidence to determine what happened and who is responsible when a crime has occurred.

criminalist 犯罪学专家；刑事专家

A police crime-scene analyst or laboratory worker versed in criminalistics.

criminal justice 刑事司法

In the strictest sense, the criminal (penal) law, the law of criminal procedure, and the array of procedures and activities having to do with the enforcement of this body of law. Criminal justice cannot be separated from social justice because the kind of justice enacted in our nation's criminal courts is a reflection of basic American understandings of right and wrong.

criminal justice system 刑事司法制度

The aggregate of all operating and administrative or technical support agencies that perform criminal justice functions. The basic divisions of the operational aspects of criminal justice are law enforcement, courts, and corrections.

criminal law 刑法

The branch of modern law that concerns itself with offenses committed against society, its members, their property, and the social order. Also called penal law.

criminal negligence 刑事疏忽

Behavior in which a person fails to reasonably perceive substantial and unjustifiable risks of dangerous consequences.

criminal proceedings 刑事程序

The regular and orderly steps, as directed or authorized by statute or a court of law, taken to determine whether an adult accused of a crime is guilty or not guilty.

criminology 犯罪学

The scientific study of the causes and prevention of crime and the rehabilitation and punishment of offenders.

Appendix III
Common Terms Used in Criminal Law

cruel and unusual punishment 残酷或非寻常的刑罚

　Punishment involving torture or a lingering death or the infliction of unnecessary and wanton pain.

culpability 应受惩罚性

　Blameworthiness; responsibility in some sense for an event or situation deserving of moral blame. Also, in Model Penal Code usage, a state of mind on the part of one who is committing an act which makes him or her potentially subject to prosecution for that act.

cultural defense 文化抗辩

　A defense to a criminal charge in which the defendant's culture is taken into account in judging his or her culpability.

custody 羁押；拘禁；监禁

　The legal or physical control of a person or a thing. Also, the legal, supervisory, or physical responsibility for a person or a thing.

cybercrime 网络犯罪

　See computer crime.

cyberstalking 网络跟踪/骚扰

　The use of the Internet, e-mail, and other electronic communication technologies to stalk another person.

cyberterrorism 网络恐怖主义

　A form of terrorism that makes use of high technology, especially computers and the Internet, in the planning and carrying out of terrorist attacks.

 Dd

dangerousness 危险

　The likelihood that a given individual will later harm society or others. Dangerousness is often measured in terms of recidivism, or the likelihood of additional crime commission within five years following arrest or release from confinement.

date rape 约会强奸

　Unlawful forced sexual intercourse with a female against her will that occurs within the context of a dating relationship. Date rape, or acquaintance rape, is a subcategory of rape that is of special concern today.

deadly force 致命武力

　Force likely to cause death or great bodily harm. Also, "the intentional use of a firearm or other instrument resulting in a high probability of death".

deadly weapon 致命武器

　An instrument designed to inflict serious bodily injury or death or capable of being used for such a purpose.

decriminalization 非刑事化

　The redefinition of certain previously criminal behaviors into regulated activities that become "ticketable" rather than "arrestable".

defendant 被告人

　A person formally accused of an offense by the filing in court of a charging document.

defense (to a criminal charge) 刑事指控抗辩

　Evidence and arguments offered by a defendant and his or her attorney to show why the defendant should not be held liable for a criminal charge.

defense attorney 辩护律师

　See defense counsel.

defense counsel 辩护律师

　A licensed trial lawyer hired or appointed to conduct the legal defense of a person accused of a crime and to represent him or her before a court of law. Also called defense attorney.

delinquency 青少年违法行为

　In the broadest usage, juvenile actions or conduct in violation of criminal law, juvenile status offenses, and other juvenile misbehavior.

delinquent 少年犯

　A juvenile who has been adjudged by a judicial officer of a juvenile court to have committed a delinquent act.

delinquent child 儿童犯

A child who has engaged in activity that would be considered a crime if the child were an adult. The term delinquent is used to avoid the stigma associated with the term criminal.

detainee 被关押人

Usually, a person held in local, very short-term confinement while awaiting consideration for pretrial release or a first appearance for arraignment.

detention 拘留

The legally authorized confinement of a person subject to criminal or juvenile court proceedings, until the point of commitment to a correctional facility or until release.

detention hearing 拘留听审

In juvenile justice usage, a hearing by a judicial officer of a juvenile court to determine whether a juvenile is to be detained, is to continue to be detained, or is to be released while juvenile proceedings are pending.

deterrence 震慑；威慑

A goal of criminal sentencing that seeks to inhibit criminal behavior through the fear of punishment.

diminished capacity 责任减等

A defense based on claims of a mental condition that may be insufficient to exonerate the defendant of guilt but that may be relevant to specific mental elements of certain crimes or degrees of crime. Also called diminished responsibility.

direct evidence 直接证据

Evidence that, if believed, directly proves a fact. Eyewitness testimony and videotaped documentation account for the majority of all direct evidence heard in the criminal courtroom.

direct-supervision jail 直接监管监狱

A temporary confinement facility that eliminates many of the traditional barriers between inmates and correctional staff. Physical barriers in direct-supervision jails are far less common than in traditional jails, allowing staff members the opportunity for greater interaction with, and control over,

residents. Also called new-generation jail.

discharge 释放

To release from confinement or supervision or to release from a legal status imposing an obligation upon the subject person.

discretion 裁量权；判断能力

See police discretion.

dispute-resolution center 争端解决中心

An informal hearing place designed to mediate interpersonal disputes without resorting to the more formal arrangements of a criminal trial court.

district attorney (DA) 地区检察官

See prosecutor.

DNA profiling DNA界定；DNA描绘

The use of biological residue, found at the scene of a crime, for genetic comparisons in aiding in the identification of criminal suspects.

docket 待审案件目录

See court calendar.

double jeopardy 双重危险；双重追诉

A common law and constitutional prohibition against a second trial for the same offense.

drug 毒品

Any chemical substance defined by social convention as bioactive or psychoactive.

drug abuse 滥用毒品

Illicit drug use that results in social, economic, psychological, or legal problems for the user.

due process 正当程序

A right guaranteed by the Fifth, Sixth, and Fourteenth Amendments of the U.S. Constitution and generally understood, in legal contexts, to mean the due course of legal proceedings according to the rules and forms established for the protection of individual rights. In criminal proceedings, due process of law is generally understood to include the following basic elements: a law creating and defining the offense, an impartial tribunal having jurisdictional authority over

Appendix III
Common Terms Used in Criminal Law

the case, accusation in proper form, notice and opportunity to defend, trial according to established procedure, and discharge from all restraints or obligations unless convicted.

Electronic Communications Privacy Act (ECPA) 《电子通信隐私法》
A law passed by Congress in 1986 establishing the due process requirements that law enforcement officers must meet in order to legally intercept wire communications.

electronic evidence 电子证据
Information and data of investigative value that are stored in or transmitted by an electronic device.

element (of a crime) 犯罪要件
In a specific crime, one of the essential features of that crime, as specified by law or statute.

embezzlement 侵占罪
The misappropriation, or illegal disposal, of legally entrusted property by the person to whom it was entrusted, with the intent to defraud the legal owner or the intended beneficiary.

emergency search 紧急搜查
A search conducted by the police without a warrant, which is justified on the basis of some immediate and overriding need, such as public safety, the likely escape of a dangerous suspect, or the removal or destruction of evidence.

entrapment 警察设陷阱/圈套
An improper or illegal inducement to crime by agents of law enforcement. Also, a defense that may be raised when such inducements have occurred.

equity 平衡
A sentencing principle, based on concerns with social equality, that holds that similar crimes should be punished with the same degree of severity, regardless of the social or personal characteristics of the offenders.

espionage 间谍罪
The "gathering, transmitting, or losing" of information related to the national defense in such a manner that the information becomes available to enemies of the United States and may be used to their advantage.

ethnocentric 种族中心主义的
Holding a belief in the superiority of one's own social or ethnic group and culture.

ethnocentrism 种族中心主义
The phenomenon of "culture-centeredness", by which one uses one's own culture as a benchmark against which to judge all other patterns of behavior.

European Police Office (Europol) 欧洲警察办公室
The integrated police-intelligence gathering and disseminating arm of the member nations of the European Union.

evidence 证据
Anything useful to a judge or jury in deciding the facts of a case. Evidence may take the form of witness testimony, written documents, videotapes, magnetic media, photographs, physical objects, and so on.

excessive force 过当武力
The application of an amount and/or frequency of force greater than that required to compel compliance from a willing or unwilling subject.

excuse 可得宽恕
A legal defense in which the defendant claims that some personal condition or circumstance at the time of the act was such that he or she should not be held accountable under the criminal law.

exemplary damages 惩罚性损害赔偿金
See punitive damages.

expert system 专家系统
Computer hardware and software that attempts to duplicate the decision-making processes used by skilled investigators in the

analysis of evidence and in the recognition of patterns that such evidence might represent.

expert witness 专家证人

A person who has special knowledge and skills recognized by the court as relevant to the determination of guilt or innocence. Unlike lay witnesses, expert witnesses may express opinions or draw conclusions in their testimony.

ex post facto 可溯及既往的；有溯及力的；事后的

Latin for "after the fact". The Constitution prohibits the enactment of ex post facto laws, which make acts committed before the laws in question were passed punishable as crimes.

extradition 引渡

The surrender by one state to another of an individual accused or convicted of an offense in the second state.

federal court system 联邦法院体系

The three-tiered structure of federal courts, comprising U.S. district courts, U.S. courts of appeals, and the U.S. Supreme Court.

federal law enforcement agency 联邦执法机构

A U.S. government agency or office whose primary functional responsibility is the enforcement of federal criminal laws.

felony 重罪

A criminal offense punishable by death or by incarceration in a prison facility for at least one year.

feminist criminology 女权主义犯罪学

A developing intellectual approach that emphasizes gender issues in criminology.

fine 罚金

The penalty imposed upon a convicted person by a court, requiring that he or she pay a specified sum of money to the court.

first appearance 初次聆讯

An appearance before a magistrate during which the legality of the defendant's arrest is initially assessed and the defendant is informed of the charges on which he or she is being held. At this stage in the criminal justice process, bail may be set or pretrial release arranged. Also called initial appearance.

force 武力

See police use of force.

forcible rape 暴力强奸

The carnal knowledge of a female forcibly and against her will. For statistical reporting purposes, the FBI defines forcible rape as "unlawful sexual intercourse with a female, by force and against her will, or without legal or factual consent". Statutory rape differs from forcible rape in that it generally involves nonforcible sexual intercourse with a minor. See also carnal knowledge and rape.

foreign terrorist organization (FTO) 外国恐怖主义组织

A foreign organization that engages in terrorist activity that threatens the security of U.S. nationals or the national security of the United States and that is so designated by the U.S. secretary of state.

forfeiture 剥夺，没收

The authorized seizure of money, negotiable instruments, securities, or other things of value. Under federal antidrug laws, judicial representatives are authorized to seize all cash, negotiable instruments, securities, or other things of value furnished or intended to be furnished by any person in exchange for a controlled substance, as well as all proceeds traceable to such an exchange. Also called asset forfeiture.

forgery 伪造文书罪

The creation or alteration of a written or printed document, which if validly executed would constitute a record of a legally binding transaction, with the intent to defraud by affirming it to be the act of an unknowing second person. Also, the creation of an art object with intent to misrepresent the identity

Appendix III
Common Terms Used in Criminal Law

of the creator.

fraud 欺诈

An offense involving deceit or intentional misrepresentation of fact, with the intent of unlawfully depriving a person of his or her property or legal rights.

frivolous suit 无意义的诉讼

A lawsuit with no foundation in fact. Frivolous suits are generally brought by lawyers and plaintiffs for reasons of publicity, politics, or other non-law-related issues and may result in fines against plaintiffs and their counsel.

fruit of the poisoned tree doctrine 毒树之果原则

A legal principle that excludes from introduction at trial any evidence later developed as a result of an illegal search or seizure.

good time 缩减的刑期

The amount of time deducted from time to be served in prison on a given sentence as a consequence of good behavior.

grand jury 大陪审团

A group of jurors who have been selected according to law and have been sworn to hear the evidence and to determine whether there is sufficient evidence to bring the accused person to trial, to investigate criminal activity generally, or to investigate the conduct of a public agency or official.

gross negligence 重大过失

The intentional failure to perform a manifest duty in reckless disregard of the consequences as affecting the life or property of another.

guilty plea 认罪答辩

A defendant's formal answer in court to the charge or charges contained in a complaint, information, or indictment, claiming that he or she did commit the offense or offenses listed.

guilty verdict 有罪判决

See verdict.

habeas corpus 人身保护令

See writ of habeas corpus.

habitual offender 惯犯；累犯

A person sentenced under the provisions of a statute declaring that people convicted of a given offense, and shown to have previously been convicted of another specified offense, shall receive a more severe penalty than that for the current offense alone.

hacker 电脑黑客

A computer hobbyist or professional, generally with advanced programming skills. Today, the term hacker has taken on a sinister connotation, referring to hobbyists who are bent on illegally accessing the computers of others or who attempt to demonstrate their technological prowess through computerized acts of vandalism.

hate crime 仇恨犯罪

A criminal offense in which the motive is "hatred, bias, or prejudice, based on the actual or perceived race, color, religion, national origin, ethnicity, gender, or sexual orientation of another individual or group of individuals". Also called bias crime.

hearing 听证

A proceeding in which arguments, witnesses, or evidence is heard by a judicial officer or an administrative body.

hearsay 传闻证据；传闻

Something that is not based on the personal knowledge of a witness. Witnesses who testify about something they have heard, for example, are offering hearsay by repeating information about a matter of which they have no direct knowledge.

hearsay rule 传闻证据规则

The long-standing precedent that hearsay cannot be used in American courtrooms. Rather than accepting testimony based on hearsay, the court will ask that the person who was the original source of the hearsay information be brought in to be questioned and cross-examined. Exceptions to the hearsay rule may occur when the person with direct knowledge is dead or is otherwise unable to testify.

high-technology crime 高科技犯罪
Violations of the criminal law whose commission depends upon, makes use of, and often targets sophisticated and advanced technology. See also computer crime.

homicide 杀人
See criminal homicide.

hung jury 悬案陪审团
A jury that, after long deliberation, is so irreconcilably divided in opinion that it is unable to reach any verdict.

identity management 身份管理
The comprehensive management and administration of a user's individual profile information, permissions, and privileges across a variety of social settings.

identity theft 盗用身份罪
A crime in which an imposter obtains key pieces of information, such as Social Security and driver's license numbers, to obtain credit, merchandise, and services in the name of the victim. The victim is often left with a ruined credit history and the time-consuming and complicated task of repairing the financial damages.

illegally seized evidence 非法采集的证据
Evidence seized without regard to the principles of due process as described by the Bill of Rights. Most illegally seized evidence is the result of police searches conducted without a proper warrant or of improperly conducted interrogations.

inchoate offense 未完成犯罪
An offense not yet completed. Also, an offense that consists of an action or conduct that is a step toward the intended commission of another offense.

included offense 包含在内的犯罪
An offense that is made up of elements that are a subset of the elements of another offense having a greater statutory penalty, and the occurrence of which is established by the same evidence or by some portion of the evidence that has been offered to establish the occurrence of the greater offense.

incompetent to stand trial 无受审能力
In criminal proceedings, a finding by a court that as a result of mental illness, defect, or disability, a defendant is incapable of understanding the nature of the charges and proceedings against him or her, of consulting with an attorney, and of aiding in his or her own defense.

indictment 公诉书；大陪审团起诉书
A formal, written accusation submitted to the court by a grand jury, alleging that a specified person has committed a specified offense, usually a felony.

individual rights 个人权利；（宪法赋予的）公民基本权利
The rights guaranteed to all members of American society by the U.S. Constitution (especially those found in the first ten amendments to the Constitution, known as the Bill of Rights). These rights are particularly important to criminal defendants facing formal processing by the criminal justice system.

information （由检察官签署的）刑事起诉书
A formal written accusation submitted to the court by a prosecutor, alleging that a specified person has committed a specific offense.

initial appearance 初次聆讯
See first appearance.

insanity defense 精神病辩护
A legal defense based on claims of mental illness or mental incapacity.

intensive probation supervision (IPS) 严格的缓刑监督
A form of probation supervision involving frequent face-to-face contact between the probationer and the probation officer.

intent 意图
The state of mind or attitude with which an

act is carried out. Also, the design, resolve, or determination with which a person acts to achieve a certain result.

intermediate appellate court 中间上诉法院

An appellate court whose primary function is to review the judgments of trial courts and the decisions of administrative agencies and whose decisions are, in turn, usually reviewable by a higher appellate court in the same state.

International Criminal Police Organization (INTERPOL) 国际刑（事）警（察）组织

An international law enforcement support organization that began operations in 1946 and today has 181 members.

international terrorism 国际恐怖主义

The unlawful use of force or violence by a group or an individual who has some connection to a foreign power, or whose activities transcend national boundaries, against people or property in order to intimidate or coerce a government, the civilian population, or any segment thereof, in furtherance of political or social objectives.

interrogation 讯问

The information-gathering activity of police officers that involves the direct questioning of suspects.

Islamic law 伊斯兰法

A system of laws, operative in some Arab countries, based on the Muslim religion and especially the holy book of Islam, the Koran.

jail 监狱；看守所

A confinement facility administered by an agency of local government, typically a law enforcement agency, intended for adults but sometimes also containing juveniles, which holds people detained pending adjudication or committed after adjudication, usually those sentenced to a year or less.

jail commitment 监禁刑

A sentence of commitment to the jurisdiction of a confinement facility system for adults which is administered by an agency of local government and whose custodial authority is usually limited to people sentenced to a year or less of confinement.

judge 法官

An elected or appointed public official who presides over a court of law and who is authorized to hear and sometimes to decide cases and to conduct trials.

judgment 判决

The statement of the decision of a court that the defendant is acquitted or convicted of the offense or offenses charged.

judicial officer 司法官员

Any person authorized by statute, constitutional provision, or court rule to exercise the powers reserved to the judicial branch of government.

judicial review 司法审查

The power of a court to review actions and decisions made by other agencies of government.

jural postulates 法律假设

Propositions developed by the famous jurist Roscoe Pound that hold that the law reflects shared needs without which members of society could not coexist. Pound's jural postulates are often linked to the idea that the law can be used to engineer the social structure to ensure certain kinds of outcomes. In capitalist societies, for example, the law of theft protects property rights.

jurisdiction 司法管辖权

The territory, subject matter, or people over which a court or other justice agency may exercise lawful authority, as determined by statute or constitution. See also venue.

juror 陪审员

A member of a trial or grand jury who has been selected for jury duty and is required to serve as an arbiter of the facts in a court of law. Jurors are expected to render verdicts of "guilty" or "not guilty" as to the charges brought against the accused, although they may sometimes fail to do so (as in the case of a hung jury).

jury panel 候选陪审员名单

The group of people summoned to appear in court as potential jurors for a particular trial. Also, the people selected from the group of potential jurors to sit in the jury box, from which those acceptable to the prosecution and the defense are finally chosen as the jury.

jury selection 陪审团挑选

The process whereby, according to law and precedent, members of a trial jury are chosen.

justification 正当理由

A legal defense in which the defendant admits to committing the act in question but claims it was necessary in order to avoid some greater evil.

juvenile 未成年人；少年

A person subject to juvenile court proceedings because a statutorily defined event or condition caused by or affecting that person was alleged to have occurred while his or her age was below the statutorily specified age limit of original jurisdiction of a juvenile court.

juvenile court 少年法庭

A court that has, as all or part of its authority, original jurisdiction over matters concerning people statutorily defined as juveniles.

kidnapping 绑架

The transportation or confinement of a person without authority of law and without his or her consent, or without the consent of his or her guardian, if a minor.

landmark case 标志性案例

A precedent-setting court decision that produces substantial changes in both the understanding of the requirements of due process and in the practical day-to-day operations of the justice system.

larceny-theft 偷盗罪

The unlawful taking or attempted taking, carrying, leading, or riding away of property, from the possession or constructive possession of another. Motor vehicles are excluded. Larceny is the most common of the eight major offenses, although probably only a small percentage of all larcenies are actually reported to the police because of the small dollar amounts involved.

latent evidence 隐蔽的证据

Evidence of relevance to a criminal investigation that is not readily seen by the unaided eye.

law 法律

A rule of conduct, generally found enacted in the form of a statute, that proscribes or mandates certain forms of behavior. Statutory law is often the result of moral enterprise by interest groups that, through the exercise of political power, are successful in seeing their valued perspectives enacted into law.

law enforcement 执法；执行法律

The generic name for the activities of the agencies responsible for maintaining public order and enforcing the law, particularly the activities of preventing, detecting, and investigating crime and apprehending criminals.

law enforcement agency 执法机构

A federal, state, or local criminal justice agency or identifiable subunit whose principal functions are the prevention, detection, and investigation of crime and the apprehension of alleged offenders.

law enforcement officer 执法人员

An officer employed by a law enforcement agency who is sworn to carry out law enforcement duties.

lawyer 律师

See attorney.

lay witness 非专家证人

An eyewitness, character witness, or other person called on to testify who is not considered an expert. Lay witnesses

Appendix III
Common Terms Used in Criminal Law

must testify to facts only and may not draw conclusions or express opinions.

legal cause 法定原因；近因

A legally recognizable cause. A legal cause must be demonstrated in court in order to hold an individual criminally liable for causing harm.

legal counsel 法律顾问

See attorney.

Mafia 黑手党

See Cosa Nostra.

major crimes 主要犯罪；重大犯罪

See Part I offenses.

mala in se [拉] 本质上的违法行为

Acts that are regarded, by tradition and convention, as wrong in themselves.

mandatory sentence 强制判决

A statutorily required penalty that must be set and carried out in all cases upon conviction for a specified offense or series of offenses.

maximum sentence 最高刑罚

In legal usage, the maximum penalty provided by law for a given criminal offense, usually stated as a maximum term of imprisonment or a maximum fine. Also, in corrections usage, in relation to a given offender, any of several quantities (expressed in days, months, or years) which vary according to whether calculated at the point of sentencing or at a later point in the correctional process and according to whether the time period referred to is the term of confinement or the total period under correctional jurisdiction.

mediation committee 调解委员会

One of the civilian dispute-resolution groups found throughout China. Mediation committees successfully divert many minor offenders from the more formal mechanisms of justice.

mens rea 犯罪意图

The state of mind that accompanies a criminal act. Also, a guilty mind.

Miranda rights 米兰达权利

The set of rights that a person accused or suspected of having committed a specific offense has during interrogation and of which he or she must be informed prior to questioning, as stated by the U.S. Supreme Court in deciding Miranda v. Arizona (1966) and related cases.

Miranda warnings 米兰达警告

The advisement of rights to criminal suspects by the police before questioning begins. Miranda warnings were first set forth by the U.S. Supreme Court in the 1966 case of Miranda v. Arizona.

misdemeanor 轻罪

An offense punishable by incarceration, usually in a local confinement facility, for a period whose upper limit is prescribed by statute in a given jurisdiction, typically one year or less.

mistrial 错误审理；无效审理

A trial that has been terminated and declared invalid by the court because of some circumstance which created a substantial and uncorrectable prejudice to the conduct of a fair trial or which made it impossible to continue the trial in accordance with prescribed procedures.

mitigating circumstances （罪行）减轻情节

Circumstances relating to the commission of a crime that may be considered to reduce the blame worthiness of the defendant. See also aggravating circumstances.

M'Naghten rule 麦那顿规则

A rule for determining insanity, which asks whether the defendant knew what he or she was doing or whether the defendant knew that what he or she was doing was wrong.

Model Penal Code (MPC)《模范刑法典》

A generalized modern codification considered basic to criminal law, published by the American Law Institute in 1962.

money laundering 洗钱

The process by which criminals or criminal organizations seek to disguise the illicit nature of their proceeds by introducing them into the stream of legitimate commerce and finance.

motion 动议；申请

An oral or written request made to a court at any time before, during, or after court proceedings, asking the court to make a specified finding, decision, or order.

motive 动机

A person's reason for committing a crime.

motor vehicle theft 机动车盗窃

The theft or attempted theft of a motor vehicle. Motor vehicle is defined as a self-propelled road vehicle that runs on land surface and not on rails. The stealing of trains, planes, boats, construction equipment, and most farm machinery is classified as larceny under the UCR Program, not as motor vehicle theft.

murder 谋杀

The unlawful killing of a human being. Murder is a generic term that in common usage may include first and second-degree murder, manslaughter, involuntary manslaughter, and other similar offenses.

murder and non-negligent manslaughter 谋杀及非过失杀人

Intentionally causing the death of another without legal justification or excuse. Also, causing the death of another while committing or attempting to commit another crime.

negligence 过失

In legal usage, generally, a state of mind accompanying a person's conduct such that he or she is not aware, though a reasonable person should be aware, that there is a risk that the conduct might cause a particular harmful result.

negligent manslaughter 过失杀人

Causing the death of another by recklessness or gross negligence.

neoclassical criminology 新古典主义犯罪学

A contemporary version of classical criminology that emphasizes deterrence and retribution and that holds that human beings are essentially free to make choices in favor of crime and deviance or conformity.

no true bill 不予起诉

The decision by a grand jury that it will not return an indictment against the person accused of a crime on the basis of the allegations and evidence presented by the prosecutor.

offender 罪犯；违法者

An adult who has been convicted of a criminal offense.

offense 犯罪

A violation of the criminal law. Also, in some jurisdictions, a minor crime, such as jaywalking, that is sometimes described as ticketable.

opening statement （律师）开庭陈述

The initial statement of the prosecution or the defense, made in a court of law to a judge, or to a judge and jury, describing the facts that he or she intends to present during trial to prove the case.

opinion 法院判决意见书

The official announcement of a decision of a court, together with the reasons for that decision.

organized crime 有组织犯罪

The unlawful activities of the members of a highly organized, disciplined association engaged in supplying illegal goods and services, including gambling, prostitution, loan-sharking, narcotics, and labor racketeering, and in other unlawful activities.

original jurisdiction 初始管辖权

The lawful authority of a court to hear or to act on a case from its beginning and to pass judgment on the law and the facts. The authority may be over a specific geographic area or over particular types of cases.

Appendix III
Common Terms Used in Criminal Law

parens patriae〈拉丁语〉国家监护原则

A common law principle that allows the state to assume a parental role and to take custody of a child when he or she becomes delinquent, is abandoned, or is in need of care that the natural parents are unable or unwilling to provide.

Parliament 议会

The British legislature, the highest law-making body of the United Kingdom.

parole 假释

The status of a convicted offender who has been conditionally released from prison by a paroling authority before the expiration of his or her sentence, is placed under the supervision of a parole agency, and is required to observe the conditions of parole.

parole board 假释委员会

A state paroling authority. Most states have parole boards that decide when an incarcerated offender is ready for conditional release. Some boards also function as revocation hearing panels. Also called parole commission.

parolee 获假释者；假释犯

A person who has been conditionally released by a paroling authority from a prison prior to the expiration of his or her sentence, is placed under the supervision of a parole agency, and is required to observe conditions of parole.

parole (probation) violation 假释（缓刑）违反行为

An act or a failure to act by a parolee (or probationer) that does not conform to the conditions of his or her parole (or probation).

parole revocation 撤销假释

The administrative action of a paroling authority removing a person from parole status in response to a violation of lawfully required conditions of parole, including the prohibition against committing a new offense, and usually resulting in a return to prison.

parole supervision 假释监督

Guidance, treatment, or regulation of the behavior of a convicted adult who is obligated to fulfill conditions of parole or conditional release. Parole supervision is authorized and required by statute, is performed by a parole agency, and occurs after a period of prison confinement.

paroling authority 假释主管机关

A board or commission which has the authority to release on parole adults committed to prison, to revoke parole or other conditional release, and to discharge from parole or other conditional release status.

Part I offenses《统一犯罪汇编》(UCR) 第一编包括的犯罪

A set of UCR categories used to report murder, rape, robbery, aggravated assault, burglary, larceny-theft, motor vehicle theft, and arson, as defined under the FBI's Uniform Crime Reporting Program. Also called major crimes.

Part II offenses《统一犯罪汇编》(UCR) 第二编包括的犯罪

A set of UCR categories used to report arrests for less serious offenses.

penal code 刑法典

The written, organized, and compiled form of the criminal laws of a jurisdiction.

penal law 刑法

See criminal law.

penitentiary 监狱

A prison. See also Pennsylvania system.

Pennsylvania system 宾夕法尼亚制

A form of imprisonment developed by the Pennsylvania Quakers around 1790 as an alternative to corporal punishments. This style of imprisonment made use of solitary confinement and encouraged rehabilitation.

peremptory challenge 无因回避

The right to challenge a potential juror without disclosing the reason for the challenge. Prosecutors and defense attorneys routinely use peremptory challenges to eliminate from juries individuals who, although they express no obvious bias, are thought to be capable of swaying the jury in an undesirable direction.

perjury 伪证罪
The intentional making of a false statement as part of the testimony by a sworn witness in a judicial proceeding on a matter relevant to the case at hand.

perpetrator 犯罪人；施害人
The chief actor in the commission of a crime—that is, the person who directly commits the criminal act.

petition 起诉状
A written request made to a court asking for the exercise of its judicial powers or asking for permission to perform some act that requires the authorization of a court.

petit jury 小陪审团
See trial jury.

Phrenology 颅相学
The study of the shape of the head to determine anatomical correlates of human behavior.

piracy 侵犯版权；盗版
See software piracy.

plaintiff 原告
A person who initiates a court action.

plea （诉讼）答辩
In criminal proceedings, the defendant's formal answer in court to the charge contained in a complaint, information, or indictment that he or she is guilty of the offense charged, is not guilty of the offense charged, or does not contest the charge.

plea bargaining 辩诉交易；控辩交易
The process of negotiating an agreement among the defendant, the prosecutor, and the court as to an appropriate plea and associated sentence in a given case. Plea bargaining circumvents the trial process and dramatically reduces the time required for the resolution of a criminal case.

political defense 政治性抗辩
An innovative defense to a criminal charge that claims that the defendant's actions stemmed from adherence to a set of political beliefs and standards significantly different from those on which the American style of government is based. A political defense questions the legitimacy and purpose of all criminal proceedings against the defendant.

precedent 先例
A legal principle that ensures that previous judicial decisions are authoritatively considered and incorporated into future cases.

preliminary hearing 预审
A proceeding before a judicial officer in which three matters must be decided: (1) whether a crime was committed, (2) whether the crime occurred within the territorial jurisdiction of the court, and (3) whether there are reasonable grounds to believe that the defendant committed the crime.

preliminary investigation 初步侦查
All of the activities undertaken by a police officer who responds to the scene of a crime, including determining whether a crime has occurred, securing the crime scene, and preserving evidence.

presentment 大陪审团起诉报告
Historically, unsolicited written notice of an offense provided to a court by a grand jury from their own knowledge or observation. In current usage, any of several presentations of alleged facts and charges to a court or a grand jury by a prosecutor.

presumptive sentencing 推定判刑
A model of criminal punishment that meets the following conditions: (1)The appropriate sentence for an offender convicted of a specific charge is presumed to fall within a range of sentences authorized by sentencing guidelines that are adopted by a legislatively created sentencing body, usually a sentencing commission. (2)Sentencing judges are expected to sentence within the range or to provide written justification for departure. (3)There is a mechanism for review, usually appellate, of any departure from the guidelines.

pretrial detention 审前羁押
Confinement occurring between the time of arrest or of being held to answer a charge

Appendix III
Common Terms Used in Criminal Law

and the conclusion of prosecution.

pretrial discovery 审前披露

In criminal proceedings, disclosure by the prosecution or the defense prior to trial of evidence or other information which is intended to be used in the trial.

pretrial release 审前释放

The release of an accused person from custody, for all or part of the time before or during prosecution, on his or her promise to appear in court when required.

prison 监狱

A state or federal confinement facility that has custodial authority over adults sentenced to confinement.

prison argot 监狱隐语

The slang characteristic of prison subcultures and prison life.

prison commitment 监禁

A sentence of commitment to the jurisdiction of a state or federal confinement facility system for adults whose custodial authority extends to offenders sentenced to more than a year of confinement, to a term expressed in years or for life, or to await execution of a death sentence.

probable cause 合理根据

A set of facts and circumstances that would induce a reasonably intelligent and prudent person to believe that a particular other person has committed a specific crime. Also, reasonable grounds to make or believe an accusation. Probable cause refers to the necessary level of belief that would allow for police seizures (arrests) of individuals and full searches of dwellings, vehicles, and possessions.

probation 缓刑

A sentence of imprisonment that is suspended. Also, the conditional freedom granted by a judicial officer to a convicted offender, as long as the person meets certain conditions of behavior.

probation revocation 撤销缓刑

A court order taking away a convicted offender's probationary status and usually withdrawing the conditional freedom associated with that status in response to a violation of the conditions of probation.

probation termination 缓刑终止

The ending of the probation status of a given person by routine expiration of the probationary period, by special early termination by the court, or by revocation of probation.

probation violation 违反缓刑规则

An act or a failure to act by a probationer that does not conform to the conditions of his or her probation.

procedural defense 程序性抗辩

A defense that claims that the defendant was in some significant way discriminated against in the justice process or that some important aspect of official procedure was not properly followed in the investigation or prosecution of the crime charged.

procedural law 程序法

The part of the law that specifies the methods to be used in enforcing substantive law.

procuratorate 检察院

An agency in many countries with powers and responsibilities similar to those of a prosecutor's office in the United States. Also called procuracy.

property crime 财产犯罪

A UCR offense category that includes burglary, larceny-theft, motor vehicle theft, and arson.

prosecution agency 检察机关

A federal, state, or local criminal justice agency or subunit whose principal function is the prosecution of alleged offenders.

prosecutor 检察官

An attorney whose official duty is to conduct criminal proceedings on behalf of the state or the people against those accused of having committed criminal offenses. Also called county attorney; district attorney (DA); state's attorney; U.S. attorney.

prostitution 卖淫罪

The act of offering or agreeing to engage in, or engaging in, a sex act with another in return for a fee.

psychosis 严重精神失常

A form of mental illness in which sufferers are said to be out of touch with reality.

public defender 公设辩护人

An attorney employed by a government agency or subagency, or by a private organization under contract to a government body, for the purpose of providing defense services to indigents, or an attorney who has volunteered such service.

public safety department 公共安全部门

A state or local agency that incorporates various law enforcement and emergency service functions.

punitive damages 惩罚性损害赔偿金

Damages requested or awarded in a civil lawsuit when the defendant's willful acts were malicious, violent, oppressive, fraudulent, wanton, or grossly reckless. Also called exemplary damages.

Racketeer Influenced and Corrupt Organizations (RICO) 《反勒索及受贿组织法》

A federal statute that allows for the federal seizure of assets derived from illegal enterprise.

rape 强奸

Unlawful sexual intercourse, achieved through force and without consent. Broadly speaking, the term rape has been applied to a wide variety of sexual attacks and may include same-sex rape and the rape of a male by a female. Some jurisdictions refer to same-sex rape as sexual battery. See also forcible rape; sexual battery.

real evidence 物证

Evidence that consists of physical material or traces of physical activity.

reasonable doubt 合理怀疑

In legal proceedings, an actual and substantial doubt arising from the evidence, from the facts or circumstances shown by the evidence, or from the lack of evidence. Also, the state of a case such that, after the comparison and consideration of all the evidence, jurors cannot say they feel an abiding conviction of the truth of the charge.

reasonable doubt standard 合理怀疑标准

The standard of proof necessary for conviction in criminal trials.

reasonable force 合理武力

A degree of force that is appropriate in a given situation and is not excessive. Also, the minimum degree of force necessary to protect oneself, one's property, a third party, or the property of another in the face of a substantial threat.

reasonable suspicion 合理嫌疑

The level of suspicion that would justify an officer in making further inquiry or in conducting further investigation. Reasonable suspicion may permit stopping a person for questioning or for a simple pat-down search. Also, a belief, based on a consideration of the facts at hand and on reasonable inferences drawn from those facts, that would induce an ordinarily prudent and cautious person under the same circumstances to conclude that criminal activity is taking place or that criminal activity has recently occurred. Reasonable suspicion is a general and reasonable belief that a crime is in progress or has occurred, whereas probable cause is a reasonable belief that a particular person has committed a specific crime. See also probable cause.

recidivism 累犯

The repetition of criminal behavior. In statistical practice, a recidivism rate may be any of a number of possible counts or instances of arrest, conviction, correctional commitment, or correctional status change related to repetitions of these events within a given period of time.

recidivist 累犯

A person who has been convicted of one or

Appendix III
Common Terms Used in Criminal Law

more crimes and who is alleged or found to have subsequently committed another crime or series of crimes.

reckless behavior 粗心大意的行为；轻率行为
Activity that increases the risk of harm.

rehabilitation （罪犯的）改造，再教育
The attempt to reform a criminal offender. Also, the state in which a reformed offender is said to be.

release on recognizance (ROR) 具结释放
The pretrial release of a criminal defendant on his or her written promise to appear in court as required. No cash or property bond is required.

reprieve 暂缓执行刑罚
An executive act temporarily suspending the execution of a sentence, usually a death sentence. A reprieve differs from other suspensions of sentence not only in that it almost always applies to the temporary withdrawing of a death sentence, but also in that it is usually an act of clemency intended to provide the prisoner with time to secure amelioration of the sentence.

restitution 恢复原状
A court requirement that an alleged or convicted offender pay money or provide services to the victim of the crime or provide services to the community.

restoration 修复
A goal of criminal sentencing that attempts to make the victim "whole again".

rights of defendant 被告人权利
The powers and privileges that are constitutionally guaranteed to every defendant.

robbery 抢劫
The unlawful taking or attempted taking of property that is in the immediate possession of another by force or violence and/or by putting the victim in fear. Armed robbery differs from unarmed, or strong-armed, robbery with regard to the presence of a weapon. Contrary to popular conceptions, highway robbery does not necessarily occur on a street-and rarely in a vehicle. The term highway robbery applies to any form of robbery that occurs outdoors in a public place.

rule of law 法治
The maxim that an orderly society must be governed by established principles and known codes that are applied uniformly and fairly to all of its members.

rules of evidence 证据规则
Court rules that govern the admissibility of evidence at criminal hearings and trials.

search warrant 搜查令、搜查证
A document issued by a judicial officer which directs a law enforcement officer to conduct a search at a specific location, for specified property or person relating to a crime, to seize the property or person if found, and to account for the results of the search to the issuing judicial officer.

self-defense 自我防卫
The protection of oneself or of one's property from unlawful injury or from the immediate risk of unlawful injury. Also, the justification that the person who committed an act that would otherwise constitute an offense reasonably believed that the act was necessary to protect self or property from immediate danger.

sentencing 科刑
The imposition of a criminal sanction by a judicial authority.

sentencing hearing 判决前听审
In criminal proceedings, a hearing during which the court or jury considers relevant information, such as evidence concerning aggravating or mitigating circumstances, for the purpose of determining a sentencing disposition for a person convicted of an offense.

sexual battery 性侵犯
Intentional and wrongful physical contact with a person, without his or her consent, that entails a sexual component or purpose.

sex offense 性犯罪

In current statistical usage, any of a broad category of varying offenses, usually consisting of all offenses having a sexual element, except forcible rape and commercial sex offenses. The category includes all unlawful sexual intercourse, unlawful sexual contact, and other unlawful behavior intended to result in sexual gratification or profit from sexual activity.

sheriff 行政司法官

The elected chief officer of a county law enforcement agency. The sheriff is usually responsible for law enforcement in unincorporated areas and for the operation of the county jail.

smuggling 走私

The unlawful movement of goods across a national frontier or state boundary or into or out of a correctional facility.

social control 社会控制

The use of sanctions and rewards within a group to influence and shape the behavior of individual members of that group. Social control is a primary concern of social groups and communities, and it is their interest in the exercise of social control that leads to the creation of both criminal and civil statutes.

social order 社会秩序

The condition of a society characterized by social integration, consensus, smooth functioning, and lack of interpersonal and institutional conflict. Also, a lack of social disorganization.

software piracy 软件盗版

The unauthorized duplication of software or the illegal transfer of data from one storage medium to another. Software piracy is one of the most prevalent computer crimes in the world.

speedy trial 迅速审判

A trial which is held in a timely manner. The right of a defendant to have a prompt trial is guaranteed by the Sixth Amendment of the U.S. Constitution, which begins, "In all criminal prosecutions, the accused shall enjoy the right to a speedy and public trial."

Speedy Trial Act 《迅速审判法》

A 1974 federal law requiring that proceedings against a defendant in a criminal case begin within a specified period of time, such as 70 working days after indictment. Some states also have speedy trial requirements.

stare decisis 遵循先例

A legal principle that requires that in subsequent cases on similar issues of law and fact, courts be bound by their own earlier decisions and by those of higher courts having jurisdiction over them. The term literally means "standing by decided matters".

state-action doctrine 遵循先例原则

The traditional legal principle that only government officials or their representatives in the criminal justice process can be held accountable for the violation of an individual's constitutional civil rights.

state court system 州法院体系

A state judicial structure. Most states have at least three court levels: generally, trial courts, appellate courts, and a state supreme court.

status offense 身份罪

An act or conduct that is declared by statute to be an offense, but only when committed by or engaged in by a juvenile, and that can be adjudicated only by a juvenile court.

statutory law 制定法

Written or codified law; the "law on the books", as enacted by a government body or agency having the power to make laws.

statutory rape 法定强奸罪；奸淫幼女罪

Sexual intercourse with a person who is under the legal age of consent.

stay of execution 执行中止

The stopping by a court of the implementation of a judgment—that is, of a court order previously issued.

strict liability 严格责任

Liability without fault or intention. Strict liability offenses do not require mens rea.

Appendix III
Common Terms Used in Criminal Law

subpoena 传票
A written order issued by a judicial officer or grand jury requiring an individual to appear in court and to give testimony or to bring material to be used as evidence. Some subpoenas mandate that books, papers, and other items be surrendered to the court.

substantive criminal law 实体性刑事法律
The part of the law that defines crimes and specifies punishments.

suspect 犯罪嫌疑人
An adult or a juvenile who has not been arrested or charged but whom a criminal justice agency believes may be the person responsible for a specific criminal offense.

suspended sentence 暂缓监禁（缓刑）
The court decision to delay imposing or executing a penalty for a specified or unspecified period. Also, a court disposition of a convicted person pronouncing a penalty of a fine or a commitment to confinement but unconditionally discharging the defendant or holding execution of the penalty in abeyance upon good behavior. Also called sentence withheld.

terrorism 恐怖主义
A violent act or an act dangerous to human life in violation of the criminal laws of the United States or of any state committed to intimidate or coerce a government, the civilian population, or any segment thereof, in furtherance of political or social objectives.

testimony 证人证言
Oral evidence offered by a sworn witness on the witness stand during a criminal trial.

theft 盗窃
Generally, any taking of the property of another with intent to deprive the rightful owner of possession permanently.

transnational crime 跨国犯罪
Unlawful activity undertaken and supported by organized criminal groups operating across national boundaries.

treason 叛国罪
A U.S. citizen's actions to help a foreign government overthrow, make war against, or seriously injure the United States. Also, the attempt to overthrow the government of the society of which one is a member.

trial 审判
In criminal proceedings, the examination in court of the issues of fact and relevant law in a case for the purpose of convicting or acquitting the defendant.

trial de novo 重新审判
Literally, "new trial". The term is applied to cases that are retried on appeal, as opposed to those that are simply reviewed on the record.

trial judge 主持庭审的法官
A judicial officer who is authorized to conduct jury and non-jury trials but who may not be authorized to hear appellate cases. Also, the judicial officer who conducts a particular trial.

unconditional release 无条件释放
The final release of an offender from the jurisdiction of a correctional agency. Also, a final release from the jurisdiction of a court.

Uniform Crime Reports (UCR) 《统一犯罪汇编》
An annual FBI publication that summarizes the incidence and rate of reported crimes throughout the United States.

vagrancy 流浪；流浪罪
An offense related to being a suspicious person, including vagrancy, begging, loitering, and vagabondage.

vandalism 破坏公共财产
The destroying or damaging, or attempting to destroy or damage, public property or

the property of another without the owner's consent. This definition of vandalism does not include burning.

venue 审判地
The particular geographic area in which a court may hear or try a case. Also, the locality within which a particular crime was committed. See also jurisdiction.

verdict 陪审团裁决
The decision of the jury in a jury trial or of a judicial officer in a non-jury trial.

victim 受害人
A person who has suffered death, physical or mental anguish, or loss of property as the result of an actual or attempted criminal offense committed by another person.

violent crime 暴力犯罪
A UCR offense category that includes murder, rape, robbery, and aggravated assault.

warden 监狱长
The official in charge of the operation of a prison, the chief administrator of a prison, or the prison superintendent.

warrant 授权书；令状
In criminal proceedings, a writ issued by a judicial officer directing a law enforcement officer to perform a specified act and affording the officer protection from damages if he or she performs it.

weapon of mass destruction (WMD) 大规模杀伤性武器
A chemical, biological, and nuclear weapon that has the potential to cause mass casualties.

white-collar crime 白领犯罪
Violations of the criminal law committed by a person of respectability and high social status in the course of his or her occupation. Also, nonviolent crime for financial gain utilizing deception and committed by anyone who has special technical and professional knowledge of business and government, irrespective of the person's occupation.

witness 目击证人
Generally, a person who has knowledge of the circumstances of a case. Also, in court usage, one who testifies as to what he or she has seen, heard, or otherwise observed or who has expert knowledge.

writ 令状
A document issued by a judicial officer ordering or forbidding the performance of a specified act.

writ of certiorari 调卷令状
A writ issued from an appellate court for the purpose of obtaining from a lower court the record of its proceedings in a particular case. In some states, this writ is the mechanism for discretionary review. A request for review is made by petitioning for a writ of certiorari, and the granting of review is indicated by the issuance of the writ.

writ of habeas corpus 人身保护令状
A writ that directs the person detaining a prisoner to bring him or her before a judicial officer to determine the lawfulness of the imprisonment.

youthful offender 未成年犯
A person, adjudicated in criminal court, who may be above the statutory age limit for juveniles but is below a specified upper age limit, for whom special correctional commitments and special record-sealing procedures are made available by statute.

Appendix IV
Glossary

附录四 词汇表

A

abide by 遵守；依照	I-6
abridge 剥夺	I-9
accession 添附	II-5
accord to 使调和	I-9
accountability（对……）负有责任（负有义务）	I-10
accretion 增加物；生长部分	I-7
action 诉讼	II-7
actual damages 实际损害赔偿	II-3
actus reus〈拉丁语〉犯罪行为	II-1
adjudicate 判决，裁判	I-2
adjudication 审判；裁判	I-5
adjudicatory 裁判的	I-10
administration 行政机关；局（署）	I-2
administrative agency 行政机关	I-1
administrative law 行政法	I-1
adopt 通过	I-2
advisory 供咨询的；顾问的	I-7
affiliated 附属的	I-8
affiliation 联系；加入	I-9
affix 使固定；附加	II-9
aggregation 集合；集合体	II-5
albeit 虽然	II-11
algorithm [数] 运算法则	II-9
allege 宣称	II-2
amalgamation（指阶级，社会，民族，公司）混合	I-7
amendment 修正案；补充条款	I-2
analogous 类似的；可比拟的	I-6
anarchy 无政府状态；无秩序；混乱	I-7
animate 赋予生命；鼓舞；使活泼	I-7
annexes 文件的附件	II-12
anti-dumping 反倾销的	II-12
antiquity 古代	I-1
aphrodisiacs 春药	II-2
appellate 上诉的	I-3
apprehend 逮捕	II-4
apprenticeship 学徒制	I-8
apprise（正式用语）通知；报告	II-10
appropriation 擅用；私用；盗用	II-9
arraignment 传讯；提讯	II-3
arson 纵火罪；放火罪	II-1
articles of association 社团章程；公司章程	II-8
articulate 清楚明白地说出	I-5
assault 恐吓；侵犯；殴击；企图伤害罪（刑法）	II-2
assembly 大会；公民大会	I-1
asset 资产	II-8
assumption of risk 自愿承担风险	II-7
attempt 企图；犯罪未遂	II-2
attorney at law 律师	II-1
Attorney General 总检察长	II-4
attorney 律师	II-2

attributable 可归于……的		I-8
attribute 特征		II-11
audiovisual 视听的		II-9
authentic 可信的		II-11
authoritative 权威的；有权威的		II-11
authorize 授权		II-9
avoid 使无效；免除		II-6

B

bail hearing 保释听证		II-3
barbarize 使变粗野；使语言芜杂		I-7
battery 非法侵犯；殴击罪（刑法）		II-7
be (left) stranded（指人）陷入无交通工具的情况；束手无策		I-7
bear out 证实		II-12
beneficiary 受益人		II-6
bilateral 有两面的；双边的		II-11
binding authority 有约束力的法律依据		I-6
bona fide〈拉丁法谚〉善意；诚实		II-8
booking（逮捕）登记		II-4
breach of contract 违反合同；违约		II-1
breathalyzer test 呼吸测试		II-4
breed 引起；造成		II-10
bring a lawsuit against sb. 对某人提起诉讼		I-6
building block（本义）积木，这里指组成部分		I-1
burglary 夜盗罪；恶意侵入他人住宅罪		II-1

C

cannibalism 食人（罪）		II-2
canton 州；行政区（尤指瑞士的州，法国的区）		II-11
caseload 待处理案件的数量		I-3
castle exception 城堡例外规则		II-2
cause of action 诉因		II-9
centre in 集中于		II-12
certification mark 证明商标		II-9
challenge 申请（法官或陪审员）回避		I-4
charge 指控		II-2
chattel 动产		II-5
check 制约；牵制		I-2
child-custody 子女监护		I-3
choreographic 舞台舞蹈的		II-9
circuit court 巡回法院		I-3
circumscribe 限制		II-2
circumvent 防治……发生		II-4
citizenry 公民成市民（集合称）		I-10
city council 市政会；市议会		I-2
civil liberties 公民自由		I-9
civil rights 民权		I-9
civil wrong 民事过错行为		II-1
claim（有权）请求；要求；向法庭请求损害赔偿的请求权		II-7
clarify 澄清；使明白		II-10
close corporation 封闭公司		II-8
code 制定法的汇编；法典		I-2
coerce 强迫某人（服从等）		II-10
collective mark 集体商标		II-9
commence 开始		I-7
commentator 评论员；讲解员		I-10
commissioners 委员；专员		I-10
comparative negligence 相对过失；比较过失		II-7
compensatory damages 补偿性损害赔偿金		II-3
compilation 编辑；编撰；编制；编撰物		I-7
compliance 顺从；听从；依从		II-10
conceptualist 概念论者		I-8
conceptually 概念的；观念的；构思的		I-10
conclusion 缔结		II-11
concurrent 同时发生的；并存的		II-5
confer 赠与；把……赠与		II-11

Appendix IV
Glossary

conform 使相似；适应	II-10	Crown Court 英国王室法院；刑事法院	I-4
confrontation clause 对质条款	II-3	crystallize（喻：指思想，计划）使变得明确	II-10
confrontation 对质；对证	II-3	cumbersome 棘手的；麻烦的	II-8
confusion 混合	II-5	custodian 管理人	I-9
Congress 国会	I-1	custody 羁押；拘留；拘禁	II-4
consensus 全体一致同意	II-12		
consent 被害人同意	II-2		

D

consideration 对价；约因	II-5	damages 损害赔偿金	I-1
constituent 选民；有权制宪或修宪的	I-9	Dark Ages 黑暗世纪	I-1
constitutional law 宪法	I-1	deadly force 致命武力	II-2
constitutional right 宪法性权利	I-2	dean（大学）系主任	I-8
constitutionality 合宪性	I-2	debased 贬低（价值，品质，品格等）	I-7
consular 领事的	II-11	decease 死亡	II-5
contradictory 矛盾的；对立的	II-4	decidendi 判决理由	I-6
contravene 违反	II-1	declare war 宣战	I-9
contributory negligence 共同过失；互有过失	II-7	deed 契据	II-5
conventional law 常规法	I-5	defense lawyers 辩护律师	II-3
conversion 侵占（动产）	II-7	defense of infancy 未成年辩护	II-2
conveyance 财产转让；让与	II-5	defense 抗辩事由	I-6
conviction 有罪判决；定罪	II-1	defer to 服从；遵从	I-3
corporate 社团的；法人的；共同的；全体的	I-10	definitive 最后的；确定的；权威性的	II-11
corporate veil 法人面纱	II-8	degenerate（由于失去被认为是正常和优良的特质而）退步；堕落	I-7
corporation limited by guarantee 担保有限公司（英国公司类型）	II-8	delegation of powers 权力的委托；授权	I-2
corporation limited by shares 股份有限公司（英国公司类型）	II-8	deliberation（陪审团）审议；评议；（刑事案件中）预谋；蓄谋	I-4
corrections 矫正	II-3	demeanor 行为；举止；风度	I-3
creditor 债权人	II-8	derivative 派生的事物	II-11
criminal justice system 刑事司法系统	II-3	despotic 专制的；暴虐的	I-9
criminal law 刑法	I-1	deter 阻碍做某事	II-10
criminal procedure 刑事诉讼；刑事程序	II-3	determinate 决定性的；限定性的	I-5
criminal prosecution 刑事诉讼	I-3	deterrence（通过威慑来）阻却（不法行为）	II-7
criminal trial 刑事审判	II-2	detriment 损害	II-6
criteria 标准	I-8	development law 发展法	II-12
cross-examine 交叉询问	II-3		

. 361 .

dicta dictum的复数形式，法官个人意见；附带意见	I-6
direct victim 直接受害者	II-1
disaffirm 否认或驳斥	II-6
disband 解散	I-4
discharge 清偿（债务）；履行（义务）；免除；撤销	II-6
disciplinary 惩罚性的；执行纪律的；纪律上的	I-10
discipline 学科	II-11
disclosure 透露；公开	I-10
discretion 自由处理；自由决定	II-10
disgruntled 不满意的；不高兴的	II-9
disintegration 分裂成小碎片	I-7
disperse 散布	I-10
disseminate 传播；散布（思想，教义等）	I-7
dissent 分歧；异议	I-6
distillation 用蒸馏法净化或制造	I-7
distinctive 区别的	I-7
distinctive 有区别的；与众不同的	II-9
divergent 分歧的	I-8
divine 神的；敬神的	I-5
divisional courts 高等法院各分庭	I-6
documentation 证据资料	II-2
Doha Development Agenda（缩写为DDA）多哈发展议程	II-12
domestic relations court 家庭关系法院	I-3
donee 受赠人	II-5
double jeopardy clause 双重追诉条款	I-3
double jeopardy 双重危险；双重追诉	II-2
drain 排出沟外	I-10
due process 正当程序；正当法律程序	II-4
dwelling 住处	II-2
dynamic 动力的；动力学的；动态的	II-11

easement（在他人土地上的）通行权；地役权	II-5
economic integration 经济整合	II-12
embezzlement 侵占罪	II-2
emblem 象征；标记	II-9
eminent domain 国家征用权	II-5
emissary 使者	II-11
emotional overtones 感情色彩	II-5
empirical 完全根据经验的；经验主义的	I-5
employment discrimination 就业歧视	I-9
emulate 仿效	I-8
enact 颁布	I-2
enactment 法令；条例	I-9
endorse（签注）认可；赞成	I-9
engender 造成	I-9
enter into 订立	I-2
entity 实体	II-8
enumeration 列举	II-11
enunciate 阐明	I-9
equitable remedies 衡平救济	II-7
equivalent 对等物	II-9
evidentiary 证据的；根据证据的	II-10
exaggerate 夸大；夸张	I-7
excuse 可得宽恕	II-2
exemplary damages 惩戒性损害赔偿金	I-1
expedient 有用的；有利的	I-6
expert witness 专家证人	II-2
exponent 倡导者；拥护者	I-5
expound 详加解释；详细说明	I-7

fact finder 事实调查人	II-1
fair use 合理使用	II-9
false imprisonment 非法限制人身自由；非法禁	

Appendix IV
Glossary

锢	II-7
fancifully 富于想象力的	II-9
far-flung 蔓延的；辽阔的	I-7
fault 过错	II-2
feature 特点；特征	II-9
federalism 联邦制	I-9
fee simple defeasible 可限定无条件继承之不动产	II-5
fee simple 无条件继承之不动产（财产）权	II-5
felonious homicide 重罪杀人；恶意杀人	II-1
felony 重罪	II-1
fen 沼泽；沼池	I-10
feudalism 封建制度	I-7
file 提交	II-9
fine 罚金	I-1
first-degree murder 一级谋杀	II-1
float（票据）流通	II-8
foreperson 陪审团主席	I-4
forfeiture of lands and goods 没收土地及货物	II-1
formalism 形式主义	I-7
formative 使成形的；形成的	I-7
formulate 确切的阐述（表达、说明）	I-10
formula 处方；配方	II-9
forseeability 可预见性	II-7
fraudulent 欺诈性的	II-8
fraud 欺诈	II-6
Freedom of Information Act《情报自由法》	I-2
frivolous 不庄重的；不重要的	II-10
fundamental law 基本法；根本法	I-9
fungible 可代替的；可互换的	II-5
future interest 未来财产权益	II-5

G

GATT 关税与贸易总协定	II-12
General Agreement on Trade In Service 简称 GATS，服务贸易总协定	II-12
general assembly 州议会	II-2
general partnership 普通合伙	II-8
genuine 真实的；真正的	II-9
gift 赠与	II-5
good behavior 廉洁行为；品行良好；（正在服刑的罪犯）遵守监规	I-3
goodwill 商誉	II-9
governance 统治；管理	I-9
government procurement 政府采购	II-12
governor 州长	I-2
gratuitous 无偿的；自愿的；无理由的	II-6
gravel 砂砾；碎石	II-5
guardian 监护人	II-4

H

hack (slang) 闯入；侵入	II-9
hail 欢呼；拥立	II-4
hearing 听审；听证	II-3
heritage 遗产；继承物	I-7
hierarch 教主；掌权者；高僧	II-11
hierarchy 层次	I-8
higher court 上级法院	I-6
hold 认定；认为	I-3
holding corporation 控股公司；持股公司	II-8
holster 手枪皮套	II-4
House of Representatives 众议院	I-1
hung jury 悬案陪审团	II-3
hybrid 杂种；混合之物	I-7

I

ideology 思维方式；意识形态	I-5
immunity 免除；豁免	I-9
implementation 执行	I-10

impose 加（税，义务等）于	II-10
imprisonment 监禁	II-1
in entirety 完全	II-9
in light of 按照；根据	II-9
in part 部分的；有几分	II-9
in perpetuity 永远	II-9
in the wake of 直接随着……	II-12
inalienable（权利等）不能让与的；不可剥夺的	I-9
incarceration 关押	II-1
inception 开始	II-6
indictment 大陪审团起诉书；公诉书	I-4
indigenous 土生的；天生的	I-7
indigent defendants 贫穷被告人	II-3
infirmity 身体虚弱	II-7
inflict 强加于	II-2
information（由检察官签署的）刑事起诉书	I-4
ingenious 制作精巧的	I-7
inheritance 继承；遗产	II-5
injunction 禁令	II-7
injunctive 命令的；指令的	I-10
injurious falsehood 诽谤；诋毁	II-7
insolvent liquidation（因资不抵债）破产清算	II-8
insolvent 支付不能的	II-8
intangible 无形的	II-5
inter alia〈拉丁语〉除了别的东西；其中	I-4
interaction 相互作用；相互影响	I-7
Internal Revenue Service (IRS) 美国国内税务署	II-8
interpose 提出（异议，否决等）	II-10
interrogation 刑事讯问	II-4
intoxication 醉态	II-2
introduce 提出议案等	I-1
invasion 侵略；侵犯	I-7
investigate 调查；侦查；审查	I-10
investigation 研究；调查	I-10
investigation 侦查	II-3
inviolable 神圣不可侵犯的	II-2
invoke 援引；调用	II-9
involuntary intoxication 非自愿醉态	II-2
irreparable 不能挽回的	I-10

J

joint tenancy 联合共有	II-5
joint venture 合资公司	II-9
judicial decisions 司法判决	I-1
judicial process 司法程序	II-3
judicial review 司法审查	I-9
judiciary 司法机构；司法机关	I-2
jurisdictional 司法权的；管辖权的	I-9
jurisdiction 司法管辖权；管辖区域	I-3
jurisprudence 法律体系；法理学；法哲学	I-1
jury summon 陪审召集令	I-4
jury trial 陪审团审判	II-3
jus civile 市民法	I-1
justification 认为有理；认为正当；理由	I-10
juvenile offense 未成年犯罪	II-2

K

King's Peace 国王的安宁	II-1

L

larceny 偷盗罪	II-1
law enforcement officer 执法人员	II-2
law enforcement 执法部门	II-3
lawsuit 诉讼	I-3
layperson 外行；非法律专业人士	I-4
legal encyclopedia 法律大百科全书	I-5

Appendix IV
Glossary

legal entity 法律实体	II-8
legal person 法人；法律拟制人	II-7
legislative 关于立法的；有立法权的；立法的	I-1
legislator 立法者；立法机关的成员	I-2
legislature 立法机关	I-10
legitimacy 合法性	I-5
libel 书面诽谤	II-7
license 特许权	II-5
life estate 终身财产；终身不动产	II-5
life tenant 土地等不动产的终身占有人	II-5
lifetime appointments 终身制任命	I-3
Limited Liability Partnership 简称LLP，有限责任合伙制	II-8
Limited Partnership 简称LP，有限合伙制	II-8
liquidate（企业破产或解散时）清算	II-8
liquidated damages 预定损害赔偿金；违约金	II-7
list（股票）上市	II-8
litigation 诉讼	I-8

M

maintain 供养；维持	I-9
malice 恶意	II-1
malicious prosecution 恶意控诉；诬告	II-7
mandamus 训令令状	I-10
mandate（法庭的）命令；要求	II-6
mandatory 命令的；强制性的	II-10
manslaughter 非预谋杀人罪	II-1
map out 计划；设计	II-12
marginal 边际的	II-10
market access 市场准入	II-12
matrimonial 婚姻的	I-7
matrix 发源地	I-8
mayhem 重伤罪	II-1
medieval 中世纪的	I-5

mens rea〈拉丁语〉犯罪意图	II-1，II-2
merchandise 商品；货物	II-12
mete 给予	I-10
migrate 迁移；迁居；移居	I-7
millennium 千年	I-7
misdemeanor 轻罪	II-1
mistake of fact 事实错误	II-2
mistake of law 法律错误	II-2
model act 模范法	I-2
Model Penal Code《模范刑法典》	II-1
monopoly 垄断；独占	I-7
monumental（指著作，研究等）不朽的	I-7
motto 座右铭；题词	II-9
municipal court 市镇法院（庭）	I-3
murder 谋杀	II-1

N

natural law school 自然法学派	I-5
natural rights 天赋权利；自然权利	I-5
necessity 紧急避险	II-2
negate 取消；使无效	II-4
negligence 过失侵权；过失	II-7
negotiable instrument 可流通票据	II-6
nondisclosure contract 不披露合同	II-9
non-discriminatory 非歧视性的	II-12
nonetheless 虽然如此；但是	II-9
non-for-profit corporation 非营利性公司	II-8
nonverbal behavior 非语言的行为或举止	I-3
norm 标准；规范；准则	I-10
normality 常态；正常	I-5
normative 标准的；规范的	II-12
notwithstanding 尽管；即使	I-6
novel 新奇的；新颖的	I-10
nuisance 滋扰；妨碍	II-7
null and void 无效的；无法律约束力的；可撤销的	I-9

· 365 ·

nullified 无效的		I-10
nullify 使无效		I-4
nullity （法律上的）无效；无效行为		II-6
numerous 众多的；许多的；无数的		II-11

O

obiter dicta 附带意见		I-6
obligatory 义不容辞的；必须的		II-11
observe 遵守		II-11
of sorts （口语）暗指名实不全		II-12
offer 提出；提供		II-2
on the grounds of 因为；根据		II-12
orator 演说者；（尤指出色的）演说家		I-7
ordain （法律）规定		I-9
ordinance 条例		I-2
originator 创作者；发明人		II-9
outlaw 宣布……为非法		I-9
output 生产量		I-7
overlap （与……）交叠；重合		I-9
override 优先于；不顾；使无效		I-2
overrule （上级法院）否决或推翻（下级法院的判决）		I-3

P

pain and suffering 痛苦与创伤		I-1
pantomime 哑剧；舞剧		II-9
paradigm 范例		I-10
parole officers 假释官员		II-3
party （诉讼）当事人		I-3
patent 专利		II-9
penalty 刑罚		II-7
per se 〈拉丁语〉自身；本身		II-9
peremptory challenge 无因回避请求		I-4
perennial 长久的；持久的		II-10
performance （合同义务的）履行		II-6

perjury 作伪证；伪证罪		II-1
persuasive authority 有说服力的法律依据		I-6
persuasive precedent 有说服力的先例		I-6
petit jury 小陪审团		I-4
petition 诉状；诉请		I-3
philosophy of law 法哲学		I-5
pictorial 图画的；用图画表示的		II-9
pigeonhole 把……分类（归档）；分类记存		I-10
plague 麻烦、困扰或灾祸的原因；祸患		I-7
plead 辩护；抗辩		I-3
pleadings 诉讼文件；民事诉状；答辩状		I-1
plenary （指权力）无限的；绝对的		II-11
police 警察		II-3
positivist school 实证主义法学派		I-5
possess 占有；支配		I-5
possession 占有；占有权；先占		II-5
practitioner 法律执业者		I-8
pragmatism 实用主义		I-8
precedent 先例		I-1
preclude 阻止做某事；使不可能		II-10
predictability 可预见性		I-6
prerogative 特权		I-10
precedential （作为）先例的		II-11
primitive 粗糙的；简单的		II-11
prior to 在前；居先		II-4
prison escape 逃狱；脱狱		II-1
Privacy Act《隐私权法》		I-2
private law 私法		I-1
privately retained counsel 私人雇用的律师		II-1
probable cause 合理依据		I-4
probate court 遗嘱检验法庭		I-3
probation officers 缓刑官员		II-3
products liability 产品责任		II-7
profit 收益权；利益		II-5
promulgate 发布；公布		II-11
proponent 提议者；支持者		I-5

Appendix IV
Glossary

proportionate 成比例的；相成的 II-2
prosecute 对……起诉；检控 I-10
prosecuting attorney 公诉律师 II-1
prosecution 起诉 II-3
prosecutor 检察官 I-1
prospectus（介绍学校，企业等优点的）说明书；简章；简介资料 I-10
provide 规定 I-3
Public Corporation〈英〉公众公司；〈美〉公益公司 II-8
public law 公法 I-1
public prosecutor 公诉人 II-1
public safety 公共安全；公众安全 II-4
publicist 国际法专家 II-11
puffing（对商品质量的）自我吹嘘；夸大说明；抬价 II-6
punishment 处罚 II-3
punitive damages 惩罚性损害赔偿金 I-1

Q

question of fact 事实问题 I-3

R

racial segregation 种族隔离 I-9
radon［化］氡 I-1
rape 强奸罪 II-1
ratification 批准 II-11
ratify 批准 I-2
rationale（某事物的）基本理由；理论基础 II-10
real estate 不动产；地产 II-5
real property 不动产 II-5
realty 不动产；地产 II-5
reasonable person (man)（法律上的）理性人 II-7
rebuttable 可以反驳的；可以反证的 I-3

reciprocally 互惠的；交互的；相互的 I-7
recourse 权力的行使 II-2
redressable 可获得救济的 II-7
register 注册；登记 II-8
regulation 条例；规章 I-2
regulatory（行政）规章的；制定规章的 I-9
reiterate 重申 I-9
rejection 被抛弃或被拒绝之物 I-7
reluctant 不愿（做某事）的；勉强的 II-10
remainder 剩余地产；剩余地产权；剩余继承权 II-5
remedy 救济 I-1, II-7
remnant 遗留下来的痕迹 I-8
render 正式宣布 I-6
reporter 案例汇编 I-6
Representative 众议院议员 I-9
reproduce 再生；复制 II-9
res ipsa loquitur 事情不言自明；事实自证 II-7
restraint 抑制；制止；克制 II-11
retain 雇用；聘请（律师，顾问） II-1
retroactive 有溯及既往力的 I-5
reverse 撤销；推翻 I-6
reversionary interest 归复权益；将来权益 II-5
revocation 撤销；撤回 II-6
rhetoric 修辞；修辞学 I-7
rigid 僵硬的；坚挺的 I-7
robbery 抢劫罪 II-1
rule 规则 I-2

S

sanction（为维护或恢复法律或权威的尊严所作的）处罚 II-10
satellite 追随者 II-10
scales 天平 I-1
scholarship 学问；学识 I-5
scrutiny 详细审查 II-12

sculptural 雕刻的	II-9	
second-degree murder 二级谋杀	II-1	
secular 尘世的；非宗教的；非精神的	I-7	
security 有价证券	II-12	
self-incrimination 自证其罪；自我归罪	II-4	
seminar 研讨会	I-8	
Senate 参议院	I-1	
sexual assault 性侵犯	II-3	
shareholder 股东	II-8	
sheriffs 行政司法官	II-3	
small claims court 小额索赔法院	I-3	
social security 社会保障	II-4	
sodomy 反自然性行为	II-1	
sole proprietorship（个人）独资企业	II-8	
sophistication 精细；复杂；高深；奥妙	I-7	
sovereign power 主权权力	I-5	
sovereign 独立自主的	II-11	
specify 指定；详细说明	I-10	
spectrum 光谱；比喻广阔的范围、领域或系列	II-12	
speedy tria〈美〉迅速审判	II-3	
spell out 详细规定；详细说明	I-1	
spouse 配偶	II-5	
stare decisis〈拉丁语〉遵循先例原则；判例拘束原则	I-2	
state trading 国营贸易	II-12	
statesmanship 政治家的才能，智慧，技巧等	I-7	
statute 制定法；成文法	I-10	
statute of limitations 时效；诉讼时效	I-1	
statutory construction 制定法的解释；法定解释	I-2	
statutory law 制定法	I-2	
statutory 法定的	II-8	
strain 种类	I-5	
strand（指船）搁浅	I-7	
subject matter 争议事项；标的	I-3	

subjugate 使屈服；使服从	II-4	
subsidiary 辅助的；补充的	II-11	
subsidies 补贴	II-12	
subtlety 微妙；灵巧；细微的差别	I-7	
supplement 增补；补充	I-7	
surviving 依然健在的	II-9	
survivor 尚存者	I-1	
syrup 糖浆	II-9	
systematic 有系统；有体系的	I-7	

T

take into account 考虑；重视	I-6	
tangible 有形的	II-5	
tariff-free 免关税；零关税	II-12	
tenancy by the entirety 夫妻共有	II-5	
tenancy in common 共同共有	II-5	
tenor 要旨；大意	I-9	
testimony 证据（指证人以誓言口头提供证明）；证言	I-3	
the accused 被告人	I-4	
the Berne Convention《伯尔尼公约》	II-9	
the board of directors 董事会	II-9	
the WTO Secretariat 秘书处	II-12	
theologian 神学家	I-5	
theoretical 理论的	I-8	
third-degree murder 三级谋杀	II-1	
throw out 驳回起诉；驳回请求	II-4	
title 产权；权利；资格	II-5	
tortfeasor 侵权行为人	II-7	
trademark 商标	II-9	
treatise 论文；论说	I-7	
treaty 条约	I-2	
trespass on the case 间接侵害行为	II-7	
trespass to chattel 侵犯动产	II-7	
trespass to land 对土地的侵犯	II-7	
trespass 侵入；侵权之诉；侵犯	II-5	

Appendix IV
Glossary

trial court 初审法院	I-3
true bill 大陪审团认可的起诉书；准予起诉	I-4
tyranny 暴政	I-9

U

umbrella agreement 总括协定	II-12
unconstitutional 违宪的；与宪法相抵触的	II-4
undercut 削弱	I-8
unequivocal 明确的；不含糊的	II-6
unicameral 一院制的；单院的	I-9
Uniform Commercial Code《统一商法典》	I-2
uniformity 一致；均匀	I-10
United States Code《美国法典》	I-2
unprecedented 空前的；史无前例的；无比的	II-12
unscathed 未受损失的	II-4
usurp 非法地占有或拥有；篡夺	I-9
utility 有用；实用；效用	II-10

V

validate 使生效；使有法律效力	I-9
vault 银行的保险箱；保险柜	II-9
vehemence 激烈；猛烈	I-5
verbose 啰嗦的；累赘的	II-10
Vermont 佛蒙特州（美国州名）	I-9
vest (in)（权力等）属于；归属	I-9
veto 否决	I-9
vetting 彻底审查	I-4
vicarious liability 替代责任	II-1
vigorously 精神旺盛的	I-10
vindicate 辩护；证明有理	I-5
violation 违犯；违反	I-5
violator 违法者；违反者	I-1
virtually 事实上；实际上	I-7
void 无效	I-2
vouch 担保	II-9

W

waiver 弃权；权利放弃	II-4
Warren Court 沃伦法院	II-4
welter 混乱；混杂；纷争	I-7
wield 具有；运用（权利）	I-1
will 遗嘱	II-5
witnesses 证人	II-2
working party 工作组；工作班子；专题调查委员会	II-12
writ of certiorari 调案复审令状	I-3
wrong 过错行为；不法行为	II-7

Appendix V
References

附录五 参考文献

BARNES A J, DWORKIN T M, RICHARDS E L. 2000. Law for business[M]. 7th ed. New York: McGraw-Hill.

BARNETT R E. 2001. Perspectives on contract law[M]. New York: Aspen Law & Business.

BRYAN A G. 2009. Black's law dictionary[M]. 9th ed. St. Paul: West Publishing Co.

BREYER S G, STEWART R B, SUNSTEIN C R, et al. 2003. Administrative law and regulatory policy[M]. Beijing: CITTC Publishing House.

GIBSON B, CAVADINO P. 2002. Criminal justice process[M]. 2nd ed. Winchester: Waterside Press.

BUERGENTHAL T, MRUPHY S. 2001. Public international law[M]. Beijing: Law Press.

CALVI J V, COKEMAN S. 2004. American law and legal system[M]. 5th ed. Upper Saddle River: Pearson Prentice Hall.

CANON D T, COLEMAN J J, MAYER K R. 1997. The enduring debate[M]. New York: W. W. Norton & Company.

CARPER D L, WEST B W. 2003. Understanding the law[M]. New York: Thomson.

CLAPP J E. 2000. A dictionary of the law[M]. New York: Random House.

CLARK D S, ANSAY T. 2002. Introduction to the law of United States[M]. 2nd ed. New York: Kluwer Law International.

DINE J. 2001. Company law[M]. New York: Palgrave Macmillan.

RUSH E G. 2000. The dictionary of criminal justice[M]. 5th ed. New York: McGraw-Hill.

FARNSWORTH E A. 1996. An Introduction to the legal system of the United States[M]. New York: Oxford University Press.

GELLHORN E, LEVIN R M. 2001. Administrative law and process[M]. Beijing: Law Press.

GLENDON M A, GORDON M W, CAROZZA P G. 2001. Comparative legal traditions[M]. Beijing: Law Press.

Appendix V

References

GOLDMAN S, SARAT A. 2000. American court system[M]. San Francisco: W. H. Freeman & Company.

GROSSMAN G S. 2000. The spirit of American law[M]. Boulder: Westview Press.

HARWOOD V. 2003. Modern tort law[M]. 5th ed. London: Caverndish Publishing Limited.

KEMPIN F G. 1990. Historical introduction to Anglo-American law[M]. St. Paul: West Publishing Co.

LOWRY J, WATSON L. 2001. Company law[M]. Toronto: Butterworths.

HALSEY D W. 1978. Macmillan contemporary dictionary[M]. London: Macmillan Publishing Co., Inc.

MARLIN-BENNETT R. 2004. Knowledge power: intellectual property, information, and privacy[M]. Boulder: Lynne Rienner Publishers.

MRRRIAM-WEBSTER. 1996. Merriam-Webster's dictionary of law. Springfield: Merriam-Webster, Inc.

MILLER R L, CROSS B F. 1993. The legal and regulatory environment today[M]. St. Paul: West Publishing Co.

MILLER R L, JENTZ G A. 2003. Business law today: the essentials: text and summarized cases: ecommerce, legal, ethical, and international environment[M]. 6th ed. Mason: Thomson.

MULLIS A, OLIPHANT K. 2003. Torts[M]. New York: Palgrave Macmillan.

QURESHI A H. 2002. Perspectives in international economic law[M]. The Hague: Kluwer Law International.

SANSON M. 2002. Essential international trade law[M]. Sydney: Cavendish Publishing Ltd.

SCHMALLEGER F. 1999. Criminal justice today[M]. 5th ed. Upper Saddle River: Prentice-Hall, Inc.

SCHMALLEGER F. 1996. Trial of the century: people of the State of California vs. Orenthal James Simpson. Upper Saddle River: Prentice-Hall, Inc.

SCHREEMAN A. 1996. The law of corporations, and other business organizations[M]. 3rd ed. Mason: Thomson.

SMITH J C, WEISSTUB D N. 1983. The western idea of law[M]. Toronto: Butterworths.

SPIRO G W. 1993. The legal environment of business: cases and principles[M]. Upper Saddle River: Prentice-Hall, Inc.

UGLOW S. 1995. Criminal justice[M]. London: Sweet and Maxwed.

陈忠诚. 1992. 法窗译话［M］. 北京：中国对外翻译出版公司.

陈忠诚. 2000. 法苑译潭 [M]. 北京：中国法制出版社.

陈忠诚. 1998. 英汉法律用语正误辨析 [M]. 北京：法律出版社.

陈忠诚. 2000. 英汉汉英法律用语辨证字典 [M]. 北京：法律出版社.

程逸群. 1999. 英汉—汉英双向法律词典 [M]. 北京：中国政法大学出版社.

郭义贵. 2004. 法律英语 [M]. 北京：北京大学出版社.

何家弘. 1997. 法律英语 [M]. 北京：法律出版社.

李宗锷，潘慧仪. 1999. 英汉法律大词典 [M]. 北京：法律出版社.

刘艺工，屈文生. 2003. 法律英语 [M]. 北京：机械工业出版社.

潘维大，刘文琦. 英美法导读 [M]. 北京：法律出版社.

薛波. 2003. 元照英美法词典 [M]. 北京：法律出版社.

赵建，夏国佐. 1999. 法学专业英语教程1—3册[M]. 北京：中国人民大学出版社.

http://patriot.net/~crouch/fln.html

http://www.courttv.com/casefiles/simpson/criminal/summary/

http://www.slwk.com/papers/paper3.htm

http://www.wto.org/index.htm

http://www.szelaw.com

http://www.udayton.edu/~grandjur/fedj/fedj.htm

http://www.constitution.org/jury/gj/fgj.htm

http://www.crfc.org/americanjury/voir_dire.html